DEFINING DOCUMENTS
IN AMERICAN HISTORY

The Vietnam War
(1956-1975)

DEFINING DOCUMENTS
IN AMERICAN HISTORY

The Vietnam War
(1956-1975)

Editor

Michael Shally-Jensen, PhD

SALEM PRESS
A Division of EBSCO Information Services
Ipswich, Massachusetts

GREY HOUSE PUBLISHING

Publisher's Cataloging-In-Publication Data
(Prepared by The Donohue Group, Inc.)

Vietnam War (1956-1975) / editor, Michael Shally-Jensen, PhD. --
[First EDITION].

    pages : illustrations ; cm. -- (Defining documents in American history)

    Edition statement supplied by publisher.
    Includes bibliographical references and index.
    ISBN: 978-1-61925-852-5 (hardcover)

    1. Vietnam War, 1961-1975--Sources. 2. Vietnam War, 1961-1975--United States--Sources. I. Shally-Jensen, Michael. II. Series: Defining documents in American history (Salem Press)

DS557.4 .V54 2015
959.704/3

FIRST PRINTING
PRINTED IN THE UNITED STATES OF AMERICA

Table of Contents

The Antiwar Movement

Nixon's War

Aftermath

Appendixes

Publisher's Note

Defining Documents in American History series, produced by Salem Press, consists of a collection of essays on important historical documents by a diverse range of writers on a broad range of subjects in American history. *Defining Documents in American History: The Vietnam War* surveys key documents produced from 1956-75, organized under five broad categories:

- Kennedy's War
- Johnson's War
- The Antiwar Movement
- Nixon's War
- Aftermath

Historical documents provide a compelling view of this unique period of American history. Designed for high school and college students, the aim of the series is to advance historical document studies as an important activity in learning about history.

Essay Format

The Vietnam War contains 44 primary source documents – many in their entirety. Each document is supported by a critical essay, written by historians and teachers, that includes a Summary Overview, Defining Moment, Author Biography, Document Analysis, and Essential Themes. Readers will appreciate the diversity of the collected texts, including journals, letters, speeches, political sermons, laws, government reports, and court cases, among other genres. An important feature of each essays is a close reading of the primary source that develops evidence of broader themes, such as the author's rhetorical purpose, social or class position, point of view, and other relevant issues. In addition, essays are organized by section themes, listed above, highlighting major issues of the period, many of which extend across eras and continue to shape American life. Each section begins with a brief introduction that defines questions and problems underlying the subjects in the historical documents. A brief glossary included at the end of each document highlights keywords important in the study of the primary source. Each essay also includes a Bibliography and Additional Reading section for further research.

Appendixes

- **Chronological List** arranges all documents by year.
- **Web Resources** is an annotated list of web sites that offer valuable supplemental resources.
- **Bibliography** lists helpful articles and books for further study.

Contributors

Salem Press would like to extend its appreciation to all involved in the development and production of this work. The essays have been written and signed by scholars of history, humanities, and other disciplines related to the essay's topics. Without these expert contributions, a project of this nature would not be possible. A full list of contributor's names and affiliations appears in the front matter of this volume.

Editor's Introduction

The Vietnam War loomed large for decades in the American consciousness. Only recently, in the wake of new military ventures abroad, has it taken on the character of a distant war from a different era. Yet there are still millions who remember the war or who have family members or relatives who fought in it or protested against it. As with all such events, it inevitably went from being a living thing to being a subject in history books. With the passage of time, the lessons the war provided about the dangers of entering a foreign conflict on tenuous grounds, without deep knowledge of one's opponent and without the full commitment of the American people—these lessons seem in many ways to have been forgotten. Now, however, that history has partially repeated itself with US military involvement in Iraq (and, to a lesser extent, in Afghanistan), the Vietnam War is once again being examined for the cautionary tales it contains.

Early Years and Expansion of the War

Before there was any US involvement in Vietnam—before there was a Vietnam War—there was the First Indochina War (1946-1954). That conflict pitted French colonial forces who had long governed the territory against Vietnamese anti-imperialist forces who sought to expel the Europeans and establish Vietnam as a self-governing nation. The result, after nearly a decade of bloodshed and hundreds of thousands of deaths, was an agreement, signed in Geneva, whereby the French would withdraw and Vietnam would be divided into northern and southern districts. Communist interests aligned under Ho Chi Minh were concentrated in the north, and non-communist interests aligned under Emperor Bao Dai and his regime, as supported by the United States, were concentrated in the south. A section in the agreement specified that a general election was to be held in 1956, the idea being that through this process a unified national government would be created. Yet neither South Vietnam nor the United States signed onto the election, largely out of fear that they would not prevail, and so it never took place. Meanwhile, Bao Dai's chosen prime minister in South Vietnam, Ngo Dinh Diem, manipulated the power structure in order to eject the emperor and make himself head of state. In consequence, communist cadres (Viet Minh) already present in South Vietnam were activated, and southern-based anti-Diem guerilla forces and

military units making up the National Liberation Front (NLF), or Viet Cong, also went into action. North Vietnam began supplying these groups with armaments and information.

This was the situation when a new American president, John F. Kennedy, took office in early 1961. Kennedy had stood up for Diem as a member of the US Senate and had earned a reputation as a committed anticommunist. His predecessor in the White House, Dwight D. Eisenhower, had spoken of the "domino"-like effect that could happen if a small country like Vietnam were to succumb to a communist advance in a region like Southeast Asia. Kennedy took that message to heart. He was not inclined to "lose" Vietnam to communism, as China had been "lost" in 1949 and Korea had been partly lost in 1955. American military advisors were sent to Vietnam under Eisenhower, and Kennedy acted to increase their number significantly, authorizing as many as 16,000 by 1963. Yet, even while Kennedy publicly supported the Diem regime, as corrupt and inept as it proved to be, privately he and his advisors harbored doubts—to the point of contemplating a manufactured coup de'état. In the end, a generals' coup took place under its own accord, albeit with CIA support, in early November 1963. Diem and his brother were killed in the affair and replaced in government by an unstable regime, and another one after that, and so on over a period of years. Kennedy, though, never came to know the extent of the problem, having falling victim to an assassin's bullet only three weeks after Diem's demise.

If the Kennedy years were the beginning of the quagmire in Vietnam, the Johnson years were when the quagmire widened and started to swallow up Vietnam—along with Johnson's own presidency. Most of Kennedy's advisers remained with the Johnson administration, and most continued to press for greater US involvement in the conflict and stronger measures in the fight against communism. In August 1964, Johnson used the excuse of a North Vietnamese patrol-boat attack on an American destroyer in the Gulf of Tonkin to release the full force of the US military on Viet Cong strongholds in South Vietnam. He would eventually authorize a variety of devastating war measures, including the dropping of napalm bombs on villages suspected of harboring Viet Cong (resulting in high civilian casualties); the removal of village residents to so-called "strategic hamlets" (relocation centers) and the bulldozing of entire villages; the use of massive B-52 bombing raids against targets in the south, on a scale comparable to those used in World War II; the spraying of toxic herbicides and defoliants such as Agent Orange over extensive areas of South Vietnam (to destroy enemy crops and clear vegetation); and the use of often inhumane prison environments together with enhanced interrogation methods, or torture, in the handling of prisoners. Notice, too, that this was all taking place *in the south*, before any large-scale US incursion into North Vietnam. Critics would later point out that for every destructive act against ordinary Vietnamese citizens, dozens of angry, anti-American Viet Cong recruits were created. Johnson increased American troop levels from 180,000 to 550,000 between 1965 and 1968. Bombing raids into North Vietnam also were begun.

As Defense Secretary Robert McNamara put it, there seemed to be "no attractive course of action" for the Americans. As long as the US government refused to pull out of Vietnam over fear that doing so would allow communism to spread and ruin the reputation of the United States, policymakers could only hope that heightened military pressure would eventually win the day. And yet as long as military escalation failed to achieve the administration's aims, and as long as US troops continued to come home in body bags, the deeper became the hole that the United States seemed to be digging itself into. Johnson had cannily started down a path of "victory without conquest" in 1965—meaning that, short of either side's total conquest of the other, a peace settlement would suffice. Yet, even as he spoke, he and his generals were pressing for a military advantage and engaging in punishing attacks against the enemy. This proved to be a losing strategy, as evidenced by the Tet Offensive of early 1968. In that series of strikes by Viet Cong guerillas against cities and towns throughout South Vietnam, the ancient capital of Hue was seized and Saigon itself was subject to unsettling attacks. Although the Viet Cong, with 40,000 dead during Tet, were eventually driven off, their morale severely damaged, the United States suffered a moral defeat, as well. It became obvious to everyone that there was no light at the end of the tunnel, as the generals had proclaimed. The quagmire seemed only to be getting murkier.

Protest and Prevarication

The antiwar movement that became one of the most prominent features of 1960s America emerged slowly, only as the prevailing anticommunist sentiment in the country began wane. Some of the first to protest were religious and pacifist groups along with members of the Old Left—socialists, progressives, and radicals. By the mid-1960s opposition had spread to many college campuses, spurred by resistance to the draft and by the increasing visibility of the war on television: news reports graphically depicted what was happening on the ground. In early 1966 Senator J. William Fulbright, chair of the Senate Foreign Relations Committee, held televised hearings regarding the war, revealing ambiguities in military policy and raising questions in the mind of the viewing public. Although a majority of Americans still supported the war effort, dissent both on campus and off spread rapidly. Protesters held marches, vigils, teach-ins, sit-ins, draft card burnings, and other forms of rebellion and agitation. The growing unpopularity of the war, and the no-win situation that it seemed to present, lay behind President Johnson's decision not to run for a second term in late March 1968. (At that point, the public had yet to learn of another debacle: the shooting, around this same time, of hundreds of unarmed civilians by a US Army patrol operating near My Lai.) One consequence of Johnson's withdrawal was the rise of prominent antiwar candidates on the Democratic side, including senators Eugene McCarthy and Robert F. Kennedy. Although Kennedy was killed before the party's August convention in Chicago, the event became a great showdown between antiwar and mainstream political and cultural forces. Protesters shouted "The whole world's watching!" as Chicago police, at Mayor Richard Daley behest, employed heavy-handed tactics to clear the scene. Johnson's vice president and, now, presidential contender, Hubert Humphrey, narrowly won the Democratic ticket over McCarthy but went on to lose the general election to the Republican nominee, Richard M. Nixon. It became clear that America was divided as it had not been divided since the time of the Civil War.

Nixon had run on a campaign message of "peace with honor," indicating that he would end the war and uphold the United States' good reputation abroad. He pledged in his victory speech to bring the divided nation together. And yet few politicians have been more polarizing than Nixon. He and his vice president, Spiro Agnew, denigrated antiwar protesters and members of the hippie counterculture, and he played on black-white tensions to win political support in the south and elsewhere. He argued that he sought an end to the war even as he widened it to Cambodia (where North Vietnamese supply lines ran) and as he resumed, on an even grander scale, the bombing of North Vietnam. He reduced American troops in the region under a policy of "Vietnamization," or the assignment of greater responsibility for the war to South Vietnam, and yet the war was still raging when he was elected to a second term in November 1972. In both prosecuting the war and undertaking peace negotiations, Nixon hoped to plant an image of himself as ruthless and unpredictable; he called it his "madman theory," expecting that the enemy would cave out of fear of this volatile president with his finger on the nuclear button.

The Cambodia operations served to stir widespread student protests, including on the campus of Kent State University, where on May 4, 1970, the National Guard shot and killed four students (not all of them protestors). War opposition generally increased as a result, coming to encompass, even, returning military veterans. Then, in June 1971, a secret Department of Defense history of US involvement in Vietnam was leaked to the press, creating an uproar. Known as the Pentagon Papers, the report revealed military operations that were unknown not only to the public but also to Congress. Even though the period covered in the document concerned years in which other administrations had held power, the Nixon administration did not welcome the revelations. Indeed, Nixon himself targeted the person who leaked the papers, former defense analyst Daniel Ellsberg, for retribution. A covert White House burglary team was sent to Ellsberg's psychiatrist's office seeking information, but nothing damaging was found. A subsequent break-in at the Democratic National Committee's headquarters in the Watergate Hotel was botched and led to the constitutional crisis known as Watergate. President Nixon found himself threatened with impeachment for high crimes and misdemeanors, but he decided to resign instead, on August 9, 1974. Fortunately for him, the Vietnam War—or, at least, America's participation in it—had already come to an end in the form of a peace accord signed in Paris in early 1973. Nixon's supporters could thus claim that

the president had delivered on his promise and was responsible for disengaging from Vietnam in an honorable manner. His critics, on the other hand, continued to blame him for prolonging the war and engaging in the same kind of deception and dissimulation that had taken place during the Johnson years—compounded, in this case, by the disaster of Watergate. When, in April 1975, the South Vietnamese capital of Saigon fell to the communists, the collapse seemed to epitomize the bright shining mess that was the Vietnam War. The war had been profoundly controversial through most of its existence, and it remained so well after it ended. Indeed, even the attempt to memorialize the soldiers, sailors, airmen, and marines who fought in it by erecting a monument on the National Mall, eight years after the American pullout, proved a difficult exercise. The abstract design chosen, created by Maya Lin, upset observers who expected a more traditional war memorial. Only after the Vietnam Veterans Memorial was erected in 1983 and visited by millions did it become an enduring icon of American culture and history. The 58,300 names it contains reflect US dead and missing; in Vietnam, the comparable figure would exceed 3 million.

Michael Shally-Jensen, PhD

Bibliography and Additional Reading

Appy, Christian G. *American Reckoning: The Vietnam War and Our National Identity.* New York: Viking, 2015.

Burr, William, and Jeffrey P. Kimball. *Nixon's Nuclear Specter: The Secret Alert of 1969, Madman Diplomacy, and the Vietnam War.* Lawrence, KS: University Press of Kansas, 2015.

Halberstam, David. *The Making of a Quagmire: America and Vietnam during the Kennedy Era.* Lanham, MD: Rowman & Littlefield, 2008.

Hunt, Michael H. *Lyndon Johnson's War: America's Cold War Crusade in Vietnam, 1945-1968.* New York: Hill & Wang, 1996.

Kaiser, David E. *American Tragedy: Kennedy, Johnson, and the Origins of the Vietnam War.* Cambridge, MA: Belknap Press, 2000.

Karnow, Stanley. *Vietnam: A History,* 2d ed. New York: Penguin Books, 1997.

Contributors

Anna Accettola, MA
University of California, Los Angeles

K.P. Dawes, MA
Chicago, IL

Steven L. Danver, PhD
Walden University

Ashleigh Fata, MA
University of California, Los Angeles

Gerald F. Goodwin, PhD
Bloomington, IN

Kevin Grimm, PhD
Regent University

Mark S. Joy, PhD
Jamestown University

Scott C. Monje, PhD
Tarrytown, NY

Michael Shally-Jensen, PhD
Amherst, MA

Robert Surbrug, PhD
Bay Path University

Anthony Vivian
University of California, Los Angeles

Donald A. Watt, PhD
Middleton, ID

DEFINING DOCUMENTS
IN AMERICAN HISTORY

The Vietnam War
(1956-1975)

KENNEDY'S WAR

The Vietnam War was, tragically, part of a larger war known as the Cold War. This larger conflict, while not always out in the open, pitted the decidedly anticommunist United States against communist powers such as the Soviet Union and China. Thus, in the United States, a policy of "containment" of communism was pursued, a policy demanding that presidents, lawmakers, and military leaders take steps to limit communist influence wherever it took root. The Truman administration, in the post–World War II years, was the first to apply the principle of containment to Southeast Asia, assisting the French in trying to put down the Viet Minh communist revolution in Indochina. President Dwight Eisenhower likened the process of containment, or rather the failure to contain, to a game of dominos: if one country fell to communism, then other countries in the same region would fall in turn. Under Eisenhower, therefore, aid to South Vietnam was continued and a small number of military advisers were sent in.

John F. Kennedy, a member of Congress during the Truman and Eisenhower years, was heir to the prevailing anticommunist thinking and came to experience its value—and its faults—first hand. First, there was the debacle of the Bay of Pigs, the failed April 1961 invasion of Cuba by CIA operatives (a project that Kennedy inherited and allowed to go forward). Then, there was the horror of the Cuban Missile Crisis of October 1962, when the United States and the Soviet Union faced off over the latter's deployment of nuclear missiles in Cuba. Between these two events, Kennedy was disposed to authorize further aid and assistance to South Vietnam in its effort to defend itself against communist forces. The problem in this case, however, was that the South Vietnamese government was an authoritarian regime very much disliked and distrusted by the majority of the Vietnamese people. Kennedy, therefore, was rather cautious in building up the American presence in Vietnam—top military leaders would have preferred a more rapid expansion—and he remained open to regime change in the country. He sent in more U.S. military advisers to assist in the fighting, and when a coup toppled the South Vietnamese government and its head, Ngo Dinh Diem, Kennedy was not disappointed. Some historians speculate that Kennedy may have continued to exhibit restraint in the region, but unfortunately he was killed soon after Diem's ouster. The baton was then passed to his successor, Lyndon B. Johnson.

■ Senator John F. Kennedy on America's Stake in Vietnam

Date: June 1, 1956
Author: John F. Kennedy
Genre: speech

Summary Overview

Vietnam was going through a period of transition in the mid-1950s. The former colonial rulers, the French, withdrew their forces and, in 1954, divided the territory into North and South Vietnam. In 1956, an election was to be held to unify the country, and the communist leaders in the North were favored to win. The organization the American Friends of Vietnam was opposed to this election and supported the government of South Vietnam. Senator John F. Kennedy was invited to give the keynote speech to a conference that was convened to influence American leaders to support this policy. Given that four and a half years later Senator Kennedy would become president, this speech is an important indicator of his thoughts prior to achieving the highest office in government. Also, his analysis of what might happen if the United States were to become involved in the war in Vietnam in 1954 proved to be an accurate view of the conflict that lay ahead.

Defining Moment

The communist movement was successful in 1917 in transforming Russia into the Soviet Union. But communism's spread soon stalled. This changed after World War II, when communist governments were put in place throughout areas in Europe and Asia that were occupied by the Soviet army. The 1949 victory by communist forces in China gave communism a strong position in Asia. When Vietnamese leaders sought to overthrow the French, communist leaders were more than willing to assist. The division of Vietnam into two countries, North and South, gave the leadership of the North to those who had adopted communist ideology, and leadership of the South was taken by Western/capitalist-leaning individuals.

By the time of this conference in June 1956, all French forces had withdrawn and an election was to be held to reunify Vietnam. There was little doubt that the leaders of North Vietnam, those who had been most active in the anti-French revolution, and who most fully adopted the communist ideology, would win the election. Thus, it was believed, if the United States was to stem the growth of communism in Asia, it must support the leaders of South Vietnam to keep communism bottled up in the North. The gathering convened by the American Friends of Vietnam proposed to influence American leaders of both parties to support South Vietnam along with its leader, Ngo Dinh Diem. John F. Kennedy, a rising star in the Democratic Party, was invited to speak. Although a majority of the American Friends of Vietnam were conservative, it was necessary to get liberals, such as Kennedy, to support the cause. Kennedy's views, as expressed in this speech, help to explain why, as president, he was willing to increase military aid to South Vietnam. While neither this speech nor this conference can be given total credit for the policy of America supporting South Vietnam, the talk sought a continuation of President Eisenhower's commitment of opposing communism. The continuity of American policy in 1961, in the transition from a Republican administration to a Democratic one, is clearly foreshadowed in this speech, as was Kennedy's strong anticommunist rhetoric during the presidential campaign. Kennedy's statement that Vietnam was the "keystone of the Free World in Southeast Asia" was a clear variant on the "domino theory," which had been put forth by President Eisenhower two years before. This speech contains the essence of what would become American policy toward Vietnam for most of the succeeding two decades.

Author Biography

John Fitzgerald Kennedy (1917–1963) was born into a wealthy Catholic family in Boston. His parents stressed success for him and all his siblings. As a student, he excelled at what he enjoyed and was mediocre at the rest. Although he spent much of his time socializing, his senior thesis at Harvard was published in 1940. A naval war hero in World War II, in 1946, he was elected to the House of Representatives. In 1952, he ran for the US Senate, defeating the Republican incumbent in a year when Republicans won the presidency, the Senate, and the House. The following year, he married Jacqueline Bouvier. He ran for and was elected president in 1960 and was the first Catholic to hold that position. His foreign policy was staunchly anticommunist throughout the world. Assassinated on November 21, 1963, Kennedy had a mixed record of accomplishments during his short term as president, but the enthusiasm and activism he inspired endeared him to many across the nation.

HISTORICAL DOCUMENT

It is a genuine pleasure to be here today at this vital Conference on the future of Vietnam, and America's stake in that new nation, sponsored by the American Friends of Vietnam, an organization of which I am proud to be a member. Your meeting today at a time when political events concerning Vietnam are approaching a climax, both in that country and in our own Congress, is most timely. Your topic and deliberations, which emphasize the promise of the future more than the failures of the past, are most constructive. I can assure you that the Congress of the United States will give considerable weight to your findings and recommendations; and I extend to all of you who have made the effort to participate in this Conference my congratulations and best wishes.

It is an ironic and tragic fact that this Conference is being held at a time when the news about Vietnam has virtually disappeared from the front pages of the American press, and the American people have all but forgotten the tiny nation for which we are in large measure responsible. This decline in public attention is due, I believe, to three factors:

(1) First, it is due in part to the amazing success of President Diem in meeting firmly and with determination the major political and economic crises which had heretofore continually plagued Vietnam. (I shall say more about this point later, for it deserves more consideration from all Americans interested in the future of Asia).

(2) Secondly, it is due in part to the traditional role of American journalism, including readers as well as writers, to be more interested in crises than in accomplishments, to give more space to the threat of wars than the need for works, and to write larger headlines on the sensational omissions of the past than the creative missions of the future.

(3) Third and finally, our neglect of Vietnam is the result of one of the most serious weaknesses that has hampered the long-range effectiveness of American foreign policy over the past several years—and that is the over emphasis upon our role as "volunteer fire department" for the world. Whenever and wherever fire breaks out—in Indo-China, in the Middle East, in Guatemala, in Cyprus, in the Formosan Straits—our firemen rush in, wheeling up all their heavy equipment, and resorting to every known method of containing and extinguishing the blaze. The crowd gathers—the usually successful efforts of our able volunteers are heartily applauded—and then the firemen rush off to the next conflagration, leaving the grateful but still stunned inhabitants to clean up the rubble, pick up the pieces and rebuild their homes with whatever resources are available.

The role, to be sure, is a necessary one; but it is not the only role to be played, and the others cannot be ignored. A volunteer fire department halts, but rarely prevents, fires. It repels but rarely rebuilds; it meets the problems of the present but not of the future. And while we are devoting our attention to the Communist arson in Korea, there is smoldering in Indo-China; we turn our efforts to Indo-China until the alarm sounds in Algeria—and so it goes.

Of course Vietnam is not completely forgotten by our policy-makers today—I could not in honesty make such a charge and the facts would easily refute it—but the unfortunate truth of the matter is that, in my opinion, Vietnam would in all likelihood be receiving more attention from our Congress and Administration, and greater assistance under our aid programs, if it were in imminent danger of Communist invasion or revolution. Like those peoples of Latin America and Africa whom we have very nearly overlooked in the past decade, the Vietnamese may find that their devotion to the cause of democracy, and their success in reducing the strength of local Communist groups, have had the ironic effect of reducing American support. Yet the need for that support has in no way been reduced. (I hope it will not be necessary for the Diem Government—or this organization—to subsidize the growth of the South Vietnam Communist Party in order to focus American attention on that nation's critical needs!)

No one contends that we should now rush all our firefighting equipment to Vietnam, ignoring the Middle East or any other part of the world. But neither should we conclude that the cessation of hostilities in Indo-China removed that area from the list of important areas of United States foreign policy. Let us briefly consider exactly what is "America's Stake in Vietnam":

(1) First, Vietnam represents the cornerstone of the Free World in Southeast Asia, the keystone to the arch, the finger in the dike. Burma, Thailand, India, Japan, the Philippines and obviously Laos and Cambodia are among those whose security would be threatened if the Red Tide of Communism overflowed into Vietnam. In the past, our policy-makers have sometimes issued contradictory statements on this point—but the long history of Chinese invasions of Southeast Asia being stopped by Vietnamese warriors should have removed all doubt on this subject.

Moreover, the independence of a Free Vietnam is crucial to the free world in fields other than the military. Her economy is essential to the economy of Southeast Asia; and her political liberty is an inspiration to those seeking to obtain or maintain their liberty in all parts of Asia—and indeed the world. The fundamental tenets of this nation's foreign policy, in short, depend in considerable measure upon a strong and free Vietnamese nation.

(2) Secondly, Vietnam represents a proving ground of democracy in Asia. However we may choose to ignore it or deprecate it, the rising prestige and influence of Communist China in Asia are unchallengeable facts. Vietnam represents the alternative to Communist dictatorship. If this democratic experiment fails, if some one million refugees have fled the totalitarianism of the North only to find neither freedom nor security in the South, then weakness, not strength, will characterize the meaning of

democracy in the minds of still more Asians. The United States is directly responsible for this experiment—it is playing an important role in the laboratory where it is being conducted. We cannot afford to permit that experiment to fail.

(3) Third and in somewhat similar fashion, Vietnam represents a test of American responsibility and determination in Asia. If we are not the parents of little Vietnam, then surely we are the godparents. We presided at its birth, we gave assistance to its life, we have helped to shape its future. As French influence in the political, economic and military spheres has declined in Vietnam, American influence has steadily grown. This is our offspring—we cannot abandon it, we cannot ignore its needs. And if it falls victim to any of the perils that threaten its existence—Communism, political anarchy, poverty and the rest—then the United States, with some justification, will be held responsible; and our prestige in Asia will sink to a new low.

(4) Fourth and finally, America's stake in Vietnam, in her strength and in her security, is a very selfish one—for it can be measured, in the last analysis, in terms of American lives and American dollars. It is now well known that we were at one time on the brink of war in Indo-China—a war which could well have been more costly, more exhausting and less conclusive than any war we have ever known. The threat to such war is not now altogether removed from the horizon. Military weakness, political instability or economic failure in the new state of Vietnam could change almost overnight the apparent security which has increasingly characterized that area under the leadership of Premier Diem. And the key position of Vietnam in Southeast Asia, as already discussed, makes inevitable the involvement of this nation's security in any new outbreak of trouble.

It is these four points, in my opinion, that represent America's stake in Vietnamese security. And before we look to the future, let us stop to review what the Diem Government has already accomplished by way of increasing that security. Most striking of all, perhaps, has been the rehabilitation of more than three-quarters of a million refugees from the North. For these courageous people dedicated to the free way of life, approximately 45,000 houses have been constructed, 2,500 wells dug, 100 schools established and dozens of medical centers and maternity homes provided.

Equally impressive has been the increased solidarity and stability of the Government, the elimination of rebellious sects and the taking of the first vital steps toward true democracy. Where once colonialism and Communism struggled for supremacy, a free and independent republic has been proclaimed, recognized by over 40 countries of the free world. Where once a playboy emperor ruled from a distant shore, a constituent assembly has been elected.

Social and economic reforms have likewise been remarkable. The living conditions of the peasants have been vastly improved, the wastelands have been cultivated, and a wider ownership of the land is gradually being encouraged. Farm cooperatives and farmer loans have modernized an outmoded agricultural economy; and a tremendous dam in the center of the country has made possible the irrigation of a vast area previously uncultivated. Legislation for better labor relations, health protection, working conditions and wages has been completed under the leadership of President Diem.

Finally, the Vietnamese army—now fighting for its own homeland and not its colonial masters - has increased tremendously in both quality and quantity. General O'Daniel can tell you more about these accomplishments.

But the responsibility of the United States for Vietnam does not conclude, obviously, with a review of what has been accomplished thus far with our help. Much more needs to be done; much more, in fact, than we have been doing up to now. Military alliances in Southeast Asia are necessary but not enough. Atomic superiority and the development of new ultimate weapons are not enough. Informational and propaganda activities, warning of the evils of Communism and the blessings of the American way of life, are not enough in a country where concepts of free enterprise and capitalism are meaningless, where poverty and hunger are not enemies across the 17th parallel but enemies within their midst. As Ambassador Chuong has recently said: "People cannot be expected to fight for the Free World unless they have their own freedom to defend, their freedom from foreign domination as well as freedom from misery, oppression, corruption."

I shall not attempt to set forth the details of the type of aid program this nation should offer the Vietnamese—for it is not the details of that program that are as important as the spirit with which it is offered and the objectives it seeks to accomplish. We should not attempt to buy the friendship of the Vietnamese. Nor can we win their hearts by making them dependent upon our handouts. What we must offer them is a revolution—a political, economic and social revolution far superior to anything the Communists can offer—far more peaceful, far more democratic and far more locally controlled. Such a Revolution will require much from the United States and much from Vietnam. We must supply capital to replace that drained by the centuries of colonial exploitation; technicians to train those handicapped by deliberate policies of illiteracy; guidance to assist a nation taking those first feeble steps toward the complexities of a republican form of government. We must assist the inspiring growth of Vietnamese democracy and economy, including the complete integration of those refugees who gave up their homes and their belongings to seek freedom. We must provide military assistance to rebuild the new Vietnamese Army, which every day faces the growing peril of Vietminh Armies across the border.

And finally, in the councils of the world, we must never permit any diplomatic action adverse to this, one of the youngest members of the family of nations—and I include in that injunction a plea that the United States never give its approval to the early nationwide elections called for by the Geneva Agreement of 1954. Neither the United States nor Free Vietnam was a party to that agreement—and neither the United States nor Free Vietnam is ever going to be a party to an election obviously stacked and subverted in advance, urged upon us by those who have already broken their own pledges under the Agreement they now seek to enforce.

All this and more we can offer Free Vietnam, as it passes through the present period of transition on its way to a new era—an era of pride and independence, and era of democratic and economic growth—an era which, when contrasted with the long years of colonial oppression, will truly represent a political, social and economic revolution.

This is the revolution we can, we should, we must offer to the people of Vietnam—not as charity, not as a business proposition, not as a political maneuver, nor simply to enlist them as soldiers against Communism or as chattels of American foreign policy—but a revolution of their own making, for their own welfare, and for the security of freedom everywhere. The Communists offer them another kind of revolution, glittering and seductive in its superficial appeal. The choice between the two can be made only by the Vietnamese people themselves. But in these times of trial and burden, true friendships stand out. As Premier Diem recently wrote a great friend of Vietnam, Senator Mansfield, "It is only in winter that you can tell which trees are evergreen." And I am confident that if this nation demonstrates that it has not forgotten the people of Vietnam, the people of Vietnam will demonstrate that they have not forgotten us.

GLOSSARY

Indo-China (also, Indochina): Southeast Asia

North: North Vietnam, the Democratic Republic of Vietnam, ally of communist nations, and the eventual victor in the war

South Vietnam: the Republic of Vietnam, ally of the United States

Vietminh Armies: originally, communist forces fighting the French; the term was later used for North Vietnamese troops and related forces

Document Analysis

While not a well-known speech, this declaration of values by then Senator Kennedy illustrates the speaker's understanding of American culture and politics as well as of America's national security policy. The focal point of the United States' foreign policy was opposition to communism. Kennedy uses Cold War rhetoric here in praising a leader, in this case Diem, who was opposed to communism. During this period, it is implied, if Diem could be useful in stopping the spread of communism, then many, more negative behaviors could be overlooked. For Kennedy and the Friends of Vietnam, and according to the American foreign policy of that day, the ideology of North Vietnam must not be allowed to spread. Thus, Kennedy concisely lays out a position of unity regarding his and Eisenhower's policy on Vietnam. In an aside, he predicts the course of the military conflict in the 1960s and early '70s.

Kennedy understood that, in 1956, Vietnam was not a topic of interest for most Americans or their political leaders. Then as now, journalists and readers preferred stories about sensational events, not about situations that seemed to be unfolding smoothly. Thus, with the withdrawal of the French, and with the Geneva Accords setting a path for Vietnamese unity, the crisis seemed to be over. Kennedy's analogy of the United States as a volunteer fire department reflects his ability to communicate important issues using everyday images and serves as an apt description of how US forces were being used. Kennedy understood that stopping communist expansion was needed, but, more importantly, he recognized the inadequacy of a policy that achieved only this end. He proclaims that to win in Vietnam, the United States needed to offer a way of life that was "far superior to anything the Communists can offer." Unfortunately for the people of Vietnam, and for American foreign policy, that which was being offered by the Diem regime did not add up to this sort of total social revolution.

Kennedy's vision of Vietnam as "the keystone to the arch" of countries surrounding China, from Japan to India, was in line with the mainstream thought of American leaders. While in retrospect this view can be questioned, the staggering advances made by communism in the decade prior to 1956 raised legitimate concerns for the United States. As is always the case in foreign policy, Kennedy had to deal with the situation and leaders at hand. Thus, he speaks words of support for Diem, even though many of the accomplishments mentioned in the speech were not benefiting the

Buddhist majority in Vietnam, but only the Catholic minority, including Diem himself. Kennedy subtly pushes for change in South Vietnam by stating that the country could be a showplace of freedom and democracy for all Vietnamese and all of Asia.

Given the steps that Kennedy would later take as president, which moved the United States into a more active military role in Vietnam, it is interesting that he presents his thoughts on what a war in that country might mean. While believing that at some point the United States might have to intervene militarily in Vietnam, he hopes that this will not happen. He reflects that if the United States had entered the previous conflict, it would have been "more costly, more exhausting and less conclusive than any war we have ever known." That essential insight ultimately became the reality when Americans had had enough of Vietnam and American troops were finally withdrawn from the country in the 1970s.

Essential Themes
While in many areas of politics Kennedy was seen as innovative or liberal, his position on Vietnam reflected the status quo. By 1956, Vietnam had become "our offspring," and the United States needed to support South Vietnam as a bulkhead against communism. If things faltered in that country, it would be "inevitable" that the United States would have to protect its interests elsewhere in the region. While Kennedy hoped that South Vietnam would progress in all areas, he indicates that he was not totally opposed to American military activity in the country. The fact that he held this view in 1956 meant that there was no real division on the issue between the major candidates in the 1960 presidential election. This speech suggests the policy that Kennedy would pursue when the situation in South Vietnam worsened under his presidency in the early 1960s. The speech may not represent a blueprint of his later actions in Vietnam, but it does reflect his thoughts on how the United States might combat a possible communist expansion. This is the most important aspect of Kennedy's speech and one that later stood as the basis of American foreign policy in the region in the decade after his death.

The speech also contains an example of Kennedy's understanding about how the success or failure of American foreign policy should be measured not merely in terms of military accomplishments or the ideology of a government. He believed, rather, that American foreign policy would be successful only when it helped the average person in Vietnam, or when it assisted the citizens of any country to live better, more secure lives. Freedom and personal security in economic, social, or political terms was what Kennedy thought should be the measure of whether American policy was a success. Thus, he talks about better living conditions, economic growth, and the implementation of democracy for the people of South Vietnam. Through these measures, Kennedy believed, the people of South Vietnam would not only advance themselves, but would also solidify themselves in opposition to communism. While Kennedy recognized that there was value in being the "volunteer fire department" stamping out a communist insurgency, he declares that it was important to follow up such actions by taking measures that allowed the values of freedom and liberty to become a part of the daily life of a country. Only then, Kennedy believed, would the revolution against oppression be complete.

—Donald A. Watt, PhD

Bibliography and Additional Reading
Dallek, Robert. *An Unfinished Life: John F. Kennedy, 1917–1963*. Boston: Little, Brown & Company, 2003. Print.
Freedman, Lawrence. *Kennedy's Wars: Berlin, Cuba, Laos, and Vietnam*. Oxford: Oxford University Press, 2002. Print.
Morgan, Joseph G. *The Vietnam Lobby: The American Friends of Vietnam, 1955–1975*. Chapel Hill and London: University of North Carolina Press, 1997. Print.
Prados, John. "JFK and the Diem Coup." *The National Security Archive*. George Washington University, 5 Nov. 2003. Web. 29 May 2015. <http://nsarchive.gwu.edu/NSAEBB/NSAEBB101/>.
Sorenson, Theodore C. *Kennedy*. New York: Harper & Row, 1965. Print.

■ "The Path of Revolution in the South"

Date: 1956
Author: Le Duan
Genre: essay

Summary Overview

In 1956, Le Duan was one of the top three leaders in the Vietnamese Communist Party and in North Vietnam. By the time he wrote this essay, it was clear that the election to unify North and South Vietnam was not going to occur. The essay had a two-fold purpose. While it was a call for a negotiated settlement, Le Duan clearly saw the reluctance of the South to negotiate and thus placed the blame for the impending conflict on South Vietnam and the United States (which was propping up the South Vietnamese government). Secondly, this was a call for support by the North Vietnamese leaders and people for the reunification of Vietnam, through an armed conflict if necessary. Although it was still a few years until large-scale military action between North and South Vietnam was undertaken, this document served as a foundation for the North's support of South Vietnamese insurgents as well as for the direct involvement of North Vietnamese forces.

Defining Moment

World War II brought about the end of colonization in many parts of the world, including Vietnam. Just as most of the French government cooperated with the Germans after the fall of Paris in 1940, so too most of the French colonial officers in Vietnam cooperated with the Japanese when the latter arrived in September of that same year. Once an Allied victory became all but assured in Europe, French nationalism began to increase among its colonial officials. Thus, in March 1945, the Japanese incarcerated the French and set up a puppet Vietnamese government. The Viet Minh, communist forces that had fought the Japanese throughout the war, were able to gain control of northern Vietnam by August and declared an independent state there. France returned after the conclusion of World War II and tried to re-establish a colony, ultimately losing in 1954 when the Geneva Accords were signed. In that agreement, two temporary states were established, a communist one in the North and a pro-Western one in the South.

When the provisions of the Geneva Accords fell apart in 1956, the communist leaders in the North had to decide whether to accept a divided country for the foreseeable future or to develop a new plan for Vietnam's unification as a communist state. There were moderates who were satisfied with the status quo, and others who wanted to try a new round of negotiations. Le Duan was the leader of the faction that wanted to reunify the country as soon as possible and by whatever means necessary. His "Path of Revolution" essay set forth the justification for military action because, to him, it was clear that peaceful negotiations were not going to occur. Having served the Communist Party in the South, Le Duan was certain that he understood the situation and what would be needed. As he lobbied other members of the Communist Party's Central Committee, he presented the idea that aggressive military action was the only alternative to negotiation.

At the 1956 meeting of North Vietnam's Central Committee, the discussions resulted in a decision as to which direction the committee would move to unify the country. As no negotiations were imminent, the committee chose the direction advocated by Le Duan. Le Duan was so successful in presenting his case, in fact, that he was elevated to membership in the secretariat at that meeting. In 1957, Le Duan was assigned the task of developing a full plan for the military struggle with the South, which was implemented in 1959. Although Ho Chi Minh was technically in charge until his death in 1969, Le Duan was the political leader of the military campaign in South Vietnam until the end of the war in 1975.

Author Biography

Le Duan (1907/08–1986) was born in the southern part of Vietnam while it was part of French Indochi-

9

na. Having received a basic education, he worked as a clerk for the railroad system. While in this job, he became acquainted with Marxism. In 1928, he joined the Revolutionary Youth League and, two years later, was a founding member of the Indochina Communist Party. Within a few more years, he was a member of the Central Committee. As a result of this group's anti-French actions, Le Duan was twice imprisoned. Released from prison in 1945, he became an assistant to the commu-

nist leader Ho Chi Minh, focusing on activities in the south. In 1956, he was elevated to membership in the Secretariat of the Communist Party, becoming first secretary in 1959 and then head of the Communist Party in 1960. While officially sharing power with Ho Chi Minh, until Ho's death in 1969, when Ho's health declined in the mid-1960s Le Duan was clearly the party leader. Until his own death, he was first among equals in the political collective leadership of Vietnam.

HISTORICAL DOCUMENT

The situation forces bellicose states such as the U.S. and Britain to recognize that if they adventurously start a world war, they themselves will be the first to be destroyed, and thus the movement to demand peace in those imperialist countries is also developing strongly.

Recently, in the U.S. Presidential election, the present Republican administration, in order to buy the people's esteem, put forward the slogan "Peace and Prosperity," which showed that even the people of an imperialist warlike country like the U.S. want peace.

The general situation shows us that the forces of peace and democracy in the world have tipped the balance toward the camp of peace and democracy. Therefore we can conclude that the world at present can maintain long-term peace.

On the other hand, however, we can also conclude that as long as the capitalist economy survives, it will always scheme to provoke war, and there will still remain the danger of war.

Based on the above the world situation, the Twentieth Congress of the Communist Party of the Soviet Union produced two important judgments:

1.   All conflicts in the world at present can be resolved by means of peaceful negotiations.
2.   The revolutionary movement in many countries at present can develop peacefully.

Naturally in the countries in which the ruling class has a powerful military-police apparatus and is using fascist policies to repress the movement, the revolutionary parties in those countries must look clearly at their concrete situation to have the appropriate methods of struggle.

Based on the general situation and that judgment, we conclude that, if all conflicts can be resolved by means of peaceful negotiations, peace can be achieved.

Because the interest and aspiration of peaceful reunification of our country are the common interest and aspiration of all the people of the Northern and Southern zones, the people of the two zones did not have any reason to provoke war, nor to prolong the division of the country. On the contrary the people of the two zones are more and more determined to oppose the U.S.-Diem scheme of division and war provocation in order to create favorable conditions for negotiations between the two zones for peaceful unification of the country.

The present situation of division is created solely by the arbitrary U.S.-Diem regime, so the fundamental problem is how to smash the U.S.-Diem scheme of division and war-provocation.

As observed above, if they want to oppose the U.S-Diem regime, there is no other path for the people of the South but the path of revolution. What, then, is the line and struggle method of the revolutionary movement in the South? If the world situation can maintain peace due to a change in the relationship of forces in the world in favor of the camp of peace and democracy, the revolutionary movement can develop following a peaceful line, and the revolutionary movement in the South can also develop following a peaceful line.

First of all, we must determine what it means for a revolutionary movement to struggle according to a peaceful line. A revolutionary movement struggling according to a peaceful line takes the political forces of the people as the base rather than using people's armed forces to struggle with the existing government to achieve their revolutionary objective. A revolutionary movement struggling according to a peaceful line is also different from a reformist movement in that a reformist movement relies fundamentally on the law and constitution to struggle, while a revolutionary movement relies on the revolutionary political forces of the masses as the base. And another difference is that a revolutionary movement struggles for revolutionary objectives, while a reformist movement struggles for reformist goals. With an imperialist, feudalist, dictatorial, fascist government like the U.S.-Diem, is it possible for a peaceful political struggle line to achieve its objectives?

We must recognize that all accomplishments in every country are due to the people. That is a definite law: it cannot be otherwise. Therefore the line of the revolutionary movement must be in accord with the inclinations and aspirations of the people. Only in that way can a revolutionary movement be mobilized and succeed.

The ardent aspiration of the Southern people is to maintain peace and achieve national unification. We must clearly recognize this longing for peace: the revolutionary movement in the South can mobilize and advance to success on the basis of grasping the flag of peace, in harmony with popular feelings. On the contrary, U.S.-Diem is using fascist violence to provoke war, contrary to the will of the people and therefore must certainly be defeated.

Can the U.S.-Diem regime, by using a clumsy policy of fascist violence, create a strong force to oppose and destroy the revolutionary movement? Definitely not, because the U.S.-Diem regime has no political strength in the country worth mentioning to rely on. On the contrary, nearly all strata of the people oppose them. Therefore the U.S.-Diem government is not a strong government it is only a vile and brutal government. Its vile and brutal character means that it not only has no mass base in the country but is on the way to being isolated internationally. Its cruelty definitely cannot shake the revolutionary movement, and it cannot survive for long.

The proof is that in the past two years, everywhere in the countryside, the sound of the gunfire of U.S.-Diem repression never ceased; not a day went by when they did not kill patriots, but the revolutionary spirit is still firm, and the revolutionary base of the people still has not been shaken.

Once the entire people have become determined to protect the revolution, there is no cruel force that can shake it. But why has the revolutionary movement not yet developed strongly? This is also due to certain objective and subjective factors.

Objectively, we see that, after nine years of waging strong armed struggle, the people's movement generally speaking now has a temporarily peaceful character that is a factor in the change of the movement for violent forms of struggle to peaceful forms. It has the correct character of rebuilding to advance later.

With the cruel repression and exploitation of the U.S.-Diem, the people's revolutionary movement definitely will rise up. The people of the South have known the blood and fire of nine years of resistance war, but the cruelty of the U.S.-Diem cannot extinguish the struggle spirit of the people.

On the other hand, subjectively, we must admit that a large number of cadres, those have responsibility for guiding the revolutionary movement, because of the change in the method of struggle and the work situation from public to secret, have not yet firmly grasped the political line of the party, have not yet firmly grasped the method of political struggle, and have not yet followed correctly the mass line, and therefore have greatly reduced the movement's possibilities for development.

At present, therefore, the political struggle movement has not yet developed equally among the people, and a primary reason is that a number of cadres and masses are not yet aware that the strength of political forces of the people can defeat the cruelty, oppression and exploitation of the U.S.-Diem, and therefore they have a halfway attitude and don't believe in the strength of their political forces.

We must admit that any revolutionary movement has times when it falls and times when it rises; any revolutionary movement has times that are favorable for development and times that are unfavorable. The basic thing is that the cadres must see clearly the character of the movement's development to lead the mass struggle to the correct degree, and find a way for the vast determined masses to participate in the movement. If they are determined to struggle from the bottom to the top, no force can resist the determination of the great masses.

In the past two years, the political struggle movement in the countryside and in the cities, either by one form or another, has shown that the masses have much capacity for political struggle with the U.S.-Diem. In those struggles, if we grasp more firmly the struggle line and method, the movement can develop further, to the advantage of the revolution. The cruel policy of U.S.-Diem clearly cannot break the movement, or the people's will to struggle.

There are those who think that the U.S.-Diem's use of violence is now aimed fundamentally at killing the leaders of the revolutionary movement to destroy the Communist Party, and that if the Communist Party is worn away to the point that it doesn't have the capacity to lead the revolution, the political struggle movement of the masses cannot develop.

This judgment is incorrect. Those who lead the revolutionary movement are determined to mingle with the masses, to protect and serve the interest of the masses and to pursue correctly the mass line. Between the masses and communists there is no distinction any more. So how can the U.S.-Diem destroy the leaders of the revolutionary movement, since they cannot destroy the masses? Therefore they cannot annihilate the cadres leading the mass movement.

In fact more than twenty years ago, the French imperialists were determined to destroy the Communists to destroy the revolutionary movement for national liberation, but the movement triumphed. It wasn't the Communist but the French imperialist themselves and their feudal lackeys who were destroyed on our soil.

Now twenty years later, U.S.-Diem are determined to destroy the Communists in the South, but the movement is still firm, and Communists are still determined to fulfill their duty. And the revolutionary movement will definitely advance and destroy the imperialist, feudalist government. U.S.-Diem will be destroyed, just as the French imperialists and their feudal lackeys were destroyed.

We believe that: the peaceful line is appropriate not only to the general situation in the world but also to the situation within the country, both nation-wide and in the South. We believe that the will for peace and the peace forces of the people throughout the country have smashed the U.S.-Diem schemes of war provocation and division.

We believe that the will for peace and Southern people's democratic and peace forces will defeat the cruel, dictatorial and fascist policy of U.S.-Diem and will advance to smash the imperialist, feudalist U.S.-Diem government. Using love and righteousness to triumph over force is a tradition of the Vietnamese nation. The aspiration for peace is an aspiration of the world's people in general and in our own country, including the people of the South, so our struggle line cannot be separated from the peaceful line.

Only the peaceful struggle line can create strong political forces to defeat the scheme of war provocation and the cruel policy of U.S.-Diem. We are determined to carry out our line correctly, and later the development of the situation will permit us to do so.

Imperialism and feudalism are on the road to disappearance. The victory belongs to our people's glorious task of unification and independence, to our glorious Communism we must pledge our lives. We shall win.

GLOSSARY

Diem: Ngo Dinh Diem, president of South Vietnam

two zones: a means of referring to a divided Vietnam (north and south) without implying the legitimacy of South Vietnam

Document Analysis

Le Duan issues a call for peace in this essay, while outlining the reasons that war is justified. He maintains that most people want peace, but he also claims that the people in both North and South Vietnam desire, even more so, to be unified. This attitude, according to Le Duan, was the result of the "imperialist warlike country" of the United States and the "fascist" government of Diem joining forces in the South. Thus, in a paradoxical way, Le Duan argues that the communists and others seeking peace must work to overthrow Diem at all costs in order to foster peace and unification. As he saw it, the time was ripe for revolution against these twin oppressors of the people (the Diem regime and his US backers).

When Le Duan circulated this essay among the party and governmental leaders of North Vietnam, he understood that a weariness regarding war had arisen owing to the long recent struggle against the French. He included material from the Communist Party's Twentieth Congress in the Soviet Union to demonstrate that he understood the rationale for not wanting immediately to push for change in South Vietnam, when one could perhaps gain the desired ends through political negotiations. However, from his perspective, the latter route was not likely to advance the goal of unifying the nation under communist rule. Thus, even though frequently he invokes the terms "peace" and "peaceful" in his essay, the central message is to unleash all "appropriate methods of struggle"—up to and including armed conflict—against the oppressors. The "imperialist, feudalist, dictatorial, fascist" regime of Diem, supported by the United States, would never allow a peaceful transition and unification.

Although the oppression Le Duan refers to was, at this time, directed mainly against Buddhist opposition elements in the south rather than against communist groups, the author is correct to note that the "masses" have not been included in the governing system of the south and therefore might be ready to follow a communist push for change. Time and again, Le Duan refers to the violence of the Diem regime. He seems certain that while violence might stop the actions of a few, it was not going to stop broader change, particularly when virtually the entire population desired it. As part of his work to move the leadership of the Communist Party to his position, Le Duan intentionally sets the peaceful communists in opposition to the violent Diem regime. He places the blame for his proposed policy of aggressive military response on the leaders of the South and on the United States. The "half-way attitude" by which Le Duan characterizes leaders of various cadres refers not only to those in the South, but also to too-moderate leaders in the North. Through emphasizing the so-called "peaceful struggle line," the essayist attempts to justify "smashing" the Diem regime and obtaining the desired "unification and independence."

who desired results rather than ideological purity. Thus, while he refers to the peaceful path toward change put forward by Soviet communist leaders, Le Duan desires quicker results. He looks beyond using solely "strong political forces" to destroy the violent Diem regime. He talks up the notion of peace, yet in seeking the desired ends, he advocates an aggressive military stance toward the enemy. Because Diem, in 1955, had used a questionable election to displace the emperor who was put in place by the Japanese in 1945, and because he also refused to allow nationwide elections for unification, Le Duan did not regard negotiation as an option. For him, rather, aggression was justified. His use of President Eisenhower's 1956 campaign slogan, "Peace and Prosperity," demonstrates his belief that the desire for peace could eventually produce results beneficial to the people of Vietnam. While he incorrectly boasts that the conflict in Vietnam would destroy the United States, he is correct in his assessment that, in most nations, there is a point at which the people would rather realize peace than continue a conflict.

While his essay cannot be viewed as a blueprint for the North's reaching its desired goals, it is a call for the reactivation of the revolutionary struggle that had defeated the French. That message ultimately carried the day with the leaders of North Vietnam. In the next year, Le Duan was given the task of developing a plan for the political and military actions that would unfold in South Vietnam. The strategy began to be implemented in 1959, with the formation of the various oppositional organizations in the South in 1960. Although at first glance "The Path of Revolution in the South" might not seem relevant to the ensuing path of war, given that so much of its space is given over to pronouncements of peace, the essay proved key in pushing the people toward war. It also illustrates the approach that North Vietnam would take in its public pronouncements, picturing itself as desiring only peace and placing all the blame for the war squarely on the other side. Le Duan was able to win the necessary political support for the war in both North and South Vietnam, ultimately resulting in the communists' successfully reaching their goal of unifying the nation under their rule.

—Donald A. Watt, PhD

Essential Themes

Although a communist from the inception of the party in Vietnam, Le Duan was often seen as a pragmatist

Bibliography and Additional Reading

Ang, Cheng Guan. *The Vietnam War From the Other Side: The Vietnamese Communists' Perspective*. London: Routledge, 2002. Print.

Duiker, William. *Sacred War: Nationalism and Revolution in a Divided Vietnam*. New York: McGraw Hill, 1994. Print.

Le, Quynh. "Vietnam Ambivalent on Le Duan's Legacy." *BBC News*. BBC, 14 Jul. 2006. Web. <http://news.bbc.co.uk/2/hi/asia-pacific/5180354.stm>.

Nguyen, Lien-Hang T. *Hanoi's War: An International History of the War for Peace in Vietnam*. (The New Cold War History) Chapel Hill, NC: University of North Carolina Press, 2012. Print.

Tucker, Spencer C. *The Encyclopedia of the Vietnam War: A Political, Social, and Military History*. 2nd ed. Santa Barbara: ABD-CLIO, 2011.

■ President Ngo Dinh Diem: Address to US Congress

Date: May 9, 1957
Author: President Ngo Dinh Diem of South Vietnam
Genre: speech

Summary Overview

Ngo Dinh Diem had been president of South Vietnam (the Republic of Vietnam) for two years at the time of this speech. During the previous year, 1956, an election was to have been held to unify the nation—North and South—under one government, and virtually everyone expected the leader of North Vietnam, Ho Chi Minh, to win that electoral contest. In line with US wishes, the election was cancelled, and communist leaders in the North therefore began agitating for change in the South. Since the United States had been the main supporter of South Vietnam, President Diem went to the US Congress to seek America's continued support. He knew that without the help of the United States, he would not stay in power, and most likely, the government of the North would take control of all of Vietnam. Using terms that he expected would resonate with members of Congress, Diem sought to cement the relationship between the two countries and solidify his position as an anticommunist leader in postcolonial Indochina.

Defining Moment

With the defeat of French forces by a communist-commanded army in 1954, negotiations led to the Geneva Accords of that year. The accords established a timeline for the withdrawal of French forces, temporarily divided of the country into two sections (North and South), and set elections for 1956 to bring about a united government at the national level. The French were able to install Emperor Bao Dai, with whom they had worked for decades, in the South, leaving the communists their stronghold in the North. When Diem challenged Bao Dai for power in the South in 1955, he was untainted by cooperation with the French and was also able to steer the election process and control the press. Winning the premiership with over 98 percent of the vote, and consequently refusing to hold the 1956 unification election, Diem had tested the limits of the political sys-

tem and was in need of outside support. Viewing Vietnam as a strategic location in which to stop communist expansion, US president Dwight D. Eisenhower decided to support Diem by sending a small number of military advisers and significant amounts of financial aid. In order for this aid to continue, the US Congress would need to authorize funding for it. Thus, it was vital that Diem's speech before a joint session of Congress be well received.

Diem was not seeking active participation by American military forces, despite the fact that various small uprisings against his regime were then taking place in South Vietnam. While some of these uprisings were communist-inspired, most were the result of local disenchantment with Diem's policies. They did not present a unified front, as was essentially the case in later years. Knowing his American audience, however, Diem sought to garner support by presenting Vietnam as a focal point for US anticommunist efforts. He depicted his administration as similar to that of any Western democracy and as holding the same values as the United States. While a realistic examination of Diem's government and its activities would not uphold such claims, it was nevertheless clear that the South Vietnamese president was willing to confront the communists opposing him. For most members of Congress, that was enough. During the 1950s, few US allies were asked to document their efforts to uphold human rights. Diem sold his regime to Congress as staunchly anticommunist—a proven method of gaining American support.

Author Biography

Ngo Dinh Diem (1901–1963) was born into a Catholic family that was part of the nobility in north-central Vietnam. Completing his education in 1921, he was appointed a provincial governor. In 1933, he served briefly as minister of the interior for the Vietnamese emperor, Bao Dai, within a figurehead government installed by the French. During World War II, Diem participated in efforts toward independence. He rejected an offer from the French to participate in a postwar government and also rejected an offer from Ho Chi Minh. In 1954, he was appointed prime minister by the emperor (who ruled only South Vietnam). The two had disputes and

Diem organized an election in 1955 designed to allow people to choose between himself and the emperor. Under questionable conditions, Diem won the election and named himself president. He ruled until November 1963, when he was killed during a coup that overthrew his government.

HISTORICAL DOCUMENT

Mr. President, Mr. Speaker, distinguished Members of the Congress of the United States, it is a rare privilege for me to have this opportunity to address you today.

To address you in the Halls of this Congress—where there has been forged the destiny of one of the great countries of the world.

I am proud to bring to the distinguished representatives of the noble Republic of the United States—the fraternal best wishes of the Vietnamese people. I bring as well the expression of their profound gratitude for the moral and material aid given by the people of the United States. My people appreciate both its great import and its profound significance.

Since the end of the last war, when Asia broke her chains, the conscience of the world has at last awakened to a profound and inevitable development, the birth of Asian independence. This realization has brought about a condemnation in the most concrete terms of the old system of exploitation which governed, in the past, the relationship between East and West. In its place firm efforts are being made to establish a new formula of international cooperation, more adapted to the real needs of the world and to the new Asian philosophy. It is the battle for independence, the growing awareness of the colonial peoples that the origin of their poverty has been the systematic withholding of technical development, coupled with the growing nationalist and social sentiment, that have combined to bring about a profound transformation in the Asian state of mind and given to its masses an irresistible dynamism.

The Asian people—long humiliated in their national aspirations, their human dignity injured—are no longer, as in the past, resigned and passive. They are impatient. They are eager to reduce their immense technical backwardness. They clamor for a rapid and immediate economic development, the only sound base for democratic political independence.

The leaders of Asia—whatever their ideologies—are all faced with the tragic urgency of the economic and social problems of their countries. Under the strong pressure of their peoples, they are compelled to adopt economic planning. Such planning is bound to cause serious political repercussions. It is for this reason that the main theme of domestic political debates in Asian countries centers around the extent of planning indispensable method required to bring urgent practical results. Should everything be planned? Or should planning be restricted to essential sectors? Should democratic or should ruthless totalitarian methods be adopted?

It is in this debate—unfortunately influenced in many countries by the false but seductive promises of fascism and communism—that the efforts being made to safeguard liberal democracy through aid given by the industrial countries of the West, play a vital role. For the honor of humanity, the United States has made the most important contribution to this end.

These, gentlemen of the Congress, in outline and general summary, are some of the problems facing the countries of Asia. These are the goals to be realized and the methods proposed. These are also the internal pressures and temptations facing Asian leaders.

In the great Asian land mass, Vietnam finds itself in the most sensitive area. Although Vietnam faces the same general problems of other Asian countries, because of her sensitive geopolitical position her problems are greatly intensified.

Placed at one of the strategic points of access for the important raw materials of Southeast Asia, the possession of which is decisive in the world, held back in her development by 100 years of foreign domination, exhausted by 15 years of war and destruction, the northern half of her territory given to the Communists, free Vietnam is in a more menaced and critical position than other Asian countries.

At great human sacrifice—and thanks to the aid given by the generous American people—free Vietnam has succeeded, in record time, to overcome the chaos brought about by war and the Geneva accords. The national rehabilitation and stability which have been achieved, have permitted the integration of over 860,000 refugees into the economy of the other 11 million people in free Vietnam, and have permitted the adoption of important economic and political reforms.

Nevertheless, at the time all Asia is passing from one civilization to another, at the moment when all the important problems come up at once to the leaders and seem to call for immediate solution, at a time when all must be done in a climate of increasing revolutionary tension, it has become necessary for Vietnam, more than for other countries, to adopt a certain number of principles, guide lines for action, not only to protect her from the totalitarian temptations but, above all, to assist her to attain independence instead of anarchy—to safeguard peace without sacrificing independence—to attain economic progress without sacrificing essential human liberties.

It was for these reasons—basing myself on fundamental sources of Asiatic culture, and within our own Vietnamese democratic tradition - that I had the honor to define this doctrine in the message of April 17, 1956, delivered to the National Constituent Assembly of Vietnam. I take the liberty of citing from it the most significant passages, for they constitute the basis of our constitution. I quote:

> In the face of the massive forces of material and political oppression which constantly menace us, we feel, more than other people—the essential need to base our political life on a solid foundation and—rigorously to hasten the successive steps of our actions along lines which, without hesitation, will bring about the largest measure of democratic progress.

> This can only be spiritualist—that line followed by human beings in their inti-mate reality as in their community life—in their vocation as in the free pursuit of intellectual, moral and spiritual perfection.

We affirm, therefore, our faith in the absolute value of the human being—whose dignity antedates society and whose destiny is greater than time.

We affirm that the sole legitimate object of the state is to protect the fundamental rights of human beings to existence—to the free development of their intellectual, moral, and spiritual life.

We affirm that democracy is neither material happiness nor the supremacy of numbers. Democracy is essentially a permanent effort to find the right political means in order to assure to all citizens the right of free development and of maximum initiative, responsibility, and spiritual life.

We are convinced that with these guiding principles as the central theme for the development of our political institutions, Vietnam will be able to make its political and economic regime—not a closed one—but an open system, broader with each passing day until it reaches the broad dimensions of man.

Mr. President, Mr. Speaker, gentlemen of the Congress, the Republic of Vietnam, the youngest Republic in Asia, soon will be two years old. Our Republic was born among great suffering. She is courageously facing up to economic competition with the Communists, despite heavy and difficult conditions, which become daily more complex. Vietnam nevertheless has good reason for confidence and hope. Her people are intelligent, have imagination and courage. They also draw strength from the moral and material aid they receive from the free world, particularly that given by the American people.

In the face of increased international tension and Communist pressure in Southeast Asia, I could not repeat too often how much the Vietnamese people are grateful for American aid, and how much they are conscious of its importance, profound significance, and amount.

In actual fact, at any other moment of history, the conflicts between peoples have never been posed in such immediate terms of civilization as they are today. It is by having made timely contributions in sufficient quantities for the rehabilitation of our economic and technical life, which permitted a higher standard of living, that the free world, under the leadership of the United States, is assuring the success of the new system of international cooperation. This action has contributed to the defense of Southeast Asia and prevented the raw materials of this area from falling into Communist hands.

Although our economy has suffered greatly from war, destruction and colonialism, the people of Vietnam are now increasing their contribution to their country. A few months ago the National Assembly voted new and higher taxes to bring in needed revenues for the national budget. A national conscription ordinance was recently promulgated, and a comprehensive declaration of policy was issued two months ago for the purpose of encouraging foreign private investment.

It is on this high moral plane that we pay tribute to the generous and unselfish assistance we have received from the people of the United States. It is on the same plane that the interests of Vietnam are identical with the interests of the people of the free world. It is on this plane that your and our fight are one and the same. We too will continue to fight Communism.

It is in this conviction and in the ardent and always present remembrance of the strong sympathetic comprehension with which the American people and Government have followed our efforts, that I close, thanking you once again, Mr. President, Mr. Speaker, and gentlemen of the Congress, for the honor you have bestowed on me and for your kind attention.

GLOSSARY

extent of planning: reference to the competition between communist, centrally planned economies/countries and capitalist, free-enterprise economies/countries

free Vietnam: South Vietnam, i.e., the Republic of Vietnam

Document Analysis

When the communists took control of the Chinese mainland in 1949, Western nations were confronted with the possibility that communism might spread even further across the continent. Even though some communist organizations, such as those in Vietnam, predated the communist Chinese victory, this victory symbolized new possibilities for communism. With this as the background, Diem focuses his comments on Asia as well as on Vietnam. He wants support for his country, and in order to obtain it, he emphasizes the key role that Vietnam might play in Asia. He depicts the new Vietnamese republic as a twin of the United States, slightly different in external features, but the same at heart. Diem hoped to communicate that South Vietnam and the United States share a mutual desire to stop communism, noting the superiority of the democratic system, which he claims the two countries also share.

Diem states correctly that Asia is different from other parts of the world. However, like leaders of other emerging countries around the world, he blames all his country's economic and social ills upon the colonial system. This is the first reason he gives to support the idea that the United States should help South Vietnam; economic support would assist the country to overcome a variety of problems. Moving on to a topic of more direct concern to the United States, Diem discusses the idea of a planned economy—a codeword for communism. For Diem, extensive economic planning is bad and symptomatic of a totalitarian state. A freer economy, close to capitalism, Diem claims, meant that the country was a democracy. This latter description, Diem asserts, described South Vietnam and was exactly what America wanted. Thanking Congress for previous economic aid, while claiming to be very similar to the United States, Diem recognizes that South Vietnam has adopted "guide lines for action," which he asserts were to "safeguard peace without sacrificing independence." He states that the people of South Vietnam have "good reason for confidence and hope." Diem is implying that it would not take long for South Vietnam to be stable and prosperous.

He closes with the reason for his speech, namely, the receiving of American foreign aid. Having cut ties with France, the United States was now the closest ally of South Vietnam. Diem makes reference to what support has been given to South Vietnam since 1954, going on to outline the benefits the United States had reaped from this. Economic stability in South Vietnam, keeping communists from making economic or political gains, and a strong partner among the nations of the "free world" are the past benefits. However, Diem notes that the struggle is not yet over, and he therefore states that his government needed "timely contributions" to continue the struggle. Having "identical" interests with the United States, Diem proposes that the two nations fight together against communism. He refers to South Vietnam's contribution to the cause, implying that the Americans would need to continue its support if it wanted to defeat the communists.

Essential Themes

In this speech, Diem reiterates a common theme of the time, that communism must be stopped and that Vietnam is the key location in which to accomplish this. While he may not have envisioned the military campaign growing as large as it would a decade later, he understood that the rivalry between the countries of North and South Vietnam encompassed all aspects of life. Diem reinforces the position that many American leaders held, namely, that keeping South Vietnam strong and independent remains vital to the United States' interests. Although keeping foreign aid flowing to South Vietnam was the reason for Diem's visit to Washington, the theme of stopping communism in Vietnam was the most important aspect of the speech. This is where the interests of the United States and South Vietnam were seen to be most closely aligned.

Related to this theme is the fact that, at the time, South Vietnam could continue to exist only with assistance from the United States. While Diem does not state this directly, it is clear in his speech that only American assistance has made it possible for South Vietnam to become stable. Having been established by the French to thwart the communists, the country had little reason to exist separately from the North. The earlier political turmoil between Diem and Bao Dai added to the instability, as did Diem's assistance of his fellow Catholics in Vietnam at the expense of the Buddhist majority. American aid would give Diem the ability to survive.

The speech Diem had given to the Vietnamese assembly in 1956, quoted in the present speech, was basically a listing of the values that had guided the founders of the United States and other Western democracies. This is how he wanted the world to see South Vietnam and himself as its leader. However, as it was pointed out by some of his critics, here was Diem proclaiming the values of the American founders even while he had managed to take office by receiving almost 400,000 more votes than there were registered voters in all of South Vietnam. This lack of integrity eventually cost him the support of many in Congress and earned him many enemies in Vietnam. Nevertheless, with this speech he carried the day and succeeded in receiving continued American support for the government of South Vietnam.

—*Donald A. Watt, PhD*

Bibliography and Additional Reading

Jacobs, Seth. *Cold War Mandarin: Ngo Dinh Diem and the Origins of America's War in Vietnam, 1950–1963.* Lanham, MD: Rowman & Littlefield, 2006. Print.

Ladenburg, Thomas. "Sink or Swim, with Ngo Dinh Diem." *Digital History*. University of Houston, 2007. Web.

Miller, Edward. *Misalliance: Ngo Dinh Diem, the United States, and the Fate of South Vietnam.* Cambridge: Harvard University Press, 2013. Print.

"The United States and Ngo Dinh Diem, 1954–1963." *The Vietnam Era.* Woodbridge, CT: Primary Source Media, 1999. Web.

■ Memo from Ambassador Durbrow to Diem

Date: October 14, 1960
Author: Elbridge Durbrow
Genre: report

Summary Overview

The year 1960 was a time of deteriorating conditions for South Vietnam and its president, Ngo Dinh Diem. It began with the first major successful attacks by the Viet Cong, or communist forces in the south, as they took control of extensive parts of the Mekong Delta. Although the South Vietnamese army eventually took back the territory, throughout that year, the Viet Cong would capture areas and then fade away rather than take large casualties. Publically, Diem gave optimistic reports of successful operations, generally with altered casualty reports.

Much of the non-communist population of South Vietnam was losing faith in Diem. In September, Durbrow had reported that this had created a two-fold threat against Diem, one communist and the other non-communists. As early as April 1960, Durbrow had asked permission to confront Diem regarding his treatment of the South Vietnamese people. Finally, in October, Durbrow was given permission to confront Diem with a series of suggestions that he and the Eisenhower administration hoped would create a better government, help unify the country, and strengthen its fight against the communists. Essentially, Durbrow was reminding Diem that, in 1954, Eisenhower had promised to support him (Diem) only if he worked to create a democracy in South Vietnam.

Defining Moment

Even though the Viet Cong did not organize nationally until December 1960, since the beginning of the year, regional groups had begun successfully pressing a guerilla-style military campaign against Diem's government. At that time, the Viet Cong never had more than 15,000 soldiers, compared to the South Vietnamese army of almost 150,000 regular and 100,000 reserve troops. Given this disparity, the Viet Cong were doing much better than would have been expected. Diem tried to reorganize his forces, including establishing his own commando units. However, officers were still appointed based on political rather than military considerations.

Similarly, Diem's administration was composed of relatives, friends, and allies, without regard to their skills in running a government. Domestically, Diem failed to understand the needs of the people. In trying to control rural areas, Diem alienated many people by forcing them to construct and move to "agrovilles"—hastily organized villages—with no compensation. This was supposed to be a means of protecting them, but in reality, it was primarily intended as a way to more effectively control the people. The operation proved so unpopular that Diem eventually was forced to discontinue it. Watching events unfold, President Eisenhower stated in May 1960 that Diem was "blind" to the needs of the people of South Vietnam. American aid was neither helping the general population nor being effectively used to combat the communists.

As the official witnessing this ongoing catastrophe, Ambassador Durbrow was greatly concerned. A career foreign service diplomat, he understood that criticizing the domestic policy of another country placed him on shaky ground. However, his concern for the people, as well as his desire not to waste American resources, drove him to request permission to confront Diem regarding the situation in South Vietnam. In mid-September, he requested permission to have a "frank and friendly" discussion with Diem regarding changes that needed to be made. The document reprinted here is the official message that Durbrow delivered to Diem. After this discussion, Durbrow reported to the State Department that Diem had listened intently, but made very few comments. Indeed, it seems that this initial confrontation caused alienation between the Diem regime and the United States. A few days later, in a meeting with Durbrow and visiting diplomats, Durbrow mentioned the "snide" comments that Diem had made on some of these issues. When some junior offices attempted a coup in November, Diem falsely accused Durbrow of supporting them. As a result of Durbrow's presenting his list of issues to Diem, what had been a close relationship came to an end.

Author Biography

Elbridge Durbrow (1903–1997) was a career diplomat serving from 1930 to 1968. He was born in San Francisco, California, and earned his bachelor's degree at Yale University. He had further studies at five schools, two in the United States (Stanford University, University of Chicago), two in France, and one in the Netherlands. From 1930 until 1941, he served in Europe. From 1941 until 1946, he was in Washington in the Eastern European division. He then spent two years in Moscow and two years at the National War College before being posted to Italy. In March 1957, he was appointed ambassador to Vietnam, serving until April 1961. He then was appointed to serve with NATO, followed by a return to the National War College. After retirement, he served as chairman of the American Foreign Policy Institute and other organizations.

HISTORICAL DOCUMENT

Mr. President, in your struggle for survival against the Viet Cong, you have taken many wise steps with respect to the security forces of the Government, and I understand that you are in the process of setting up a national Internal Security Council and a centralized intelligence agency as important and necessary additional steps toward giving effective guidance to and making maximum use of the security forces. We have recognized the increased security threat to your Government and the additional needs of your security forces. We have shown this recognition by the comprehensive program for training, equipping and arming the Civil Guard which I have just explained, by our furnishing special forces personnel needs of ARVN for the war against the guerrillas.

Our serious concern about the present situation is based, however, not only on the security threat posed by the Viet Cong, but also on what to us seems to be a decline in the popular political support of your Government brought on in part, of course, by Viet Cong intimidation. As your friend and supporter, Mr. President, I would like to have a frank and friendly talk with you on what seems to be the serious political situation confronting your Government. While I am aware that the matters I am raising deal primarily with internal affairs and, therefore, in ordinary circumstances would be no concern of mine, I would like with your permission and indulgence to talk to you frankly as a friend and try to be as helpful as I can by giving you the considered judgment of myself and some of my friends and your friends in Washington on what we hope would be appropriate measures to assist you in this present crucial situation.

I believe that your speech to the National Assembly on October 3, in which you stated that your Government has decided to reorganize certain of its institutions and to rationalize and simplify its working methods, indicates that we may be thinking to some extent at least along the same lines.

I would like particularly to stress the desirability of actions to broaden and increase your popular support prior to the 1961 Presidential elections. It would seem to me that some sort of a psychological shock effect would be helpful in order to take the initiative from the Communist propagandists as well as the non-Communist oppositionists, and to convince the population that your Government is taking effective political as well as security measures to deal with the present situation. It would appear that, unless fully effective steps are taken to reverse the present adverse political trend, your Government will face an increasingly difficult internal security situation. It is our carefully considered view that small or gradual moves are not adequate. To attain the desired effect, moves, major in scope and with extensive popular appeal, should be taken at once. Specific actions which we would suggest are as follows:

(1) We suggest that you consider Cabinet changes as a necessary part of the effective moves needed to build up popular interest and support. One Cabinet change that we believe would be helpful would be the appointment of a full-time Minister of National Defense in order to permit you to devote your attention to developing over-all

policies. To achieve maximum benefit it is suggested that you issue firm directives to assure that there is adherence to channels of command both up and down and that firm action be taken to eliminate any feeling that favoritism and political considerations enter into the promotion and assignment of personnel in the armed forces. Removal of this latter feeling is of great importance if the morale of the armed forces is not to be adversely affected during their mortal struggle against the Viet Cong.

We suggest that one or two members of the non-Communist opposition be given Cabinet posts in order to demonstrate to the people your desire for the establishment of national unity in the fight against the Viet Cong, and to weaken the criticisms of the opposition which have attracted considerable attention both in Saigon and abroad.

(2) In rationalizing and simplifying the Government's methods of work, we suggest you seek to find new methods to encourage your Cabinet Members to assume more responsibility rather than frequently submitting relatively minor matters to the Presidency for decision, thus allowing you more time to deal with basic policy matters; that the new national Internal Security Council be so constituted as to be the top level policy-making institution by having it meet frequently under your chairmanship for full discussion of all the major problems confronting the Government and proposed solutions thereto; and that the Government be operated as much as possible through well defined channels of authority from you in direct line to the department and agency heads properly concerned. Under this system Cabinet Ministers and agency heads can be held fully responsible for the operation of their departments and agencies, because of the full authority you have bestowed upon them. If a Cabinet Minister cannot fulfill his responsibilities under this system, we would then suggest that you replace him.

(3) We would suggest that you consider altering the nature of the Can Lao Party from its present secret character to that of a normal political party which operates publicly, or even consider disbanding it. If the first alternative is adopted, various methods of convincing the population that the action has been taken might be used, such as party publication of a list of its members.

The purpose of this action would be to eliminate the atmosphere of secrecy and fear and reduce the public suspicion of favoritism and corruption, which the Can Lao Party's secret status has fostered according to many reports we have heard in and out of the Government.

(4) We suggest that the National Assembly be authorized to investigate any department or agency of the Government. The Assembly should be authorized to conduct its investigations through public hearings and to publish the findings. This investigative authority for the Assembly would have a three-fold purpose: (a) to find some mechanism for dispelling through public investigation the persistent rumors about the Government and its personalities; (b) to provide the people with an avenue of recourse against arbitrary actions by certain Government officials; and (c) to assuage some of the non-Communist opposition to the Government.

We further suggest that the National Assembly be asked to establish requirements for the behavior of public servants.

We also suggest that the National Assembly be encouraged to take wider legislative initiative through the introduction of bills sponsored by individual Deputies or groups of Deputies, as well as to broaden area of public debate on all bills, whether Government-sponsored or introduced on a Deputy's initiative.

(5) We suggest that you issue a warning that you may require every public official to make a declaration, for possible publication, listing his property and sources of income.

(6) We suggest that you announce that, if the press will take a responsible role in policing itself, the controls exercised over it by the Government would be reduced. In this connection you might wish to consider the appointment of a committee, including representatives of the press and some members of the opposition, to draft a press code which the press would police. Within the framework of such a code the press could be a means of disseminating facts in order to reduce rumor-mongering against the Government, malicious or not, much of which stems from lack of information.

Providing timely and more ample information would also help to reduce anti-Government rumors. Means to accomplish this include freer access for the press to responsible members of the Government, and frequent public statements from the Presidency and fireside chats, transmitted to the people by radio, sound film, tape recordings, and through the press. The more these media are encouraged to reach the provinces, the more effective will they be in bringing the people closer to your Government by providing a means of transmitting ideas from one to the other.

(7) We would like to suggest that you liberalize arrangements for Vietnamese wishing to study abroad, and for this purpose make more foreign exchange available.

We also suggest that you ease restrictions on the entry into and departure from Viet-Nam of Vietnamese nationals, in order to encourage Vietnamese well trained abroad to return and make their contribution to the development of their country.

(8) We suggest that you consider some appropriate means by which villagers could elect at least some of their own officials. Such elections at the village level would be a means of associating the population with the Government and of eliminating arbitrary actions by local government officials by demonstrating to them that they will periodically be judged at the polls.

(9) We suggest prompt adoption of the following measures for the enhancement of the Government's support in rural areas:

a. Take action which will result in an increase in the price which peasants actually will receive for paddy before the new harvest.

b. Liberalize the terms of credit extended to the small rice farmers.

c. Continue to expand expenditures for agricultural development and diversification, particularly in the Mekong Delta area.

d. Institute a system of modest Government payment for all community development labor whether on agrovilles or on other Government projects.

e. Institute a system of limited subsidies to the inhabitants of agrovilles during the period of their readjustment. While the two situations are not completely comparable, the subsidies helped to bridge the period of adjustment for the settlers in the High Plateau. This should help to develop a favorable popular attitude toward the agrovilles by covering some of the expenses incurred in moving to and getting settled in the agrovilles.

f. Give appropriate and adequate compensation to the 2800 village health workers. These workers can serve as an important arm of the Government in establishing friendly relations with villagers.

g. Increase compensation paid to the Self Guard Youth.

(10) We suggest that as many of the steps recommended above as possible be announced dramatically to the public in your message to the people on October 26. We would envisage this message as a ringing effort to obtain the support of all non-Communist elements for your Government and to create national unity to win the fight against the Viet Cong.

GLOSSARY

agrovilles: villages created by the government and on which people were forced to live

ARVN: Army of the Republic of Viet Nam (South Vietnam)

Can Lao Party: political party created by Diem

Document Analysis

Ever since Ngo Dinh Diem gained power in 1954, the United States had supported his leadership in South Vietnam. Durbrow begins by reminding Diem that the United States is responsible for providing his military strength. Then Durbrow talks about the failure of the Diem government to be truly open and at least somewhat democratic. His suggestions are an implicit criticism of Diem and his policies, but are presented as a means toward achieving the shared goal of stopping communist advances. Durbrow points out the need to have individuals in positions where they can do the most to help the people, rather than where they or Diem desire them to be. Durbrow discusses the agricultural policies of the South Vietnamese government, including the agroville policy that was widely despised by the rural population. Focusing on South Vietnamese domestic concerns rather than on anti-communist operations, Durbrow moves boldly into areas that the United States had previously been reticent to address. Durbrow believes that if Diem implements these suggestions, he will become a stronger leader and regain the support of the people in the battle against communism.

The containment of communism was the reason the United States was involved in Vietnam. It was a goal about which the government of South Vietnam and the United States were in complete agreement. In his presentation to Diem, however, Durbrow discusses this topic only passingly. His concern is that Diem is losing ground to the communists not just on the battlefield, but in the hearts of the people. By alienating the general population, Diem, says Durbrow, effectively encourages people to be receptive to communist leaders and their ideas. The ambassador points out several areas in which the government is not working effectively. He wants Diem to shuffle his cabinet to get rid of those who are not able to meet the demands of their offices and bring in others who can help key programs to succeed.

Related to creating a better government, Durbrow pushes for some basic democratic reforms. Allowing the newspapers some freedom is one suggestion. Having local leaders elected, rather than appointed by the central government, is an additional step. As a check on the possible abuse of power, he suggests that the legislature actually be given power, including the power to review the actions of the executive branch. Having those in government be open about their sources of income is one way Durbrow hopes to reduce corruption by those in office. While, if followed scrupulously, the suggestions that the ambassador makes would transform Diem's government, Durbrow is not pushing for South Vietnam to become a full-blown Western democracy; rather, he seeks only to see some movement in that direction.

Point 9 in Durbrow's memo represents an attempt to help Diem become more popular in the rural areas. This is where the Viet Cong made great inroads. When Diem first came to power, one of his earliest moves was to follow American advice to limit the rent that could be charged tenant farmers. The recommendations that Durbrow delivers to Diem include the idea of helping to improve the standard of living for farmers and others in rural areas. Fair wages for rural government workers, government assistance to those producing rice, and a futures system aimed at stabilizing crop prices are widely accepted ideas elsewhere. These types of policies would, according to Durbrow, increase rural support for Diem, making it harder for the communists to operate in those areas.

Essential Themes

Few people like to hear criticism and then begin working with their critic. At the same time, few people have the ability to raise criticisms with the president of a country. Ambassador Durbrow, however, does take on that responsibility. He believes that the only way communism can be stopped in South Vietnam is by transforming the government. He is not pushing for a change in leadership, but only a change in those around Diem and in some of Diem's basic policies. Basically, he states that the Diem government is inept and fails to serve the people. He presses for more openness and basic democratic reforms. What seem to be obvious steps for Diem to take, however, are not understood in that way by Diem himself.

Unfortunately for the people of South Vietnam, Durbrow's criticism of Diem's government does not end up changing things. It is just the first of a number of confrontations between Diem and American officials regarding the South Vietnamese president's domestic policies. Diem would not change, and his style of government would remain the norm through the short history of that country. In later years, a major criticism of American policy in Vietnam was that the United States was supporting an oppressive, non-democratic regime. Durbrow knows this and tries to institute change, but winds up merely alienating Diem.

Durbrow continued to press for changes in Diem's domestic policies and forwarded various plans to the State Department until he was replaced in May 1961. Kennedy's advisers told Durbrow that if his recommendations were implemented, it would weaken Diem's government and the communists would take over South Vietnam. This, of course, was just the opposite of Durbrow's own conclusion. Soon enough, Kennedy's

advisers pushed for a new ambassador. While Diem did stop the construction of agrovilles, he made only token progress on the other suggestions. Durbrow's confrontation with Diem, authorized by Eisenhower, failed to bring about substantive changes or transform the situation in South Vietnam. It did, nonetheless, put the American government on record as opposing many of the weaknesses of the Diem regime.

—Donald A. Watt, PhD

Bibliography and Additional Reading

"Interview with Eldridge Durbrow, 1979." *Open Vault.* WGBH Educational Foundation, 2015. Web. <http://openvault.wgbh.org/catalog/vietnam-078fff-interview-with-eldridge-durbrow-1979-part-1-of-2>.

Jacobs, Seth. *Cold War Mandarin: Ngo Dinh Diem and the Origins of America's War in Vietnam, 1950–1963.* Lanham, MD: Rowman & Littlefield, 2006. Print.

Ladenburg, Thomas. "Sink or Swim, with Ngo Dinh Diem." *Digital History.* University of Houston, 2007. Web.

Miller, Edward. *Misalliance: Ngo Dinh Diem, the United States, and the Fate of South Vietnam.* Cambridge: Harvard University Press, 2013.

US Department of State. "Foreign Relations of the United States, 1958–1960, Vietnam, Volume I." *Office of the Historian.* US Department of State, 2015. Web.

■ Notes on a National Security Council Meeting

Date: November 15, 1961
Authors/Participants: John F. Kennedy and members of the National Security Council
Genre: discussion; meeting minutes

Summary Overview

During his first ten months in office, President John F. Kennedy had sent several individuals and groups to South Vietnam to assess the situation and recommend a course of action. The last group had arrived in mid-October, headed by General Maxwell Taylor. Taylor recommended that thousands of American soldiers be sent to Vietnam, not only to advise but to fight. Thus, when President Kennedy met with the National Security Council on November 15, 1961, it was to consider what steps to take in Vietnam. The decision that was to be made based upon this discussion would set the extent of American involvement in Vietnam and could affect the relations that the United States would have with many other countries. Kennedy had an agreement with Lyndon Johnson that the vice president review national security decisions. These notes were taken by one of Johnson's aides. While Kennedy did not make the final decision at this meeting, it can be seen from the text that he was not interested in a large-scale escalation of American forces.

Defining Moment

In 1961, the Cold War was at its height. Since the end of World War II, communism had spread from the Soviet Union to encompass all the Eastern European countries, as well as China and Cuba. Two governments had been established in Germany based upon the territory occupied by Soviet or Western troops. At the time of this meeting, tension, caused by the building of the Berlin Wall, had just eased. Soviet and American tank units had faced each other across the barbed wire barrier, and after negotiations, they slowly backed away from each other, preserving the peace. It had only been seven months since the failed US invasion of Cuba at the Bay of Pigs. Kennedy's record against the communists was one clear loss and one draw.

In this context, President Kennedy had to make a crucial decision regarding how heavily the United States

should invest in supporting South Vietnam against communist incursions. The struggle in Vietnam, between the communist North and the pro-Western South, had been going on for seven years. Those who had studied the situation in Vietnam gave conflicting advice. Some were optimistic that victory would be easy, others thought it would be impossible. Some thought that simply by inserting American forces the balance of power would shift, while others believed that there needed to be a change in the governing style of President Ngo Dinh Diem of South Vietnam—or perhaps that he needed to be replaced. Since Kennedy's inauguration, there had been ongoing discussions of numerous matters, but now that other areas of the world had calmed down, Vietnam became the focus of anti-communist activity. Kennedy had always advocated stopping the spread of communism, but he was not eager to produce another failure. Thus, in the NSC meeting, Kennedy asked questions about the appropriateness of American involvement in the conflict, as well as some questions regarding possible steps that could be taken.

While the decisions made after this meeting were not monumental in terms of numbers of troops or advisers, or the scope of the mission, they did reflect a significant increase in the level of US involvement. Kennedy did not go as far as many had wished, or as the Department of Defense had expected, but his thinking in this discussion proved important in his decision to continue aid to South Vietnam, at an increased level. The stage became set for the eventual assignment of a combat role to American forces.

Author Biography

The National Security Council (NSC) was formally established in 1947. However, a group functioning in this manner has always been part of the executive branch. Under law, there are several positions that automatically are part of the NSC, such as the vice president, the secretaries of Defense and the Treasury, and the chairman of the Joint Chiefs of Staff. However, other individuals may be invited to attend some, or all, of the NSC meetings at the discretion of the president. There were twenty-six individuals noted as in attendance at this meeting, with Vice President Johnson the only regular member absent, owing to his travel schedule.

HISTORICAL DOCUMENT

Washington, *November 15, 1961, 10 a.m.*

A brief outline of the size and disposition of Chinese armed forces was given. The President then asked what routes of movement are available for these troops from China to North Viet Nam. Mr. Amory pointed out and described the condition of railway and roads of access and cited the generally inadequate aspects of these avenues. Mr. Dulles cautioned that it should not be assumed that the Chinese setbacks as well as the ideological rift were such that the Soviets and Chinese would not be able nor willing to engage jointly any nation which threatened Communist interests.

Mr. Rusk explained the Draft of Memorandum on South Viet Nam. He added the hope that, in spite of the magnitude of the proposal, any U.S. actions would not be hampered by lack of funds nor failure to pursue the program vigorously. The President expressed the fear of becoming involved simultaneously on two fronts on opposite sides of the world. He questioned the wisdom of involvement in Viet Nam since the basis thereof is not completely clear. By comparison he noted that Korea was a case of clear aggression which was opposed by the United States and other members of the U.N. The conflict in Viet Nam is more obscure and less flagrant. The President then expressed his strong feeling that in such a situation the United States needs even more the support of allies in such an endeavor as Viet Nam in order to avoid sharp domestic partisan criticism as well as strong objections from other nations of the world. The President said that he could even make a rather strong case against intervening in an area 10,000 miles away against 16,000 guerrillas with a native army of 200,000, where millions have been spent for years with no success. The President repeated his apprehension concerning support, adding that none could be expected from the French, and Mr. Rusk interrupted to say that the British were tending more and more to take the French point of view. The President compared the obscurity of the issues in Viet Nam to the clarity of the positions in Berlin, the contrast of which could even make leading Democrats wary of proposed activities in the Far East.

Mr. Rusk suggested that firmness in Viet Nam in the manner and form of that in Berlin might achieve desired results in Viet Nam without resort to combat. The President disagreed with the suggestion on the basis that the issue was clearly defined in Berlin and opposing forces identified whereas in Viet Nam the issue is vague and action is by guerrillas, sometimes in a phantom-like fashion. Mr. McNamara expressed an opinion that action would become clear if U.S. forces were involved since this power would be applied against sources of Viet Cong power including those in North Viet Nam. The President observed that it was not clear to him just where these U.S. forces would base their operations other than from aircraft carriers which seemed to him to be quite vulnerable. General Lemnitzer confirmed that carriers would be involved to a considerable degree and stated that Taiwan and the Philippines would also become principal bases of action.

With regard to sources of power in North Viet Nam, Mr. Rusk cited Hanoi as the most important center in North Viet Nam and it would be hit. However, he considered it more a political target than a military one and under these circumstances such an attack would "raise serious questions." He expressed the hope that any plan of action in North Viet Nam would strike first of all any Viet Cong airlift into South Viet Nam in order to avoid the establishment of a procedure of supply similar to that which the Soviets have conducted for so long with impunity in Laos.

Mr. Bundy raised the question as to whether or not U.S. action in Viet Nam would not render the Laotian settlement more difficult. Mr. Rusk said that it would to a certain degree but qualified his statement with the caveat that the difficulties could be controlled somewhat by the manner in which actions in Viet Nam are initiated.

The President returned the discussion to the point of what will be done next in Viet Nam rather than whether or not the U.S. would become involved. He cautioned that the technique of U.S. actions should not have the effect of unilaterally violating Geneva accords. He felt that a technique and timing must be devised which will place the onus of breaking the accords on the other side and require them to defend their actions. Even so, he realized that it would take some time to achieve this condition and even more to build up world opinion against Viet Cong. He felt that the Jorden Report might be utilized in this effort.

The President discussed tactics in dealing with the International Control Commission. He delineated a clever plan to charge North Viet Nam with the onus for breaking accords. Following this he envisioned the initiation of certain U.S. actions. He realized that these actions would be criticized and subject to justification in world opinion but felt that it would be much less difficult if this particular U.S. action were secondary rather than primary. He directed State to study possible courses of action with consideration for his views relating to timing and to the Geneva Accords. He asked State also to consider the position of the individual members of the ICC and further suggested that the time was appropriate to induce India to agree to follow U.S. suggestion.

Mr. Murrow reported that parts of the Jorden Report are already in the hands of the ICC. He questioned the value of utilizing the report in the suggested manner since to do so would simply be to place a U.S. stamp on the report. Such action might not reap the desired effects.

The President asked what nations would possibly support the U.S. intervention in Viet Nam, listing Pakistan, Thailand, the Philippines, Australia, New Zealand (?). Mr. Rusk replied that they all would but the President implied doubts because of the pitfalls of the particular type of war in Viet Nam. He described it as being more a political issue, of different magnitude and (again) less defined than the Korean War.

Mr. Fowler said that the studies suggested to him that the job to be done has been magnified, thereby leading to pessimistic conclusions as to outcome. Taylor responded that although the discussion and even some of the draft memoranda were somewhat pessimistic, he returned from Viet Nam with optimism over what could be done if certain clearcut actions were taken. He envisioned two phases: (1) the revival of Viet Nam morale and (2) the initiation of the guerrilla suppression program. Mr. McNamara cautioned that the program was in fact complex and that in all probability U.S. troops, planes and resources would have to be supplied in additional quantities at a later date.

The President asked the Secretary of Defense if he would take action if SEATO did not exist and McNamara replied in the affirmative. The President asked for justification and Lemnitzer replied that the world would be divided in the area of Southeast Asia on the sea, in the air and in communications. He said that Communist conquest would deal a severe blow to freedom and extend Communism to a great portion of the world. The President asked how he could justify the proposed courses of action in Viet Nam while at the same time ignoring Cuba. General Lemnitzer hastened to add that the JCS [Joint Chiefs of Staff] feel that even at this point the United States should go into Cuba.

The President stated the time had come for neutral nations as well as others to be in support of U.S. policy publicly. He felt that we should aggressively determine which nations are in support of U.S. policy and that these nations should identify themselves. The President again expressed apprehension on support of the proposed action by the Congress as well as by the American people. He felt that the next two or three weeks should be utilized in making the determination as to whether or not the proposed program for Viet Nam could be supported. His impression was that even the Democratic side of Congress was not fully convinced. The President stated that he would like to have the Vice President's views in this regard and at that point asked if there was information on the Vice President's arrival. The President then stated that no action would be taken during the meeting on the proposed memorandum and that he would discuss these subjects with the Vice President. He asked State to report to him when the directed studies had been completed.

"The meeting proceeded in the normal fashion with the first hour being consumed by the presentation of reports. Discussion continued until about 11:30, at which time the President asked me if I had further information on your arrival and, when I replied in the negative, he asked if I would check. I went outside the meeting and called Walter [Jenkins] and discovered that you had informed him around midnight of your difficulty in returning to Washington last night by private plane because of weather and of the possibility that you might not return to Washington as scheduled but might proceed to Seattle. I returned to the meeting and informed the President that I could not ascertain the details of your flight and arrival at the moment. The President then suggested that the meeting be adjourned and that he would discuss the subject with you later." (Johnson Library, Vice Presidential Security File, National Security Council (II))

No record was found of a subsequent meeting between the President and Vice President regarding Vietnam.

GLOSSARY

Draft (of) Memorandum on South Vietnam: a joint State/Defense memo regarding increasing aid to South Vietnam, sent November 11

International Control Commission (ICC): organization overseeing the 1954 Geneva Accords

Jorden Report: William Jorden's report on North Vietnamese aggression, publically released in December

SEATO: Southeast Asia Treaty Organization

Viet Cong: communist forces from, and operating in, South Vietnam

Document Analysis

Whether to continue assistance to South Vietnam, and if so how much, and how to justify it: these were questions about which the National Security Council needed advise the president. While ultimately Kennedy had to make the decision, the more information he could acquire, the better his decision would be. While the first question is dealt with relatively quickly in the meeting, the latter two seem to present more of a dilemma for the president and the NSC members. In addition, one always needed to have the support of Congress in order to fund any such proposed actions.

The continuation of aid to South Vietnam does not really seem to be an issue to be decided. Two days prior to this meeting, Kennedy indicated his understanding that a significant number of American troops might be needed in South Vietnam. On the day before this meeting, in response to the Draft Memorandum on South Vietnam mentioned in the meeting notes, Kennedy directed Dean Rusk of the Department of State and Robert McNamara from the Department of Defense to prepare an additional shipment of rifles for the South Vietnamese and to select a general to head up military operations in the country. Both of these directions seem to indicate continued assistance. After stating how easy it would be to make a "strong case against intervening," Kennedy directs the group to focus on the next steps, rather than the question of whether to continue involvement.

The type and amount of aid is the major point upon which a decision needs to be made. The early statement by Rusk, hoping that American efforts will not be "hampered by lack of funds," reflects a large deployment of military personnel and equipment, which is in the Draft Memorandum. In those previous discussions, the president had agreed that sending only a token force would not be helpful. The probable use of American air power raised the question of where to locate secure naval aircraft carriers or terrestrial air bases. Moreover, the expansion of the use of American air power would necessitate the expansion of allowable targets. In addition to South Vietnam, reference is made to targets in Laos and North Vietnam. Army deployments would be the basis for the "revival of Viet Nam morale" and, of course, direct combat action by the

Americans—hence, Kennedy's point about needing the Democrats in Congress to stand with him.

The international repercussions of sending further military assistance to South Vietnam is the third area that was discussed. Which countries were capable and willing to be active allies in the fight against the North Vietnamese and the Viet Cong? How would increased aid to South Vietnam affect neighboring countries? How can matters be finessed in order not to have it seem that the United States is blatantly disregarding the Geneva Accords? (The Jorden Report, documenting North Vietnamese aid to the Viet Cong, was a major help in efforts to strengthen the United States' position within the international community.) These types of concerns were at the heart of how the United States would respond to the needs of the South Vietnamese. If only Vietnam were considered, the members indicate, a large response would seem to be best. If, however, the international community is taking into consideration, the range of actions becomes more restricted. The meeting ends without a decision. Kennedy, however, does seem to have a good grasp of the situation and the various options available.

Essential Themes

This meeting of the National Security Council represents the continuation of a process that had been going on for several years. With the French having pulled out of their former colonies in Indochina and the communist Viet Minh having taken control of North Vietnam, the United States stepped forward to support the South Vietnamese. From time to time, decisions were made that continued and expanded that involvement. This meeting represents one of those times. The memos exchanged in the days leading up to this meeting were supportive of increasing assistance. This meeting does the same.

At this point, President Kennedy recognizes that continued growth will create problems external to Vietnam. Time is spent, therefore, discussing alliances, communist responses, as well as the International Control Commission (ICC). While the ICC was not that important in and of itself, it is noted that if it took issue with the United States, it could create problems within the wider global community. Thus, Kennedy cares about how American actions would be perceived and the types of justifications that could be presented to support them.

The direct outcome of this meeting came one week later, in the form of National Security Action Memorandum No. 111. In that document, Kennedy authorized greatly expanding aid to South Vietnam, including military hardware, especially aircraft. It authorized not only more assistance on training the South Vietnamese army, but also greater participation in surveillance and intelligence operations. Even then, though, Kennedy did not authorize combat troops. In a separate authorization, Kennedy gave the go-ahead for defoliation efforts—that is, the beginning of the use of Agent Orange. All of these are relatively small steps in the context of what would later become a major war, yet they are precisely the steps that wound up drawing the United States more deeply into the conflict.

—*Donald A. Watt, PhD*

Bibliography and Additional Reading

Keefer, Edward C., ed. "Foreign Relations of the United States, 1961–1963, Volume I, Vietnam, 1961." *Office of the Historian.* US Department of State, 2015. Web. <https://history.state.gov/historicaldocuments/frus1961-63v04>.

Logevall, Fredrik. *Choosing War: The Lost Chance for Peace and the Escalation of War in Vietnam.* Berkeley: University of California Press, 1999. Print.

Miller, Edward. *Misalliance: Ngo Dinh Diem, the United States, and the Fate of South Vietnam.* Cambridge: Harvard University Press, 2013. Print.

Rusk, Dean. *As I Saw It.* Ed. Daniel S. Papp. New York: W.W. Norton & Company, 1990. Print.

Schlesinger, Arthur M., Jr. *A Thousand Days: John F. Kennedy in the White House.* 1965. First Mariner Books Ed. New York: Houghton Mifflin Harcourt, 2002. Print.

Letter from JFK to Diem

Date: December 14, 1961
Author: John F. Kennedy
Genre: letter

Summary Overview

Having been president for less than a year, John F. Kennedy received an appeal from the leader of South Vietnam, Ngo Dinh Diem, for military support to help prop up Diem's failing regime. The North Vietnamese and anti-government South Vietnamese forces had been gaining ground for most of the year. President Kennedy faced the decision of allowing what seemed to be the inevitable fall of South Vietnam, or taking steps to strengthen the military and government of that nation. In this letter, he communicates that he has decided to assist the South Vietnamese government with increased military aid. While Vietnam had been divided into two countries, North and South Vietnam, for seven years, this was the first time Kennedy faced a request for major military aid. His decision to grant this aid can be seen as a significant step toward full-scale war in Vietnam, in which the United States would soon become embroiled.

Defining Moment

John Kennedy had been an advocate of the containment of communism throughout his political career. As president, one of the areas in which an American ally confronted communist forces was Vietnam. When the French gave Vietnam its independence in 1954, the Geneva Accords divided the nation into two parts, with communist leadership in the North and capitalist in the South. The agreement also mandated an election in 1956 to unify the nation, an election that the communist leaders would most probably have won. Thus, President Diem of South Vietnam, with the support of the United States, refused to allow the vote. Ever since that time, the leaders of North Vietnam had sought unification at any cost, including a military struggle. They kept increasing the level of armed conflict until, by 1961, they were gaining the upper hand throughout most areas of South Vietnam. Diem realized that to have any chance of staying in power, he needed more assistance from the United States. While American leaders had continually asked Diem to take steps to improve the standard of living for the citizens in the South, he did very little. Diem knew that the Americans feared the further expansion of communism and believed that this would be enough for him to get the necessary support.

Fortunately for Diem, Kennedy had previously sent his own advisors to South Vietnam to assess the situation, and they had recommended actions similar to those Diem requested. Thus, while Kennedy wanted changes in the way average South Vietnamese citizens were treated, he did not seem to have any choice if the communist forces were to be contained. The decision, communicated in this letter, was the first step toward the major deployment of American advisers in Vietnam. Rather than just hundreds, as was the case prior to the letter, they numbered in the thousands within months, in addition to major grants of military equipment to the South Vietnamese armed forces. While no one could know at that time, this major deployment of military advisers to South Vietnam was the last major step creating a foundation for President Johnson sending hundreds of thousands of US military forces to South Vietnam.

Author Biography

President John Fitzgerald Kennedy (1917–1963) was the second youngest president in US history at the time of his inauguration and the first Catholic president. A graduate of Harvard, and having served with distinction in the Navy during World War II, Kennedy spent six years in the House and eight years in the Senate prior to becoming president. He married to Jacqueline Bouvier in 1953. He was a Cold War politician, which meant a strong anticommunist stance. Born into a wealthy Boston family, Kennedy saw public service as a calling and approached it from a politically liberal perspective. He was a Pulitzer Prize-winning author, as well as a politician. He used his family's wealth to aid in his political career, as well as employing many innovative campaign techniques. He was assassinated on November, 21, 1963, a traumatic event for the nation. Although scholars debate the quality of his political achievements as president, most in the nation saw his brief time in office reflected in the term often applied to it, "Camelot."

HISTORICAL DOCUMENT

Dear Mr. President:

I have received your recent letter in which you described so cogently the dangerous conditions caused by North Vietnam's effort to take over your country. The situation in your embattled country is well known to me and to the American people. We have been deeply disturbed by the assault on your country. Our indignation has mounted as the deliberate savagery of the Communist programs of assassination, kidnapping, and wanton violence became clear.

Your letter underlines what our own information has convincingly shown—that the campaign of force and terror now being waged against your people and your Government is supported and directed from outside by the authorities at Hanoi. They have thus violated the provisions of the Geneva Accords designed to ensure peace in Vietnam and to which they bound themselves in 1954.

At that time, the United States, although not a party to the Accords, declared that it "would view any renewal of the aggression in violation of the Agreements with grave concern and as seriously threatening international peace and security." We continue to maintain that view.

In accordance with that declaration, and in response to your request, we are prepared to help the Republic of Vietnam to protect its people and to preserve its independence. We shall promptly increase our assistance to your defense effort as well as help relieve the destruction of the floods which you describe. I have already given the orders to get these programs underway.

The United States, like the Republic of Vietnam, remains devoted to the cause of peace and our primary purpose is to help your people maintain their independence. If the Communist authorities in North Vietnam will stop their campaign to destroy the Republic of Vietnam, the measures we are taking to assist your defense efforts will no longer be necessary. We shall seek to persuade the Communists to give up their attempts to force and subversion. In any case, we are confident that the Vietnamese people will preserve their independence and gain the peace and prosperity for which they have sought so hard and so long.

GLOSSARY

Geneva Accords: the agreement ending Vietnam's rebellion against France.

Hanoi: the capital of North Vietnam.

North Vietnam: the Democratic Republic of Vietnam, communist and the ultimate victor in the Vietnam War.

Republic of Vietnam: South Vietnam.

Document Analysis

Communications between two friendly heads of state tend to use generalities, rather than specifics. This letter of assurance, from President Kennedy to President Diem, follows this pattern. Most of it is a litany of grievances caused by North Vietnamese leaders, with only a brief affirmation of support for Diem. Kennedy communicates to Diem that his support was only due to the immediate need to confront the communists, a reminder that Kennedy expected Diem to change some of his policies if he was going to continue receiving support from the United States.

Beginning with the grievances that Diem lodged against the North Vietnamese leaders, Kennedy summarizes them as "deliberate savagery." He then refers to the report he received from the team he had sent to Vietnam in October, 1961. Maxwell Taylor and Walt Rostow were the leaders of that mission. They stated that Vietnam was the key to keeping communism from spreading in Southeast Asia. Their advice was to send more advisers and a limited number of combat troops. This was the information that Kennedy had prior to Diem's request for further assistance. The US mission had verified to its satisfaction what Kennedy repeated in the letter, that the North Vietnamese leaders were directing attacks against the South Vietnamese government and people. The Geneva Accords, to which Kennedy refers, were the documents that had divided Vietnam into two countries with the promise of peace between the two factions. The fact that the North was directing attacks was a direct violation of these accords; that was clear. However, Kennedy conveniently forgets that the accords also called for an election in 1956 to unify the nation and that that election had not been held by Diem, in line with US preferences. Thus, it could be said that both sides were in violation of the accords, not just the North.

When it was convenient, the United States had argued that it was not its responsibility to enforce the accords, since it had not been part of the group that had negotiated that treaty. However, now that America's ally was under attack, America's leaders wanted to enforce part of the agreement. This violation was seen as a threat to "international peace and security." Based on this argument, Kennedy agrees to send more advisers to South Vietnam, as well as military hardware. The unrelated matter of the floods that were devastating parts of South Vietnam is mentioned not just for the humanitarian relief being offered, but because Kennedy's advisers had recommended that some of the American troops sent to Vietnam should be presented as having been deployed to help with flood relief. While Diem did not request American combat troops, and Kennedy did not wish to send them, mentioning the relief effort in the letter leaves open the possibility of sending in combat troops masquerading as relief workers, if they were needed in the future.

Kennedy's closing paragraph represents a not very subtle warning to Diem that American assistance was not unconditional. By mentioning that the military aid was for fighting communists, Kennedy is giving an indirect warning to Diem about the need to rein in his brother, who had been using units of the South Viet-

namese army to oppress factions within the country. The hope of "peace and prosperity" for the people of South Vietnam would occur, it is noted, only if North Vietnamese forces would cease their attacks and if Diem's government were less brutal in its suppression of domestic political opponents.

Essential Themes

During the early years of Diem's presidency, political opposition (including communist) was not highly organized. However, things started to change, and, by 1960, the anti-Diem forces in South Vietnam had organized and were supported by North Vietnam. Thus, in 1961, the push by these groups, and more directly by North Vietnamese agents, started to pay off for them. A large area of rural South Vietnam was no longer under the control of the government. Diem was forced to request greater assistance from the United States. For Kennedy, the Bay of Pigs disaster in Cuba and the construction of the Berlin Wall in Germany, were setbacks in trying to defeat communism. This made Vietnam a key location in which to try to turn the tide against communism. When the request for more assistance came from President Diem, President Kennedy was willing to respond with people, equipment, and funds.

While the immediate increase in American troops was not large in absolute terms (from about 900 in December 1960 to over 3,000 at the end of December 1961), the decision that Vietnam represented a key battleground with communism set the stage for the future commitment of hundreds of thousands of troop and staggering amounts of money. With Kennedy's commitment, documented in this letter, the United States was spending, by the end of December, about one million dollars a day to support the South Vietnamese regime. Many would see this investment of American resources as the beginning of what was to become almost unconditional support for successive South Vietnamese governments for the next decade. While there have been numerous debates regarding what might have been Kennedy's plans for Vietnam if he had not been assassinated, this decision in December 1961 led to his eventual deployment of 16,000 advisers in Vietnam. Whether he would have expanded it into the war that eventually occurred can never be known, but it was clear that in December 1961, he was setting the stage for this possibility.

—Donald A. Watt, PhD

Bibliography and Additional Reading

Chomsky, Noam. *Rethinking Camelot: JFK, the Vietnam War, and US Political Culture.* Cambridge, MA: South End Press, 1993. Print.

Dallek, Robert. *An Unfinished Life: John F. Kennedy, 1917–1963.* Boston: Little, Brown & Company, 2003. Print.

Freedman, Lawrence. *Kennedy's Wars: Berlin, Cuba, Laos, and Vietnam.* Oxford: Oxford University Press, 2002. Print.

"Military Advisors in Vietnam: 1963 Lesson Plan." *John F. Kennedy Presidential Library and Museum.* John F. Kennedy Presidential Library and Museum, 2015. Web. <http://www.jfklibrary.org/Education/Teachers/Curricular-Resources-Image-List/High-School-Curricular-Resources/Military-Advisors-Vietnam.aspx>.

Schlesinger, Arthur M., Jr. *A Thousand Days: John F. Kennedy in the White House.* 1965. First Mariner Books edition. New York: Houghton Mifflin Harcourt Publishing Company, 2002. Print.

Sorenson, Theodore C. *Kennedy.* New York: Harper & Row, 1965. Print.

■ Senate Majority Leader Mike Mansfield on US Policy in Southeast Asia

Date: December 18, 1962
Author: Michael J. Mansfield
Genre: report

Summary Overview

The United States had been assisting President Diem in South Vietnam ever since he came to power in 1955. This included military advisers since the late 1950s, as Diem sought to contain domestic rebels as well as others who were inspired and supported by North Vietnam. In December 1961, the United States' president, John F. Kennedy, authorized a rapid expansion in the number of advisers and in the amount of aid to Diem's regime. In the latter part of 1962, Kennedy asked Senate Majority Leader Mike Mansfield to travel to Vietnam and give a report on what he experienced. Since Mansfield had supported Kennedy's Vietnam policy in the past, Kennedy expected continued support. However, in his assessment of the situation, Mansfield was very negative. This was the first public criticism of American policy in Vietnam and the rest of Southeast Asia. Mansfield doubted that Diem would be able to implement the types of policies desired by the United States and needed by his country. Thus, in Mansfield's view, it was time to re-evaluate American policy in that region.

Defining Moment

New forces were at work within Vietnam by 1962. In South Vietnam, support for President Diem was decreasing rapidly. Having been elected president in 1955, albeit with many electoral irregularities, Diem initially enjoyed broad support. While that support had slowly diminished over the succeeding years, by 1960, it had plummeted. The Vietcong, formally organized in 1960, had not only become a solid fighting force, but the political wing of the organization began offering rural South Vietnamese alternative policies for those areas. As a result, the South Vietnamese government was constructing new "strategic hamlets" and moving the people from their homes into "modern" compounds. South Vietnam was doing this theoretically to offer bet-

ter services to the people than had been the case in their old villages, but, in reality, South Vietnam was trying to move people away from the Vietcong and undercut rural support for that movement. All of this was happening while the Vietcong were gaining strength and partial control of many South Vietnamese rural areas.

1962 was also a pivotal year for American involvement in Vietnam. The number of military advisers had nearly tripled to more than 9,000. While not specifically executing combat missions, the US Air Force began dropping Agent Orange, a defoliant, on what were believed to be transportation corridors used by North Vietnamese and Vietcong forces. This was an attempt to make it easier for the South Vietnamese army to intercept supplies meant for communist forces or to attack them on what would be a more advantageous terrain. Millions of dollars a month were being given to the Diem government in South Vietnam to assist it militarily and to help it with needed civilian programs. The Americans also decided to bypass the South Vietnamese government by beginning to work directly with an ethnic minority in a key location, the Montagnards. President Kennedy wanted a person he could trust to review the situation and report on it. He choose his former Senate Democratic colleague and supporter, Majority Leader Mike Mansfield. With the American midterm elections completed, and the Democrats holding strong control of both houses, Mansfield was free to plainly express his view of the situation. All things considered, Mansfield's estimation was that American policy in South Vietnam was not working. In light of this, he raised the question as to whether the current American goal of using South Vietnam as a barrier to communist expansion should be kept or modified. If this was to be the location for the confrontation, one should examine the strengths and weaknesses of the current policies.

Author Biography

Michael Joseph Mansfield (1903–2001) was born in New York, but moved to Montana as a child. A naval veteran of World War I, he later served in the army and then in the marines. Mansfield's last posting was in East Asia, through which he developed a special interest in that region. He married Maureen Hayes in 1932, and she pushed him to continue his education. In just a few years, he went from a person without a high school diploma to one who had earned a master's degree. This enabled him to change occupations, from working in the copper mines to being a college professor. A member of the Democratic Party, he served in the House from 1943–53. Defeating a Republican incumbent in the 1952 election, he moved to the Senate, serving there until 1977. He was elected majority leader in 1961 and served there until his retirement, which made him the longest serving majority leader in history. In 1977, he was appointed ambassador to Japan and served there for the next ten years.

HISTORICAL DOCUMENT

SOUTHEAST ASIA—VIETNAM

We have problems of varying complexity with all of the nations in Southeast Asia. Clearly, however, the critical focus is south Viet Nam. Developments there in the next two or three years may well influence greatly the trends in the whole region for the following ten or twenty.

And at this point it is far from certain what will develop in Viet Nam. One thing is reasonably clear: From somewhere about 1956 or '57, the unusual combination of factors which had resulted in the establishment of the Republic under Ngo Dinh Diem began to lose its impulse. A drift set in at about that time, responsibility for which is only partially ascribable to the shortcomings of the Vietnamese government. Our aid programs, military and non-military, after all, were one of the principal sources of the origin and the continuance of that government's power and these were properly open to charges of being ill-conceived and badly administered. They did little with the time which was bought at Geneva in the sense of stimulating the growth of indigenous roots for the political structure in Saigon. That structure is, today, far more dependent on us for its existence than it was five years ago. If Vietnam is the cork in the Southeast Asian bottle then American aid is more than ever the cork in the Vietnamese bottle.

We have now had for some months new concepts and a new American approach in Viet Nam. But the purpose of both remains, in essentials, what the purpose of other approaches have been from the outset. Indeed, it was distressing on this visit to hear the situation described in much the same terms as on my last visit although it is seven years and billions of dollars later. Viet Nam, outside the cities, is still an insecure place which is run at least at night largely by the Vietcong. The government in Saigon is still seeking acceptance by the ordinary people in large areas of the countryside. Out of fear or indifference or hostility the peasants still withhold acquiescence, let alone approval of that government. In short, it would be well to face the fact that we are once again at the beginning of the beginning.

But as noted there are now new concepts and a new American approach. The new concepts, as undoubtedly you are aware, center on the strategic hamlets. The new approach involves the re-oriented and expanded economic aid program and the use of many thousands of supporting American military personnel as well as the special forces which are concentrating their efforts on the tribal people, the Montagnards.

Although the first results have scarcely been registered, the evaluations of the new approach—Vietnamese and American—in Saigon are extremely optimistic. Those bearing responsibility—Vietnamese and American—speak of success in the solution of the problem in terms of a year or two.

Having heard optimistic predictions of this kind, with the introduction of other "new concepts," beginning with French General Navarre in Hanoi in 1953, certain reservations seem to me to be in order. It is true that Vietminh casualty counts have been rising but the accuracy of these counts is open to question. Moreover, it should be noted that the estimates of Vietcong core strength have also been rising. The total of 20,000 which is now calculated at CINCPAC is the highest which I have ever encountered since the Geneva accords of 1954.

Responsible Americans in Saigon believe that exceptional progress has been made in winning over the Montagnards by the special forces. This is an important achievement because the location of these tribal people has considerable strategic significance in terms of north-south supply trails. But it should also be recognized that in terms of the major struggle the Montagnards are peripheral. In the last analysis, the Saigon government will stand or fall on the basis not of the several hundred thousand primitive Montagnards, but the millions of Vietnamese in the villages, towns and cities.

Apart from these two tangibles—higher Vietminh casualties and progress in winning over the Montagnards—there are also reports of improvements in the security of road travel and in the movement of rice and other commodities out of the countryside into the cities. These are excellent indicators of progress but the reports are not yet conclusive as to trends.

At this point, therefore, the optimistic predictions of success must be regarded as deriving primarily from the development of the theory of the strategic hamlets by Mr. Ngo Dinh Nhu and by the injection of new energy which has been provided by additional American aid and personnel. The real tests are yet to come.

Reservations are in order because in the first place, the rapid success of the concept of the strategic hamlet would seem to depend on the assumption that the Vietminh will remain wedded to their present tactics and will be unable to devise significant and effective revisions to meet the new concepts and the new highly mobile firepower of the American-trained forces. That may be the case but it would be unwise to underestimate the resourcefulness of any group which has managed to survive years of the most rugged kind of warfare. In the second place, rapid success of the new concepts depends upon the assumption that the great bulk of the people in the countryside sustain the Vietminh merely out of fear or, at best, indifference. There is really no effective measure of the accuracy of this assumption. It may indeed contain a good deal of truth but the critical question is how much truth. The temptation to extrapolate our own reactions on to the Vietnamese peasant in this kind of a situation is as obvious as it is dangerous.

The fact is that only experience and the most acute observation and objective reporting will throw real light on the accuracy of this assumption. To date we have not had enough of any of those essential ingredients of sound judgment. If experience should prove that there is less rather than more truth in the assumption that fear or indifference are the keystones of the Vietcong hold over the countryside, the target date for success will be delayed indefinitely beyond the year or two of the present predictions.

This is not to say that even a serious error in this assumption renders success impossible. If we were prepared to increase the commitment of men and military aid to compensate for the error it is not impossible that the concept of the strategic hamlet could still be brought into existence, in time, despite widespread support of the peasants for the Vietcong. And if the Vietnamese government, with more aid, could then turn the secured hamlets into a significantly more satisfactory way of life than the peasants have known, then it is conceivable that a deep disaffection towards the Vietcong could be induced. But it would be well to recognize that any such reorientation involves an immense job of social engineering, dependent on great outlays of aid on our part for many years and a most responsive, alert and enlightened leadership in the government of Vietnam.

Even assuming that aid over a prolonged period would be available, the question still remains as to the capacity of the present Saigon government to carry out the task of social engineering. Ngo Dinh Diem remains a dedicated, sincere, hardworking, incorruptible and patriotic leader. But he is older and the problems which confront him are more complex than those which he faced when he pitted his genuine nationalism against, first, the French and Bao Dai and then against the sects with such effectiveness. The energizing role which he played in the past appears to be passing to other members of his family, particularly to Ngo Dinh Nhu. The latter is a person of great energy and intellect who is fascinated by the operations of political power and has consummate eagerness and ability in organizing and manipulating it. But it is Ngo Dinh Diem, not Ngo Dinh Nhu, who has such popular mandate to exercise power as there is in south Vietnam. In a situation of this kind there is a great danger of the corruption of unbridled power. This has implications far beyond the persistent reports and rumors of fiscal and similar irregularities which are, in any event, undocumented. More important is its effect on the organization of the machinery for carrying out the new concepts. The difficulties in Vietnam are not likely to be overcome by a handful of paid retainers and sycophants. The success of the new approach in Vietnam presupposes a great contribution of initiative and self-sacrifice from a substantial body of Vietnamese with capacities for leadership at all levels. Whether that contribution can be obtained remains to be seen. For in the last analysis it depends upon a diffusion of political power, essentially in a democratic pattern. The trends in the political life of Vietnam have not been until now in that direction despite lip service to the theory of developing democratic and popular institutions "from the bottom up" through the strategic hamlet program.

To summarize, our policies and activities are designed to meet an existing set of internal problems in south Vietnam. North Vietnam infiltrates some supplies and cadres into the south; together with the Vietnamese we are trying to shut off this flow. The Vietcong has had the offensive in guerrilla warfare in the countryside; we are attempting to aid the Vietnamese military in putting them on the defensive with the hope of eventually reducing them at least to ineffectiveness. Finally, the Vietnamese peasants have sustained the Vietcong guerrillas out of fear, indifference or blandishment and we are helping the Vietnamese in an effort to win the peasants away by offering them the security and other benefits which may be provided in the strategic hamlets.

That, in brief, is the present situation. As noted, there is optimism that success will be achieved quickly. My own view is that the problems can be made to yield to present remedies, provided the problems and their magnitude do not change significantly and provided that the remedies are pursued by both Vietnamese and Americans (and particularly the former) with great vigor and self-dedication.

Certainly, if these remedies do not work, it is difficult to conceive of alternatives, with the possible exception of a truly massive commitment of American military personnel and other resources—in short going to war fully ourselves against the guerrillas—and the establishment of some form of neocolonial rule in south Vietnam. That

is an alternative which I most emphatically do not recommend. On the contrary, it seems to me most essential that we make crystal clear to the Vietnamese government and to our own people that while we will go to great lengths to help, the primary responsibility rests with the Vietnamese. Our role is and must remain secondary in present circumstances. It is their country, their future which is most at stake, not ours.

To ignore that reality will not only be immensely costly in terms of American lives and resources but it may also draw us inexorably into some variation of the unenviable position in Vietnam which was formerly occupied by the French. We are not, of course, at that point at this time. But the great increase in American military commitment this year has tended to point us in that general direction and we may well begin to slide rapidly toward it if any of the present remedies begin to falter in practice.

As indicated, our planning appears to be predicated on the assumption that existing internal problems in south Vietnam will remain about the same and can be overcome by greater effort and better techniques. But what if the problems do not remain the same? To all outward appearances, little if any thought has been given in Saigon, at least, to the possibilities of a change in the nature of the problems themselves. Nevertheless, they are very real possibilities and the initiative for instituting change rests in enemy hands largely because of the weakness of the Saigon government. The range of possible change includes a step-up in the infiltration of cadres and supplies by land or sea. It includes the use of part or all of the regular armed forces of north Vietnam, reported to be about 300,000 strong, under Vo Nguyen Giap. It includes, in the last analysis, the possibility of a major increase in any of many possible forms of Chinese Communist support for the Vietcong.

None of these possibilities may materialize. It would be folly, however, not to recognize their existence and to have as much clarification in advance of what our response to them will be if they do.

This sort of anticipatory thinking cannot be undertaken with respect to the situation in Vietnam alone. The problem there can be grasped, it seems to me, only as we have clearly in mind our interests with respect to all of Southeast Asia. If it is essential in our interests to maintain a quasi-permanent position of power on the

Asian mainland as against the Chinese then we must be prepared to continue to pay the present cost in Vietnam indefinitely and to meet any escalation on the other side with at least a commensurate escalation of commitment of our own. This can go very far, indeed, in terms of lives and resources. Yet if it is essential to our interests then we would have no choice.

But if on the other hand it is, at best, only desirable rather than essential that a position of power be maintained on the mainland, then other courses are indicated. We would, then, properly view such improvement as may be obtained by the new approach in Vietnam primarily in terms of what it might contribute to strengthening our diplomatic hand in the Southeast Asian region. And we would use that hand as vigorously as possible and in every way possible not to deepen our costly involvement on the Asian mainland but to lighten it.

It is uncertain what the prospects for doing so may be, even if we were inclined to the latter course. The experience in Laos which, in effect, is an essay in that direction is not cause for sanguine expectation. On the one hand, there are the anticipated difficulties with the Pathet Lao. Their leader in Vientiane, Prince Souphanovong, is brilliant and capable but he is also hard-bitten and relentless. His relations with Souvanna Phouma are delicate and uncertain and there are reports that even the limited degree of cooperation which he has extended has come under attack from his own faction. The cooperation with Souvanna Phouma from the other Laotian group headed by Phoumi Nosavan has also been circumscribed and uncertain.

These difficulties, of course, were to be anticipated and much depends on Souvanna Phouma if they are to be surmounted. It is our policy to support him fully and the American Ambassador is making a noble effort to carry out that policy. The latter needs and must have the cooperation of all departments in this effort. Moreover, his views as to what is necessary should be most carefully regarded in the design of his instructions. This point needs stressing, for one has the distinct impression in Laos that a great deal of executive branch energy is going into the preparation for contingencies in anticipation of the failure of the policy of neutralization under Souvanna Phouma and not enough into making the policy work. The job will be sufficiently difficult even in the best of

circumstances and it is not at all unlikely that Souvanna Phouma may tire of it and abandon it unless the efforts of every department and agency of our own government which may be involved are bent energetically to the achievement of our policy under the direction of the Ambassador.

If Laos does not yet offer much hope of an eventual lightening of our burdens throughout Southeast Asia, Cambodia stands in stark contrast. Its internal stability is exceptional for contemporary Southeast Asia. It is led by Prince Sihanouk with dedication, energy and astuteness. And it has made steady and most impressive social and economic progress in the past few years. It is an illustration of what can be achieved in the lush lands of the region in conditions of peace, with a vigorous and progressive indigenous leadership and a judicious and limited use of outside aid. It is also an experience which can shed light on the possibilities of eventually lightening our burdens in Southeast Asia.

For that reason if for no other, it seems to me essential that we go very far in attempting to find practicable solutions which will meet the Cambodian desire for reassurance that it will not be overwhelmed from either Vietnam on the east or Thailand on the west. Cambodian fears exist. They are probably excessive fears at least in present circumstances. Nevertheless, they are powerful and deeply felt fears based in part on history and it would be most unwise to underestimate their potential influence on Cambodian policy. It would be most unfortunate if they pushed Cambodia further in the direction of China.

Our relations with this little country have been, to say the least, erratic from the outset and, it seems to me, largely unnecessarily so. There have been unfortunate clashes of personality, lack of understanding and even more serious matters involved. Official relations now seem to me to be well-handled and insofar as we may be responsible for such strains as exist, they would appear ascribable to policy as it is formulated in Washington not as it is administered in Phnom Penh.

The Cambodians are apparently prepared for a further reduction in the remaining one-sided aid commitment which has already been reduced considerably. We should welcome this opportunity and at the same time seek to broaden mutually advantageous relationships. The key to bringing about this transition without alienating Cambodia is to be found in its interrelationships and ours with its neighbors, Thailand and Vietnam. It is, in my opinion, clearly desirable to search vigorously for this key.

It is apparent that in Thailand, the bent of our policy with respect not only to Cambodia but to Laos as well is not appreciated and, at best, enjoys only a grudging tolerance. Cambodia is held in low esteem and the resentments over the recent adverse International Court decision still smolder.

With respect to Laos, the Thais have either not wanted the policy of neutralization to work or have not believed that it would work from the outset. They are still clearly skeptical. It is probable that once it became clear that we would not commit ourselves militarily to the recapture of all of Laos, the Thais preferred a solution by military partition rather than the attempt at neutralization, with the United States committed to the defense of at least southern Laos. This may still be their expectation.

American actions in Thailand appear to support the Thai skepticism at least to the point of providing heavily for contingencies in the event neutralization fails in Laos. Several new jet-ports have been built in eastern Thailand. In the recent withdrawal of the American combat unit, a great deal of heavy transport equipment, particularly for fuel, has been left behind. And, finally, the United States military command intends to put back into Thailand in the near future, a contingent of forces about equal in number to those being withdrawn for the purpose of constructing a fuel pipe line across that country.

The cost of these various operations when added to the already immense and continuing input of aid of various kinds is cause for serious concern. Thailand is relatively prosperous. It has a very substantial foreign trade from which other nations such as Japan and Western Germany profit greatly along with Thailand. There is talk of aid from other sources but it is almost entirely talk of aid on a loan or trade basis, with a clear expectation of direct and tangible returns to the donors. At the same time, we are carrying, virtually, the entire burden of aid for Thailand's defense and other purposes which carry little in the way of tangible return. This sort of an arrangement leaves us with the onerous burdens while others reap the fruits.

It is an arrangement that will probably be continued as long as we are prepared to countenance it. Sudden changes in our willingness to sustain these burdens might produce serious adverse consequences. But it seems to me that a constant pressure must be maintained to bring about a progressive reduction in our commitment by having the Thais themselves and others take on more of the onerous burdens. That pressure is not in evidence in our policies and their administration at the present time.

Elsewhere in Southeast Asia, in Burma and in Malaya, we have a minimum of commitment. In the case of Burma, this fortuitous state of affairs would appear to be largely one of Burmese choice. The Burmese have settled the border question with China along the McCarthy line (an extension of the McMahon line) and to their satisfaction. They are fumed inward in their attitudes, seeking only to stay clear of the India-China dispute. They are also fearful of antagonizing China by too close dealings with us. But there is no assurance that in the future a Burmese government, hard-pressed to maintain itself in an internal political situation which is never far from chaos, will not seek substantial aid from the United States. It seems to me that we must steel ourselves against that day. And, in all honesty, it seems to me that the key to staying clear of still another costly commitment on the Asian mainland is to be found in restraining our own bureaucratic eagerness to help.

In the case of Malaya, except for a large and expanding Peace Corps, we are maintaining relatively orthodox and inexpensive relationships with a minimum of commitment on our part. However, this excellent state of affairs may be strained by the effort to bring Malaysia into existence. It is probable that the British hope, by the unification of Malaya, Singapore, Brunei, Sarawak, and North Borneo, to lighten their burdens in that region while retaining as much as possible of their influence and their highly profitable economic position.

Without criticizing this attempt, it should be noted that our approach must be one of the greatest delicacy, primarily because of the attitudes of the Philippines. There are already indications of a measure of collaboration developing between the Philippines and Indonesia in resisting the formation of Malaysia. It is a collaboration which we should do nothing to stimulate by inadvertent statements or actions.

It is likely that Malaysia will come into existence some time next year. There are already feelers being put out for the establishment of an aid program from the United States. It seems to me, again, that we must resist this effort to deepen our commitment and, again, the key is to put restraints on our own bureaucratic eagernesses. It is one thing to provide loans to a nation such as Malaysia which is clearly a good risk or to send Peace Corpsmen to the remote areas of Brunei, Sarawak and North Borneo where a little technical knowledge can go a long way. But it is quite another thing to take on major and continuing tasks of military organization and supply and the internal development of still one more country in Southeast Asia, responsibilities which we assume in name at least and also to some degree in fact, every time we establish these aid-missions. It would seem appropriate that any continuing aid to Malaysia should remain the responsibility of the U.K. and the Commonwealth rather than being shifted to the United States.

Viewing Southeast Asia as a whole, the situation is one of varying conditions of stability. The future of freedom in the area is far from certain. Except for some significant and effective French efforts in Cambodia and Commonwealth efforts in the Malayan situation, the principal externally borne burdens fall upon us.

If we were to withdraw abruptly from beneath these burdens, there would be a major collapse in many places and what would follow is by no means certain. Obviously, much would depend upon the capacity and urge of the Chinese to move into the vacuum.

We cannot afford to withdraw suddenly from these burdens. While we must make every effort to have others share them, we would, I believe, be deluding ourselves if we expected very much help from other outside sources in the near future.

The real question which confronts us, therefore, is how much are we ourselves prepared to put into Southeast Asia and for how long in order to serve such interests as we may have in that region? Before we can answer this question, we must reassess our interests, using the words "vital" or "essential" with the greatest realism and restraint in the reassessment. When that has been done, we will be in a better position to estimate what we must, in fact, expend in the way of scarce resources, energy and lives in order to preserve those interests. We may well discover that it is in our interests to do less rather than more than we are now doing. If that is the case, we will do well to concentrate on a vigorous diplomacy which would be designed to lighten our commitments without bringing about sudden and catastrophic upheavals in Southeast Asia.

GLOSSARY

McMahon Line: the boundary between China and India, agreed on by Britain and Tibet in the 1914 Simla Accord; contested by China, this line was at the heart of the 1962 Sino-Indian War.

Pathet Lao: a Laotian communist group co-ruling with pro-West and neutral groups

Vietcong: South Vietnamese communist forces

Vietminh (also, Viet Minh): the communist forces that had fought the French and the name used for any communist forces existing early on in the US involvement with Vietnam.

Document Analysis

Mike Mansfield had been a friend and legislative ally to President Kennedy, which is why Kennedy asked him to travel to South Vietnam and assess the situation. Thus, when Kennedy read Mansfield's report on his visit, it may have surprised him that it was not the affirmation that Kennedy had expected. Mansfield had the luxury of being independent of the executive branch, so that although he did have to be a little cautious in criticizing an American ally, he did not have to worry about keeping his job if he criticized the president's policy. His negative view of the Diem regime's activities and the failure of South Vietnam to move forward in the eight years since the Geneva Accord should, therefore, be seen in that light. While he saw glimmers of success, Mansfield mainly saw the repetition of history, which if allowed to continue would see the United States on the losing side. Given this pessimistic vision of South Vietnam, Mansfield spends half of his report evaluating other potential allies in the region. He closes his analysis by stating that, in the future, it might be better "to do less rather than more" in Southeast Asia.

As in the case of any good report, Mansfield gets to the point very quickly. While he sees Diem's leadership in South Vietnam as a failure, he regards the American policy as a greater failure for its granting of aid to Diem. Mansfield correctly understood that, without American aid, Diem would likely not have remained in office following the 1955 election. Although Diem was the one who was taking inadequate actions, it was, according to Mansfield, American foreign policy that was failing. He reports that the American assistance was "ill-conceived and badly administered." Not mincing any words, Mansfield states that the South Vietnamese government was dependent on the United States for its existence, rather than on the people of South Vietnam upon finding themselves duly satisfied with his policies—as would be the case in a truly democratic system.

During these early years, the work of the US military with the Montagnards had been a success, and Mansfield points to this as a positive thing. As for most of the rest of the effort, however, Mansfield believes that the American and Vietnamese optimism about these programs merely repeats the optimism that French leaders had had in their programs only a year prior to their defeat. Mansfield reminds Kennedy (and the others who read the report) that such optimistic projections were based upon their own assumptions about what type of costs the communist forces were willing to endure and that the communist leaders would not be smart enough to change their tactics when the American and South Vietnamese leaders changed theirs. For Mansfield, then, neither of these is a sound foundation upon which to build an American policy for Vietnam.

Widening his perspective, Mansfield spends several pages going through the other Southeast Asian countries. He recognizes that these nations did not really want to get involved with the Vietnamese conflict, yet all depended, to a certain extent, upon US aid. In his summary, Mansfield questions why the United States was so deeply involved in Southeast Asia. He knows a quick withdrawal would cause great harm for the region, but he believes that it would be better "to concentrate on a vigorous diplomacy" rather than to continue to expend "energy and lives" in the support of American interests in the region.

Essential Themes

In 1962, the Vietnam conflict had not yet become the war that would divide American society. Although in later years this report would give ammunition to some of those opposing the Vietnam War, this was not the report's original intent. Rather, the report was an honest assessment of what had transpired from the Geneva Accords, which ended French rule in 1954, up to 1962. The United States was the primary country supporting the South Vietnamese government during that period. Mansfield calls into question whether that should continue to be the case. One point that Mansfield makes repeatedly is that the United States alone could not achieve the ends desired. The South Vietnamese government, under Diem's leadership, must fulfill its responsibilities; and in Mansfield's eyes, this has not yet happened. Without a South Vietnamese government willing to undertake programs to assist its people, Mansfield feels that American actions are doomed.

Because of this report, Mansfield was seen as one of the early antiwar senators. He did vote for the Gulf of Tonkin Resolution and the main funding bills for the war. However, this trip to Vietnam caused him to question many of the assumptions maintained by the executive branch. More importantly, his report called for the United States to clearly examine its priorities in foreign policy and to be certain that its activities reflected those priorities. This message served to carry the report well beyond the Vietnam War era.

—*Donald A. Watt, PhD*

Bibliography and Additional Reading

Glennon, John P., David M. Baehler, & Charles S. Sampson, eds. "Foreign Relations of the United States, 1961–1962, Volume II, Vietnam, 1962." *Office of the Historian*. US Department of State, 2015. Web.

Mansfield Foundation. "Mike Mansfield: Great American Statesman." *The Maureen and Mike Mansfield Foundation*. The Maureen and Mike Mansfield Foundation, 2009. Web.

Oberdorfer, Don. *Senator Mansfield: The Extraordinary Life of a Great American Statesman and Diplomat.* Washington, DC: Smithsonian Books, 2003. Print.

Olson, Gregory A. *Mansfield and Vietnam: A Study in Rhetorical Adaptation.* Lansing: Michigan State University Press, 1995.

■ On the Prospect of a Generals' Coup

Date: August 29, 1963
Author: Henry Cabot Lodge, Jr.
Genre: report

Summary Overview

Ambassador Henry Cabot Lodge, Jr. sent this report to Admiral Harry Felt, the commander in chief of the US Pacific Command (USPACOM) and the superior to General Harkins, who is mentioned in the letter. By August 1963, South Vietnam was, domestically, falling apart. President Ngo Dinh Diem of South Vietnam had alienated the majority of the population. Having come into office via a rigged election, Diem ruled with an iron fist and reinforced his authority through his brother Nhu (Ngo Dinh Nhu), who served as Diem's unofficial political advisor and directed the ARVN Special Forces. As a result, there was no easy way to institute a change of government in South Vietnam; only the military would have the power to bring about change. Thus, the possibility of a coup had been discussed by many different individuals in the administration of President John F. Kennedy. Lodge had just become ambassador, replacing Frederick Nolting, who had been a strong supporter of Diem and was against any discussion of a coup. Thus, Lodge's support for a coup brought about a change in the dynamics within the American administration.

Defining Moment

The government of South Vietnam's president, Ngo Dinh Diem, had been biased toward Catholics and against Buddhists since its formal inception in 1955. In May 1963, this bias reached a critical point, when Buddhists in the city of Hue were attacked by government troops as they tried to celebrate the anniversary of Buddha's birth by displaying flags. The conflict continued to escalate, with a Buddhist monk burning himself to death in protest that June. Although American officials had known about the problem for a number of years, the monk's death brought the issue to the front pages of American newspapers. This increased the American public's concern about American policy in Vietnam. Within Vietnam, some military leaders had also been concerned for some time. On August 21, Diem instituted martial law, and his brother Nhu arrested more than a thousand Buddhist leaders. These events forced American and Vietnamese leaders to consider action against Diem sooner rather than later. One day prior to the release of Lodge's report, a communication referred to as Deptel 268 had been sent from Secretary of State Dean Rusk to Lodge with a request that Lodge respond the following day, when Rusk had a meeting scheduled with President Kennedy. Deptel 268 was basically an affirmation that the United States supported and encouraged a coup, and it requested Lodge assess the situation and work to make any attempt more likely to succeed. Deptel 268 was in response to a previous communication from Lodge that outlined which forces and leader were expected to take part in a coup against Diem in the very near future.

Any attempted coup tends to be a life-or-death struggle. If successful, all may or may not turn out well; but if unsuccessful, the death penalty is usually brought into play. Thus, while it was relatively easy for American officials to encourage this course of action, for the Vietnamese military officers and troops who might consider participating, there was great danger. Lodge's support for a coup, as contrasted with former Ambassador Nolting's opposition, made a significant difference in the discussion of American support. Although no coup was attempted in August, this discussion, and related communication with Vietnamese leaders, were part of the process that eventually did lead to one in November. By sending this communication via military channels rather than straight to Rusk, Lodge was attempting to insure that all individuals who would be needed to support a coup understood what was being recommended.

Author Biography

Henry Cabot Lodge, Jr. (1902–1985) was part of a wealthy Massachusetts family. Having graduated from

Harvard, Lodge entered the Massachusetts legislature in 1933, after working as a journalist. Elected to the US Senate, he served from 1937 to 1944, when he resigned to continue to serve in the army. Having served with distinction, he returned to the Senate in 1947 for one term. He lost his bid for re-election to John F. Kennedy in 1952, as he focused on helping Dwight Eisenhower win the presidency. In 1953, Eisenhower appointed him as the ambassador to the United Nations, where he served until 1960. He was on the 1960 Republican ticket as the vice-presidential candidate, but the Democratic ticket headed by Kennedy won the election. He served as ambassador to South Vietnam under Kennedy, and later, under President Johnson, Lodge was ambassador to West Germany. His final position was as the US representative to the Vatican, from which he retired in 1977.

HISTORICAL DOCUMENT

Saigon, *August 29, 1963, 6 p.m.*
375. CINCPAC Exclusive for Felt.

1. We are launched on a course from which there is no respectable turning back: The overthrow of the Diem government. There is no turning back in part because U.S. prestige is already publicly committed to this end in large measure and will become more so as facts leak out. In a more fundamental sense, there is no turning back because there is no possibility, in my view, that the war can be won under a Diem administration, still less that Diem or any member of the family can govern the country in a way to gain the support of the people who count, i.e., the educated class in and out of government service, civil and military—not to mention the American people. In the last few months (and especially days), they have in fact positively alienated these people to an incalculable degree. So that I am personally in full agreement with the policy which I was instructed to carry out by last Sunday's telegram.

2. The chance of bringing off a Generals' coup depends on them to some extent; but it depends at least as much on us.

3. We should proceed to make all-out effort to get Generals to move promptly. To do so we should have authority to do following:

(a) That General Harkins repeat to Generals personally messages previously transmitted by CAS officers. This should establish their authenticity. (General Harkins should have order from President on this.)

(b) If nevertheless Generals insist on public statement that all U.S. aid to Vietnam through Diem regime has been stopped, we would agree, on express understanding that Generals will have started at same time. (We would seek persuade Generals that it would be better to hold this card for use in event of stalemate. We hope it will not be necessary to do this at all.)

4. Vietnamese Generals doubt that we have the will power, courage, and determination to see this thing through. They are haunted by the idea that we will run out on them even though we have told them pursuant to instructions, that the game had started.

5. We must press on for many reasons. Some of these are:

(a) Explosiveness of the present situation which may well lead to riots and violence if issue of discontent with regime is not met. Out of this could come a pro-Communist or at best a neutralist set of politicians.

(b) The fact that war cannot be won with the present regime.

(c) Our own reputation for steadfastness and our unwillingness to stultify ourselves.

(d) If proposed action is suspended, I believe a body blow will be dealt to respect for us by Vietnamese Generals. Also, all those who expect U.S. to straighten out this situation will feel let down. Our help to the regime in past years inescapably gives us a large responsibility which we cannot avoid.

6. I realize that this course involves a very substantial risk of losing Vietnam. It also involves some additional

risk to American lives. I would never propose it if I felt there was a reasonable chance of holding Vietnam with Diem.

7. In response to specific question (c) in Deptel 268, I would not hesitate to use financial inducements if I saw a useful opportunity.

As to (d) I favor such moves, provided it is made clear they are not connected with evacuation Americans. As for (e); I fear evacuation of U.S. personnel now would alarm the Generals and demoralize the people.

8. In response to your para 4, General Harkins thinks that I should ask Diem to get rid of the Nhus before starting the Generals' action. But I believe that such a step has no chance of getting the desired result and would have the very serious effect of being regarded by the Generals as a sign of American indecision and delay. I believe this is a risk which we should not run. The Generals distrust us too much already. Another point is that Diem would certainly ask for time to consider such a far-reaching request. This would give the ball to Nhu.

9. With the exception of paragraph 8 above General Harkins concurs in this telegram.
Lodge

GLOSSARY

CINCPAC: a US military acronym meaning Commander in Chief, Pacific

Deptel 268: a telegram from the Department of State to the US embassy in Vietnam, sent August 28, 1963

stultify: in this context, to cause or allow someone or something to appear foolish

Document Analysis

Ambassador Lodge communicates one definite assertion and raises a related area of uncertainty. He believes a coup against South Vietnam president Diem should happen immediately. However, he is seeking to gain a better understanding of how the United States could help those planning the coup. This telegram makes it clear that he believes a decision has already been made, by the "Generals" and the United States to "overthrow the Diem government." This had been the subject of many previous communiqués, including one, Deptel 268, sent on the previous day. Lodge argues that this course of action is for the best and tries to encourage the "Generals to move promptly."

What is not clear to him is how the United States could help. In point 2, Lodge makes it clear that there is a role to play, although not in the actual fighting that might occur. He mentions some kinds of pressure that might be put on Diem, such as cutting aid, or assistance, to the generals by publically supporting them once the coup had started. However, for the generals, there is uncertainty because if the United States is willing to sacrifice an ally of the past eight years, will it stand by that ally or "run out on them?" This uncertainty probably played a role in the coup not moving forward at that time.

Lodge was in a unique position to advise President Kennedy. Historically, he was a political rival of President Kennedy. However, as the longest-serving American ambassador to the United Nations in the first seventy years of the UN's history, Lodge had developed a strong understanding of international relations and how to deal with various governments. He was able to make decisions based on what he thought was best for the United States rather than saying what Kennedy might want to hear. Thus, his statement that the "war cannot be won with the present regime" is not said to please Kennedy; it is his own analysis of the situation. This change in government is necessary, from Lodge's perspective, if the United States wants any chance of defeating the communist attempt to take over South Vietnam. On all of these points, Lodge had consulted with the military commander for American forces in Vietnam, General Paul Harkins. The one point of disagreement between the two is whether Diem should be given the option to dismiss his brother, Nhu (and his powerful wife, known as Madame Nhu), from his position as de facto commander of a special-forces military group that acted as secret police for Diem.

The containment of communism was at stake, in the eyes of the writer. Because of this, the United States was concerned about the government of South Vietnam. Diem had to be removed for there to be a chance at victory. This was the way Lodge saw the situation. The raids on the pagodas, which resulted in massive arrests of Buddhist monks and nuns, seem to have been the action that both made US officials ready to accept a coup and pushed the South Vietnamese military to the point of considering one. Although Lodge seems to acknowledge that there was a wide gap between American and South Vietnamese military leaders on the specifics of undertaking such an action, he sees that all are unified on the need for change.

Essential Themes

This report from Ambassador Lodge to Admiral Felt, and in reality for Secretary Rusk and President Kennedy, continues a discussion that had been taking place since Lodge was appointed to be the United States ambassador to South Vietnam about two weeks prior. Basically, the turmoil in South Vietnam seems to have only one solution: Diem no longer being president of the country. And the only way to achieve that is for the military to force Diem from office. The wedge that Diem had driven between his government and the people of Vietnam, in Lodge's opinion, makes it impossible for reconciliation or for South Vietnam to have the focus needed to defeat the communists. Thus, he holds that a coup is necessary and the sooner the better. Although the administration's support was not as overt as in some coups that the Americans had engineered in other countries, pushing the idea with Vietnamese military leaders was in the same vein. Perhaps not unexpectedly, Lodge and other American leaders put American goals first, which, in this case, entail the overthrow of Diem. The same policy of doing whatever it took to repel communist advances in Southeast Asia would drive American policy for the next several years.

While there are records (such as an August 27 telegram) about General Tran Thien Khiem's meeting with CIA operatives—during which he gave them the names of six generals who were planning to participate in the coup—the leading general (Duong Van Minh) seemed to waver about the timing. Obviously, the fact that the coup was delayed by about nine weeks meant that the latter's sentiment carried the day. After the coup, about two years passed before a stable government appeared in South Vietnam; four individuals exchanged power eight times during that period. While the Buddhist persecution that Diem had instigated stopped, during this two-year period, the needs of the people were not well served. Therefore, the statement with which Lodge opens his report comes to mean more than just the coup against Diem. "We are launched on a course from which there is no respectable turning back." Once a coup is seen as acceptable to the United States, in other words, there is no reason for those seeking power to reconsider.

—Donald A. Watt, PhD

Bibliography and Additional Reading

Blair, Anne E. *Lodge in Vietnam: A Patriot Abroad.* New Haven: Yale University Press, 1995. Print.

Lodge, Henry Cabot, Jr. *As It Was: An Inside View of Politics and Power in the '50s and '60s.* New York: W.W. Norton & Company Inc., 1976. Print.

Miller, Edward. *Misalliance: Ngo Dinh Diem, the United States, and the Fate of South Vietnam.* Cambridge: Harvard University Press, 2013.

"Vietnam, Diem, the Buddhist Crisis." *JFK in History.* John F. Kennedy Presidential Library and Museum, 2015. Web. <http://www.jfklibrary.org/JFK/JFK-in-History/Vietnam-Diem-and-the-Buddhist-Crisis.aspx>.

■ Televised Interview with President Kennedy

Date: September 9, 1963
Author(s): John F. Kennedy, Chet Huntley, and David Brinkley
Genre: interview; transcript

Summary Overview

There are times when it is hard to pin down presidents as to what their thoughts are regarding certain issues or situations. A news conference, or televised interview, is one way to get the president on record. The TV co-anchors Chet Huntley and David Brinkley wanted the president to address the issues of the day on their news program. At the same time, Kennedy wanted to present an image of a president who was in control of major events and in tune with what the American people desired.

While the interview covered more than just the events in Vietnam, what was happening in that country formed a significant portion of the dialogue. Although Kennedy stated that the anti-communist operations were proving successful, he acknowledged that there were other South Vietnamese domestic concerns that were also concerns for the United States. In retrospect, what Kennedy had to say about these issues foreshadowed what came to pass within a few months.

Defining Moment

Television had helped Kennedy win the presidency, and he used it to communicate his thoughts not only to American, but also to foreign leaders. Thus, in September 1963, he allowed the anchors of evening news broadcasts to interview him. Having conducted one with CBS, this second one was with NBC news co-anchors, Chet Huntley and David Brinkley. At that time, the two hosted the top-rated evening news program, which meant that any interview they conducted was guaranteed to have a large audience.

Having been in office for more than two and a half years, Kennedy had been dealing with Vietnam since day one. The increase in military advisors and economic aid had been a consistent part of his foreign policy. For over a year, there had been some in the administration who had questioned American policy, especially as it related to supporting the South Vietnamese govern-

ment headed by President Ngo Dinh Diem. In private conversations earlier in the year, Kennedy himself had expressed such concerns. Only a month earlier, Kennedy had replaced the American ambassador to South Vietnam, Frederick Nolting, a strong supporter of Diem, with Henry Cabot Lodge, Jr., a skeptic regarding Diem's government. In addition, rumors were circulating of the CIA pushing some South Vietnamese generals to undertake a coup, adding uncertainty to the situation.

With those events in the background, President Kennedy sat down with Huntley and Brinkley to answer questions regarding current programs and proposals of his administration. His obvious hope was to strengthen support for his administration from the American populace and from members of Congress. As regards the questions related to South Vietnam, Kennedy made it clear that he had concerns about the South Vietnamese government, without overtly withdrawing his support for it. The fact, however, that he mentions some of these concerns makes it clear that they were more serious than he wanted to let on. His refusal to answer a question about the CIA should have been expected, although that was the question that probably needed answering the most.

Author Biography

John Fitzgerald Kennedy (1917–1963) was born into a wealthy family in Boston. His parents pushed all their children to succeed. He graduated from Harvard, having written his senior thesis—published in 1940—on the topic of why Britain was unprepared for World War II. He served as a naval officer World War II, winning medals for courage. In 1946, he was elected to the House of Representatives. In 1952, he was elected to the US Senate. The following year, he married Jacqueline Bouvier. He was elected president in 1960, the first Catholic to hold that position. His foreign policy was staunchly anti-communist, while domestically, he pushed for equality and an increase in emphasis upon the space program. Kennedy was assassinated on November 21, 1963. Since he was president for a relatively short period, a number of his programs and ideas had not yet been implemented. Nevertheless, his youthful image and enthusiasm inspired many throughout the country.

Chester "Chet" Huntley (1911–1974) was a journalist from Montana who worked his way up on radio and television. His big break came when he co-anchored the 1956 national political convention coverage. In 1956, he became co-anchor, with David Brinkley, of the NBC evening news until his retirement in 1970.

David Brinkley (1920–2003) was born in North Carolina and began his journalism career while still in high school. In 1943, he moved to Washington and became the NBC White House correspondent. Co-anchoring the evening news with Huntley, Brinkley then continued with NBC after Huntley's retirement. In 1981, he moved to ABC and initiated a new Sunday morning news format, staying with that network until his retirement in 1997.

HISTORICAL DOCUMENT

THE PRESIDENT. On the whole, I think this country has done an outstanding job. A good many countries today are free that would not be free. Communism's gains since 1945 in spite of chaos and poverty have been limited, and I think the balance of power still rests with the West, and I think it can increase our strength if we make the right decisions this year, economically, here at home and in the field of foreign policy. Two matters that we have been talking about are examples of that. One is the tax cut which affects our economic growth, which affects the whole movement of this country internally; the test ban treaty which affects our security abroad and our leadership. That is why I think it is very important that the Senate pass it. You know the old story that who prepares for battle that the trumpet blows an uncertain sound. Well, I think that if the United States Senate rejected that treaty after the Government has committed itself to it, the sound from the United States around the world would be very uncertain.

Mr. Huntley: Mr. President, in respect to our difficulties in South Viet-Nam, could it be that our Government tends occasionally to get locked into a policy or an attitude and then finds it difficult to alter or shift that policy?

THE PRESIDENT. Yes, that is true. I think in the case of South Viet-Nam we have been dealing with a government which is in control, has been in control for 10 years. In addition, we have felt for the last 2 years that the struggle against the Communists was going better.

Since June, however, the difficulties with the Buddhists, we have been concerned about a deterioration, particularly in the Saigon area, which hasn't been felt greatly in the outlying areas but may spread. So we are faced with the problem of wanting to protect the area against the Communists. On the other hand, we have to deal with the government there. That produces a kind of ambivalence in our efforts which exposes us to some criticism. We are using our influence to persuade the government there to take those steps which will win back support. That takes some time and we must be patient, we must persist.

Mr. Huntley: Are we likely to reduce our aid to South Viet-Nam now?

THE PRESIDENT. I don't think we think that would be helpful at this time. If you reduce your aid, it is possible you could have some effect upon the government structure there. On the other hand, you might have a situation which could bring about a collapse. Strongly in our mind is what happened in the case of China at the end of World War II, where China was lost, a weak government became increasingly unable to control events. We don't want that.

Mr. Brinkley: Mr. President, have you had any reason to doubt this so-called "domino theory," that if South Viet-Nam falls, the rest of southeast Asia will go behind it?

THE PRESIDENT. No, I believe it. I believe it. I think that the struggle is close enough. China is so large, looms so high just beyond the frontiers, that if South Viet-Nam went, it would not only give them an improved geographic position for a guerrilla assault on Malaya, but would also give the impression that the wave of the future in southeast Asia was China and the Communists. So I believe it.

Mr. Brinkley: In the last 48 hours there have been a great many conflicting reports from there about what the CIA was up to. Can you give us any enlightenment on it?

THE PRESIDENT. No.

Mr. Huntley: Does the CIA tend to make its own policy? That seems to be the debate here.

THE PRESIDENT. NO, that is the frequent charge, but that isn't so. Mr. McCone, head of the CIA, sits in the National Security Council. We have had a number of meetings in the past few days about events in South Viet-Nam. Mr. McCone participated in every one, and the CIA coordinates its efforts with the State Department and the Defense Department.

Mr. Brinkley: With so much of our prestige, money, so on, committed in South Viet-Nam, why can't we exercise a little more influence there, Mr. President?

THE PRESIDENT. We have some influence. We have some influence, and we are attempting to carry it out. I think we don't—we can't expect these countries to do everything the way we want to do them. They have their own interest, their own personalities, their own tradition. We can't make everyone in our image, and there are a good many people who don't want to go in our image. In addition, we have ancient struggles between countries. In the case of India and Pakistan, we would like to have them settle Kashmir. That is our view of the best way to defend the subcontinent against communism. But that struggle between India and Pakistan is more important to a good many people in that area than the struggle against the Communists. We would like to have Cambodia, Thailand, and South Viet-Nam all in harmony, but there are ancient differences there. We can't make the world over, but we can influence the world. The fact of the matter is that with the assistance of the United States, SEATO, southeast Asia and indeed all of Asia has been maintained independent against a powerful force, the Chinese Communists. What I am concerned about is that Americans will get impatient and say because they don't like events in southeast Asia or they don't like the government in Saigon, that we should withdraw. That only makes it easy for the Communists. I think we should stay. We should use our influence in as effective a way as we can, but we should not withdraw.

Mr. Huntley: Someone called the civil rights issue in 1964, I think, the fear of the political unknown. Would you agree?

THE PRESIDENT. Yes. I think that what they are wondering is what effect this will have, whether the North, which has supported civil rights in the past, will continue to support it. I think they will. I think the bill we put in is a reasonable bill, and I think that—my judgment is that we will not divide this country politically into Negroes and whites. That would be a fatal mistake for a society which should be as united as ours is. I think it should be divided, in other words, Republicans and Democrats, but not by race.

Mr. Huntley: But in the Congress, do you see the issue coming down to a full scale test of strength, or do you see it ending in a compromise?

THE PRESIDENT. We don't start off with a compromise. I hope it is going to pass as close to the form in which we sent it up as possible.

Mr. Brinkley: Do you plan to see President Tito this fall, Mr. President?

THE PRESIDENT. Well, I don't know. It would depend in part, and there are other Presidents who will be coming to the United Nations, and I would expect to see most of them.

Mr. Brinkley: Mr. President, Harry Truman was out for his walk this morning and he said he did not think we should have a tax cut until we get the budget balanced, and the other day Senator Humphrey was saying in the Senate that what the American people think is true is very often more important than what actually is true. In view of all that, what do you think about cutting taxes while the budget is still in deficit?

THE PRESIDENT. The reason the Government is in deficit is because you have more than 4 million people unemployed, and because the last 5 years you have had rather a sluggish growth, much slower than any other Western country. I am in favor of a tax cut because I am concerned that if we don't get the tax cut that we are going to have an increase in unemployment and that we may move into a period of economic downturn. We had a recession in '58, a recession in 1960. We have done pretty well since then, but we still have over 4 million unemployed. I think this tax cut can give the stimulus to our economy over the next 2 or 3 years. I think it will provide for greater national wealth. I think it will reduce unemployment. I think it will strengthen our gold position. So I think that the proposal we made is responsible and in the best interests of the country. Otherwise, if we don't get the tax cut, I would think that our prospects are much less certain. I think the Federal Reserve Board has indicated that. Nineteen hundred and sixty-four is going to be an uncertain time if we don't get the tax cut. I think that to delay it to 1964 would be very unwise. I think our whole experience in the late fifties shows us how necessary and desirable it is. My guess is that if we can get the tax cut, with the stimulus it will give to the economy, that we will get our budget in balance quicker than we will if we don't have it.

Mr. Huntley: The affirmative economic response to Britain's tax cut seemed to be almost immediate. Would it be as immediate in this country, do you think?

THE PRESIDENT. I think it would be. Interestingly enough, the British came forward with their tax cut in April, passed it within a month. They have experienced economic benefits from it. Unemployment has been substantially reduced. They have a larger deficit than we do. Yet the only criticism was that it wasn't enough. Nearly every economist has supported us. I think it is in the best economic interests of the country, unless this country just wants to drag along, have 5 or 6 million people unemployed, have profits reduced, have economic prospects, have our budgets unbalanced by a much larger proportion. The largest unbalanced budget in the history of this country was in 1958 because of the recession—$12 1/2 billion. The fact of the matter is that, of course, Government expenditures do go up in every administration, but the country's wealth goes up. President Eisenhower spent $185 billion more than President Truman. But the country was much wealthier. It is much wealthier now than it was in the last year of President Eisenhower's administration. I think our economic situation can be very good. I think what we have proposed is a responsible answer to a problem which has been part of our economic life for 5 or 6 years, and that is slack, failure to grow sufficiently, relatively high unemployment. If you put that together with the fact that we have to find 35,000 new jobs a week, I think the situation in this country calls for a tax reduction this year.

Mr. Huntley: Thank you, Mr. President.

GLOSSARY

difficulties with the Buddhists: a reference to the massive social protests taking place against the Diem government over the latter's treatment of Buddhist groups

Kashmir: a disputed territory bordering northwest India and northeast Pakistan

Saigon: the capital of South Vietnam; today, Ho Chi Minh City

Document Analysis

By the time President Kennedy came into office, television had truly become a national media. He used it extensively, including being the first chief executive to have his press conferences broadcast live. Kennedy held sixty-four press conferences in his thirty-four months in office, with additional interviews, as in the case of this one, also taking place. The relationship between Kennedy and the news media was less adversarial than has been the case for presidents in recent years. The status of events in South Vietnam was of interest to the nation. One item emerging from the interview is how the United States can support a government with which it has major disagreements. The other principal concern is the ongoing struggle with communism. The anticommunist tone of Kennedy's responses is in line with his political orientation throughout his life. Whether or not he was as optimistic as his responses indicate, Kennedy did try to assure the American public that the communist push for expansion was being thwarted. His counsel is for patience, as American interests would ultimately prevail.

In the midst of questions on civil rights, the test ban treaty, the upcoming United Nations session and a tax cut, Huntley and Brinkley raise the issue of Vietnam. The videos available from this interview show a friendly atmosphere, but that does not mean that the newsmen do not want to get the scoop on other reporters. Unlike four years later, when Vietnam became a central issue for all of America, it is still an emerging concern in 1963. When asked by Huntley, Kennedy does acknowledge that the United States sometimes gets "locked into a policy" even when change might be needed. As part of the response to that question, Kennedy raises the issue of the Buddhist protests against the Diem regime. (Diem had focused on the needs of the Catholic Vietnamese rather than the Buddhist majority.) While, to a certain extent, Kennedy tries to reduce the importance of the protests by stating that they were in "the Saigon area," in reality, this is an acknowledgement of the seriousness of the situation. Anti-government protests normally occurred outside the capital, which was always under tight security. The Buddhist protests had started in Hue in May and, by September, were spreading widely throughout the country. Kennedy's reference to the Saigon demonstrations is an indirect indication that the policy of supporting Diem might be moving toward a conclusion.

Several of the questions deal with what steps might be taken to pressure the Diem government into changing its policy toward South Vietnamese Buddhists. This had moved to the front pages of the American media in 1963 because, in an act of ultimate protest, a Buddhist monk had set himself on fire in Saigon that June. While not directly addressing the specifics of the Buddhist protests or their cause, Kennedy asserts that the United States "should use our influence in as effective a way as we can" regarding these and other issues. He also acknowledges that the United States should not "expect these countries to do everything the way we want." Related, yet not acknowledged in this interview, is the question about CIA activity. Kennedy refuses to say anything about it, although the question is raised because of rumors that the CIA was trying to instigate a coup. Declassified documents show that the CIA had indeed discussed a coup with some Vietnamese generals, but had not necessarily instigated the conversations.

Essential Themes

Kennedy responds more directly to some questions regarding Vietnam than was the case for other presidents in similar situations. One point that he makes clearly is that there's a limit to what foreign aid can buy. To expect that any nation receiving assistance from the United States will do whatever the United States desires, is misguided. Thus, there are various things happening in South Vietnam of which the United States does not approve. However, it also is apparent that there are limits to what is acceptable to the United States. Thus are the (not incorrect) rumors about the CIA discussing a South Vietnamese coup raised. While nothing Kennedy ever says points directly to allowing a South Vietnamese-led coup to take place in South Vietnam only two months later, his intimation of having problems with the Diem regime suggests encouragement of those considering such an action. As was seen in November, the patience that Kennedy counseled did have its limits.

Throughout his discussion of South Vietnam, and various regions of Asia, Kennedy makes it clear that the ultimate goal is stopping communism. When asked about the domino theory, that if South Vietnam fell other Southeast Asian countries would as well, Kennedy responds that he does "believe it." Throughout the interview, when asked about possible changes in the American position or actions in South Vietnam, Kennedy always raises the concern about how these things will affect the effort to stop the spread of communism. Having the majority of the South Vietnamese population support the government of South Vietnam, or questions as to whether the United States should cut its foreign aid, are questions and concerns that Kennedy accepts as valid. However, overriding all of these interests is the need to stop communism from taking control in new countries. This was one of America's and Kennedy's guiding principles. And ultimately, it was this concern that drew the United States further into the conflict in South Vietnam. The Vietnam War was the result of this strong anti-communist mindset dominating the scene in the post-World War II era.

—Donald A. Watt, PhD

Bibliography and Additional Reading

Chomsky, Noam. *Rethinking Camelot: JFK, the Vietnam War, and US Political Culture.* Cambridge: South End Press, 1993. Print.

Freedman, Lawrence. *Kennedy's Wars: Berlin, Cuba, Laos, and Vietnam.* Oxford: Oxford UP, 2002. Print.

Schlesinger, Arthur M., Jr. *A Thousand Days: John F. Kennedy in the White House.* 1965. New York: Houghton Mifflin Harcourt, 2002. Print.

Sorenson, Theodore C. *Kennedy.* New York: Harper & Row, 1965. Print.

■ Ambassador Lodge on the Worsening Situation

Date: September 11, 1963
Author: Henry Cabot Lodge, Jr.
Genre: Report

Summary Overview

One month into his appointment as ambassador to South Vietnam, Henry Cabot Lodge, Jr. sent another assessment of the situation there to President Kennedy, via the secretary of state. American involvement in Vietnam had been escalating during the past few years. Almost 15,000 military advisers were in the country, some of whom were participating in battles. The United States was putting more than a million dollars a day into supporting South Vietnam's government. Lodge wanted officials in Washington to know that these efforts were failing to produce positive results. Essentially, he called for a change in government, as President Ngo Dinh Diem had undertaken policies that were totally alienating the general population of South Vietnam. Most of the reports that were being sent to Washington from Vietnam were very optimistic because the authors did not want to seem to be failing. Lodge, who had just arrived and had been a political rival of Kennedy, had no qualms about being totally honest with him.

Defining Moment

In 1960, the communist forces in South Vietnam, known as the Viet Cong, organized across the country with help from North Vietnam. They became a more effective military force and were able to confront the forces of South Vietnam. Shortly after that, the ever-multiplying American military advisers, who previously were just advisers, began to take an active role on the battlefield. This greatly increased the investment that the United States was making in that country, in addition to the skyrocketing monetary costs of economic assistance. At the same time this pressure was being applied by the communists, President Diem was alienating 70 to 80 percent of South Vietnam's population, or those identifying as Buddhist. Diem and most of his close advisers were Catholic, and their policies were mainly directed toward the 20 to 30 percent of the population that was Catholic. This created discon-

tent, which the communists could use to support their cause. Diem's brother, Ngo Dinh Nhu, was in charge of security and had no compassion when dealing with average citizens. He viewed anyone who was not fully behind Diem as a communist, even though most were just disenchanted citizens. Most believed that if Diem continued these policies and his support of his brother, not only would his government fall, but South Vietnam would fall as well. Ambassador Henry Cabot Lodge, Jr., was among those with this belief. This spurred him to write to Secretary of State Dean Rusk, in order that the president and his cabinet might take the appropriate action.

Lodge made clear in this report that he understood the culture of 'yes men.' Having twice lost elections to Kennedy and being a Republican, Lodge understood that Kennedy had appointed him to the position because of the Lodge's experience at the United Nations. Kennedy wanted someone who would be honest about a situation that was becoming very tenuous. Although because of his own death, Kennedy ultimately did not make the decision to greatly expand the American commitment, and it was clear to him that very soon a decision would have to be made regarding American involvement in the struggle. From other documents, it is clear that Kennedy had lost faith in Diem, and this report by Lodge would have strengthened that view.

Author Biography

Henry Cabot Lodge, Jr. (1902–1985) was born into an influential family in Massachusetts. After graduating from Harvard and working at a newspaper, he began his political career in 1933, winning election to the Massachusetts legislature. In 1936, he was elected to the US Senate, serving from 1937 to 1944 and 1947 to 1953. After having served one tour of duty in World War II, he had to choose between being in the army or the Senate. In 1944, he resigned from the Senate to undertake a second tour, winning several medals for distinguished service. Re-elected to the Senate, he helped convince Dwight Eisenhower to run for president and focused on Eisenhower's campaign, which resulted in Lodge losing his Senate seat to John F. Kennedy. He then served as ambassador to the United Nations until 1960, when he was the Republican vice-presidential candidate. He served as ambassador to South Vietnam and, later, to West Germany. His final position was as the US representative to the Vatican, from which he retired in 1977.

HISTORICAL DOCUMENT

Saigon, *September 11, 1963, 2 p.m.*
Eyes only for the Secretary from Lodge.

My best estimate of the current situation in Viet Nam is:

   a.   That it is worsening rapidly;

   b.   That the time has arrived for the US to use what effective sanctions it has to bring about the fall of the existing government and the installation of another; and

   c.   That intensive study should be given by the best brains in the government to all the details, procedures and variants in connection with the suspension of aid.

Herewith is the background for this proposal:

1. I do not doubt the military judgment that the war in the countryside is going well now. But, as one who has had long connection with the military, I do doubt the value of the answers which are given by young officers to direct questions by Generals—or, for that matter, by Ambassadors. The urge to give an optimistic and favorable answer is quite unsurmountable—and understandable. I, therefore, doubt the statement often made that the military are not affected by developments in Saigon and cities generally.

2. The fact that Saigon is "only one-seventh" of the population does not allow for the fact that there are a number of other cities and that the cities in the long run must play a vital military role. For example, the junior officers in the Vietnamese Army come, as they do in all countries, largely from families which are educated, the so-called elite. These people live largely in the cities. The evidence grows that this elite is filled with hostility towards the Govt of Viet Nam, consider therefore the lieutenant in the Vietnamese Army whose father has probably been imprisoned; whose mother has seen her religion insulted, if not persecuted, whose older brother has had an arbitrary fine imposed on him—and who all hate the government with good reason. Can the lieutenant be indifferent to that? Now come the high school demonstrations and the fact that the lieutenant's younger brother has probably been dragged off in a truck (bearing the US insignia) to camping areas with the result that our lieutenant also has a deeply disaffected younger brother, if not a sister, who has been handled disrespectfully by the police.

3. Is it conceivable that this will not affect the energy with which the lieutenant will do his job in supporting his government? Is it any wonder that I hear reports of a major in the G-3 section of a corps headquarters who simply sits and does nothing because he is disgusted with the government? Must there not inevitably be a tendency—not for something spectacular and mutinous—but for the soldiers to get less aggressive and for the populations to get less sympathetic to the war effort? And as this happens will not the popularity of the US inevitably suffer because we are so closely supporting a regime which is now brutalizing children, although we are clearly able, in the opinion of Vietnamese, to change it if we wanted to?

4. Does not all of this mean that time is not on the side of the military effort and that if the situation in the cities is not improved, the military effort is bound to suffer?

5. But instead of improving, everything I can learn shows me that the situation is getting worse. The demonstrations in the schools are to me extremely curious and impressive manifestations. Out of nowhere apparently appears a banner and a plan to put up a roadblock or a scheme for conducting a parade. Perhaps this is the work of Communist agents, even though the students are undoubtedly not Communists. The latest rumor is that there will soon be similar demonstrations by civil

servants—and what a fantastic confusion this will create and the government is obviously cut off from reality—not looking at anything objectively but solely concerned with fighting back, proving how right it has been-and privately thumbing its nose at the US.

6. For these reasons it seems to me that the ship of state here is slowly sinking. This brings me to the conclusion, that if there are effective sanctions which we can apply, we should apply them in order to force a drastic change in government. The only sanction which I can see is the suspension of aid and therefore I recommend that the best brains in the government study precise details of suspending aid so as to do ourselves the most good and the least harm.

7. Let us, for example, assume that our aim is to get rid of Nhu. I use this purely for illustrative purposes, as we may think of something better. Once we have made up our minds that we are willing to suspend aid, should we not make a private threat that unless Nhu was removed we would suspend aid? This procedure might have two advantages: First it might result in Nhu's being removed. But, secondly, it would seem to put us on the popular side of the question and would then, when news of it leaked, tend to separate the government from the people. Also, when the tremendous shock of aid suspension took place, it should lessen the hatred which would be visited on us. This should be a period of action with perhaps a few leaks and with a minimum of statements by us—certainly not emotion-stirring statements which would arouse the xenophobia which is always latent here and the arousing of which would strengthen the GVN. We might, for example, be able to express our horror at the brutalization of children, but even this is risky if we are the ones who are doing the talking.

8. Renewed efforts should be made to activate by whatever positive inducements we can offer the man who would take over the government—Big Minh or whoever we might suggest. We do not want to substitute a Castro for a Batista.

9. We should at the same time start evacuation of all dependents. Both in order to avoid the dangers to dependents which would inevitably ensue, but also for the startling effect which this might have.

10. As the aid suspension went publicly into effect, we should be prepared to launch a massive program to protect the lives of the little people in the cities from starvation. Should this be soup kitchens, or should it mean taking anti-inflationary measures?

11. As aid suspension went into effect publicly, should we not start another quiet program to keep the Army supplied so that the war against the Viet-Cong should go on? Should not the Army be supplied by totally bypassing the Govt of Viet Nam, with supplies coming directly from the US to the Vietnamese Army?

12. Might we not thus bring sanctions to bear on the government without impeding the war effort and without making ourselves hated all over the world, as would be the case were there famines and misery?

13. Admittedly this is difficult and intricate and perhaps impossible, but it is also utterly vital and I recommend that it be studied without delay. We are giving it as much study as we can here in the Embassy.

14. If we decide to wait and see, we run certain risks:
a. That the future leadership of Viet Nam, the educated classes—already completely out of sympathy with the regime, and disillusioned with and distrustful of us as the instruments of change—will lose heart. (For while waiting we shall have to resume the role of supporters of the regime.)
b. More importantly, those individuals whom the regime regards as proximate threats will be systematically eliminated from contention in one way or another.

In short, by a wait-and-see approach, we insure that when and if we decide that we cannot win with the present regime, we shall have even less to work with in terms of opposition than we have now.

What is even more dangerous is that the situation here may not wait for us. The student demonstrations in Saigon, for example, are profoundly disturbing. At the very least, these reflect in the most unmistakable way the deep discontent of the middle and upper-class population of Saigon. They are also the classic vehicle for Communist action. There is thus the real possibility of the situation getting out of hand in such a way that only the Communists will be in a position to act—when and if we decide that we cannot win with this regime.

Lodge

GLOSSARY

Big Minh: Duong Van Minh, general and leader of the November 1963 coup

Castro/Batista: in Cuba, communist Fidel Castro had taken power from the dictatorial American ally Fulgencio Batista

GVN: Government of the Republic of Vietnam (South Vietnam)

Nhu: President Diem's brother, Ngo Dinh Nhu

Document Analysis

Ambassador Lodge gets to the point quickly in his report to the secretary of state. The South Vietnamese government is declining in its ability to do anything positive. The dire situation cannot be rectified by the current government. A new government is needed and until then, the United States should figure out how to cut its foreign aid without hurting the people or the war effort; it is that simple and yet that complex. The United States had propped up the Diem government for eight years and, therefore, was closely identified with it. Officials in Washington needed to figure out how to meet this challenge: how could they support Vietnamese anticommunist efforts without supporting the government that had undertaken those actions. If Diem could fire his brother, Lodge thought, there might be hope for a substantial change within the current government. However, he does not believe that this is a real possibility. Lodge gives descriptive examples and an analysis of the deteriorating situation to help the Washington officials understand what he has come to know since his arrival in Vietnam the previous month.

Lodge calls for quick action to resolve the situation. As he states toward the end of the report, waiting and watching means that the United States will have to continue to prop up a failed government against the will of virtually all of the people in South Vietnam. Continued demonstrations against the government will play into the hands of the communists, and waiting will allow Diem to not only repress any demonstrators, but to imprison or kill anyone loyal to South Vietnam who might be seen as a threat to the regime. Inaction means losing potential allies when a new government is formed and having less influence with whomever becomes the new ruler. Lodge understands that it is essential for the United States to be able to work with the new government, if the anticommunist efforts are to succeed and the people of South Vietnam are to have any hope of a better life.

Lodge knew that Diem was not a true supporter of democracy, so that a change in government likely meant a coup. He comments that the "ship of state here is slowly sinking." As a result, what is needed is the United States to cooperate with the right people—"to force drastic change in government." He believes that the United States needs to take a very public stance showing its lack of support for Diem. Cutting aid and removing American dependents are both things that Lodge expects would have a "startling effect" on Diem, on the population of South Vietnam, and on observers around the world. He does not want America's withdrawal of support for the government to hurt the people, or to make America "hated all over the world." But change is necessary. This needs to be communicated to those who might undertake the change, without hurting the programs in South Vietnam in which the United States has become involved.

Essential Themes

Ambassador Lodge was not the first American official who thought that the time had come for President Diem to leave office. However, the force of this report is much greater than that of many of the previous ones. It adds weight to the arguments for change and helps tip the scales in the direction of the United States supporting a coup. Although no decisive action was taken when this report was first received, less than a month after Lodge sent his report, he was informed of an impending coup. Those planning it wanted to be certain that the United States would not interfere. Within two months, a successful coup cost Diem and his brother not only their positions, but their lives as well. Big Minh (Duong Van Minh), who is mentioned in this report, was the leader of the coup. It is unclear whether he ordered Diem's execution, but as leader of the coup, he must take responsibility for all actions. Minh and the military council he established were not ready to rule, however, and within three months, his government was toppled and Minh went into retirement.

While the lack of support for Diem's government is the main focus of this report, Lodge also raises the question of how the United States could support people and programs within a country while not supporting its government. This was a major issue in Vietnam in 1963, as it has been elsewhere at other times. Lodge does not have an answer to this question, but he underscores the need to find an answer through the various illustrations he includes in the report. It continued to be an issue throughout most of the Vietnam War.

One result of Lodge's report supporting a change in government was not only the coup in November 1963, but all the later changes in government. The proposal he puts forth to accept one change in government meant that in later years, other individuals would feel little compunction about staging a coup. In less than two years, there were eight changes in government before a stable regime—that of Nguyen Van Thiêu—took control for the final ten years of South Vietnam's existence. Lodge's report points out the need for a government in the midst of conflict to serve its own people in addition to confronting the enemy. The various regimes that ruled during South Vietnam's twenty year existence never seemed to meet the criteria that Lodge set out for a successful government, thus contributing to the North's ultimate victory.

—*Donald A. Watt, PhD*

Bibliography and Additional Reading

Blair, Anne E. *Lodge in Vietnam: A Patriot Abroad.* New Haven: Yale University Press, 1995. Print.

Lodge, Henry Cabot, Jr. *As It Was: An Inside View of Politics and Power in the '50s and '60s.* New York: W.W. Norton & Company Inc., 1976. Print.

Logevall, Fredrik. *Choosing War: The Lost Chance for Peace and the Escalation of War in Vietnam.* Berkeley: University of California Press, 1999. Print.

Miller, Edward. *Misalliance: Ngo Dinh Diem, the United States, and the Fate of South Vietnam.* Cambridge: Harvard UP, 2013. Print.

"Vietnam, Diem, the Buddhist Crisis." *JFK in History.* John F. Kennedy Presidential Library and Museum, 2015. Web. <http://www.jfklibrary.org/JFK/JFK-in-History/Vietnam-Diem-and-the-Buddhist-Crisis.aspx>.

JOHNSON'S WAR

If Kennedy was cautiously optimistic about finding a resolution to the conflict without expending great amounts of blood and treasure, Johnson was hopeful that a strong military response would put the communists on the defensive and allow the United States a way out. He termed this scenario "peace without conquest." That is, Johnson had no intention of occupying the region. Under pressure from his advisers, however, he did believe that it was necessary to pursue the war in order to force a peaceful settlement. Thus, Johnson was pleased to have the excuse of a minor naval incident in the Gulf of Tonkin in August 1964 to enable him to turn US involvement in Vietnam from "cold" to "hot." He supplemented American military advisers with large numbers of combat troops and brought in substantial amounts of military weaponry and supplies. He authorized major bombing raids in North Vietnam and the use of air bombing, napalm, and toxic defoliants (such as Agent Orange) in South Vietnam. Between 1965 and 1968, the number of US troops skyrocketed from 6,000 to 536,000; and between 1965 and 1967, the tonnage of bombs used against the North expanded from 63,000 to 226,000. Tough search-and-destroy missions and a misguided "strategic hamlet" program impacted civilian populations and turned many of them against the United States.

Johnson was faced with a situation where the more he tried to do, the less he seemed to achieve. The National Liberation Front (NLF) in the South continued to grow and wage an effective guerilla war, augmented by North Vietnamese forces. The South Vietnamese Army (ARVN), assigned primarily to back-up and pacification duties, did not acquire the training or experience it needed to assume a greater share of the fighting—even though by 1968 its numbers had reached 800,000. Meanwhile, the influx of foreign fighters and of billions of dollars in aid inside a small, undeveloped country had profound effects on the society and the economy: the entire region was destabilized and corruption flourished. Millions of refugees were created in the countryside. Moreover, the North was not persuaded to compromise. Instead, the ultimate result of Johnson's expansion was a grand stalemate in which neither side had the upper hand. On top of that, opposition to the war in the United States was gaining momentum. Critics complained not merely of the war's military failure but of its moral indefensibility, the havoc it wreaked in Vietnam in the name of a loose theory about stopping communism in the Third World.

The problem, too, was that Johnson's heart was never in the subject of international relations or global political dynamics. He cared far more about his ambitious domestic policy agenda, the so-called Great Society (civil rights, antipoverty measures, educational opportunities, etc.). Thus, following the latest series of questionable US "successes" in the Vietnam War, including the quelling of the Tet Offensive in early 1968, Johnson, under increasing political pressure at home, chose to wash his hands of the matter and not seek the presidency for a second term.

■ CIA Memo on National Liberation Front Methods

Date: November 29, 1963
Author: John A. McCone
Genre: memorandum

Summary Overview

One of the largest blunders made by American war planners in the years leading up the war in Vietnam was a near complete lack of understanding of not only Vietnamese culture, but also the deep resentment of the South Vietnamese government among the population. By late 1963, southern Vietnamese revolutionaries had already been for years working in towns and villages across the south to win popular support for their cause to put down the repressive regime of Ngo Dinh Diem. But fearful of the spread of communism, the United States took a position against the majority of the population in support of the Diem regime. In fact, one could argue that by entering what was essentially a civil war, the United States helped hasten the fall of the south to communism. In a memo commissioned by John A. McCone, then director of the Central Intelligence Agency (CIA), for delivery to Dean Rusk, the secretary of state under both Kennedy and Johnson, American intelligence officers outlined the various methods used by the National Liberation Front (NLF) to ingratiate themselves to the South Vietnamese people. The document stands as a detailed analysis of all the NLF was doing to improve the lives of the people of the south, and serves to demonstrate the eagerness with which American officials sought to link southern revolutionaries to an international communist conspiracy.

Defining Moment

The strategy of "containment" as developed by American officials at the end of World War II, held that through the careful use of military force the spread of communism could be limited as not to overwhelm any single region. It was this idea that led to American intervention in the Korean Conflict, ultimately resulting in the creation of two distinct Koreas: a communist north and democratic south. After the French withdraw from Vietnam, the same approach was used in that country. Although neither north nor south wanted division, the Western powers meeting in Geneva separated the two along the seventeenth parallel. Vietnam, however, was very different from Korea. The weak, and often repressive regime of Ngo Dinh Diem in the south, standing in contrast to the popular and well-supported communist revolutionary movement of Ho Chi Minh in the north, instilled first resentment and then open revolt. What was in fact a civil and, in part, sectarian war in the south the West came to interpret as an attempted communist coup directed by the Soviet Union and China.

As the violence escalated, southern activists consolidated the various communist and noncommunist anti-Diem forces operating in the south into a single paramilitary force that came to be known as the National Liberation Front, or Viet Cong. These various groups, having operated across the south since the 1940s, had pushed through massive land reforms, seizing farmland from wealthy landlords and redistributing it to the poor. In 1960, the Diem government, in a move it hoped would weaken the Viet Cong, brought back landlords to the farms and villages, often violently ejecting people from land that they had farmed for over a decade. To make matters worse, these landlords then demanded the poor, and now landless farmers, to pay back rent for the years of use. Seeing an opportunity, Ho Chi Minh began to support southern guerrilla fighters and sent North Vietnamese forces into Laos to create supply routes into the south.

With the election of John F. Kennedy, the United States, still badly misunderstanding the realities on the ground, further tied itself to the Diem regime. Vice President Lyndon Johnson even went so far as to declare Diem "the Winston Churchill of Asia." Among Diem's chief American supporters was John A. McCone, appointed director of the Central Intelligence Agency after the ousting of Allen W. Dulles following the Bay of Pigs. McCone believed, wrongly, that the Viet Cong had been agents of northern communists since the end of World War II and advocated for immediate American military involvement in support of the repressive Diem regime. When Diem was finally overthrown in early November of 1963, McCone bitterly objected to American support for the coup. He continued to advocate for greater American involvement, and although the information he and the CIA provided the Johnson administration did eventually lead to full American military intervention, McCone grew increasingly frustrated over what he considered a weak and feckless response to the communist takeover of Southeast Asia.

Author Biography

John Alexander McCone was born in California in 1902. Heir to an iron fortune, McCone attended the University of California at Berkeley, where he received a degree in mechanical engineering. Rising in private industry, he became an executive vice president at Consolidated Steel Corporation and, as a leading industrialist, served as an advisor for the Atomic Energy Commission. As his profile rose, McCone became ever more involved with the Central Intelligence Agency (CIA), until ultimately he was named as director following the resignation of Allen W. Dulles following the disastrous Bay of Pigs invasion of 1961. A proponent of the use of force during the Cuban Missile Crisis, McCone was the mastermind behind numerous covert plots while director of the CIA, including the overthrow of several democratically elected governments. Opposed to the 1963 plot to overthrow Ngo Dinh Diem, McCone became increasingly disillusioned by the Johnson administration's involvement in Vietnam, until he finally resigned as director in 1965. McCone died in 1991.

HISTORICAL DOCUMENT

Memorandum Prepared for the Director of Central Intelligence
Washington, *November 29, 1963.*
SUBJECT

Viet Cong Quasi-Governmental Activities

1. In the "armed liberation" strategy of both Mao Tse-Tung and Ho Chi Minh, the establishment and gradual extension of "secure" base areas is a primary objective in the struggle. Within such secure areas, the Viet Cong have, since the beginning of resistance against the French in 1945–46, attempted to carry out quasi-governmental functions. Their purpose is two-fold and sometimes contradictory. They seek to win the voluntary support of the population by various activities of a welfare or civic-action nature. By example they try to show that they are more efficient, honest, and humane as administrators than the enemy regime. At the same time, they are concerned with exercising control and extracting support in the form of manpower, food and labor; these requirements frequently take priority and undo any favorable effects from their psychological operations.

2. In areas still not "secure" or not under strong Viet Cong influence, the guerrilla forces must live a hit-and-run existence and have little opportunity to act as the effective local administration. In these areas they must nonetheless rely upon support, shelter, and supply from the civilian populace, which is obtained not only by force but by positive steps to convince the population that its aspirations are those of the Viet Cong.

3. Much of our detailed knowledge with respect to Viet Cong activities in these directions comes from the period of Viet Minh resistance against the French. There is sufficient current reporting, however, to leave little doubt that the same pattern of activity is still being followed.

4. Viet Minh documents captured during the Indochina war frequently dealt with a program to raise rural living standards—the "new life" program. Such documents often contained statistics on the establishment of schools, numbers of children and adults in school, medical dispensaries, numbers of trained medical aides and midwives, sanitation efforts including numbers of wells and latrines dug, and food and livestock production. This effort and various other governmental activities were

carried out under the authority of Administrative-Resistance Councils set up at the regional, provincial, district, and town levels.

5. A similar Viet Cong hierarchy of military, politico-administrative, and Liberation Front Committees now exists in South Vietnam, but Viet Cong troops themselves are frequently the agents of both governmental and civic-action tasks. While force and terrorism remain a major Viet Cong instrument against local officials of the South Vietnamese Government and recalcitrant villagers, recently captured Viet Cong documents clearly show that Viet Cong troops and agents are ordered to provide assistance to peasants and to avoid antagonisms and abuses, such as looting or violation of churches and pagodas.

6. A Communist land reform program in South Vietnam, begun by the Viet Minh, is still being carried out under the Viet Cong, but some difficulties have been encountered. This is reflected in the attitude of the Liberation Front, which watered down its initial emphasis on land reform, although free and unconditional distribution of land to poor peasants is still a part of its platform. Informants and Viet Cong prisoners indicate that early attempts by the Viet Cong to force "middle-class" peasants to give land to the poor were too harsh, caused peasant disputes and loss of production, and depleted the source of funds available for peasant loans and for support of Viet Cong troops. As a result, there appears to have been some modification of Viet Cong land reform activities to lessen pressure on "middle-class" peasants and encourage higher production. Although there are some references to communal farms, the Viet Cong do not appear to have stressed land collectivization in South Vietnam, where popular reaction to North Vietnam's brutal agrarian reform policies has been adverse.

7. Current reports also indicate that the Viet Cong provide assistance to peasants in land clearance, seed distribution, and harvesting, and in turn persuade or force peasants to store rice in excess of their own needs for the use of guerrilla troops. Controls are apparently imposed in Viet Cong zones to prevent shipments for commercial marketing in Saigon, or to collect taxes on such shipments. The Viet Cong themselves often pay cash or give promissory notes for the food they acquire.

8. Little detailed information is available on current Communist health and sanitation activities. Captured Viet Cong doctors or medical personnel indicate that dispensaries for treatment of Viet Cong wounded often are scattered inconspicuously among several peasant homes in a village, and that civilians are treated as facilities and supplies permit. Civilians as well as guerrilla forces are almost certainly instructed in methods of sanitation and disease prevention, but apparent shortages of medical personnel and medicines in some areas suggest that medical care for civilians in Viet Cong-dominated areas may be spotty.

9. There are also references to primary and adult education, much of it in the form of indoctrination, and to Viet Cong-run schools operating almost side by side with government schools, under the excuse that peasants lack the necessary documentation required to enter government schools. A Liberation Front broadcast of 19 November 1963 claimed that there were some 1,000 schools with 2 million pupils in "freed areas" of South Vietnam. These figures are doubtless exaggerated, but may be a gauge of a fairly extensive Communist educational effort.

10. A standard Viet Cong technique of gaining a foothold among tribal minorities in the highland areas of South Vietnam—where Communist encouragement of tribal autonomy gives them a political appeal—has been to select promising tribesmen, take them to North Vietnam for training in welfare activities as well as for political indoctrination, and return them to tribal villages where their new skills tend to assure them positions of prestige and leadership.

11. The Viet Cong also promote cultural activities-heavily flavored with propaganda—through press, radio and film media, as well as live drama and festivals. A student informant reported attending dramatic performances in a Viet Cong-held area, where plays, song, and dances provided entertainment and a dose of propaganda—often enthusiastically received.

12. There is little firm information about the Viet Cong effort to develop "combat hamlets." They appear to exist in areas where control by either side is missing or tenuous, and sometimes are located near government "strategic hamlets." Reports indicate that, like strategic hamlets, they are fortified externally, and their inhabitants are carefully trained in defensive procedures and escape routes, often interrelated with other nearby hamlets. Similar defensive systems have long prevailed in Viet Cong-controlled areas, although Viet Cong installations themselves may be innocent looking and easily evacuated buildings or huts.

13. A Viet Cong document discussing the successful construction of a "combat hamlet" indicates that primary stress is laid on determining the basic wants and needs of the inhabitants—frequently their concern for their own land. Propaganda is directed at convincing them that the government is threatening their interests, that defensive measures must be taken, and finally that offensive actions against government officials and troops are needed. The peasants presumably come to regard the Viet Cong as their protectors and to cooperate voluntarily with the Viet Cong military effort.

GLOSSARY

propaganda: biased or misleading information used to promote a political point of view

Viet Cong: South Vietnamese communist guerrillas

Viet Minh: North Vietnamese communists

Document Analysis

The memo, titled "Viet Cong Quasi-Governmental Activities," is laid out into thirteen points, documenting the various ways in which forces of the National Liberation Front are trying to win the hearts and minds of the South Vietnamese people. From the beginning, the memo makes clear that the strategy of the NLF is one of "armed liberation," harking back to Mao Tse-Tung and Ho Chi Minh, the leaders of China and North Vietnam, respectively. These are communist tactics, at work since the 1940s, meant to win the support of South Vietnam's population, and take control of the region. The authority of the Viet Cong is limited, as in many regions where the NLF does not have complete control, communist forces can only conduct "hit and run" attacks.

Much of the intelligence, the memo continues, derives from captured Viet Minh documents, which outline efforts to improve the quality of life for the population, including education, medical care, and infrastructure. The Viet Cong are careful to treat the populace well in order to win them to their side. This is all done for propaganda purposes, by improving conditions for the peasantry of South Vietnam, the Viet Cong hope to turn the people against their government. As an example, the memo cites the NLF land reform program in which, the memo charges, middle-class farmers were forced to give their land to the poor. Perhaps aware that the evidence of such allegations is weak, the writer concedes that some modification to the policy must have occurred as many middle-class farmers have remained on their land and there appears to be little evidence of collectivization.

Food distribution, seed collecting, and sanitation improvements have all been implemented to turn the population. The Viet Cong has even set up schools to educate the poor, but, the writer assures their audience, the numbers of this programs success are surely exaggerated and used, it assumes, to spread communist propaganda. The writer does admit that many tribes in the region have been allowed autonomy, but this too, the writer assures their audience, is part of the same communist strategy. Most alarmingly, the Viet Cong appear to be setting up defenses and training the population in combat. The result is that the population now, mistakenly, considers the Viet Cong their protectors and cooperates with them in their efforts.

Essential Themes

The November 1963 memo commissioned by John McCone on Viet Cong activities in South Vietnam, is a clear example of the colossal misalignment in American understanding of the situation in Vietnam. Contorting the facts to try and fit the narrative of a communist conspiracy to spread an insidious ideology across the globe, the memo paints a cynical picture of communist agents using medicine, education, and food to trick the people into resenting their government. Despite evidence of local autonomy, fair land distribution policies, and a lack of a strong NLF political-military establishment, the memo tells a tale of a south on the brink of hostile takeover, of a poor, naive population, being tricked into supporting an insidious enemy.

It is astounding to consider that at no point did American intelligence analysts stop to consider the repressive policies of the South Vietnamese government, that NLF forces could actually be working to better the lives of the South Vietnamese people, or that the general consensus of the population had swung wildly toward regime change. It was an attitude born out of a kind of colonial arrogance. Surely the United States, the most powerful, most sophisticated country in the world, knew what was best for Vietnam, even better than the Vietnamese. It was this lack of understanding—born out of notions of cultural superiority that propelled American strategy in Southeast Asia for two decades—that ultimately led to American military intervention in what was essentially a civil war.

As the conflict escalated, as more and more American soldiers lost their lives, military planners would continue to grow ever more frustrated by a lack of support from the local population. In time, the very people that the United States claimed it was fighting to liberate, would be come to be seen as the enemy. Atrocities committed by American troops and indiscriminant killing started to become more common, and the very nature of the war took on an ever darker turn. Before long the entire region was destabilized as the American war against a nation's own people spread to Laos and Cambodia, and at every step, American political and military leaders viewed events not for what they were, but for what they in some sense wanted them to be.

—KP Dawes, MA

Bibliography and Additional Reading

Herring, George. *America's Longest War*. New York: McGraw-Hill, 1996. Print.

McNamara, Robert & Brian VanDeMark. *In Retrospect: The Tragedy and Lessons of Vietnam*. New York: Random House, 1995. Print.

VanDeMark, Brian. *Into the Quagmire: Lyndon Johnson and the Escalation of the Vietnam War*. New York: Oxford University Press, 1995. Print.

■ The Gulf of Tonkin Incident

Date: August 4–7, 1964
Author/s: Lyndon B. Johnson and United States Congress
Genre: speech; address

Summary Overview

After the defeat of the French colonial forces in 1954, the United States became the guarantor of security for the pro-Western government of South Vietnam, which was threatened not only by the government and army of communist North Vietnam, but by pro-communist guerilla fighters among their own people. In August 1964, two American destroyers, USS Maddox and USS Turner Joy, were conducting intelligence-gathering operations off the coast of North Vietnam, in the Gulf of Tonkin, when they were reportedly attacked by North Vietnamese torpedo boats. Though he claimed the American ships were in international waters rather than being close to the North Vietnamese coast, and though he was aware that the evidence for the attacks being unprovoked was dubious, President Lyndon B. Johnson wasted no time in presenting a resolution to Congress seeking to defend American interests in the region by any means the president deemed necessary and proper.

Defining Moment

After their defeat at the Battle of Dien Bien Phu in 1954, the French colonial army left Southeast Asia, and the Vietnamese nationalist and communist leader, Ho Chi Minh, declared an independent Vietnam. However, the peace conference held at Geneva, Switzerland, divided the country into two halves, with Ho Chi Minh's nationalists in the north and a corrupt, but pro-Western, government under President Ngo Dinh Diem in the south, with elections to reunify the country scheduled for 1956. Diem, however, refused to hold the elections, establishing a dictatorship in South Vietnam. The ensuing years saw the rapid growth of the Viet Cong: nationalists living in the south, but supportive of a unified Vietnam under Ho Chi Minh's leadership. By 1960, the Viet Cong had the official support of the government and armed forces of North Vietnam.

Diem's popularity among his own people (who were overwhelmingly Buddhist, while Diem was Catholic) faded during the early 1960s, and when a Buddhist monk set himself on fire in Saigon in June 1963, many South Vietnamese turned against him. A coup d'état, supported by the CIA, overthrew Diem on November 1, 1963, and he was assassinated the next day. With the upheaval in South Vietnam and the continued growth of the Viet Cong with material support from North Vietnam, the US government was more committed than ever to preventing the North Vietnamese from unifying the country under communist rule. As this was in the midst of the Cold War, American policy was heavily influenced by the so-called Domino Theory, which stated that if one country were to be allowed to fall to communism it would only lead to more and more communist uprisings throughout the region.

During the early 1960s, President John F. Kennedy began to increase American aid to South Vietnam, sending large amounts of military hardware and, beginning in 1961, American military advisors. By the end of 1962, the number of military advisors had increased to 12,000, and American helicopter crews began flying missions in the country. By the time of Kennedy's assassination in November 1963, about 16,700 American military advisors were in South Vietnam, though he remained opposed to direct American involvement in combat operations.

By the summer of 1964, President Lyndon B. Johnson, who advocated a more proactive American role in protecting the independence of South Vietnam, was increasing American military presence both in South Vietnam and in the waters off the coast of both North and South Vietnam. The South Vietnamese military had proven no more able to stabilize the country than had Diem, and Johnson was convinced that only the American military and American intelligence efforts would be able to prevent the North Vietnamese from taking over.

Author Biography

President Lyndon B. Johnson and the vast majority of the members of the United States Congress shared a common vision of the world order in some of the tensest years of the Cold War between the Soviet Union and the United States. Every conflict was viewed in the context of the geopolitical struggle between the superpowers, and Vietnam is perhaps the greatest example of this. Rather than seeing it as a fight between Vietnamese nationalists and French colonizers or pro-Western Vietnamese, the American government as a whole viewed the conflict as a simple matter of communism vs. anti-communism. Any actions taken by the United States in Vietnam were taken to prevent not only Vietnam from becoming a communist nation, and thus, a Soviet puppet state, but also to prevent all of Southeast Asia from falling to a series of communist uprisings.

HISTORICAL DOCUMENT

President Johnson's Address to the Public
August 4, 1964

My fellow Americans:

As President and Commander in Chief, it is my duty to the American people to report that renewed hostile actions against United States ships on the high seas in the Gulf of Tonkin have today required me to order the military forces of the United States to take action in reply.

The initial attack on the destroyer Maddox, on August 2, was repeated today by a number of hostile vessels attacking two U.S. destroyers with torpedoes. The destroyers and supporting aircraft acted at once on the orders I gave after the initial act of aggression. We believe at least two of the attacking boats were sunk. There were no U.S. losses.

The performance of commanders and crews in this engagement is in the highest tradition of the United States Navy. But repeated acts of violence against the Armed Forces of the United States must be met not only with alert defense, but with positive reply. That reply is being given as I speak to you tonight. Air action is now in execution against gunboats and certain supporting facilities in North Viet-Nam which have been used in these hostile operations.

In the larger sense this new act of aggression, aimed directly at our own forces, again brings home to all of us in the United States the importance of the struggle for peace and security in southeast Asia. Aggression by terror against the peaceful villagers of South Viet-Nam has now been joined by open aggression on the high seas against the United States of America.

The determination of all Americans to carry out our full commitment to the people and to the government of South Viet-Nam will be redoubled by this outrage. Yet our response, for the present, will be limited and fitting. We Americans know, although others appear to forget, the risks of spreading conflict. We still seek no wider war.

I have instructed the Secretary of State to make this position totally clear to friends and to adversaries and, indeed, to all. I have instructed Ambassador Stevenson to raise this matter immediately and urgently before the Security Council of the United Nations. Finally, I have today met with the leaders of both parties in the Congress of the United States and I have informed them that I shall immediately request the Congress to pass a resolution making it clear that our Government is united in its determination to take all necessary measures in support of freedom and in defense of peace in southeast Asia.

I have been given encouraging assurance by these leaders of both parties that such a resolution will be promptly introduced, freely and expeditiously debated, and passed with overwhelming support. And just a few minutes ago I was able to reach Senator Goldwater and I am glad to say that he has expressed his support of the statement that I am making to you tonight.

It is a solemn responsibility to have to order even limited military action by forces whose overall strength is as vast and as awesome as those of the United States of America, but it is my considered conviction, shared throughout your Government, that firmness in the right is indispensable today for peace; that firmness will always be measured. Its mission is peace.

* * *

Gulf of Tonkin Resolution
August 7, 1964

Joint Resolution

To promote the maintenance of international peace and security in southeast Asia.

Whereas naval units of the Communist regime in Vietnam, in violation of the principles of the Charter of the United Nations and of international law, have deliberately and repeatedly attacked United Stated naval vessels lawfully present in international waters, and have thereby created a serious threat to international peace; and

Whereas these attackers are part of deliberate and systematic campaign of aggression that the Communist regime in North Vietnam has been waging against its neighbors and the nations joined with them in the collective defense of their freedom; and

Whereas the United States is assisting the peoples of southeast Asia to protest their freedom and has no territorial, military or political ambitions in that area, but desires only that these people should be left in peace to work out their destinies in their own way: Now, therefore be it

Resolved by the Senate and House of Representatives of the United States of America in Congress assembled, That the Congress approves and supports the determination of the President, as Commander in Chief, to take all necessary measures to repel any armed attack against the forces of the United States and to prevent further aggression.

Section 2. The United States regards as vital to its national interest and to world peace the maintenance of international peace and security in southeast Asia. Consonant with the Constitution of the United States and the Charter of the United Nations and in accordance with its obligations under the Southeast Asia Collective Defense Treaty, the United States is, therefore, prepared, as the President determines, to take all necessary steps, including the use of armed force, to assist any member or protocol state of the Southeast Asia Collective Defense Treaty requesting assistance in defense of its freedom.

Section 3. This resolution shall expire when the President shall determine that the peace and security of the area is reasonably assured by international conditions created by action of the United Nations or otherwise, except that it may be terminated earlier by concurrent resolution of the Congress.

Document Analysis

On August 2, 1962, the USS Maddox, an American naval destroyer, was reportedly attacked with torpedoes by a number of small North Vietnamese patrol boats in the Gulf of Tonkin, off the coast of North Vietnam. A second encounter, including the *Maddox* and a second American destroyer, the USS *Turner Joy*, was reported two days later. On the date of the second attack President Lyndon B. Johnson went on television to inform the American public of the incidents and to recommend immediate reprisals, including a bombing campaign to be carried out by the Air Force.

Behind the actions in the Gulf of Tonkin, however, was a determination reached by the Johnson administration by August 1964 that the only way to prevent a North Vietnamese takeover of South Vietnam was direct American military action. American surveillance, such as that being carried out in North Vietnamese waters by ships like the *Maddox* and *Turner Joy*, revealed large amounts of supplies and personnel flowing from the north to the south. However, when the incidents on August 2 and August 4 were reported to the American public, no mention was made of this or the fact that the actions did not take place in international waters. As it turned out, the attack on the *Turner Joy* may have never taken place at all.

Johnson's response to the attacks was to inform the American public and immediately call for Congress to authorize the use of force to defend American military installations in Southeast Asia. This led to the Gulf of Tonkin Resolution, which passed House of Representatives unanimously and the Senate with only two opposing votes.

Rather than viewing the conflict in Vietnam as an internal civil war, the resolution put the actions in stark, Cold War terms, declaring that "these attackers are part of deliberate and systematic campaign of aggression that the communist regime in North Vietnam has been waging against its neighbors and the nations joined with them in the collective defense of their freedom". It authorized President Johnson "to take all necessary steps, including the use of armed force, to assist any member or protocol state of the Southeast Asia Collective Defense Treaty requesting assistance in defense of its freedom." Johnson's television address had the desired effect, at least for the time being, in that it gave the American people and the Congress a tangible reason to support American military involvement in Vietnam.

Essential Themes

The joint resolution that Congress passed on August 7, 1964, declared that the North Vietnamese had "deliberately and repeatedly attacked United Stated naval vessels lawfully present in international waters", which was based on the information that the Johnson administration had provided. The resolution was for the express purpose of promoting and maintaining "international peace and security in southeast Asia," but had the effect of acting as a de facto declaration of war against North Vietnam. Congress did not see it that way, as they expected that the president, as commander-in-chief, would have to ask Congress for any additional expansion of the conflict. Johnson, however, repeatedly used the Gulf of Tonkin Resolution as justification for expanding American military involvement in what became the Vietnam War, stating that he the resolution was "like grandma's night shirt—it covered everything."

Though neither Johnson nor Secretary of Defense Robert McNamara were sure of the veracity of the reports of the second attack, Johnson did not hesitate to use the attack to drum up support for expanded American involvement in Vietnam. The Maddox, which carried electronic spy equipment, had not been in international waters as Johnson claimed, but was collecting intelligence close to the coast of North Vietnam. Though stories of the Gulf of Tonkin crisis being manufactured for political reasons increasingly gained traction as the Vietnam War became increasingly unpopular, evidence supporting the allegations gradually accumulated.

However, by that time, the war was on. Retaliatory air strikes began immediately, and American forces bombed the so-called Ho Chi Minh Trail, the main supply line carrying materials from North Vietnam to Viet Cong guerrilla fighters in South Vietnam. In March 1965, the United States commenced Operation Rolling Thunder, a three-year-long massive strategic bombing campaign against North Vietnamese targets in order to reduce North Vietnam's ability to support the insurgency in the south. Also in March 1965, the first American combat troops arrived to defend the Da Nang Air Base in South Vietnam, beginning an escalation that would see over a half million American troops in the region at its height.

—*Steven L. Danver, PhD*

Bibliography and Additional Reading

Caputo, Philip. *A Rumor of War*. New York: Holt, 1999.

MacLear, Michael. *Vietnam: The Ten Thousand Day War*. Toronto: Methuen, 1981. Print.

Sheehan, Neil. A *Bright Shining Lie: John Paul Vann and America in Vietnam*. New York: Vintage Books, 1988. Print.

Siff, Ezra Y. *Why the Senate Slept: The Gulf of Tonkin Resolution and the Beginning of America's Vietnam War*. Westport, CT: Praeger, 1999. Print.

■ A New Approach to Retaliation

Date: February 7, 1965
Author: McGeorge Bundy
Genre: memorandum

Summary Overview

Today we know that many of escalation's greatest champions within the United States government, secretly harbored doubts about America's chances at victory in Vietnam, chief among them McGeorge Bundy, national security advisor to both presidents Kennedy and Johnson. An influential policy maker, often referred to as one of the "wise men" of the White House, Bundy was one of the staunchest hawks in both administrations. He pushed relentlessly for greater action against North Vietnam, all the while realizing fully that greater engagement might mean disaster. For this reason, Bundy's memo of February 1965 is especially illuminating. Outlining a strategy of sustained military reprisals against North Vietnam, Bundy all but confirms that the war in Vietnam is not about Vietnam at all, but greater gains internationally and domestically. American lives could be and would be lost, but, on the whole, those losses were acceptable, even beneficial. The memorandum stands as a shocking indictment of not just the war, but the men who conceived it.

Defining Moment

By the latter half of 1964, thousands of American "military advisors" had already been deployed in South Vietnam, and the United States Navy patrolled the waters beyond. As violence in the south spread, spurred on by an ever more repressive government, and as tension with North Vietnam increased, policy makers within the White House, led primarily by Secretary of Defense Robert McNamara, were putting greater and greater pressure on President Lyndon Baines Johnson to act. The longtime Texas Democrat, although committed to keeping America's pledge to preserve a communist-free South Vietnam, was apprehensive about sending American troops into Southeast Asia. Johnson's fear was that, like the French, American forces would be unable to adequately fight against an entrenched guerrilla force, resulting in a prolonged quagmire and the loss of thou-

sands of American lives. Then, in August 1964, the *USS Maddox*, on an intelligence mission in the Gulf of Tonkin, reportedly fired on North Vietnamese torpedo boats that had allegedly fired upon the Maddox first. A second report of attack and counterattack came in two days later. Although it became clear within military and intelligence circles that no outright North Vietnamese attack had occurred, the hawks in the Johnson administration used the event, which came to be known as the Gulf of Tonkin Incident, to rally the nation to war.

Some evidence suggests that even Johnson himself was misled, although to what extent remains unclear. Nonetheless, within days, Congress passed a resolution empowering the president to conduct military operations in Southeast Asia. The authorization, left purposefully vague, allowed foreign policy planners to essentially wage war without a declaration of war. Within months, memos and policy statements started circulating throughout the White House, recommending various kinds of military operations, including a sharp increase in ground troops and a prolonged bombing campaign against the North. Among the memos that were produced that winter, was a call to action from National Security Advisor McGeorge Bundy. Bundy argued for what he called sustained reprisals against the North Vietnamese and Viet Cong forces operating in the South. Memos such as this one not only helped to push Johnson to action, but also defined the uneven, at times counterproductive American policy. More importantly, these memos helped demonstrate that policy makers working within the White House were very willing to sacrifice American lives for the sake of political achievements.

Author Biography

McGeorge "Mac" Bundy was born in Boston in 1919. The second son of a wealthy and politically well-connected family, Bundy attended two prestigious prep schools before going on to Yale, where he received a degree in mathematics. After World War II, Bundy went to work for the Council of Foreign Relations, where he was involved in various intelligence related programs focused on anti-Soviet efforts. After a stint as dean at Harvard University, Bundy was appointed national security advisor by John F. Kennedy in 1961. In his role at the White House, Bundy was crucial to events such as the Bay of Pigs invasion, the Cuban Missile Crisis, and of course the Vietnam War. In 1966, Bundy became president of the Ford Foundation and, in 1979, returned to teaching at New York University. In his later years, Bundy became an influential in helping to mold American nuclear policy. He died in 1996.

HISTORICAL DOCUMENT

A POLICY OF SUSTAINED REPRISAL

I. Introductory

We believe that the best available way of increasing our chance of success in Vietnam is the development and execution of a policy of sustained reprisal against North Vietnam--a policy in which air and naval action against the North is justified by and related to the whole Viet Cong campaign of violence and terror in the South.

While we believe that the risks of such a policy are acceptable, we emphasize that its costs are real. It implies significant U.S. air losses even if no full air war is joined, and it seems likely that it would eventually require an extensive and costly effort against the whole air defense system of North Vietnam. U.S. casualties would be higher--and more visible to American feelings--than those sustained in the struggle in South Vietnam.

Yet measured against the costs of defeat in Vietnam, this program seems cheap. And even if it fails to turn the tide--as it may--the value of the effort seems to us to exceed its cost.

II. Outline of the Policy

1. In partnership with the Government of Vietnam, we should develop and exercise the option to retaliate against any VC act of violence to persons or property.

2. In practice, we may wish at the outset to relate our reprisals to those acts of relatively high visibility such as the Pleiku incident. Later, we might retaliate against the assassination of a province chief, but not necessarily the murder of a hamlet official; we might retaliate against a grenade thrown into a crowded cafe in Saigon, but not necessarily to a shot fired into a small shop in the countryside.

3. Once a program of reprisals is clearly underway, it should not be necessary to connect each specific act against North Vietnam to a particular outrage in the South. It should be possible, for example, to publish weekly lists of outrages in the South and to have it clearly understood that these outrages are the cause of such action against the North as may be occurring in the current period. Such a more generalized pattern of reprisal would remove much of the difficulty involved in finding precisely matching targets in response to specific atrocities. Even in such a more general pattern, however, it would be important to insure that the general level of reprisal action remained in close correspondence with the level of outrages in the South. We must keep it clear at every stage both to Hanoi and to the world, that our reprisals will be reduced or stopped when outrages in the South are reduced or stopped--and that we are not attempting to destroy or conquer North Vietnam.

4. In the early stages of such a course, we should take the appropriate occasion to make clear our firm intent to undertake reprisals on any further acts, major or minor, that appear to us and the GVN as indicating Hanoi's support. We would announce that our two governments have been patient and forbearing in the hope that Hanoi would come to its senses without the necessity of our having to take further action; but the outrages continue and now we must react against those who are responsible; we will not provoke; we will not use our force indiscriminately; but

we can no longer sit by in the face of repeated acts of terror and violence for which the DRV is responsible.

5. Having once made this announcement, we should execute our reprisal policy with as low a level of public noise as possible. It is to our interest that our acts should be seen--but we do not wish to boast about them in ways that make it hard for Hanoi to shift its ground. We should instead direct maximum attention to the continuing acts of violence which are the cause of our continuing reprisals.

6. This reprisal policy should begin at a low level. Its level of force and pressure should be increased only gradually--and as indicated above it should be decreased if VC terror visibly decreases. The object would not be to "win" an air war against Hanoi, but rather to influence the course of the struggle in the South.

7. At the same time it should be recognized that in order to maintain the power of reprisal without risk of excessive loss, an "air war" may in fact be necessary. We should therefore be ready to develop a separate justification for energetic flak suppression and if necessary for the destruction of Communist air power. The essence of such an explanation should be that these actions are intended solely to insure the effectiveness of a policy of reprisal, and in no sense represent any intent to wage offensive war against the North. These distinctions should not be difficult to develop.

8. It remains quite possible, however, that this reprisal policy would get us quickly into the level of military activity contemplated in the so-called Phase II of our December planning. It may even get us beyond this level with both Hanoi and Peiping, if there is Communist counter-action. We and the GVN should also be prepared for a spurt of VC terrorism, especially in urban areas, that would dwarf anything yet experienced. These are the risks of any action. They should be carefully reviewed--but we believe them to be acceptable.

9. We are convinced that the political values of reprisal require a continuous operation. Episodic responses geared on a one-for-one basis to "spectacular" outrages would lack the persuasive force of sustained pressure. More important still, they would leave it open to the Communists to avoid reprisals entirely by giving up only a small element of their own program. The Gulf of Tonkin affair produced a sharp upturn in morale in South Vietnam. When it remained an isolated episode, however, there was a severe relapse. It is the great merit of the proposed scheme that to stop it the Communists would have to stop enough of their activity in the South to permit the probable success of a determined pacification effort.

III. Expected Effect of Sustained Reprisal Policy

1. We emphasize that our primary target in advocating a reprisal policy is the improvement of the situation in South Vietnam. Action against the North is usually urged as a means of affecting the will of Hanoi to direct and support the VC. We consider this an important but longer-range purpose. The immediate and critical targets are in the South--in the minds of the South Vietnamese and in the minds of the Viet Cong cadres.

2. Predictions of the effect of any given course of action upon the states of mind of people are difficult. It seems very clear that if the United States and the Government of Vietnam join in a policy of reprisal, there will be a sharp immediate increase in optimism in the South, among nearly all articulate groups. The Mission believes--and our own conversations confirm--that in all sectors of Vietnamese opinion there is a strong belief that the United States could do much more if it would, and that they are suspicious of our failure to use more of our obviously enormous power. At least in the short run, the reaction to reprisal policy would be very favorable.

3. This favorable reaction should offer opportunity for increased American influence in pressing for a more effective government--at least in

the short run. Joint reprisals would imply military planning in which the American role would necessarily be controlling, and this new relation should add to our bargaining power in other military efforts--and conceivably on a wider plane as well if a more stable government is formed. We have the whip hand in reprisals as we do not in other fields.

4. The Vietnamese increase in hope could well increase the readiness of Vietnamese factions themselves to join together in forming a more effective government.

5. We think it plausible that effective and sustained reprisals, even in a low key, would have a substantial depressing effect upon the morale of Viet Cong cadres in South Vietnam. This is the strong opinion of CIA Saigon. It is based upon reliable reports of the initial Viet Cong reaction to the Gulf of Tonkin episode, and also upon the solid general assessment that the determination of Hanoi and the apparent timidity of the mighty United States are both major items in Viet Cong confidence.

6. The long-run effect of reprisals in the South is far less clear. It may be that like other stimulants, the value of this one would decline over time. Indeed the risk of this result is large enough so that we ourselves believe that a very major effort all along the line should be made in South Vietnam to take full advantage of the immediate stimulus of reprisal policy in its early stages. Our object should be to use this new policy to effect a visible upward turn in pacification, in governmental effectiveness, in operations against the Viet Cong, and in the whole U.S./GVN relationship. It is changes in these areas that can have enduring long-term effects.

7. While emphasizing the importance of reprisals in the South, we do not exclude the impact on Hanoi. We believe, indeed, that it is of great importance that the level of reprisal be adjusted rapidly and visibly to both upward and downward shifts in the level of Viet Cong offenses. We want to keep before Hanoi the carrot of our desisting as well as the stick of continued pressure. We also need to conduct the application of the force so that there is always a prospect of worse to come.

8. We cannot assert that a policy of sustained reprisal will succeed in changing the course of the contest in Vietnam. It may fail, and we cannot estimate the odds of success with any accuracy--they may be somewhere between 25% and 75%. What we can say is that even if it fails, the policy will be worth it. At a minimum it will damp down the charge that we did not do all that we could have done, and this charge will be important in many countries, including our own. Beyond that, a reprisal policy--to the extent that it demonstrates U.S. willingness to employ this new norm in counter-insurgency--will set a higher price for the future upon all adventures of guerrilla warfare, and it should therefore somewhat increase our ability to deter such adventures. We must recognize, however, that that ability will be gravely weakened if there is failure for any reason in Vietnam.

IV. Present Action Recommendations

1. This general recommendation was developed in intensive discussions in the days just before the attacks on Pleiku. These attacks and our reaction to them have created an ideal opportunity for the prompt development and execution of sustained reprisals. Conversely, if no such policy is now developed, we face the grave danger that Pleiku, like the Gulf of Tonkin, may be a short-run stimulant and a long-term depressant. We therefore recommend that the necessary preparations be made for continuing reprisals. The major necessary steps to be taken appear to us to be the following:

1. We should complete the evacuation of dependents.

2. We should quietly start the necessary westward deployments of back-up contingency forces.

3. We should develop and refine a running catalogue of Viet Cong offenses which can be published regularly and related clearly to our own reprisals. Such a catalogue should perhaps build on the foundation of an initial White Paper.

4. We should initiate joint planning with the GVN on both the civil and military level. Specifically, we should give a clear and strong signal to those now forming a government that we will be ready for this policy when they are.

5. We should develop the necessary public and diplomatic statements to accompany the initiation and continuation of this program.

6. We should insure that a reprisal program is matched by renewed public commitment to our family of programs in the South, so that the central importance of the southern struggle may never be neglected.

7. We should plan quiet diplomatic communication of the precise meaning of what we are and are not doing, to Hanoi, to Peking and to Moscow.

8. We should be prepared to defend and to justify this new policy by concentrating attention in every forum upon its cause--the aggression in the South.

9. We should accept discussion on these terms in any forum, but we should not now accept the idea of negotiations of any sort except on the basis of a stand down of Viet Cong violence. A program of sustained reprisal, with its direct link to Hanoi's continuing aggressive actions in the South, will not involve us in nearly the level of international recrimination which would be precipitated by a go-North program which was not so connected. For this reason the international pressures for negotiation should be quite manageable.

GLOSSARY

counter-insurgency: action taken against guerillas

Hanoi: capital of North Vietnam

pacification: to forcibly eliminate hostile population

Viet Cong: Vietnamese communist guerrillas

White Paper: a government report

Document Analysis

The main thrust of Bundy's memo is a strategy he outlines for "sustained reprisal against North Vietnam." In some way loosely based on the perceived events surrounding the Gulf of Tonkin Incident, the notion is that American military forces will only respond to the hostile actions of the North Vietnamese and Viet Cong. This was in some ways also reflective of Johnson's insistence on achieving, rather paradoxically, peace through force. The policy as outlined would be adopted in cooperation with the government of South Vietnam. In practice, the sustained reprisal would essentially force American military planners to grade hostile incidents, thus determining which ones required a response and which ones did not. The assassination of a South Vietnamese official might garner retaliation, for example, while the indiscriminant killing of villagers might not.

Propaganda would serve a necessary function, as every act of reprisal would have to be closely linked with an act of violence perpetrated by the North Vietnamese. The idea would be that the general public, both within and outside of Vietnam, would be able to perceive clear linkages between action and reaction.

Bundy points out that the best possible way to justify reprisal is to stress the strategy as one of last resort. It is the North Vietnamese who have forced the United States into this position. Reprisal would most often take the form of strategic bombing of the North, thus it is also vital to destroy whatever air combat capabilities the North Vietnamese might possess as quickly as possible. To work effectively, reprisal would need to go on without pause. Sustained, deliberate, military action must be maintained. The results of this policy? The immediate effect would be a shift in perception and loyalty toward the American side. The South Vietnamese people, having had few options outside the Viet Cong, would recognize that they now had a powerful ally on their side. For the United States, the payoff would be even greater. Win or lose, Bundy stresses, the effect for the United States would be ultimately positive, as America would demonstrate both its strength and resolve to the larger international community. Even if the military failed in pacifying the enemy, the political gains are simply too good to abandon. In the best case scenario, communist forces would become demoralized and eventually give up the fight, but again, this is a perk, rather than a clear objective. In the end, Bundy proposes nine action recommendations to be carried out immediately in order to begin implementation of the policy. Most of these, tellingly, emphasize the need to shape perception.

Essential Themes

Was the war in Vietnam inevitable? No, but if anything is clear from the memos and policy statements circling throughout the White House during the first years of the Johnson administration, it is that some of the smartest men in the nation were determined to see it happen, despite their own very real doubts about final victory. In his memo of February 1965, former mathematician turned national security advisor McGeorge Bundy outlines a strategy of attack against North Vietnam, founded heavily in a plan to shift world opinion, which turned real human death and suffering into cold calculation. If the North Vietnamese do x, we respond with y. But even more striking is Bundy's acceptance that his strategy may fail. Yes, he concedes, sustained retaliation might not help achieve military objectives, the United States might lose the war, American troops will, most likely, suffer many casualties; but the political gains, in Bundy's opinion, outweigh the risks. Here the conflict in Vietnam is presented not as war, but as a political chess match. The loss of human life, both Vietnamese and American, is little more than a means to an end: the growth of American prestige.

In the weeks following this memo, President Johnson launched Operation Flaming Dart, Operation Rolling Thunder, and Operation Arc Light. All told the three bombing campaigns lasted for three years, devastating parts of North Vietnam, Cambodia, and Laos and resulting in innumerable deaths and casualties. By December of that year, over 200,000 ground troops were sent in to protect the air bases launching the attacks. At every step, McGeorge Bundy advocated for greater and greater escalation. By the time Johnson left office, troop numbers had doubled, and American casualties were climbing into the tens of thousands. And as for Bundy's long-term goal of growing American prestige? The war in Vietnam had very much the opposite effect. Once seen as a champion of freedom and liberation, the United States was transformed in the eyes of many to an oversized empire no better than the communist forces it hoped to defeat.

—KP Dawes, MA

Bibliography and Additional Reading

Bird, Kai. *McGeorge Bundy and William Bundy: Brothers in Arms.* New York: Simon & Schuster, 1999. Print.

Herring, George. *America's Longest War.* New York: McGraw-Hill, 1996. Print.

McNamara, Robert & Brian VanDeMark. *In Retrospect: The Tragedy and Lessons of Vietnam.* New York: Random House, 1995. Print.

VanDeMark, Brian. *Into the Quagmire: Lyndon Johnson and the Escalation of the Vietnam War.* New York: Oxford University Press, 1995. Print.

■ LBJ: "Peace Without Conquest"

Date: April 7, 1965
Author: Lyndon Baines Johnson
Genre: speech

Summary Overview

For all of his great achievements, Lyndon Baines Johnson, the thirty-sixth president of the United States, is perhaps best remembered, rightly or wrongly, for taking America to war in Vietnam. What ultimately became one of the costliest wars in United States history, in both material and lives, had its roots in a profound fear of communism and a loss of American international standing. Johnson's rationale for the war, and his strategy for fighting it, were best laid out in a speech he delivered at Johns Hopkins University on April 7, 1965. Considered perhaps the most important foreign policy statement of the Johnson administration, the speech, billed as "Peace Without Conquest," was an attempt to stem the growing alarm across the United States at the sudden escalation of the war by a man who had run for president the previous year on promises of peace. Ultimately, the speech offers insight into Johnson's flawed understanding of the Vietnam conflict, and why, in hindsight, his strategy for war was doomed to failure from the start.

Defining Moment

After the defeat of the Axis powers at the end of World War II, after Soviet forces occupied the countries they "liberated" from the Nazis, and after China fell to the Communist forces of Mao Zedong, Western leaders began to fear what they called the "Domino Effect." If one country in a region were to succumb to communism, then, the theory held, eventually all countries in the region would succumb to communism. It was belief in this theory that led to Western intervention in the Korean conflict, and why, beginning with Eisenhower and continuing with Kennedy, the United States began to take an ever greater interest in the small Southeast Asian country of Vietnam.

Long under French colonial rule, the Vietnamese had successfully overthrown their European masters in what was called the First Indochina War. As part of the negotiated peace, Vietnam was divided, much as Korea had been, between the communist north and the loyalist south. However, in 1954, pro-communist forces, known as the Viet Cong, began a guerilla campaign to bring the south under northern rule. As fighting escalated and the despotic regime of South Vietnam took ever harsher measures to deal with the insurrection, the superpowers began to take interest. While China and the Soviet Union began sending aid to the North, the United States became ever more involved in the South.

Tensions ran high until 1963, when South Vietnam's government was overthrown and the conflict with communist forces escalated. Up until the assassination of President Kennedy, the United States had limited its involvement to a financial and advisory role; however, this quickly changed after the election of President Johnson. Despite having run as a peace candidate, Johnson greatly increased US-aid to South Vietnam. Using the Gulf of Tonkin Incident as a pretext, and armed with Congressional approval, Johnson began a coordinated bombing campaign of the North, while bolstering the South's defenses with American ground troops.

The sudden escalation in American involvement was strongly criticized by many across the nation, especially a small, but highly influential minority in the media. American allies as well complained about what they saw as a kind of neo-imperialism perpetrated by the United States. It was amidst this backdrop that Johnson decided to address not only the nation, but the world, as to justify American military intervention in Vietnam. If the Johnson administration were to wage a war abroad, it would need to win the war of public opinion at home.

Author Biography

Lyndon Baines Johnson was born in Stonewall, Texas, in August 1908. The oldest of five children, Johnson gravitated toward debate and public speaking at an early age. After receiving a degree in education, Johnson first went into teaching and then, in 1930, politics. After receiving a law degree and having worked as a congressional aide, Johnson was elected to Congress as a Democrat in 1937 to represent Texas' tenth congressional district. A devoted member of Roosevelt's New Deal coalition, Johnson soon made a name for himself as a wheeler and dealer, able to convince even the most obstinate foes of the righteousness of his cause. After a distinguished naval career during World War II, Johnson was elected to the United States Senate and quickly rose through the ranks, first to become majority whip and later the leader of the Senate Democrats.

Respected, admired, and feared, Johnson ran for president in the 1960 Democratic primary. Having lost to his chief rival, the junior Senator from Massachusetts, John F. Kennedy, Johnson begrudgingly, and much to the chagrin of the Kennedys, accepted the nomination as vice president. Often marginalized by the Kennedy administration, Johnson became president after Kennedy's assassination in November 1963 and was elected in his own right in 1964 by an impressive margin. Despite having done considerable work on social welfare and civil rights, Johnson's presidency was marred by the growing war in Vietnam. Facing ever more hostile public opinion, Johnson chose not to run for reelection in 1968 and withdrew from public life. Lyndon Baines Johnson died in January 1973.

HISTORICAL DOCUMENT

Mr. Garland, Senator Brewster, Senator Tydings, Members of the congressional delegation, members of the faculty of Johns Hopkins, student body, my fellow Americans:

Last week 17 nations sent their views to some two dozen countries having an interest in southeast Asia. We are joining those 17 countries and stating our American policy tonight which we believe will contribute toward peace in this area of the world.

I have come here to review once again with my own people the views of the American Government.

Tonight Americans and Asians are dying for a world where each people may choose its own path to change.

This is the principle for which our ancestors fought in the valleys of Pennsylvania. It is the principle for which our sons fight tonight in the jungles of Viet-Nam.

Viet-Nam is far away from this quiet campus. We have no territory there, nor do we seek any. The war is dirty and brutal and difficult. And some 400 young men, born into an America that is bursting with opportunity and promise, have ended their lives on Viet-Nam's steaming soil.

Why must we take this painful road?

Why must this Nation hazard its ease, and its interest, and its power for the sake of a people so far away?

We fight because we must fight if we are to live in a world where every country can shape its own destiny.

And only in such a world will our own freedom be finally secure.

This kind of world will never be built by bombs or bullets. Yet the infirmities of man are such that force must often precede reason, and the waste of war, the works of peace.

We wish that this were not so. But we must deal with the world as it is, if it is ever to be as we wish.

THE NATURE OF THE CONFLICT
The world as it is in Asia is not a serene or peaceful place.

The first reality is that North Viet-Nam has attacked the independent nation of South Viet-Nam. Its object is total conquest.

Of course, some of the people of South Viet-Nam are participating in attack on their own government. But trained men and supplies, orders and arms, flow in a constant stream from north to south.

This support is the heartbeat of the war.

And it is a war of unparalleled brutality. Simple farmers are the targets of assassination and kidnapping. Women and children are strangled in the night because their men are loyal to their government. And helpless villages are ravaged by sneak attacks. Large-scale raids are conducted on towns, and terror strikes in the heart of cities.

The confused nature of this conflict cannot mask the fact that it is the new face of an old enemy.

Over this war—and all Asia—is another reality: the deepening shadow of Communist China. The rulers in Hanoi are urged on by Peking. This is a regime which has destroyed freedom in Tibet, which has attacked India, and has been condemned by the United Nations for aggression in Korea. It is a nation which is helping the forces of violence in almost every continent. The contest in Viet-Nam is part of a wider pattern of aggressive purposes.

Why are these realities our concern? Why are we in South Viet-Nam?

We are there because we have a promise to keep. Since 1954 every American President has offered support to the people of South Viet-Nam. We have helped to build, and we have helped to defend. Thus, over many years, we have made a national pledge to help South Viet-Nam defend its independence.

And I intend to keep that promise.

To dishonor that pledge, to abandon this small and brave nation to its enemies, and to the terror that must follow, would be an unforgivable wrong.

We are also there to strengthen world order. Around the globe, from Berlin to Thailand, are people whose well-being rests, in part, on the belief that they can count on us if they are attacked. To leave Viet-Nam to its fate would shake the confidence of all these people in the value of an American commitment and in the value of America's word. The result would be increased unrest and instability, and even wider war.

We are also there because there are great stakes in the balance. Let no one think for a moment that retreat from Viet-Nam would bring an end to conflict. The battle would be renewed in one country and then another. The central lesson of our time is that the appetite of aggression is never satisfied. To withdraw from one battlefield means only to prepare for the next. We must say in southeast Asia—as we did in Europe—in the words of the Bible: "Hitherto shalt thou come, but no further."

There are those who say that all our effort there will be futile—that China's power is such that it is bound to dominate all southeast Asia. But there is no end to that argument until all of the nations of Asia are swallowed up.

There are those who wonder why we have a responsibility there. Well, we have it there for the same reason that we have a responsibility for the defense of Europe. World War II was fought in both Europe and Asia, and when it ended we found ourselves with continued responsibility for the defense of freedom.

OUR OBJECTIVE IN VIET-NAM

Our objective is the independence of South Viet-Nam, and its freedom from attack. We want nothing for ourselves—only that the people of South Viet-Nam be allowed to guide their own country in their own way.

We will do everything necessary to reach that objective. And we will do only what is absolutely necessary.

In recent months attacks on South Viet-Nam were stepped up. Thus, it became necessary for us to increase our response and to make attacks by air. This is not a change of purpose. It is a change in what we believe that purpose requires.

We do this in order to slow down aggression.

We do this to increase the confidence of the brave people of South Viet-Nam who have bravely borne this brutal battle for so many years with so many casualties.

And we do this to convince the leaders of North Viet-Nam—and all who seek to share their conquest—of a very simple fact: We will not be defeated. We will not grow tired.

We will not withdraw, either openly or under the cloak of a meaningless agreement.

We know that air attacks alone will not accomplish all of these purposes. But it is our best and prayerful judgment that they are a necessary part of the surest road to peace.

We hope that peace will come swiftly. But that is in the hands of others besides ourselves. And we must be prepared for a long continued conflict. It will require patience as well as bravery, the will to endure as well as the will to resist.

I wish it were possible to convince others with words of what we now find it necessary to say with guns and planes: Armed hostility is futile. Our resources are equal to any challenge. Because we fight for values and we fight for principles, rather than territory or colonies, our patience and our determination are unending.

Once this is clear, then it should also be clear that the only path for reasonable men is the path of peaceful settlement.

Such peace demands an independent South Viet-Nam—securely guaranteed and able to shape its own relationships to all others—free from outside interference—tied to no alliance—a military base for no other country.

These are the essentials of any final settlement.

We will never be second in the search for such a peaceful settlement in Viet-Nam.

There may be many ways to this kind of peace: in discussion or negotiation with the governments concerned; in large groups or in small ones; in the reaffirmation of old agreements or their strengthening with new ones.

We have stated this position over and over again, fifty times and more, to friend and foe alike. And we remain ready, with this purpose, for unconditional discussions.

And until that bright and necessary day of peace we will try to keep conflict from spreading. We have no desire to see thousands die in battle—Asians or Americans. We have no desire to devastate that which the people of North Viet-Nam have built with toil and sacrifice. We will use our power with restraint and with all the wisdom that we can command.

But we will use it.

This war, like most wars, is filled with terrible irony. For what do the people of North Viet-Nam want? They want what their neighbors also desire: food for their hunger; health for their bodies; a chance to learn; progress for their country; and an end to the bondage of material misery. And they would find all these things far more readily in peaceful association with others than in the endless course of battle.

These countries of southeast Asia are homes for millions of impoverished people. Each day these people rise at dawn and struggle through until the night to wrestle existence from the soil. They are often wracked by disease, plagued by hunger, and death comes at the early age of 40.

Stability and peace do not come easily in such a land. Neither independence nor human dignity will ever be won, though, by arms alone. It also requires the work of peace. The American people have helped generously in times past in these works. Now there must be a much more massive effort to improve the life of man in that conflict-torn corner of our world.

The first step is for the countries of southeast Asia to associate themselves in a greatly expanded cooperative effort for development. We would hope that North Viet-Nam would take its place in the common effort just as soon as peaceful cooperation is possible.

The United Nations is already actively engaged in development in this area. As far back as 1961 I conferred with our authorities in Viet-Nam in connection with their work there. And I would hope tonight that the Secretary General of the United Nations could use the prestige of his great office, and his deep knowledge of Asia, to initiate, as soon as possible, with the countries of that area, a plan for cooperation in increased development.

For our part I will ask the Congress to join in a billion dollar American investment in this effort as soon as it is underway.

And I would hope that all other industrialized countries, including the Soviet Union, will join in this effort to replace despair with hope, and terror with progress.

The task is nothing less than to enrich the hopes and the existence of more than a hundred million people. And there is much to be done.

The vast Mekong River can provide food and water and power on a scale to dwarf even our own TVA [Tennessee Valley Authority].

The wonders of modern medicine can be spread through villages where thousands die every year from lack of care.

Schools can be established to train people in the skills that are needed to manage the process of development.

And these objectives, and more, are within the reach of a cooperative and determined effort.

I also intend to expand and speed up a program to make available our farm surpluses to assist in feeding and clothing the needy in Asia. We should not allow people to go hungry and wear rags while our own warehouses overflow with an abundance of wheat and corn, rice and cotton.

So I will very shortly name a special team of outstanding, patriotic, distinguished Americans to inaugurate our participation in these programs. This team will be headed by Mr. Eugene Black, the very able former President of the World Bank.

In areas that are still ripped by conflict, of course development will not be easy. Peace will be necessary for final success. But we cannot and must not wait for peace to begin this job.

THE DREAM OF WORLD ORDER

This will be a disorderly planet for a long time. In Asia, as elsewhere, the forces of the modern world are shaking old ways and uprooting ancient civilizations. There will be turbulence and struggle and even violence. Great social change—as we see in our own country now—does not always come without conflict.

We must also expect that nations will on occasion be in dispute with us. It may be because we are rich, or powerful; or because we have made some mistakes; or because they honestly fear our intentions. However, no nation need ever fear that we desire their land, or to impose our will, or to dictate their institutions.

But we will always oppose the effort of one nation to conquer another nation.

We will do this because our own security is at stake.

But there is more to it than that. For our generation has a dream. It is a very old dream. But we have the power and now we have the opportunity to make that dream come true.

For centuries nations have struggled among each other. But we dream of a world where disputes are settled by law and reason. And we will try to make it so.

For most of history men have hated and killed one another in battle. But we dream of an end to war. And we will try to make it so.

For all existence most men have lived in poverty, threatened by hunger. But we dream of a world where all are fed and charged with hope. And we will help to make it so.

The ordinary men and women of North Viet-Nam and South Viet-Nam—of China and India—of Russia and America—are brave people. They are filled with the same proportions of hate and fear, of love and hope. Most of them want the same things for themselves and their families. Most of them do not want their sons to ever die in battle, or to see their homes, or the homes of others, destroyed.

Well, this can be their world yet. Man now has the knowledge—always before denied—to make this planet serve the real needs of the people who live on it.

I know this will not be easy. I know how difficult it is for reason to guide passion, and love to master hate. The complexities of this world do not bow easily to pure and consistent answers.

But the simple truths are there just the same. We must all try to follow them as best we can.

We often say how impressive power is. But I do not find it impressive at all. The guns and the bombs, the rockets and the warships, are all symbols of human failure. They are necessary symbols. They protect what we cherish. But they are witness to human folly. A dam built across a great river is impressive.

In the countryside where I was born, and where I live, I have seen the night illuminated, and the kitchens warmed, and the homes heated, where once the cheerless night and the ceaseless cold held sway. And all this happened because electricity came to our area along the humming wires of the REA [Rural Electric Authority]. Electrification of the countryside—yes, that, too, is impressive.

A rich harvest in a hungry land is impressive.

The sight of healthy children in a classroom is impressive.

These—not mighty arms—are the achievements which the American Nation believes to be impressive.

And, if we are steadfast, the time may come when all other nations will also find it so.

Every night before I turn out the lights to sleep I ask myself this question: Have I done everything that I can do to unite this country? Have I done everything I can to help unite the world, to try to bring peace and hope to all the peoples of the world? Have I done enough?

Ask yourselves that question in your homes—and in this hall tonight. Have we, each of us, all done all we could? Have we done enough?

We may well be living in the time foretold many years ago when it was said: "I call heaven and earth to record this day against you, that I have set before you life and death, blessing and cursing: therefore choose life, that both thou and thy seed may live."

This generation of the world must choose: destroy or build, kill or aid, hate or understand.

We can do all these things on a scale never dreamed of before.

Well, we will choose life. In so doing we will prevail over the enemies within man, and over the natural enemies of all mankind.

To Dr. Eisenhower and Mr. Garland, and this great

institution, Johns Hopkins, I thank you for this opportunity to convey my thoughts to you and to the American people.

Good night.

GLOSSARY

delegation: a group of representatives

infirmities: physical or mental weaknesses

turbulence: violent movement; upheaval

Document Analysis

In his speech, Johnson attempts to do several things. Foremost, the president tries to reassure critics that he is focused on peace. He affirms that he is willing to do everything and anything, including one-on-on or multiparty negotiations to come to a fair and equitable agreement. If the aims of keeping South Vietnam free can be achieved through diplomacy, his administration will exhaust every option.

He also tries to win over the people of South Vietnam by offering a billion dollars in aid to help develop the Mekong River basin. Very much in keeping with Johnson's New Deal roots, the massive UN-led project would transform South Vietnam and perhaps the region. He recalls the changes brought about to the United States thanks to massive public works projects. The message Johnson hoped this would send to the Vietnamese and the peoples of Southeast Asia was that the United States was not just bringing war, it was going to help remake and revitalize the region. However, amidst the promises of aid and peace, Johnson also warns that the United States will use whatever military power is at its disposal to forcefully keep communism at bay.

The war in Vietnam, Johnson reasons, is not a small squabble over an insignificant third world country, this is a direct conflict with China and the Soviet Union. At stake is not just the freedom of South Vietnam, but the freedom of the world, and perhaps more importantly, the prestige and international standing of the United States. Johnson states clearly that American military forces will stay in Vietnam no matter how long it takes: "We will not be defeated. We will not grow tired." Cen-

tral to his military policy in Vietnam, Johnson points to the bombing of the north. Through airstrikes he hopes to weaken and demoralize the North Vietnamese and their allies to the point where they are forced to seek peace. Although all options are on the table, Johnson reiterates again and again that South Vietnam must remain a free nation. America made a promise, and it is a promise that Johnson intends to keep.

Essential Themes

Lyndon Johnson's attempt to turn domestic public opinion in favor of military action in Vietnam was a resounding success. Promising both peace and strength, Johnson was able to walk a tight line, reassuring both critics and supporters. In a sense he was echoing the sentiments of past presidents, such as Woodrow Wilson, and his mentor Franklin Roosevelt, that America wants only freedom and equality for all and is willing to use force, albeit reluctantly, to achieve it. Peace advocates could rally around Johnson's willingness to negotiate, while hawks could applaud his renewed pledge to continue attacking the enemy until victory was achieved. Here was the carrot and the stick.

America's allies too, generally approved of the speech, praising Johnson's focus on aid and diplomacy. Not surprisingly, communist countries reacted with hostility, focusing almost entirely on the warmongering rhetoric. In Vietnam, both north and south reacted with a mixture of confusion and unease. This feeling of anxiety soon seeped into all corners, as in the months following the speech, the Johnson administration escalated the bombing campaign, pausing here and there in an awkward strategy to allow the North Vietnamese to negotiate. In the end, the speech was little more than empty rhetoric. With a blank check from Congress, Johnson ramped up American military involvement in Vietnam. Within months, thousands more troops were sent to Southeast Asia, and American bombers were dropping unimagined quantities of ordnance (explosive weapons) on Hanoi and other North Vietnamese cities.

As the war in Vietnam became ever bloodier, Johnson's domestic agenda, including the War on Poverty and the Great Society, began to lose support. Soon a new and vocal antiwar movement began to gain ever more traction, especially from those of fighting age, and Johnson, who in 1964 had won the presidency with an impressive 486 out of 538 electoral votes, became one of the most unpopular presidents in modern history. The "Peace Without Conquest" speech was the high-water mark for the Johnson administration. It was height of Johnson's popularity and also the beginning of the end of his presidency. It was only four years later, facing opposition from all sides, and an unwinnable war abroad, that Lyndon Baines Johnson decided not to run for a second term.

—*KP Dawes, MA*

Bibliography and Additional Reading

Herring, George. *America's Longest War*. New York: Mc-Graw-Hill, 1996. Print.

VanDeMark, Brian. *Into the Quagmire: Lyndon Johnson and the Escalation of the Vietnam War*. New York: Oxford University Press, 1995. Print.

Yuravlivker, Dror. "'Peace without Conquest': Lyndon Johnson's Speech of April 7, 1965." *Presidential Studies Quarterly*. 36.3 (2006): 457–481. Print.

■ Meeting Between the President and His Advisors

Date: July 21, 1965
Author: Lyndon Baines Johnson; Robert McNamara; George Ball; Dean Rusk; various others
Genre: discussion; transcript

Summary Overview

Of all the discussion around America's role in the escalating conflict in Vietnam, perhaps none was more crucial to the issue of war and peace than the meeting President Lyndon Baines Johnson held with his advisors in the summer of 1965. The culmination of months, if not years, of debate and hand-wringing, this single, fateful meeting was the final confirmation of full-scale military intervention. Caught between two camps—the doves, represented by Undersecretary of State George Ball, and the hawks, represented by Secretary of Defense Robert McNamara—Johnson, facing the real prospect of abandoning his ambitious domestic agenda, had to decide to either withdraw from Southeast Asia and risk the loss of American prestige, or commit to war and risk a prolonged and bloody quagmire. The arguments laid out in the meeting document the false assumptions and tragic misconceptions held by American war planners harking back to the Eisenhower administration. These arguments also provide a prescient warning as to what lay ahead.

Defining Moment

The United States first became interested in the small Southeast Asian country of Vietnam, after the defeat and ousting of French colonial forces in the years following World War II. Fearful of the growing power of North Vietnamese communists, American administrations, beginning with Truman and continuing under Eisenhower and Kennedy, had made commitments to keep South Vietnam free. In the case of South Vietnam, "free" was a relative term, as one despotic regime after another ruled over the country with an iron fist. As the population of the south became increasingly sympathetic to the north, tensions turned into open conflict, until they finally boiled over in the early 1960s. By 1965, it was clear that the government of South Vietnam was barely able to stand on its own, and it fell to Lyndon Baines Johnson to make a seismic decision: to either abandon South Vietnam to communist forces, or commit American military forces to a potentially long and costly war.

Representing the two sides of the debate were Undersecretary of State George Ball and Secretary of Defense Robert McNamara. Ball, a life-long diplomat, had been arguing against intervention in Vietnam since the moment John F. Kennedy sent the first 16,000 military "advisors" into the country, famously, and prophetically, warning the president that if the United States were to begin sending troops into Vietnam it would only be a matter of time before the number would top 300,000. Under Johnson, Ball continued to lobby against American involvement, outlining his dire and, in hindsight, accurate warnings of disaster, culminating in a memo he sent to Johnson in February 1965. McNamara— previously one of Ford Motor Company's ten "Whiz Kids" and the corporation's youngest president—was resolutely in favor of American military intervention in Vietnam. A champion of using statistical analysis to make warfare more efficient and considered to be the chief architect of the Vietnam War, McNamara pushed for full-scale commitment, arguing that the conflict in Southeast Asia was crucial to America's long term international security interests. In fact, McNamara was so hawkish that he occasionally withheld crucial information from President Johnson, as he did in the Gulf of Tonkin Incident of August 1964, which led directly to both American military attacks against North Vietnamese forces and the Gulf of Tonkin Resolution, which effectively gave Johnson Congressional approval to launch a war in Vietnam.

The debate between Ball and McNamara came to a head in the summer of 1965, when Johnson— struggling to pass key provisions of his Great Society domestic agenda through Congress and facing an ever more tenuous situation in Vietnam—had to decide between full military commitment and complete withdraw.

Author Biography

George W. Ball was born in Iowa in 1909. Having grown up just north of Chicago, he received a law degree from Northwestern University and eventually became an aide to Adlai Stevenson, the Democratic presidential candidate in 1952 and 1956. After serving in an administrative role during World War II, helping to manage Roosevelt's Lend Lease program, he joined the State Department, where he served as undersecretary for economic and agricultural affairs under both the Kennedy and Johnson administrations. In 1968, he briefly served as American ambassador to the United Nations. He died in 1994.

Robert S. McNamara was born in California in 1916. After attending the University of California at Berkeley, he went on to get an MBA from Harvard Business School. During World War II, he worked under Major General Curtis LeMay in the Office of Statistical Control, analyzing the effectiveness of Allied bombing on enemy cities. After the war, McNamara joined the Ford Motor Company, eventually rising to become the youngest CEO in the company's history, and, in 1960, was made secretary of defense, first under Kennedy and then under Johnson. Considered the architect of the Vietnam War, McNamara eventually resigned his post as the war soon proved unwinnable. In 1968, he was appointed to the World Bank, where he served as president until 1981. He died in 2009.

HISTORICAL DOCUMENT

President: What has happened in recent past that requires this decision on my part? What are the alternatives? Also, I want more discussions on what we expect to flow from this decision. Discuss in detail.

Have we wrung every single soldier out of every country we can? Who else can help? Are we the sole defenders of freedom in the world? Have we done all we can in this direction? The reasons for the call up? The results we can expect? What are the alternatives? We must make no snap judgments. We must consider carefully all our options.

We know we can tell SVN "we're coming home." Is that the option we should take? What flows from that.

The negotiations, the pause, all the other approaches—have all been explored. It makes us look weak—with cup in hand. We have tried.

Let's look at all our options so that every man at this table understands fully the total picture.

McNamara: This is our position a year ago (shows President a map of the country with legends). Estimated by country team that VC controls 25%—SVN 50%—rest in white area, VC in red areas.

VC tactics are terror, and sniping.

President: Looks dangerous to put US forces in those red areas.

McNamara: You're right. We're placing our people with their backs to the sea—for protection. Our mission would be to seek out the VC in large scale units.

Wheeler: Big problem in Vietnam is good combat intelligence. The VC is a creature of habit. By continuing to probe we think we can make headway.

Ball: Isn't it possible that the VC will do what they did against the French—stay away from confrontation and not accommodate us?

Wheeler: Yes, but by constantly harassing them, they will have to fight somewhere.

McNamara: If VC doesn't fight in large units, it will give ARVN a chance to re-secure hostile areas.

We don't know what VC tactics will be when VC is confronted by 175,000 Americans.

Raborn: We agree—by 1965, we expect NVN will increase their forces. They will attempt to gain a substantial victory before our build-up is complete.

President: Is anyone of the opinion we should not do what the memo says—If so, I'd like to hear from them.

Ball: I can foresee a perilous voyage—very dangerous—great apprehensions that we can win under these conditions. But, let me be clear, if the decision is to go ahead, I'm committed.

President: But is there another course in the national interest that is better than the McNamara course? We know it's dangerous and perilous. But can it be avoided?

Ball: There is no course that will allow us to cut our losses. If we get bogged down, our cost might be substantially greater. The pressures to create a larger war would be irresistible. Qualifications I have are not due to the fact that I think we are in a bad moral position.

President: What other road can I go?

Ball: Take what precautions we can—take losses—let their government fall apart—negotiate—probable take over by Communists. This is disagreeable, I know.

President: Can we make a case for this—discuss it fully?

Ball: We have discussed it. I have had my day in court.

President: I don't think we have made a full commitment. You have pointed out the danger, but you haven't proposed an alternative course. We haven't always been right. We have no mortgage on victory.

I feel we have very little alternative to what we are doing.

I want another meeting before we take this action. We should look at all other courses carefully. Right now I feel it would be more dangerous for us to lose this now, than endanger a greater number of troops.

Rusk: What we have done since 1954–61 has not been good enough. We should have probably committed ourselves heavier in 1961.

Rowan: What bothers me most is the weakness of the Ky government. Unless we put the screws on the Ky government, 175,000 men will do us no good.

Lodge: There is no tradition of a national government

in Saigon. There are no roots in the country. Not until there is tranquility can you have any stability. I don't think we ought to take this government seriously. There is no one who can do anything. We have to do what we think we ought to do regardless of what the Saigon government does.

As we move ahead on a new phase—it gives us the right and duty to do certain things with or without the government's approval.

President: George, do you think we have another course?

Ball: I would not recommend that you follow McNamara's course.

President: Are you able to outline your doubts—and offer another course of action? I think it is desirable to hear you out—and determine if your suggestions are sound and ready to be followed.

Ball: Yes. I think I can present to you the least bad of two courses. What I would present is a course that is costly, but can be limited to short term costs.

President: Then, let's meet at 2:30 this afternoon to discuss Ball's proposals. Now let Bob tell us why we need to risk those 600,000 lives.

(McNamara and Wheeler outlined the reasons for more troops.) 75,000 now just enough to protect bases—it will let us lose slowly instead of rapidly. The extra men will stabilize the situation and improve it. It will give ARVN breathing room. We limit it to another 100,000 because VN can't absorb any more. There is no major risk of catastrophe.

President: But you will lose greater number of men.

Wheeler: The more men we have the greater the likelihood of smaller losses.

President: What makes you think if we put in 100,000 men Ho Chi Minh won't put in another 100,000?

Wheeler: This means greater bodies of men—which will allow us to cream them.

President: What are the chances of more NVN men coming?

Wheeler: 50–50 chance. He would be foolhardy to put 1/4 of his forces in SVN. It would expose him too greatly in NVN.

President: (to Raborn) Do you have people in NVN?

Raborn: Not enough. We think it is reliable.

President: Can't we improve intelligence in NVN?

Raborn: We have a task force working on this.

1:00 pm—Meeting adjourned until 2:30 pm.
https://history.state.gov/historicaldocuments/frus1964-68v03/d71 - fn4
Resume same meeting at 2:45 pm

Ball: We can't win. Long protracted. The most we can hope for is messy conclusion. There remains a great danger of intrusion by Chicoms.

Problem of long war in US:
1. Korean experience was galling one. Correlation between Korean casualties and public opinion (Ball showed Pres. a chart) showed support stabilized at 50%. As casualties increase, pressure to strike at jugular of the NVN will become very great.
2. World opinion. If we could win in a year's time—win decisively—world opinion would be alright. However, if long and protracted we will suffer because a great power cannot beat guerrillas.
3. National politics. Every great captain in history is not afraid to make a tactical withdrawal if conditions are unfavorable to him. The enemy cannot even be seen; he is indigenous to the country.
Have serious doubt if an army of westerners can fight orientals in Asian jungle and succeed.
President: This is important—can westerners, in absence of intelligence, successfully fight orientals in jungle rice-paddies? I want McNamara and Wheeler to seriously ponder this question.

Ball: I think we have all underestimated the seriousness of this situation. Like giving cobalt treatment to a terminal cancer case. I think a long protracted war will disclose our weakness, not our strength.

The least harmful way to cut losses in SVN is to let the government decide it doesn't want us to stay there. Therefore, put such proposals to SVN government that they can't accept, then it would move into a neutralist position—and I have no illusions that after we were asked to leave, SVN would be under Hanoi control.

What about Thailand? It would be our main problem. Thailand has proven a good ally so far—though history shows it has never been a staunch ally. If we wanted to make a stand in Thailand, we might be able to make it.

Another problem would be South Korea. We have two divisions there now. There would be a problem with Taiwan, but as long as Generalissimo is there, they have no place to go. Indonesia is a problem—insofar as Malaysia. There we might have to help the British in military way. Japan thinks we are propping up a lifeless government and are on a sticky wicket. Between long war and cutting our losses, the Japanese would go for the latter…

President: Wouldn't all those countries say Uncle Sam is a paper tiger—wouldn't we lose credibility breaking the word of three presidents—if we set it up as you proposed. It would seem to be an irreparable blow. But, I gather you don't think so.

Ball: The worse blow would be that the mightiest power in the world is unable to defeat guerrillas.

President: Then you are not basically troubled by what the world would say about pulling out?

Ball: If we were actively helping a country with a stable, viable government, it would be a vastly different story. Western Europeans look at us as if we got ourselves into an imprudent fashion [situation].

President: But I believe that these people are trying to fight. They're like Republicans who try to stay in power, but don't stay there long.

(aside—amid laughter—"excuse me, Cabot")

Ball: Thiêu spoke the other day and said the Communists would win the election.

President: I don't believe that. Does anyone believe that?

(There was no agreement from anyone—McNamara, Lodge, B. Bundy, Unger—all said they didn't believe it.)

McNamara: Ky will fall soon. He is weak. We can't have elections until there is physical security, and even then there will be no elections because as Cabot said, there is no democratic tradition. (Wheeler agreed about Ky—but said Thiêu impressed him)

President: Two basic troublings:
1. That Westerners can ever win in Asia.
2. Don't see how you can fight a war under direction of other people whose government changes every month.
Now go ahead, George, and make your other points.

Ball: The cost, as well as our Western European allies, is not relevant to their situation. What they are concerned about is their own security—troops in Berlin have real meaning, none in VN.

President: Are you saying pulling out of Korea would be akin to pulling out of Vietnam?

Bundy: It is not analogous. We had a status quo in Korea. It would not be that way in Vietnam.

Ball: We will pay a higher cost in Vietnam.
This is a decision one makes against an alternative.
On one hand—long protracted war, costly, NVN is digging in for long term. This is their life and driving force. Chinese are taking long term view—ordering blood plasma from Japan.
On the other hand—short-term losses. On balance, come out ahead of McNamara plan. Distasteful on either hand.

Bundy: Two important questions to be raised—I agree with the main thrust of McNamara. It is the function of my staff to argue both sides.
To Ball's argument: The difficulty in adopting it now would be a radical switch without evidence that it should be done. It goes in the face of all we have said and done.
His whole analytical argument gives no weight to loss suffered by other side. A great many elements in his argument are correct.
We need to make clear this is a somber matter—that it will not be quick—no single action will bring quick victory.
I think it is clear that we are not going to be thrown out.

Ball: My problem is not that we don't get thrown out, but that we get bogged down and don't win.

Bundy: I would sum up: The world, the country, and the VN would have alarming reactions if we got out.

Rusk: If the Communist world finds out we will not pursue our commitment to the end, I don't know where they will stay their hand.
I am more optimistic than some of my colleagues. I don't believe the VC have made large advances among the VN people.
We can't worry about massive casualties when we say we can't find the enemy. I don't see great casualties unless the Chinese come in.

Lodge: There is a greater threat to World War III if we don't go in. Similarity to our indolence at Munich.
I can't be as pessimistic as Ball. We have great seaports in Vietnam. We don't need to fight on roads. We have the sea. Visualize our meeting VC on our own terms. We don't have to spend all our time in the jungles.

GLOSSARY

ARVN: Army of the Republic of Vietnam, also known as, the army of South Vietnam

Chicoms: a disparaging reference to Chinese communist forces

Ho Chi Minh: the leader of North Vietnam

paper tiger: a person or thing that appears threatening but is not

Saigon: the capital city of South Vietnam

SVN: South Vietnam

VC: Viet Cong, also known as South Vietnamese communist guerillas

Document Analysis

The transcript outlines the debate between George Ball and Robert McNamara on the subject of American intervention in Vietnam. As Lyndon Johnson agonizes over what to do and questions his advisors, he focuses on the memorandum written by McNamara, which pushes for full military commitment. In this way, the various arguments—military, political, and diplomatic—are laid out. What is clear is that George Ball is in the minority. Frustrated, although still passionate, Ball is asked—and once again restates—his case against escalation. Ball makes clear that he would support whatever course Johnson decides on, but states unequivocally that, although pulling out of Vietnam would be fraught with problems, increasing troop levels and committing to the long course of war would be disastrous.

The hawks, such as McNamara and Wheeler, counter that greater troop numbers might actually mean fewer losses. The strategy is to overwhelm the enemy with greater numbers, allowing the South Vietnamese to take the lead. Ball argues that the war would be long and states simply that the United States cannot win a long war. As casualties mount, support for the war would decrease. Eventually, world opinion would turn against the United States, and the Viet Cong, fighting in their home territory, would prevail. A vital factor, as the war drags on, Ball argues, is the loss of regional allies, but even more damaging would be the change in perception of America as a superpower. How would the United States be perceived around the globe,

by foe and friend alike, if it was unable to defeat a guerrilla force?

Unfortunately for Ball, and for the country overall, the other men at the meeting, Rusk, Wheeler, Bundy, and Lodge all disparage Ball's warnings. In their view, the United States is already at war in Vietnam. To leave now would be disastrous for both countries, if not the world. That's neither here nor there because how could a small force hiding in the jungle ever defeat the military might of the United States? Besides, as Henry Cabot Lodge, ambassador to Vietnam, says: it is unlikely American troops would ever have to fight in the jungle at all.

Essential Themes

The meeting between Johnson and his advisors in July 1965 represented the last real chance to pull American troops out of Vietnam. As he had done so many times in the weeks and months prior to the meeting, the president questioned those closest to him in an attempt to assuage his fears of disaster in Southeast Asia. The lone voice against war, George Ball, having perhaps a clearer understanding of what lay ahead than anyone else in the government, argued as best as he could against escalation. The war in Vietnam would be a long and bloody struggle, he warned, one that the United States would eventually lose. But the hawks, led by Robert McNamara, were stronger in force. America could not withdraw without losing too much, and only if more troops were committed to the fight, they argued, would victory be assured.

Following the meeting, President Johnson continued to debate and deliberate. Fearful of large numbers of casualties and the collapse of his domestic agenda, and perhaps seeing the reason in Ball's arguments, he stalled. If one strong voice had come out in support of Ball, it is possible that Johnson would have rethought his plans, but faced with increasing pressure from the majority of his advisors and the Joint Chiefs of Staff, the president finally gave in. Troop levels and bombing runs were ramped up. The United States committed fully to the struggle for South Vietnam. And, with every escalation, it became harder and harder to pull out.

In the end, facing ever increasing unpopularity, Johnson decided not to seek a second term. Robert McNamara, realizing too late that the war had turned into a quagmire, left to run the World Bank, eventually even coming out against the war. As for Ball, after the Johnson administration, he largely withdrew from public life. Cast out as a defeatist by a political establishment too embarrassed to admit that he was right, he returned to work as an investment banker, quietly advocating until the end of his life, for a more united, peaceful world.

—*KP Dawes, MA*

Bibliography and Additional Reading

Herring, George. *America's Longest War.* New York: McGraw-Hill, 1996. Print.

McNamara, Robert & Brian VanDeMark. *In Retrospect: The Tragedy and Lessons of Vietnam.* New York: Random House, 1995. Print.

VanDeMark, Brian. *Into the Quagmire: Lyndon Johnson and the Escalation of the Vietnam War.* New York: Oxford University Press, 1995. Print.

■ "Why We Are in Vietnam"

Date: July 28, 1965
Author: Lyndon B. Johnson
Genre: Speech

Summary Overview

In this excerpt from Johnson's speech, with which he began a White House press conference, the president attempts to explain the reasons for the US involvement in the war in Vietnam. While he speaks of a reluctance to commit American forces and material support to a distant war, he also draws upon the perceived lessons of pre-World War II Europe—the belief that appeasement of Hitler's demands had led to further aggression and that this course should not be repeated in Southeast Asia in the face of perceived communist aggression. Johnson also puts major emphasis on treaty commitments that the US had made to the Republic of Vietnam. Over a period of eleven years, three presidents—Eisenhower, Kennedy, and Johnson—had promised that the United States would aid in defending the South Vietnamese from internal communist insurgency and from attack by the forces of the Democratic Republic of Vietnam (North Vietnam).

Defining Moment

When Lyndon Johnson acceded to the presidency upon the death of President John F. Kennedy on November 22, 1963, the United States had approximately 16,000 servicemen serving in Vietnam. Johnson noted in his memoirs that of all the crises confronting him when he became president, Vietnam did not seem to be one that required a great deal of immediate attention. Over the course of the next two years, however, Vietnam demanded more and more attention from the president and his administration. As Johnson's cabinet and civilian advisors, as well as military leaders, debated the proper course of action, several proposals emerged. One was to seek negotiations immediately, in order to begin disengaging from the war. Another option was to maintain the status quo—using US military advisors to help the forces of the Republic of Vietnam (South Vietnam) and supplying money and supplies to help the South Vietnamese defend themselves; this plan called

for only a small number of US troops, acting principally as advisors, helicopter pilots, and aircraft maintenance crews. By the spring and summer of 1965, however, Johnson had decided on a third option—to dramatically increase the number of US troops in Vietnam and to move toward an active combat mission rather than just an advisory or support operation.

The first step toward this escalation was the beginning of a sustained bombing campaign against North Vietnam, named Operation Rolling Thunder. Another step was taken in March 1965, when a Marine expeditionary brigade (about 5,000 men) was sent to defend the air base at Da Nang, on the northeastern coast of South Vietnam. Then, in the summer of 1965, General William C. Westmoreland, the commander of the Military Assistance Command Vietnam (MACV), requested that substantial US Army forces be committed to the war effort. In this speech, Johnson is reporting that he had approved Westmoreland's request and is seeking to explain and justify the reasons why Americans should be a part of the war effort in Vietnam. In the weeks prior to this announcement, most of Johnson's advisors and a significant number of US Senators had agreed that further escalation of American involvement was the only possible course of action. In this speech, Johnson stresses the perceived lessons of history, referring to the appeasement of Hitler's demands at the Munich Conference, and the necessity of honoring commitments that the United States had made to South Vietnam.

Author Biography

Lyndon Baines Johnson was born on August 27, 1908 on his family's ranch near Johnson City, Texas. After graduating from Southwest Texas State Teacher's College at San Marcos in 1934, he taught school briefly, but his interest soon turned to politics. Johnson was elected to the US House in 1937 and served six terms there. He was elected to the US Senate in 1948 and became the majority leader in 1954. In 1960, John F. Kennedy chose Johnson as his vice presidential candidate in an attempt to reassure conservative Southern Democrats. When Kennedy was assassinated on November 22, 1963, Johnson became President. In 1964, he defeated the Republican challenger Barry Goldwater in a landslide victory. While Johnson's presidency was marked by the passage of significant civil rights and social welfare legislation, the Vietnam War increasingly alienated the public, and Johnson chose not to run for re-election in 1968. He retired to his ranch in Texas, where he died on January 22, 1973, shortly before a treaty to end US involvement in Vietnam was finalized.

HISTORICAL DOCUMENT

Why We Are in Vietnam?

My fellow Americans:

Not long ago I received a letter from a woman in the Midwest. She wrote:

"Dear Mr. President:

"In my humble way I am writing 'to you about the crisis in Viet-Nam. I have a son who is now in Viet-Nam. My husband served in World War II. Our country was at war, but now, this time, it is just something that I don't understand. Why?"

Well, I have tried to answer that question dozens of times and more in practically every State in this Union. I have discussed it fully in Baltimore in April, in Washington in May, in San Francisco in June. Let me again, now, discuss it here in the East Room of the White House.

Why must young Americans, born into a land exultant with hope and with golden promise, toil and suffer and sometimes die in such a remote and distant place?

The answer, like the war itself, is not an easy one, but it echoes clearly from the painful lessons of half a century. Three times in my lifetime, in two World Wars and in Korea, Americans have gone to far lands to fight for freedom. We have learned at a terrible and a brutal cost that retreat does not bring safety and weakness does not bring peace.

It is this lesson that has brought us to Viet-Nam.

This is a different kind of war. There are no marching armies or solemn declarations. Some citizens of South Viet-Nam at times, with understandable grievances, have joined in the attack on their own government.

But we must not let this mask the central fact that this is really war. It is guided by North Viet-Nam and it is spurred by Communist China. Its goal is to conquer the South, to defeat American power, and to extend the Asiatic dominion of communism. There are great stakes in the balance. Most of the non-Communist nations of Asia cannot, by themselves and alone, resist the growing might and the grasping ambition of Asian communism.

Our power, therefore, is a very vital shield. If we are driven from the field in Viet-Nam, then no nation can ever again have the same confidence in American promise, or in American protection.

In each land the forces of independence would be considerably weakened, and an Asia so threatened by Communist domination would certainly imperil the security of the United States itself.

We did not choose to be the guardians at the gate, but there is no one else.

Nor would surrender in Viet-Nam bring peace, because we learned from Hitler at Munich that success only feeds the appetite of aggression. The battle would be renewed in one country and then another country, bringing with it perhaps even larger and crueler conflict, as we have learned from the lessons of history.

Moreover, we are in Viet-Nam to fulfill one of the most solemn pledges of the American Nation. Three Presidents—President Eisenhower, President Kennedy, and your present President—over 11 years have committed themselves and have promised to help defend this small and valiant nation.

Strengthened by that promise, the people of South Viet-Nam have fought for many long years. Thousands of them have died. Thousands more have been crippled and scarred by war. We just cannot now dishonor our word, or abandon our commitment, or leave those who believed us and who trusted us to the terror and repression and murder that would follow.

This, then, my fellow Americans, is why we are in Viet-Nam.

What are our goals in that war-strained land?

First, we intend to convince the Communists that we cannot be defeated by force of arms or by superior power. They are not easily convinced. In recent months they have greatly increased their fighting forces and their attacks and the number of incidents.

I have asked the Commanding General, General Westmoreland, what more he needs to meet this mounting aggression. He has told me. We will meet his needs.

I have today ordered to Viet-Nam the Air Mobile Division and certain other forces which will raise our fighting strength from 75,000 to 125,000 men almost immediately. Additional forces will be needed later, and they will be sent as requested.

This will make it necessary to increase our active fighting forces by raising the monthly draft call from 17,000 over a period of time to 35,000 per month, and for us to step up our campaign for voluntary enlistments.

After this past week of deliberations, I have concluded that it is not essential to order Reserve units into service now. If that necessity should later be indicated, I will give the matter most careful consideration and I will give the country—you—an adequate notice before taking such action, but only after full preparations.

We have also discussed with the Government of South Viet-Nam lately, the steps that we will take to substantially increase their own effort, both on the battlefield and toward reform and progress in the villages. Ambassador Lodge is now formulating a new program to be tested upon his return to that area.

I have directed Secretary Rusk and Secretary McNamara to be available immediately to the Congress to review with these committees, the appropriate congressional committees, what we plan to do in these areas. I have asked them to be able to answer the questions of any Member of Congress.

Secretary McNamara, in addition, will ask the Senate Appropriations Committee to add a limited amount to present legislation to help meet part of this new cost until a supplemental measure is ready and hearings can be held when the Congress assembles in January. In the meantime, we will use the authority contained in the present Defense appropriation bill under consideration to transfer funds in addition to the additional money that we will ask.

These steps, like our actions in the past, are carefully measured to do what must be done to bring an end to aggression and a peaceful settlement.

We do not want an expanding struggle with consequences that no one can perceive, nor will we bluster or bully or flaunt our power, but we will not surrender and we will not retreat.

For behind our American pledge lies the determination and resources, I believe, of all of the American Nation.

Second, once the Communists know, as we know, that a violent solution is impossible, then a peaceful solution is inevitable.

We are ready now, as we have always been, to move from the battlefield to the conference table. I have stated publicly and many times, again and again, America's willingness to begin unconditional discussions with any government, at any place, at any time. Fifteen efforts have been made to start these discussions with the help of 40 nations throughout the world, but there has been no answer.

But we are going to continue to persist, if persist we must, until death and desolation have led to the same conference table where others could now join us at a much smaller cost.

I have spoken many times of our objectives in Viet-Nam. So has the Government of South Viet-Nam. Hanoi has set forth its own proposals. We are ready to discuss their proposals and our proposals and any proposals of any government whose people may be affected, for we fear the meeting room no more than we fear the battlefield.

In this pursuit we welcome and we ask for the concern and the assistance of any nation and all nations. If the United Nations and its officials or any one of its 114 members can by deed or word, private initiative or public action, bring us nearer an honorable peace, then they will have the support and the gratitude of the United States of America.

I have directed Ambassador Goldberg to go to New York today and to present immediately to Secretary General U Thant a letter from me requesting that all the resources, energy, and immense prestige of the United Nations be employed to find ways to halt aggression and to bring peace in Viet-Nam.

I made a similar request at San Francisco a few weeks ago, because we do not seek the destruction of any government, nor do we covet a foot of any territory. But we insist and we will always insist that the people of South Viet-Nam shall have the right of choice, the right to shape their own destiny in free elections in the South or throughout all Viet-Nam under international supervision, and they shall not have any government imposed upon them by force and terror so long as we can prevent it.

This was the purpose of the 1954 agreements which the Communists have now cruelly shattered. If the machinery of those agreements was tragically weak, its purposes still guide our action. As battle rages, we will continue as best we can to help the good people of South Viet-Nam enrich the condition of their life, to feed the hungry and to tend the sick, and teach the young, and shelter the homeless, and to help the farmer to increase his crops, and the worker to find a job.

It is an ancient but still terrible irony that while many leaders of men create division in pursuit of grand ambitions, the children of man are really united in the simple, elusive desire for a life of fruitful and rewarding toil.

As I said at Johns Hopkins in Baltimore, I hope that one day we can help all the people of Asia toward that desire. Eugene Black has made great progress since my appearance in Baltimore in that direction—not as the price of peace, for we are ready always to bear a more painful cost, but rather as a part of our obligations of justice toward our fellow man.

Let me also add now a personal note. I do not find it easy to send the flower of our youth, our finest young men, into battle. I have spoken to you today of the divisions and the forces and the battalions and the units, but I know them all, every one. I have seen them in a thousand streets, of a hundred towns, in every State in this Union—working and laughing and building, and filled with hope and life. I think I know, too, how their mothers weep and how their families sorrow.

This is the most agonizing and the most painful duty of your President.

There is something else, too. When I was young, poverty was so common that we didn't know it had a name. An education was something that you had to fight for, and water was really life itself. I have now been in public life 35 years, more than three decades, and in each of those 35 years I have seen good men, and wise leaders, struggle to bring the blessings of this land to all of our people.

And now I am the President. It is now my opportunity to help every child get an education, to help every Negro and every American citizen have an equal opportunity, to have every family get a decent home, and to help bring healing to the sick and dignity to the old.

As I have said before, that is what I have lived for, that is what I have wanted all my life since I was a little boy, and I do not want to see all those hopes and all those dreams of so many people for so many years now drowned in the wasteful ravages of cruel wars. I am going to do all I can do to see that that never happens.

But I also know, as a realistic public servant, that as long as there are men who hate and destroy, we must have the courage to resist, or we will see it all, all that we have built, all that we hope to build, all of our dreams for freedom—all, all will be swept away on the flood of conquest.

So, too, this shall not happen. We will stand in Viet-Nam.

Document Analysis

President Johnson begins this speech with a reference to a letter in which a woman had asked why it was necessary for her son to be serving in Vietnam. In response, Johnson says that he had tried to answer that question in many places and at many times. He admits that the answer is not an easy one, and that the war is difficult to understand. He refers to lessons he believes can be found in the nation's past. Three times in his own lifetime—World War I, World War II, and Korea—American forces had gone to "far lands to fight for freedom." Johnson believed that these previous experiences had taught that aggression had to be met with force. Like many Cold War-era American politicians and policy makers, Johnson believed that the appeasement of Hitler's demands for territory in the years leading up to

World War II had only led to further aggression. Now, Johnson believes that the People's Republic of China is intent on dominating Southeast Asia and is supporting the communist forces fighting in Vietnam. He believes that this attempted aggression should not be appeased and that the United States had to make a stand in Vietnam. Johnson also argues that the US had to honor commitments made to aid the Republic of Vietnam (the formal name of South Vietnam). If America did not keep these commitments, no other nation in the future would be able to have confidence in promises made by the US government.

Johnson admits that it is difficult to order young Americans into combat. He also feared that this foreign war could detract attention from his domestic reform agenda. Johnson promised to do all he could to see that this did not happen, but he also believed that the United States had to meet the communist threat in Vietnam. Later in this address, Johnson announces that he has approved the request of the American commander in Vietnam for additional US ground troops. While not noted in Johnson's speech, with this commitment of large-scale forces, the United States moved from the role of advising and assisting the Republic of Vietnam to a position of carrying out most of the fighting, as assisted by South Vietnamese forces. Once this fundamental change of policy had been made, the US presence in Vietnam grew dramatically. From the approximately 75,000 US personnel in Vietnam at the time of this speech, the number would increase to more than a half-million by the time Johnson left office in January 1969.

Essential Themes

Two themes prominent in President Johnson's address are resolve in the face of a challenge, even though there may be a measure of reluctance in considering the matter. He notes his reluctance to send "the flower of our youth, our finest young men into battle," and he also says that taking this action is "the most agonizing and painful duty" he has faced as president. Yet despite this reluctance, Johnson speaks of a resolve to do whatever he and the others in his administration believed was necessary. Referring to the lessons of pre-World War II Europe, he argues that aggression left unchecked would only become more expansive and destructive. Johnson believed that the stakes were high in Vietnam and that a victory by communist forces in South Vietnam would lead to further communist advances throughout Southeast Asia.

Johnson also emphasizes the theme that the war in Vietnam is a different kind of war, one that is perhaps difficult to understand. After the massive effort by the US and its allies in World War II, in which "unconditional surrender" by the enemy was the only acceptable course, the present war was a limited one aiming at limited objectives; there were no clear-cut battle lines. He also makes a slight reference to the fact that the fighting in Vietnam was at least in part a civil war, as he notes that some citizens of South Vietnam had joined in the fight against their own government.

A theme that was very close to Johnson's own heart was his fear that this war could derail efforts toward social reform and expanded justice at home. Johnson speaks of the hard times he had witnessed in his youth. Now, as president, he has an opportunity to address many of the problems of poverty, access to education, and equal opportunity, but he fears that the war may take attention away from these domestic issues. Many scholars would argue that this was one of the great tragedies of the Vietnam War—that the divisiveness the war brought to American society indeed had the effect of limiting progress on Johnson's "Great Society" reforms.

—*Mark S. Joy, PhD*

Bibliography and Additional Reading

Gardner, Lloyd C. *Pay Any Price: Lyndon Johnson and the Wars for Vietnam.* Chicago: Ivan R. Dee, 1995. Print.

Herring, George C. *LBJ and Vietnam: A Different Kind of War.* Austin: University of Texas Press, 1996. Print.

Johnson, Lyndon B. *The Vantage Point: Perspectives on the Presidency, 1963–1969.* New York: Holt, Rinehart and Winston, 1971. Print.

Kaiser, David. *American Tragedy: Kennedy, Johnson, and the Origins of the Vietnam War.* Cambridge, MA: The Belknap Press of Harvard University Press, 2000. Print.

VanDeMark, Brian. *Into the Quagmire: Lyndon Johnson and the Escalation of the Vietnam War.* New York: Oxford University Press, 1995. Print.

■ A Recommendation for Troop Increases

Date: November 30, 1965
Author: Robert McNamara
Genre: memorandum

Summary Overview

Although President Lyndon Baines Johnson shouldered much of the blame for the war in Vietnam, it was Secretary of Defense Robert McNamara who holds the most responsibility. A brilliant statistician and manager, McNamara has often been described as the architect of the Vietnam War. It was his insistence throughout the 1960s that escalation would bring about ultimate American victory, which led first to the sustained bombing campaign of the north and, later, to the deployment of over half a million troops in the south. Unlike many of the other hawks advising Johnson, McNamara was, at least for a time, a true believer in both his mission and his strategy. The United States would win, he insisted, if only enough American troops were sent into the fight. His strategy is best exemplified in a memo he penned in November 1965, which became the overall strategy for the first phase of the war in Vietnam.

Defining Moment

After initially refusing to commit American military forces to the growing conflict in Vietnam, in early 1965, President Johnson launched a series of bombing operations against the north. Following a strategy of "sustained retaliation" as outlined by National Security Advisor McGeorge Bundy, the United States Air Force began bombing North Vietnam, along with parts of Cambodia and Laos, as a means by which to demoralize the enemy and force them into surrender. As part of the strategy, bombing operations would halt for days or weeks at a time as a means to give the North Vietnamese time to negotiate (a fact that was not communicated to the North Vietnamese).

Soon after, as Viet Cong forces began launching attacks on American air force bases, Johnson sent 3,500 Marines to defend American personnel. This was the first time American troops were introduced into Vietnam in a non-advisory capacity. As throughout the summer of 1965, South Vietnamese forces were repeatedly

defeated by military elements from the north, and with American ground forces already having been introduced in the south, the military leadership began to press the White House for ever larger troop commitments. The argument coming from most in the military, especially General William Westmoreland, commander of all American military forces in Vietnam, was that only through offensive measures could the United States hope to achieve victory in Southeast Asia. The American military, it was argued, could not sustain a solely defensive position for long. Westmoreland favored a strategy by which the United States would push the South Vietnamese back and take the lead in combat operations, thus putting the unmatched power of the United States directly against North Vietnamese forces. He was so convinced of the soundness of this strategy that he predicted total victory by the end of 1967.

Perhaps the biggest advocate of this approach within the cabinet was Secretary of Defense Robert McNamara. Long a proponent of using military strength as a means by which to defeat communism, McNamara used the same kind of statistical analysis in his approach to Vietnam, as he had used in his capacity to plan bombing operations against the Japanese in World War II. Creating several mathematical models, he concluded that if American forces were able to inflict a significant amount of casualties on the North Vietnamese, which he believed had a very limited number of troops, the war could be won in a matter of two to three years. To add weight to his argument, McNamara travelled to Southeast Asia in late 1965. Upon his return he set out his strategy in a memo to the president, which would, eventually, become the primary plan by which the United States would fight a ground war in Vietnam.

Author Biography

Robert S. McNamara was born in California in 1916. After attending the University of California at Berkeley, he went on to get an MBA from Harvard Business School. During World War II, he worked under Major General Curtis LeMay in the Office of Statistical Control, analyzing the effectiveness of Allied bombing on enemy cities. After the war, McNamara joined the Ford Motor Company as one of the ten so-called "whiz kids" and eventually rose to become the youngest CEO in the company's history. In 1960, he was appointed secretary of defense, first under Kennedy and then under Johnson, and made great efforts to restructure the military. McNamara was instrumental in some of the most important events of the Cold War, including the Bay of Pigs invasion, the Cuban Missile Crisis, and of course the Vietnam War, of which he was considered to be the chief architect. McNamara eventually resigned his post as the war soon proved unwinnable. In 1968, he was appointed to the World Bank, where he served as President until 1981. He died in 2009.

HISTORICAL DOCUMENT

Washington, *November 30, 1965.*

This is a supplement to my memorandum to you dated November 3. This memorandum incorporates the implications of events since then and information gained on General Wheeler's and my visit with Ambassador Lodge, Admiral Sharp and General Westmoreland in Vietnam on November 28–29.

1. Introductory comments. Before giving my assessment of the situation and recommendations, I want to report that United States personnel in Vietnam are performing admirably. The massive Cam Ranh Bay complex has sprung into operation since our last visit in July; the troops that we visited (the 173rd Airborne Brigade and the 1st Cavalry Division) have fought and are fighting well and their morale is high; and the team in Saigon is working harmoniously.

2. The situation. There has been no substantial change since my November 3 memorandum in the economic, political or pacification situation. There is a serious threat of inflation because of the mixture of US force build-up and GVN deficit on the one hand and the tightly stretched Vietnamese economy on the other; the Ky "government of generals" is surviving, but not acquiring wide support or generating actions; pacification is thoroughly stalled, with no guarantee that security anywhere is permanent and no indications that able and willing leadership will emerge in the absence of that permanent security. (Prime Minister Ky estimates his government controls only 25% of the population today and reports that his pacification chief hopes to increase that to 50% two years from now.)

The dramatic recent changes in the situation are on the military side. They are the increased infiltration from the North and the increased willingness of the Communist forces to stand and fight, even in large-scale engagements. The Ia Drang River Campaign of early November is an example. The Communists appear to have decided to increase their forces in South Vietnam both by heavy recruitment in the South (especially in the Delta) and by infiltration of regular North Vietnamese forces from the North. Nine regular North Vietnamese regiments (27 infantry battalions) have been infiltrated in the past year, joining the estimated 83 VC battalions in the South. The rate of infiltration has increased from three battalion equivalents a month in late 1964 to a high of 9 or 12 during one month this past fall. General Westmoreland estimates that through 1966 North Vietnam will have the capability to expand its armed forces in order to infiltrate three regiments (nine battalion equivalents, or 4500 men) a month, and that the VC in South Vietnam can train seven new battalion equivalents a month—together adding 16 battalion equivalents a month to the enemy forces. Communist casualties and desertions can be expected to go up if my recommendations for increased US, South Vietnamese and third country forces are accepted. Nevertheless, the enemy can be expected to enlarge his present strength of 110 battalion equivalents to more than 150 battalion equivalents by the end of calendar 1966, when hopefully his losses can be made to equal his input.

As for the Communist ability to supply this force, it is estimated that, even taking account of interdiction of routes by air and sea, more than 200 tons of supplies a day can be infiltrated—more than enough, allowing for the extent to which the enemy lives off the land, to support the likely PAVN/VC force at the likely level of operations.

To meet this possible—and in my view likely—Communist build-up, the presently contemplated Phase I forces will not be enough. Phase I forces, almost all in place by the end of this year, involve 130 South Vietnamese, 9 Korean, 1 Australian and 34 US combat battalions (approximately 220,000 Americans). Bearing in mind the nature of the war, the expected weighted combat force ratio of less than 2-to-1 will not be good enough. Nor will the originally contemplated Phase II addition of 28 more US battalions (112,000 men) be enough; the combat force ratio, even with 32 new South Vietnamese battalions, would still be little better than 2-to-1 at the end of 1966. The initiative which we have held since August would pass to the enemy; we would fall far short of what we expected to achieve in terms of population control and disruption of enemy bases and lines of communications. Indeed, it is estimated that, with the contemplated Phase II addition of 28 US battalions, we would be able only to hold our present geographical positions.

3. Military options and recommendations. We have but two options, it seems to me. One is to go now for a compromise solution (something substantially less than the "favorable outcome" I described in my memorandum of November 3), and hold further deployments to a minimum. The other is to stick with our stated objectives and with the war, and provide what it takes in men and materiel. If it is decided not to move now toward a compromise, I recommend that the United States both send a substantial number of additional troops and very gradually intensify the bombing of North Vietnam. Ambassador Lodge, General Wheeler, Admiral Sharp and General Westmoreland concur in this pronged course of action, although General Wheeler and Admiral Sharp would intensify the bombing of the North more quickly.

a. Troop deployments. With respect to additional forces in South Vietnam to maintain the initiative against the growing Communist forces, I recommend:

1. That the Republic of Korea be requested to increase their present deployment of nine com-

bat battalions to 18 combat battalions (the addition of one division) before July 1966 and to 21 combat battalions (the addition of another brigade) before October 1966.

2. That the Government of Australia be requested to increase their present deployment of one combat battalion to two combat battalions before October 1966.

3. That the deployment of US ground troops be increased by the end of 1966 from 34 combat battalions to 74 combat battalions.

4. That the FY '67 Budget for the Defense Department and the January Supplement to the FY '66 Budget be revised to reflect the expansion of US forces required to support the additional deployments.

The 74 US battalions—together with increases in air squadrons, naval units, air defense, combat support, construction units and miscellaneous logistic support and advisory personnel which I also recommend—would bring the total US personnel in Vietnam to approximately 400,000 by the end of 1966. And it should be understood that further deployments (perhaps exceeding 200,000) may be needed in 1967.

b. Bombing of North Vietnam. With respect to the program of bombing North Vietnam, I recommend that we maintain present levels of activity in the three quadrants west and south of Hanoi, but that over a period of the next six months we gradually enlarge the target system in the northeast (Hanoi-Haiphong) quadrant until, at the end of the period, it includes "controlled" armed reconnaissance of lines of communication throughout the area, bombing of petroleum storage facilities and power plants, and mining of the harbors. (Left unstruck would be population targets, industrial plants, locks and dams.)

4. Pause in bombing North Vietnam. It is my belief that there should be a three- or four-week pause in the program of bombing the North before we either greatly increase our troop deployments to Vietnam or intensify our strikes against the North. The reasons for this belief are, first, that we must lay a foundation in the mind of

the American public and in world opinion for such an enlarged phase of the war and, second, we should give North Vietnam a face-saving chance to stop the aggression. I am not seriously concerned about the risk of alienating the South Vietnamese, misleading Hanoi, or being "trapped" in a pause; if we take reasonable precautions, we can avoid these pitfalls. I am seriously concerned about embarking on a markedly higher level of war in Vietnam without having tried, through a pause, to end the war or at least having made it clear to our people that we did our best to end it.

5. Evaluation. We should be aware that deployments of the kind I have recommended will not guarantee success. US killed-in-action can be expected to reach 1000 a month, and the odds are even that we will be faced in early 1967 with a "no-decision" at an even higher level. My overall evaluation, nevertheless, is that the best chance of achieving our stated objectives lies in a pause followed, if it fails, by the deployments mentioned above.

Robert S. McNamara

GLOSSARY

battalion: a large body of troops

GVN: Government of North Vietnam

pacification: the forcible eliminate of a hostile population

Saigon: capital of South Vietnam

VC: Viet Cong, or communist forces in the south

Document Analysis

McNamara begins by stating that American forces in South Vietnam are performing well. Operations conducted by the United States military have been successful. However, the South Vietnamese government and military apparatus are unequal to the task before them. McNamara cites several examples of poor decisions and poor performance. The South Vietnamese government, he informs Johnson, only has the support of some 25 percent of the population. The North Vietnamese, he reports, are launching successful attacks on the south and have greatly increased the size of their army. In addition, Viet Cong forces operating throughout the south have continued to grow. Unless the American presence in Vietnam is expanded, North Vietnam's power will continue to grow unchecked. McNamara makes it clear: if the North Vietnamese build-up is to be stopped, and if the United States is to hold the momentum, additional American troops must be sent to Vietnam at once.

His recommendation is for a substantial troop increase and an escalation of the bombing campaigns already underway. By the end of 1966, McNamara estimates, American ground troops should number 400,000, with an additional 200,000 to come the following year. Bombing should be escalated and additional targets, including civilian targets, should be identified. The United States Air Force would first halt all operations for a number of weeks, as a means to allow North Vietnam to possibly seek peace and for the American public to accept the escalation, followed by an intensification of attack.

Primary in all of this, McNamara emphasizes, is public opinion both at home and abroad. A pause would also give people the perception that the United States government was making a good faith effort toward peace. However, it is the last part of McNamara's memo that is most interesting. In his final evaluation, he states that extra deployments will not guarantee success and that American casualties might reach 1,000 a month. However, in the end, he reasons, there is no greater strategy for success. Will sending ground troops be risky? Yes. Will it guarantee victory? No. But, in McNamara's mind, the potential benefits outweigh the risks. The

United States must win in Vietnam, and troop escalation is the only definite way to achieve it.

Essential Themes

In the mid-1960s, Robert McNamara was a true believer. A seasoned Cold War warrior, who had stared down the Soviets during the Cuban Missile Crisis, he traveled to Vietnam and weighed all the options. Escalation was, in his mind, the only option. Using the same dehumanizing statistical models that perfected bombing runs on Japanese cities in World War II, the secretary of defense came to agree with the military leadership that the best way to achieve victory in Southeast Asia was through a war of attrition. When faced with the unchecked spread of communism, a thousand dead Americans every month was a small price to pay. In 1965, he lay out his strategy recommendations in a memo to President Johnson, a series of initiatives that were approved in the weeks and months to come: 400,000 troops by the end of 1966 and more to follow after.

As several thousand American troops became several hundred thousand, the cost of the war became ever bloodier, and withdraw became ever more difficult. The year 1965 gave way to 1966, then on to 1967, with no end in sight. As the number of American dead increased, McNamara became ever more disillusioned with the war he helped to create. More and more, he began to countermand the orders of the generals on the ground and, privately and publically, began to doubt America's chances for victory. In late 1967, he recommended a freeze on more American troop increases and a complete stop to all bombing operations against North Vietnam. It was too little too late. President Johnson rejected the recommendations. Not even McNamara, it seemed, could stop the machine he helped start. Increasingly criticized by the media, and marginalized in the White House for his shift, McNamara resigned his post as secretary of defense in November of that year. He would go on to serve as president of the World Bank and transform international nuclear policy; but until the end of his days, it would be the Vietnam War that would remain his greatest and most enduring legacy.

—KP Dawes, MA

Bibliography and Additional Reading

Herring, George. *America's Longest War*. New York: McGraw-Hill, 1996. Print.

McNamara, Robert & Brian VanDeMark. *In Retrospect: The Tragedy and Lessons of Vietnam*. New York: Random House, 1995. Print.

VanDeMark, Brian. *Into the Quagmire: Lyndon Johnson and the Escalation of the Vietnam War*. New York: Oxford University Press, 1995. Print.

■ General Westmoreland on Military Operations

Date: August 26, 1966
Author: William C. Westmoreland
Genre: report

Summary Overview

General William C. Westmoreland wrote this report to be included as part of an extensive memorandum from the Joint Chiefs of Staff to Secretary of Defense Robert McNamara. As chief commander of the US Military Assistance Command—Vietnam (MACV), Westmoreland was the highest ranking military officer in Vietnam. In this report, he summarized the current strength of enemy forces, the status of US military operations, and his plans for going forward in the next several months. Westmoreland believed that US operations in Vietnam were on the verge of a "new phase," where the buildup of US forces, combined with continued air support and the use of the best military technology, would lead to greater success than had been the case in the past. However, he was guarded in his optimism and admitted that the communist forces were a formidable enemy that was resolute and highly motivated to maintain their military resistance.

Defining Moment

Westmoreland became commander of MACV in June 1964. The first US ground combat troops came to Vietnam in the spring of 1965, followed by substantially larger forces the following summer. In this report, written a little over a year later, Westmoreland addressed what he believed had been accomplished and what the prospects for the immediate future might be.

The immediate context of this report involved a massive study undertaken by the Army on the course of the war. The chief of staff of the Army, General Harold K. Johnson, had ordered this study, which was completed in March 1966. The study, which ran to over 900 pages, was known as "A Program for the Pacification and Long-Term Development of South Vietnam," usually referred to by the acronym PROVN. Westmoreland's document, which was a top-secret cable sent from Vietnam, was an attachment to a summary of the PROVN study that was sent from the Joint Chiefs of Staff to Secretary of

Defense Robert McNamara. In the introduction to the PROVN study, Army staffers had argued that the situation in South Vietnam had "seriously deteriorated" and that 1966 might be the last chance the US had to rectify the situation and achieve eventual success. Many of the military and political leaders of that time, in retrospect, saw this period in a similar light. The commitment of large numbers of US ground combat troops had changed the nature of the war; US troops were no longer simply advising and assisting South Vietnamese forces, but were now doing much of the fighting themselves.

Building up the logistical support for such a large number of troops had taken time, but by the summer of 1966, American forces were undertaking large-scale missions with some success. Westmoreland wrote that the war was entering a "new phase" and many at the time agreed. But in the long run, these signs of progress were misleading. As Westmoreland admitted in this document, the enemy's resolve did not seem to be weakening. As American troop levels were raised, the enemy matched the numbers. The attempts to build a stable government in the Republic of Vietnam that had the support of its own people proved futile. At home, public opinion became more sharply divided over the war, and the number of people who supported negotiations to end the war was growing. Even some members of Johnson's own administration were losing hope that the war could be brought to an acceptably positive conclusion any time soon.

Author Biography

William C. Westmoreland was born in Saxon, South Carolina, on March 26, 1914. After graduating from The Citadel, a state-supported military college in Charleston, South Carolina, he attended the US Military Academy at West Point. During World War II, he served in the campaigns for North Africa, Sicily, and

Italy. During the Korean War, where he commanded an airborne unit, he was promoted to Brigadier General. He was the commandant of West Point from 1960 to 1963. In January 1964, he was sent to Vietnam to serve as a deputy under General Paul D. Harkins of Military Assistance Command (MACV), and subsequently, he succeeded Harkins in that position. He was promoted to General (four-star rank) on August 1, 1964. In the spring of 1968, Westmoreland was appointed chief of staff of the US Army. He retired from the Army in 1972. In 1982, he filed a libel suit against CBS concerning a documentary that charged that Westmoreland had deliberately understated enemy strength in Vietnam, but withdrew the suit when CBS agreed to issue a clarifying statement. Westmoreland died in a retirement home in Charleston, South Carolina, on July 18, 2005.

HISTORICAL DOCUMENT

In order to promote a better understanding of the role which military operations play in the overall effort in South Vietnam, I discern a need at this time to review the military situation in South Vietnam as it relates to our concepts; past, present and future. This is an appropriate time in light of the fact that we are on the threshold of a new phase in the conflict resulting from our recent battlefield successes and from the continuing US/Free World military buildup.

The enemy has launched a determined campaign to gain control of South Vietnam—its land, its people, and its government. There are no indications that the enemy has reduced his resolve. He has increased his rate of infiltration, formed divisions in South Vietnam, introduced new weapons, and maintained his lines of communications into South Vietnam in spite of our increased air efforts. He continues to use Laos and the border regions of Cambodia as sanctuaries and recently moved a division through the Demilitarized Zone (DMZ) into the First Corps Tactical Zone. His campaign of terror, assassination, intimidation, sabotage, propaganda and guerilla warfare continues unabated. The enemy still holds sway over large segments of the land and population. Although thwarted in his overt large scale campaign, he is still determined.

As a companion of the foregoing appreciation of the present enemy situation, a review of our strategic concept for the past year would appear to be useful.

A. During the period 1 May 1965 to 1 November 1965, our task was to build up our combat and logistical forces; learn to employ them effectively; gain confidence in ourselves in fighting in the counterinsurgency and Southeast Asian environment; gain the trust of the Vietnamese in our military skills, courage and ability; and protect our installations and forces from distraction by the enemy.

B. During the period 1 November 1965 to 1 May 1966, our objectives were to extend our deployments toward the frontiers; exercise our logistics in furnishing support to troops in sustained combat; indoctrinate commanders on the techniques of sustained ground combat; interdict intensively by air the lines of communications leading from North Vietnam to South Vietnam; disrupt enemy bases by B–52 strikes; deny the enemy rice by protecting harvests and capturing caches in storage areas; increase our surveillance along the coast; and initiate a program of patrolling certain vital inland waterways. In summary, our purpose was to disrupt the enemy's effort to prepare his battlefield, to throw his plans off balance by offensive operations, and to continue to gain experience and self-confidence in this environment.

C. During the period 1 May to 1 November 1966—the Southwest monsoon season—our strategy has been and is to contain the enemy through offensive tactical operations (referred to as "spoiling attacks" because they catch the enemy in the preparation phases of his offensives), force him to fight under conditions of our choosing, and deny him attainment of his own tactical objectives. At the same time we have utilized all forces that could be made available for area and population security in support of revolutionary development, rice harvests heretofore available to the enemy have been protected, lines of communication required by us have been opened, and some of the inland waterways used by the enemy have been interdicted to disrupt his communication and supply systems. The threat of the enemy main forces (Viet Cong and North Vietnamese Army) has been of such magnitude that fewer friendly troops could be devoted to general area security and support of revolutionary development than visualized at the time our plans were prepared for the period.

During the period 1 November 1966 to 1 May 1967—the Northeast monsoon season—we will maintain and increase the momentum of our operations. Our strategy will be one of a general offensive with maximum practical support to area and population security in further support of revolutionary development.

A. The essential tasks of revolutionary development and nation building cannot be accomplished if enemy main forces can gain access to the population centers and destroy our efforts. US/Free World forces, with their mobility and in coordination with Vietnamese Armed Forces, must take the fight to the enemy by attacking his main forces and invading his base areas. Our ability to do this is improving steadily. Maximum emphasis will be given to the use of long range patrols and other means to find the enemy and locate his bases. Forces and bases thus discovered will be subjected to either ground attack or quick reaction B–52 and tactical air strikes. When feasible, B–52 strikes will be followed by ground forces to search the area. Sustained ground combat operations will maintain pressure on the enemy.

B. The growing strength of US/Free World forces will provide the shield that will permit ARVN to shift its weight of effort to an extent not heretofore feasible to direct support of revolutionary development. Also, I visualize that a significant number of the US/Free World Maneuver Battalions will be committed to Tactical Areas of Responsibility (TOAR) missions. These missions encompass base security and at the same time support revolutionary development by spreading security radially from the bases to protect more of the population. Saturation patrolling, civic action, and close association with ARVN, regional and popular forces to bolster their combat effectiveness are among the tasks of the ground force elements. At the same time ARVN troops will be available if required to reinforce offensive operations and to serve as reaction forces for outlying security posts and government centers under attack. Our strategy will include opening, constructing and using roads, as well as a start toward opening and reconstructing the National Railroad. The priority effort of ARVN forces will be in direct support of the revolutionary development program; in many instances, the province chief will exercise operational control over these units. This fact not-withstanding, the ARVN division structure must be maintained and it is essential that the division commander enthusiastically support revolutionary development. Our highly capable US division commanders, who are closely associated with corresponding ARVN commanders, are in a position to influence them to do what is required.

C. We intend to employ all forces to get the best results, measured, among other things, in terms of population secured; territory cleared of enemy influence; Viet Cong/North Vietnamese Army bases eliminated; and enemy guerrillas, local forces, and main forces destroyed.

D. Barring unforeseen change in enemy strategy, I visualize that our strategy for South Vietnam will remain essentially the same throughout 1967.

In summation, the MACV mission, which is to assist the Government of Vietnam to defeat the Viet Cong/North Vietnamese Army forces and extend Government control throughout South Vietnam, prescribes our two principal tasks.

We must defeat the enemy through offensive operations against his main forces and bases.

We must assist the Government to gain control of the people by providing direct military support of revolutionary development in coordination with the other agencies of the U.S. Mission.

The simultaneous accomplishment of these tasks is required to allow the people of South Vietnam to get on with the job of nation building.

Ambassador Lodge concurs, with the following comment:

"I wish to stress my agreement with the attention paid in this message to the importance of military support for revolutionary development. After all, the main purpose of defeating the enemy through offensive operations against his main forces and bases must be to provide the opportunity through revolutionary development to get at the heart of the matter, which is the population of South Vietnam. If this goal is achieved, we will be denying manpower and other support to the Viet Cong."

Document Analysis

In this memo, General Westmoreland reviewed the military situation in Vietnam as it related to the "overall effort" of US forces there. US goals in Vietnam were not strictly military; there were social and political missions as well—to help the Republic of Vietnam establish a stable internal government with the support of its own people. One of the methods used to pursue this goal was often labelled "revolutionary development and nation building." These terms referred to efforts to pacify the civilian population of South Vietnam and to dissuade them from supporting the communist forces. These efforts also included constructing needed infrastructure so that the people could see benefits from supporting their government. Westmoreland believed these missions were important, but also noted that they could not succeed without sustained military progress. As more US and "Free World" forces entered the war, Westmoreland envisioned that ARVN forces (Army of the Republic of Vietnam) could shift to the work of revolutionary development. "Free World" forces refers to other nations involved in Vietnam, such as substantial numbers of troops from Australia and the Republic of Korea (South Korea).

Westmoreland described a number of tactical missions that US forces had been involved in and would continue throughout the rest of 1966 and into the following year. These tactics included a number of defensive and offensive measures. In the early days of the buildup of US forces, much effort was devoted to providing the logistical support needed for such a large number of troops and for the defense of US bases and of large civilian population centers. As the US forces were more firmly established, more offensive operations were undertaken, specifically, attacks on known enemy

bases or large concentrations of troops. Involving both ground troops and large-scale air support, these "spoiling attacks" were designed to disrupt planned enemy offensives and represented efforts to deny the enemy access to key resources, such as rice. Westmoreland summarized the US efforts as consisting of two main tasks: defeating the enemy forces through offensive operations and supporting the government of the Republic of Vietnam in gaining the support of the population through programs such as revolutionary development. While Westmoreland's report exhibits an overall tone of can-do-it optimism, he also realistically assessed the enemy's tenacity and resolve to resist.

Attached to Westmoreland's report was a statement of support from Henry Cabot Lodge, the American ambassador to the Republic of Vietnam. Lodge seconded the connection between military operations and revolutionary development; offensive operations against the enemy would provide the security for revolutionary development programs to be pursued.

Essential Themes

A key theme that runs through Westmoreland's report is a note of guarded optimism. In the aftermath of the Vietnam War, Westmoreland has often been both praised and vilified as the quintessential American general—one who had a firm faith that the American military could succeed in carrying out the tasks that the elected leaders of the nation had assigned them. While written in a rather formal, detached style, this document betrays no sense of any despair or doubt about the military's ultimate success. Westmoreland notes that, during the early days of the buildup of US forces, much effort was devoted to building the bases and logistical framework required; but, with these forces now suitably supplied and equipped, he suggests that the war was moving into a new phase.

At the same time, Westmoreland considered the communist forces to be a formidable enemy. He refers in the memo to their resolve and determination and admits that, even as US and Free World forces increased their presence in Vietnam, the enemy also increased the rate of infiltration of forces from North Vietnam and that they still controlled "large segments of the land and population." He also admits that enemy strength and pressure was greater than anticipated, and therefore, the goal of directing the ARVN forces more into the work of revolutionary development has not yet been achieved.

In the years since the conclusion of the Vietnam War, Westmoreland has often been associated with the use of "search and destroy" missions and a commitment to attrition (the gradual wearing down of the enemy's forces) as the major goal of military operations. Interestingly, neither of these terms appear in this document. Likewise, Westmoreland has often been critiqued for focusing on the military operations and the "body count" of enemy dead and ignoring the social and political aspect of the war. But in this document, he makes repeated references to the goals of "revolutionary development and nation building," and sees military operations and offensive success as providing the essential shield that will allow these efforts to proceed without disruption by the enemy.

—*Mark S. Joy, PhD*

Bibliography and Additional Reading

Birtle, Andrew J. "PROVN, Westmoreland, and the Historians: A Reappraisal." *The Journal of Military History* 72.4 (October 2008): 1213–1247.

Carland, John M. "Winning the Vietnam War: Westmoreland's Approach in Two Documents." *The Journal of Military History* 68.2 (April 2004): 553–574.

Sorley, Lewis. *Westmoreland: The General Who Lost Vietnam.* New York: Houghton Mifflin Harcourt, 2011.

Westmoreland, William C. *A Soldier Reports.* Garden City, NY: Doubleday, 1976.

Zaffiri, Samuel. *Westmoreland: A Biography of General William C. Westmoreland.* New York: William Morrow, 1994.

■ "No Attractive Course of Action"

Date: May 19, 1967
Author: Robert S. McNamara
Genre: memorandum

Summary Overview

Six years into his tenure as secretary of defense, Robert McNamara, one of the main architects of the Vietnam War, sent this memorandum to President Lyndon B. Johnson. It details a request by US military commanders for more troops before it moves to an argument arguing such a proposal. While acknowledging recent military successes, the memo's author takes a pessimistic view with respect to a troop surge, holding that it will not have any real effect on American prospects in Vietnam. Ultimately, Johnson failed to heed his secretary of defense's advice, and McNamara went on to announce his resignation by the end of that year. The momentum of the war continued to rise, and the conflict, in the end, lasted for eight more years.

Defining Moment

In the spring of 1967, American's involvement in Vietnam was still on the ascent. The growth of a US military presence in the region began under the Kennedy administration and vastly escalated under Lyndon B. Johnson. On August 7, 1964, five days after the Gulf of Tonkin Incident, Congress passed the Gulf of Tonkin Resolution, awarding the president the military power "to take all necessary measures to repel any armed attack against the forces of the United States and to prevent further aggression." In early 1965, President Johnson began the long-term bombing campaign known as Operation Rolling Thunder. That year also saw the first purely offensive actions into enemy territory and the first major battle of the war. American troops continued to increase until reaching over 385,000 men on the ground by the end of 1966, more than ten times the amount at the end of 1964.

Even at this relatively early stage, the war was becoming unpopular among many in the American pub-lic. McNamara's enthusiasm likewise had begun to wane. As secretary of defense, he ushered in the escalation of the American engagement in Vietnam, and yet in this memorandum, we see evidence of his increasing skepticism. Later, in November 1967, he sent another memorandum calling for a more drastic (and more specific) reversal of military policy. Johnson rejected the proposals outright, and McNamara resigned shortly thereafter. As for the American public, by 1968 both the Tet Offensive (a major communist surge in South Vietnam) and the My Lai Massacre (the slaughter of civilians there) only increased antiwar sentiments.

Author Biography

Robert S. McNamara was born June 9, 1916 in San Francisco, California. He obtained a bachelor's degree in economics from the University of California in Berkeley in 1937 and a master's degree from the Harvard Business School in 1939. In early 1943, he entered the United State Air Force. Disqualified from combat duty owing to his poor eyesight, he served the majority of the war's remainder in the Office of Statistical Control. Ford Motor Company hired him as one of the so-called "whiz kids," and he rose in the ranks until becoming president in 1960, the first president of the company from outside the Ford family. Shortly thereafter, John F. Kennedy appointed him as secretary of defense. He served seven years in that post, the longest tenure of any secretary of defense to date. He oversaw the escalation of America's military engagement in Vietnam before growing skeptical of the war, as attested to in this memorandum. At the end of 1967, following President Johnson's refusal of another memorandum, McNamara announced his resignation. He became president of the World Bank, a position that he held until 1981. He died in 2009 at the age of 93.

HISTORICAL DOCUMENT

General Westmoreland and Admiral Sharp have requested 200,000 additional men (100,000 as soon as possible with the remainder probably required in FY 1969) and 13 additional tactical air squadrons for South Vietnam. The program they propose would require Congressional action authorizing a call-up of the Reserves, the addition of approximately 500,000 men to our military forces, and an increase of approximately $10 billion in the FY 68 Defense budget. It would involve the virtual certainty of irresistible pressures for ground actions against "sanctuaries" in Cambodia and Laos; for intensification of the air campaign against North Vietnam; for the blockage of rail, road, and sea imports into North Vietnam; and ultimately for invasion of North Vietnam to control infiltration routes. The Joint Chiefs of Staff recognize that these operations may cause the Soviet Union and/or Red China to apply military pressure against us in other places of the world, such as in Korea or Western Europe. They therefore believe it essential that we also take steps to prepare to face such hostile military pressures. The purpose of this paper is to examine the recommendations of our military commanders and to consider alternative courses of action.

This memorandum is written at a time when there appears to be no attractive course of action. The probabilities are that Hanoi has decided not to negotiate until the American electorate has been heard in November 1968. Continuation of our present moderate policy, while avoiding a larger war, will not change Hanoi's mind, so is not enough to satisfy the American people; increased force levels and actions against the North are likewise unlikely to change Hanoi's mind, and are likely to get us in even deeper in Southeast Asia and into a serious confrontation, if not war, with China and Russia; and we are not willing to yield. So we must choose among imperfect alternatives....

The Vietnam war is unpopular in this country. It is becoming increasingly unpopular as it escalates—causing more American casualties, more fear of its growing into a wider war, more privation of the domestic sector, and more distress at the amount of suffering being visited on the non-combatants in Vietnam, South and North. Most Americans do not know how we got where we are,

and most, without knowing why, but taking advantage of hindsight, are convinced that somehow we should not have gotten this deeply in. All want the war ended and expect their President to end it. Successfully. Or else.

This state of mind in the US generates impatience in the political structure of the United States. It unfortunately also generates patience in Hanoi. (It is commonly supposed that Hanoi will not give anything away pending the trial of the US elections in November 1968.)

The "big war" in the South between the US and the North Vietnamese military units (NVA) is going well. We staved off military defeat in 1965; we gained the military initiative in 1966; and since then we have been hurting the enemy badly, spoiling some of his ability to strike. "In the final analysis," General Westmoreland said, "we are fighting a war of attrition." In that connection, the enemy has been losing between 1500 and 2000 killed-in-action a week, while we and the South Vietnamese have been losing 175 and 250 respectively. The VC/NVA 287,000-man order of battle is leveling off, and General Westmoreland believes that, as of March, we "reached the crossover point"—we began attriting more men than Hanoi can recruit or infiltrate each month. The concentration of NVA forces across the Demilitarized Zone (DMZ) and the enemy use of long-range artillery are matters of concern. There are now four NVA divisions in the DMZ area. The men infiltrate directly across the western part of the DMZ, and supplies swing around through the Ho Chi Minh Trail. The NVA apparently plans to nibble at our forces, seeking to inflict heavy casualties, perhaps to stage a "spectacular" (perhaps against Quang Tri City or Hue), and/or to try a major thrust into the Western Highlands. They are forcing us to transfer some forces from elsewhere in Vietnam to the I Corps area.

Throughout South Vietnam, supplies continue to flow in ample quantities, with Cambodia becoming more and more important as a supply base—now of food and medicines, perhaps ammunition later. The enemy retains the ability to initiate both large- and small-scale attacks. Small-scale attacks in the first quarter of 1967 are running at double the 1966 average; larger-scale attacks are again on the increase after falling off substantially in

1966. Acts of terrorism and harassment have continued at about the same rate.

The over-all troop strengths of friendly and VC/NVA forces by Corps Area are shown in Attachments I and II.

All things considered, there is consensus that we are no longer in danger of losing this war militarily.

Regrettably, the "other war" against the VC is still not going well. Corruption is widespread. Real government control is confined to enclaves. There is rot in the fabric. Our efforts to enliven the moribund political infrastructure have been matched by VC efforts—more now through coercion than was formerly the case. So the VC are hurting badly too. In the Delta, because of the redeployment of some VC/NVA troops to the area north of Saigon, the VC have lost their momentum and appear to be conducting essentially a holding operation. On the government side there, the tempo of operations has been correspondingly low. The population remains apathetic, and many local government officials seem to have working arrangements with the VC which they are reluctant to disturb.

The National Liberation Front (NLF) continues to control large parts of South Vietnam, and there is little evidence that the revolutionary development program is gaining any momentum. The Army of South Vietnam (ARVN) is tired, passive and accommodation-prone, and is moving too slowly if at all into pacification work.

The enemy no doubt continues to believe that we will not be able to translate our military success in the "big war" into the desired "end products"—namely, broken enemy morale and political achievements by the Government of Vietnam (GVN). At the same time, the VC must be concerned about decline in morale among their ranks. Defections, which averaged 400 per week last year, have, until a slump near the end of April, been running at more than 1000 a week; very few defectors, however, are important people.

Hanoi's attitude towards negotiations has never been soft nor open-minded. Any concession on their part would involve an enormous loss of face. Whether or not the Polish and Burchett-Kosygin initiatives had much substance to them, it is clear that Hanoi's attitude currently is hard and rigid. They seem uninterested in a political settlement and determined to match US military expansion of the conflict. This change prob-

ably reflects these factors: (1) increased assurances of help from the Soviets received during Pham Van Dong's April trip to Moscow; (2) arrangements providing for the unhindered passage of matériel from the Soviet Union through China; and (3) a decision to wait for the results of the US elections in 1968. Hanoi appears to have concluded that she cannot secure her objectives at the conference table and has reaffirmed her strategy of seeking to erode our ability to remain in the South. The Hanoi leadership has apparently decided that it has no choice but to submit to the increased bombing. There continues to be no sign that the bombing has reduced Hanoi's will to resist or her ability to ship the necessary supplies south. Hanoi shows no signs of ending the large war and advising the VC to melt into the jungles. The North Vietnamese believe they are right; they consider the Ky regime to be puppets; they believe the world is with them and that the American public will not have staying power against them. Thus, although they may have factions in the regime favoring different approaches, they believe that, in the long run, they are stronger than we are for the purpose. They probably do not want to make significant concessions, and could not do so without serious loss of face.

Most interested governments and individuals appear to assume that the possibility of initiating negotiations has declined over the last several months. Following the failure of Kosygin's efforts while in London, the Soviets apparently have been unwilling to use whatever influence they may have in Hanoi to persuade North Vietnam to come to the conference table while the bombing continues.

The dominant Soviet objectives seem to continue to be to avoid direct involvement in the military conflict and to prevent Vietnam from interfering with other aspects of Soviet-American relations, while supporting Hanoi to an extent sufficient to maintain Soviet prestige in International Communism.

China remains largely preoccupied with its own Cultural Revolution. The Peking Government continues to advise Hanoi not to negotiate and continues to resist Soviet efforts to forge a united front in defense of North Vietnam. There is no reason to doubt that China would honor its commitment to intervene at Hanoi's request, and it remains likely that Peking would intervene on her own initiative if she believed that the existence of the Hanoi regime was at stake....

The war in Vietnam is acquiring a momentum of its own that must be stopped. Dramatic increases in US troop deployments, in attacks on the North, or in ground actions in Laos or Cambodia are not necessary and are not the answer. The enemy can absorb them or counter them, bogging us down further and risking even more serious escalation of the war.

GLOSSARY

attriting/attrit: to wear down an adversary by constant opposition

Delta: the Mekong Delta, also known as the Western Region, the southernmost and westernmost part of South Vietnam

FY: fiscal year, or financial year

VC: Viet Cong, a South Vietnamese military and political organization that opposed the South Vietnamese government and the United States

Document Analysis

McNamara begins with the requests of General West-moreland and Admiral Sharp for more troops. Their requests stand as a foil against which he frames the rest of his argument. At the bottom of the first paragraph, McNamara offers his programmatic statement, observing that his purpose "is to examine the recommendations of our military commanders and to consider alternative courses of action." He follows through on the first half of this statement, extensively scrutinizing the recommendations in their larger context. Tellingly, however, he does not fulfill the second half of this proposal, offering no feasible alternatives to the commanders' plans. Instead, in order to steer the president away from the commanders' proposal for a troop surge, he paints the circumstances in bleak terms. Two years earlier, in 1965, journalist David Halberstam famously called American involvement in Vietnam a quagmire. McNamara does not use that term in this memorandum, but the atmosphere that he details and the fact that he offers no feasible course of action implicitly lend weight to Halberstam's label.

As part of his pessimistic portrayal, McNamara contrasts the American public's growing distaste for the war with the resolve of the North Vietnamese. Yet his depiction of the American public proves more complex than a simple comparison would allow. Elaborating on their distaste for war, he goes as far as to say "All [Americans] want the war ended and expect their President to end it. Successfully. Or else." This is unmistakably direct language, particularly considering that it is addressed to a sitting president. While outlining the different, unfavorable courses of action, he states that the "present moderate policy" would not change Hanoi's firm stance and, therefore, "is not enough to satisfy the American people." This implies that the American people would be satisfied only with an outcome that altered North Vietnam's hardline approach (achieving, that is, a form of "success"). Seemingly speaking for all Americans, including those in the administration, he adds "we are not willing to yield." But is that a good thing or a bad thing in the eyes of the writer? He seems, perhaps, ambivalent about it.

The bulk of McNamara's examination consists of his description of two different wars. The first he labels the "big war." This is the more conventional war against the NVA, or North Vietnamese Army. According to McNamara, America has the upper-hand in this war. He is able to support this view with objective numbers. He quotes General Westmoreland, who says that they are fighting and winning a war of attrition. After detailing the positive state of this "big war," McNamara ends on a positive note: "All things considered, there is consensus that we are no longer in danger of losing this war militarily."

The "other war," which is not being fought militarily and which America is in danger of losing, is against the more localized VC, or Viet Cong. The VC are sometimes backed by and/or fight alongside the NVA. However, they are autonomous from the North and are able to fight against the Americans and South Vietnamese government both militarily and in other ways. They are corrupting the infrastructure of the government. Although McNamara usually sticks to straightforward prose befitting a government document, he is not above the occasional dramatic flourish, as witnessed by the vivid metaphor: "There is rot in the fabric." According to McNamara, this rot cannot be conquered by additional troops.

Although the programmatic statement near the beginning claims, with an air of neutrality, that the paper will "examine the recommendations of our military commanders," McNamara's opposition to these recommendations is apparent throughout and increases over the course of his account. While outlining the recommendations themselves, he details the additional, major steps necessary for them to be met with success and identifies the reaction that these actions could provoke from the Soviet Union or China. His opposition becomes clearer with each unfavorable circumstance he details. By the final paragraph, he succinctly states that "The war in Vietnam is acquiring a momentum of its own that must be stopped." The commanders' proposals, therefore, "are not necessary and are not the answer." They would only add to the momentum.

Essential Themes

David Halberstam called American intervention in Vietnam a quagmire two years before this memorandum. Robert McNamara paints a picture that supports that view. Another term that might be used in such a situation is *aporia*, meaning "baffling," "impassable"—a situation with no escape. Though it is more common in a philosophical or rhetorical setting, the term fittingly describes McNamara's outlook.

McNamara uses contrasting pairs—Hanoi's steadfastness and the American public's weariness— to make his point. Yet these contrasts fulfill different functions in his memorandum. He uses the "hard and rigid" attitude in North Vietnam to define the inverse of the sentiment in America, and vice versa. He also contrasts the "big war" with the "other war," as outlined above, but this pairing proves more nuanced. Though American success differs in the two wars, the wars come across not as opposites but as merely different. The distinction allows McNamara to concede the general's assessment of the military situation, while still depicting American prospects as unfavorable.

—*Anthony Vivian*

Bibliography and Additional Reading

Barrett, David M. *Uncertain Warriors: Lyndon Johnson and His Vietnam Advisors*. Lawrence, KS: U of Kansas P, 1993. Print.

Halberstam, David & Daniel Joseph Singal. *The Making of a Quagmire: America and Vietnam during the Kennedy Era*. Lanham, MD: Rowman & Littlefield, 2008. Print.

McNamara, Robert S. *The Essence of Security: Reflections in Office*. New York: Harper & Row, 1968. Print.

_____. & Brian VanDeMark. *In Retrospect: The Tragedy and Lessons of Vietnam*. New York. Vintage Books, 1996. Print.

■ The Tet Offensive: A CIA Assessment

Date: February 12, 1968
Author: CIA official(s)
Genre: report

Summary Overview

On January 30, 1968, Viet Cong and North Vietnamese troops launched a massive, coordinated offensive across South Vietnam. The offensive was beaten back, and the attackers faced heavy causalities. The mission summarily failed its purpose of raising a local uprising and overthrowing the South Vietnamese government. Nevertheless, the assault garnered national media attention in the United States and diminished the already wavering support for the war among the American public. This report shows signs that it is directly responding to this external perception of the assault. Written two weeks after the first onslaught, the author(s) detail the failures of the offensive and depict the state of affairs in terms that were as positive as possible for American prospects in Vietnam.

Defining Moment

From the end of 1964 to the end of 1966, the number of American troops on the ground in Vietnam ballooned tenfold. Secretary of Defense Robert McNamara lost faith in American prospects in the region and tried to convince President Lyndon B. Johnson to reverse policy throughout 1967. He failed to do so and announced his resignation by the end of 1967. Although troop increases did not match the massive increases of 1965, and 1966, 100,000 additional American troops were on the ground in Vietnam by the end of 1967.

With such a surge in troops and the United States meeting with success, at least militarily, the Tet Offensive served as a blow to current American preconceptions. Breaking a temporary truce for the Tet holiday, Viet Cong and North Vietnamese made a massive, coordinated assault on local governments and allied forces throughout South Vietnam. By military standards, the onslaught was a failure. The South Vietnamese government did not fall; American troops were not forced out. Nevertheless, the offensive had a lasting effect on international perceptions of the war, particularly among the American public. Together with the later revelations concerning the My Lai slaughter, the Tet Offensive strained the American support for the war as no other event had.

The author of the CIA report attempted to curb the negative perception of the Tet Offensive. Written just two weeks after the launching of the assault, the report depicts the results of the assault and the greater circumstances of the war in terms favorable for the United States. Although the report appears to react to public opinion, it does not try to alter the views of the public directly. With US governmental officials as its targeted audience, the report aims to use a positive portrayal to argue for a continuance of American war efforts in the region. However, its success in that regard can be questioned, for, ultimately, it represented only one of many voices in the debate concerning troop levels and war objectives.

Author Biography

The names of the author or authors of this document have not been released. Given the nature of the document as a declassified CIA report, this should come as no surprise. The report was sent by Richard Helms, the director of the Central Intelligence Agency, to Walt Rostow, President Johnson's special assistant for national security affairs. Helms had risen through the ranks of the CIA since its inception in 1947; he served as director from 1966 to 1973. He then transitioned to ambassador to Iran, where he served until 1977.

HISTORICAL DOCUMENT

The Year of the Monkey had an inauspicious beginning for the people of South Vietnam as the VC/NVA forces violated the sacred Tet holidays and launched virtually simultaneous attacks against 36 province capitals, five of the six autonomous cities, and numerous other population centers throughout the country. Their objectives have been clearly spelled out in captured documents—to destroy or subvert the GVN/allied forces, eliminate the GVN governmental structure, create a general uprising among the people, and establish a revolutionary government dominated by the National Liberation Front. In what appears to be an almost incredible miscalculation of their own military capabilities and the degree of support they could command from the people, the Communists failed to achieve these stated objectives. It has cost them dearly in manpower—in 12 days some 31,000 killed, 5,700 detained, probably another 10,000 dead from wounds, and unknown number dead from air and artillery strikes—a total probably amounting to more than half of the forces used in this attack. Nevertheless, the enemy's well-planned, coordinated series of attacks was an impressive display of strength which has given him a major psychological victory abroad, dealt a serious blow to the pacification program, and created problems that will tax the energies and resources of the government for many months to come.

The enemy's military strategy consisted of a two-phase offensive. Wherever possible, the first phase assaults were conducted by VC local forces. Psychologically, this was more appropriate than using NVA units, given the enemy's objective of winning the support of the people. NVA forces were used in I and II Corps where VC forces were inadequate, but throughout the country most VC/NVA main forces were withheld for the second phase when they would move in to capitalize on the expected chaos and general uprising.

The passive reaction of the population, the fierceness of Free World and ARVN counteroffensives after the initial surprise and confusion, and the effectiveness of massive air and artillery fire obviously forced cancellation of the commitment of VC/NVA main forces. It is estimated that slightly less than half of the enemy's main force maneuver units outside of those in the DMZ, but well over half of his local force units, participated in the attacks. Thus, he still has substantial uncommitted forces available for a new "second phase" attack.

In spite of the enemy's heavy losses, he apparently still plans a resumption of the offensive on a large scale in the near future. The failure of committed forces to withdraw completely to safehavens and current disposition of previously uncommitted units lend credence to prisoners' statements that the second phase offensive will soon be initiated. Although the VC/NVA main forces would supposedly be better equipped, trained, and disciplined than the primarily low-level troops (cannon fodder) which launched the first offensive, the enemy has lost the element of surprise, does not have the cover of a Tet truce, and has already expended a great deal in the way of men and matériel. The consequence of a second "all-out" series of attacks would probably be as disastrous militarily as the first phase. If, indeed, the enemy is preparing for large-scale attacks at Khe Sanh, Quang Tri, Hue, Danang, Dak To, Phu My, Tuy Hoa, Saigon, Can Tho, and My Tho, then he must strike quickly. Though stretched thin, allied forces have consolidated their gains, regrouped, and initiated offensive operations against the enemy's massed main forces with notable success. As time passed, his position is becoming more tenuous and there will be less and less opportunity to achieve his immediate objectives.

Although the enemy has been seriously weakened, he is not on the verge of desperation. He has over half of his main forces basically intact with more men and matériel enroute or available from NVN. He has taken substantial losses in the past and shown an amazing degree of resiliency. On the other hand, his logistics and recruitment problems will be greatly increased with such heavy losses from the local and guerrilla forces who provide manpower for support and combat.

As an alternative to a second assault against the cities, the enemy could elect to cut his losses by reverting to more traditional harassing attacks while attempting to improve his position in the countryside. The recent well-coordinated attacks over widespread areas proved the enemy's capability to utilize this tactic. Such attacks on a smaller scale would still gain headlines and have considerable psychological appeal and value to the enemy as they re-raise questions in SVN and the world as to the ability of the allies to provide security to the people. However, after such extensive indoctrination of the inevitability of imminent victory, a reversion to essentially guerrilla warfare would probably cause severe problems of morale among the cadres and a loss of impetus for the revolutionary effort.

It is not yet possible to make a firm assessment of the damage which has been caused to the pacification program, but it probably has been extensive. The pacified areas did not at least initially appear to have been a priority target, probably because most of the VC guerrillas were drawn into local force units for the city battles or were engaged in interdicting LOC's. However, GVN forces providing security for the pacified areas and the RD teams were in many cases withdrawn to assist in the defense of urban areas, leaving the VC free to penetrate previously secured hamlets and conduct propaganda, recruit, acquire food, eliminate the GVN administration, and occasionally terrorize the population. The impact of the VC presence was especially severe in the larger hamlets which generally are located close to the population centers and were on the VC route of entry. This activity was responsible for part of the large refugee flow into the cities.

With many of the cities in shambles and requiring priority reconstruction and rehabilitation efforts, the development aspects of the program almost inevitably will suffer. In any event, it will be many months before the confidence of the people in the previously secured hamlets can be restored, some of whom felt the VC presence for the first time. One possibly hopeful sign is that many of the VC expressed surprise at the relative prosperity of the people in the GVN areas, contrary to what they had been led to believe. This, together with the military defeat and heavy losses, should contribute to some future defections.

There has naturally been a mixed reaction from the people to the Communist onslaught—initially, it was one of shock at the strength of the attack, and anger at its perfidy. However, even those skeptics who would not previously acknowledge that the large electoral turnouts, the inability of the VC to get a response to calls for a general strike, and the almost totally conscript nature

of the VC forces were proof that the VC lacked popular support, can hardly deny it now. Despite the creation of a revolutionary administration, supposedly untainted by association with the NLF, no significant element of the population or of the armed forces defected. The refusal of the people to respond to the VC call for an uprising, and in fact often to render assistance to the government forces, was the key to the failure of the VC plan, and is one of most encouraging aspects of the whole affair.

There are negative factors, of course—the people now have a greater respect for the capabilities of the VC, and this will probably result in some cases in a more cautious attitude toward open support for the government. There is criticism over the government's lack of preparedness, charges of excessive property damage and civilian casualties, and looting by the counterreaction forces, and a persistent belief that somehow the U.S. was in collusion with the VC. However, the population is universally angry at the VC for violating both a sacred holiday and their own truce, and the blame for all of the ills is generally placed on the VC. There was left no doubt in the minds of the people as to the superiority of the government forces and as to who won this engagement. On balance, we feel that in the contest for the hearts and minds of the people, the VC have so far suffered a severe loss. In common danger, there was a tendency to unite behind the government. With a residue of ill will toward the VC which will not be easily erased, the task of nation-building, at least in those areas still under government control, should become a little easier. Much will depend, however, on the skill and alacrity with which the government handles the severe social and economic problems it faces.

The days ahead constitute a severe test for the GVN. There is no question but that the government suffered a serious loss of prestige by its inability to defend its cities. Notwithstanding, there has been at least a temporary tendency on the part of nationalist elements to set aside their parochial interests and rally behind the leadership. This is by no means universal—the militant Buddhists, the Dai Viets, and some others still have refused either publicly to condemn the VC or to support the government actively. Although it was an American idea, clearly the most effective action by the government so far was the creation of the joint Vietnamese/American task force under Vice President Ky to handle the immediate problems of rehabilitation. Whatever closing of ranks behind the government that has accrued can be credited largely to Ky, who has emerged as the "man of the hour." Despite aggravating and bureaucratic problems, some forward movement has been made in reestablishing essential facilities and services. Ky may well have saved the GVN from projecting its usual image of inactivity.

We are not sanguine about future political problems. The schisms which divide this society are deeply rooted, and will inevitably arise again as the first flush of unity begins to fade. Demands will be made for the removal of officials, both national and local, who proved unequal to the task in a crisis, and this will be certain to restore the endemic factional infighting. The military, some of the Catholics, and those favoring a rough, directed system will fault the government for not being tough enough, while others will be concerned over even the temporary sacrifice of democratic processes and the continued preeminent role of the military. The crisis has ignited a spark of unity, but to sustain it will require a successful relief and recovery operation, and a sublimation of personal and partisan political interests which this society has never before demonstrated.

The Communists can be credited with having maintained excellent security for such a comprehensive plan, but they are guilty of a massive intelligence failure. Documents captured over the past four months and interrogations of the prisoners involved in the recent attacks indicate quite clearly that the VC did intend to take and hold the cities, did expect a general uprising, and did plan to install a revolutionary government, as evidenced by the presence of a standby VC administrative structure in the major cities. It may seem incredible that VC expectations should have been so divorced from reality, but there are three factors which probably explain this.

First, the Communists are and always have been victims of their doctrine, and in the present case the articles of faith were: "The longer we fight, the stronger we become;" and, "The more viciously the enemy fights, the closer he is to collapse;" and "The people support us and when the urban people have the chance to rise up, our victory will be assured." Second, the leaders have been consistently and greatly misinformed by lower cadres. Given the doctrinal bias alluded to above and the Oriental penchant for telling people what they want to hear, the reports going upward have so misinterpreted the facts that the leaders could not base their decisions on reality. Third, the need for a significant victory after two years of drought may have introduced a lack of prudence. By any rational standard, North Vietnam has been losing too much in order to gain too little. For too long, VC strength and support has been dwindling. The entire nature of the war, the entire environment of the struggle, changed with the massive U.S. involvement. The Tet assault must have been part of an expected VC plan to inflict heavy physical and psychological damage in hope of gaining, if not all their objectives, something which could be construed as a victory.

We are very much aware that we have probably seen only the first of a two-act drama. If the second act repeats the scenario, we will seriously question the ability of Hanoi to continue to carry on this kind of conventional warfare for a protracted period. Whatever else may follow, the Tet offensive in South Vietnam, contrary to much foreign opinion, is not popularly regarded here either as a VC victory or even as an indication of their eventual success. There is a sobering thought for the future, however—if it were not for the presence of U.S. forces, the VC flag would be flying over much of South Vietnam today.

GLOSSARY

GVN/allied forces: the Government of Vietnam, American troops, and troops allied with them

VC/NVA: the Viet Cong, a South Vietnamese political and military organization, and the North Vietnamese Army

Document Analysis

The director of Central Intelligence Richard Helms sent this report to Walt Rostow, President Johnson's special assistant for national security affairs, two weeks after the Tet Offensive began. Rostow then showed the report to President Johnson. In the cover memorandum to the president, Rostow called it "extremely well balanced," adding, "We are unlikely to have anything better right away." A month later, Rostow was among those who advised the president not to immediately fill General Westmoreland's request for more troops. It must be assumed that this document played a role in that advisement. The document presents a detailed account of the state of affairs in the aftermath of the offensive. It also showcases a discernible perspective and agenda at a time of broad uncertainty in American policy-making.

Although part of an occupying force, the authors position themselves as the ultimate insiders. They begin with a religious flourish: "The Year of the Monkey had an inauspicious beginning for the people of South Vietnam...." Throughout the document, they speak with confidence for the South Vietnamese people. For example, later in the document they again mention the Tet holiday: "The population is universally angry at the VC for violating both a sacred holiday and their own truce, and the blame for all of the ills is generally placed on the VC." This role as supposed insider allows them to label the shocked international reaction as foreign (and, therefore, uninformed.) They argue that: "contrary to much foreign opinion," the Tet Offensive was not a victory for the attacking VC and NVA forces. There is also a touch of racism in the report, when the authors remark on "the Oriental penchant for telling people what they want to hear."

While surveying the aftermath of the offensive, the authors take account of both the allied and the enemy forces. They depict, in a fashion common at the time (and continuing into the present), the enemy in the masculine singular: "He is not on the verge of desperation. He has over half of his main forces basically intact… On the other hand, his logistics…" By representing the enemy in this way, "he" becomes more tangible, an individual man with strengths and weaknesses. This paints a different picture than representing the enemy as, say, a complex military and political organization centered in, but not restricted to, Hanoi or other circumstances.

While the authors open with "The Year of the Monkey" to assume the role of the local insider and, therefore, underscore the reliability of their information, they end with glimpses of their American patriotism, as well as peeks at their agenda. They mark American intervention in Vietnam as a turning point in the region: "The entire nature of the war, the entire environment of the struggle, changed with the massive U.S. involvement." Likewise, their final sentence combines flag-waving American patriotism with a proclamation of the necessity to continue to commit to the region militarily: "There is a sobering thought for the future, however—if it were not for the presence of U.S. forces, the VC flag would be flying over much of South Vietnam today." The authors thus offer an optimistic take on the Tet Offensive and its aftermath and credit American forces. This provides a perspective strikingly different from that of Secretary of Defense Robert McNamara a year earlier.

Essential Themes

The authors of this report establish a tone of balanced optimism. This tone was tailored to their intended audience: high-ranking US governmental officials, including President Johnson. For two weeks, the international media had been in a frenzy over the unexpected offensive. This report uses balance to showcase its own objectivity and engage with the existing narrative, and it employs optimism to offer an alternative perspective on the event. The details within the report constantly fluctuate between positive and negative, yet the authors continually apply a positive twist on the circumstances. This tone is witnessed throughout the document, but one example should sufficiently display its functioning: "The Communists can be credited with having maintained excellent security for such a comprehensive plan, but they are guilty of a massive intelligence failure." Here, the authors discuss the enemy's intelligence apparatus. As CIA agents, they are quite attuned to this topic. They balance a complement of the enemy's ability to retain the element of surprise with an insult against the enemy's assessment of the feasibility of obtaining their objectives.

In the year before, Secretary of Defense Robert McNamara sent memoranda to President Johnson expressing his skepticism that America could achieve military victory in Vietnam. In the CIA report, by contrast, the authors laud American efforts in the region and portray American prospects as difficult, but achievable. These opposing perspectives came at a time of growing war weariness among the American public.

—Anthony Vivian

Bibliography and Additional Reading

Ahern, Thomas, Jr.. *Vietnam Declassified: The CIA and Counterinsurgency.* Lexington, KY: U P of Kentucky, 2010. Print.

Allison, William Thomas. *The Tet Offensive: A Brief History with Documents.* New York: Taylor & Francis, 2008. Print.

Wirtz, James J. *The Tet Offensive: Intelligence Failure in War.* Ithaca, NY: Cornell U P, 1994. Print.

■ The President and His Advisors Review the Situation

Date: March 4-5, 1968
Author: Lyndon B. Johnson; Walt Rostow; Clark Clifford; Earle Wheeler; Paul Nitze; Dean Rusk
Genre: discussion; meeting minutes

Summary Overview

In early March 1968, President Lyndon B. Johnson and his advisors faced a quandary. The war in Vietnam had ballooned under Johnson's administration. With upwards of 500,000 men already on the ground, the military commanders were calling for over 200,000 more men. A little over a month prior, the enemy's Tet Offensive had failed to gain a military victory, but further diminished support for the war among the American public. President Johnson tasked his advisors to assess the commanders' proposal. They returned with a report, which they summarized for him in the meetings recorded in this document. Their plan granted the field commanders only 22,000 more men, a little more than one tenth of the requested amount. The war would drag on for seven more years, and yet this meeting marked a shift in US tactics and a cap on American troop numbers. Beginning in 1969, under a new president, the troop total dropped every year.

Defining Moment

At the time of these meetings in early March of 1968, President Johnson had been in office for over five years. As president, he had overseen significant policy victories in the case of his Great Society domestic programs, including the landmark Civil Rights Act of 1964. At the same time, US involvement in Vietnam had skyrocketed under his leadership. Around 20,000 American troops were on the ground in Vietnam when he was sworn in. Just five years later, the total stood at approximately 500,000, twenty-five times the original total.

Up until this time, the Johnson administration had been accustomed to fulfilling field commanders' requests for troops. This latest request was no small plea. General Westmoreland was asking for a 140 percent increase to an already massive force. A month before, the CIA had sent a report on the Tet Offensive, em-

ploying a sort of balanced optimism to underscore the continuing need for an American military presence in the region. In the year before that, Robert McNamara had advised President Johnson that American objectives could not be obtained militarily. At the time of the present meetings, McNamara's replacement, Clark Clifford, had been on the job for less than a week. Nevertheless, he performed the lion's share of the speaking, at least in the sections of the meeting recorded here.

The proposals that Clifford and the other advisors present here heed McNamara's previous calls for change. These meetings occurred at a watershed moment for troop numbers. Richard Nixon was elected to replace President Johnson later in 1968. Troop totals peaked and started to drop in 1969. These numbers corresponded to a deeper shift in American tactics in Vietnam. These meetings display the infancy of such later policies as the switch to South Vietnamese troops and the increased role of helicopters. The shift in tactics proved indecisive as the fighting continued for seven more years.

Author Biography

Several voices appear in these notes. Lyndon B. Johnson had been president for over five years; he did not seek reelection at the end of 1968. Walt Rostow was the special assistant for national security affairs from 1966 to 1969; a month before these meetings, he was the one who received the CIA report in the aftermath of the Tet Offensive. Clark Clifford had taken over as secretary of defense less than a week before these meetings, following Robert McNamara's departure. Earle Wheeler served as chairman of the Joint Chiefs of Staff from 1964 to 1970. Paul Nitze was the deputy secretary of defense from 1967 to 1969. Dean Rusk served as secretary of state from 1961 to 1969.

HISTORICAL DOCUMENT

Washington, *March 4, 1968.*

The President: As I told you last week, I wanted you to return today with your recommendations in response to General Westmoreland's request. Among the things I asked you to study were the following questions:

1. What particular forces are you recommending that we dispatch immediately? How do we get these forces?
2. How soon could we formulate what we want from the South Vietnamese?
3. What difficulties do you foresee with your recommendations, both with the Congress and financially? . . .

As I understand it, Clark Clifford, Secretary Rusk, and Rostow and others have been meeting on these questions in conjunction with the Joint Chiefs of Staff.

Walt Rostow: That is correct.

Clark Clifford: ... The subject is a very profound one, and I consider it advisable to outline the difficulty we face and the central problem which your advisers see you facing.

As you know, from time to time, the military leaders in the field ask for additional forces. We have, in the past, met these requests until we are now at the point where we have agreed to supply up to 525,000 men to General Westmoreland.

He now has asked for 205,000 additional troops. There are three questions:

1. Should the President send 205,000?
2. Should the President not send any more?
3. Should the President approve a figure somewhere in between and send an alternative number?

Your senior advisers have conferred on this matter at very great length. There is a deep-seated concern by your advisers. There is a concern that if we say, yes, and step up with the addition of 205,000 more men that we might continue down the road as we have been without accomplishing our purpose—which is for a viable South Vietnam which can live in peace.

We are not convinced that our present policy will bring us to that objective.

As I said before, we spent hours discussing this matter. For a while, we thought and had the feeling that we understood the strength of the Viet Cong and the North Vietnamese. You will remember the rather optimistic reports of General Westmoreland and Ambassador Bunker last year.

Frankly, it came as a shock that the Vietcong-North Vietnamese had the strength of force and skill to mount the Tet offensive—as they did. They struck 34 cities, made strong inroads in Saigon and in Hue. There have been very definite effects felt in the countryside.

At this stage, it is clear that this new request by General Westmoreland brings the President to a clearly defined watershed:

1. Do you continue to go down that same road of "more troops, more guns, more planes, more ships?"
2. Do you go on killing more Viet Cong and more North Vietnamese and killing more Vietcong and more North Vietnamese?

There are grave doubts that we have made the type of progress we had hoped to have made by this time. As we build up our forces, they build up theirs. We continue to fight at a higher level of intensity.

Even were we to meet this full request of 205,000 men, and the pattern continues as it has, it is likely that by March he (General Westmoreland) may want another 200,000 to 300,000 men with no end in sight.

The country we are trying to save is being subjected to enormous damage. Perhaps the country we are trying to save is relying on the United States too much. When we look ahead, we may find that we may actually be denigrating their ability to take over their own country rather than contributing to their ability to do it.

We recommend in this paper that you meet the requirement for only those forces that may be needed to deal with any exigencies of the next 3–4 months. March–April–May could be an important period.

We recommend an immediate decision to deploy to Vietnam an estimated total of 22,000 additional personnel. We would agree to get them to General Westmoreland right away. It would be valuable for the general to know they are coming so he can make plans accordingly.

This is as far as we are willing to go. We would go ahead, however, and call up a sufficient number of men. If later the President decides Westmoreland needs additional reinforcements, you will have men to meet that contingency.

The President: Westmoreland is asking for 200,000 men, and you are recommending 20,000 or so?

Clark Clifford: The strategic reserves in the United States are deeply depleted. They must be built up. Senator Russell has said this. We do not know what might happen anywhere around the world, but to face any emergency we will need to strengthen the reserve.

Out of this buildup you can meet additional requests from Westmoreland in the event you decide he needs more than the 22,000 later. The first increment will meet his needs for the next three to four months.

Westmoreland must not have realized it, but it would have taken much longer than he had anticipated to provide the men and units he originally requested anyway. We could not meet that schedule.

We suggest that you go ahead and get the manpower ready. If they are not really necessary for Vietnam, they can be added to the Strategic Reserve to strengthen it.

We also feel strongly that there should be a comprehensive study of the strategic guidance to be given General Westmoreland in the future.

We are not sure the present strategy is the right strategy—that of being spread out all over the country with a seek and destroy policy.

We are not convinced that this is the right way, that it is the right long-term course to take. We are not sure under the circumstances which exist that a conventional military victory, as commonly defined, can be had.

After this study is made—if there is no clear resolution in the actions of the next 3–4 months except long drawn-out procedure—we may want to change the strategic guidance given Westmoreland. Perhaps we should not be trying to protect all of the countryside, and instead concentrate on the cities and important areas in the country.

There will be considerably higher casualties if we follow the Westmoreland plan. It just follows that if we increase our troop commitment by 200,000 men, there will be significantly higher casualties.

We may want to consider using our men as a "shield" behind which the government of South Vietnam could strengthen itself and permit the ARVN to be strengthened.

Under the present situation, there is a good deal of talk about what the ARVN "will do" but when the crunch is on, when the crunch comes, they look to us for more. When they got into the Tet offensive, Thiêu's statement wasn't what more they could do but that "it is time for more U.S. troops." There is no easy answer to this.

If we continue with our present policy of adding more troops and increasing our commitment, this policy may lead us into Laos and Cambodia.

The reserve forces in North Vietnam are a cause for concern as well. They have a very substantial population from which to draw. They have no trouble whatever organizing, equipping, and training their forces.

We seem to have a sinkhole. We put in more—they match it. We put in more—they match it.

The South Vietnamese are not doing all they should do.

The Soviets and the Chinese have agreed to keep the North Vietnamese well armed and well supplied.

The Vietcong are now better armed than the ARVN. They have:

- better rifles
- better training
- more sophisticated weapons (mortars, artillery, rockets).

I see more and more fighting with more and more casualties on the U.S. side and no end in sight to the action.

I want to give a whole new look at the whole situation. There is strong unanimity on this. If it were possible, we would want to look at the situation without sending more troops to him. But we should send the 22,000—that is, until a new policy decision is reached. And that 22,000—that will be it until that decision is made.

We can no longer rely just on the field commander. He can want troops and want troops and want troops. We must look at the overall impact on us, including the situation here in the United States. We must look at our economic stability, our other problems in the world, our other problems at home; we must consider whether or not this thing is tieing [sic] us down so that we cannot do some of the other things we should be doing; and finally, we must consider the effects of our actions on the rest of the world—are we setting an example in Vietnam through which other nations would rather not go if they are faced with a similar threat?

It is out of caution and for protection that we recommend these additional forces.

Now the time has come to decide where do we go from here.

I can assure the President that we can reexamine this situation with complete protection to our present position.

We do recommend the following actions:

- A callup of reserve units and individuals totaling approximately 262,000 (194,000 in units; 68,000 as individuals).
- An increase in the draft calls.
- Extension of terms of service.

These actions would produce a total increase in strength in the Armed Forces of approximately 511,000 by June 30, 1969.

This proposal includes 31,600 troops for deployment to South Korea. I would oppose that. It also includes a U.S. navy unit.

If the troops for South Korea and the naval units are disapproved, the figures would be decreased to approximately 242,000 reservists called up and 454,000 total increase in troop strength.

If you do wish to meet the additional troop request, or further demands of Westmoreland you can do it out of this pool of 242,000.

If you did not, the Strategic Reserve would be strengthened by their addition. This would, in the opinion of the JCS [Joint Chiefs of Staff], put the Strategic Reserve "just about right."

You need to have that type of reserve in times such as these.

As part and parcel of policy decisions, it is important to have a very clear understanding with the government of South Vietnam. They should know that your eventual decision about more troops and more use of U.S. support depends to a large part on their attitude.

We should tell the South Vietnamese that the General has asked for 200,000 more troops, but we are giving only 25,000. We should let them know that you are delaying your decision until you know what the GVN [South Vietnamese government] will do about:

- removal of the poor unit commanders
- meaningful steps to eliminate corruption
- meeting their own leadership responsibilities
- not only saying they will do something, but meaning it as well.

If they are not, we should know it now.

I suggest you allow yourself greater degree of latitude and flexibility. There possibly is another plan which can be utilized. There may be another way to avoid more bloodshed to us, possibly by letting go some areas.

We should consider changing our concept from one of protecting real estate to protecting people. We need to see if these people are really going to take care of themselves eventually. I am not sure we can ever find our way out if we continue to shovel men into Vietnam.

We have looked at all your questions. The answers to each of them are included in the context of the document before you tonight.

We say, for example, that this is not the time to negotiate.

We have spent the last three days trying to reach a consensus. As we sat together and cross-fertilized, we have reached a general consensus on this.

Of course, if we had to vote on sending the straight 200,000 men or no men, we would come out all over the lot … we would be split all over the place.

But we wonder if we are really making progress toward our goal under the plan we have been following.

This is the overall approach we would recommend.

The President: Does this change the tour of duty?

General Wheeler: The tour of duty in Vietnam is not changed. We feel this is an essential reason for the high morale. It is the total length of service which will be lengthened.

The President: Does it affect the man with 4 years' service the same as the draftee?

General Wheeler: Yes, sir. It would apply to all types. Of course, there are some men we would not want to extend.

The President: Have we done this before (extend tours)?

Undersecretary Nitze: Yes, sir. At least twice. At one time, the Secretary of the Navy had the authority to do this. I did it for a period during Vietnam. The Congress took this authority away last year to put it on an equal basis with the other services.

General Wheeler: We did it at the same time of the Berlin airlift. Also during the Cuban missile crisis, I believe.

Secretary Rusk: Mr. President, without a doubt, this will be one of the most serious decisions you will have made since becoming President. This has implications for all of our society.

First, on the review of strategic guidance: we want the Vietnamese to do their full share and be able to survive when we leave. This was one of the things that saved us in Korea. The question is whether substantial additional troops would eventually increase or decrease South Vietnamese strength.

We may very well find that there are equipment factors that would create competition among our new U.S. forces being sent out to Vietnam and the South Vietnamese. Many of us would like to see the ARVN equipped better and supplied with the M-16 rifles.

We must also consider what would happen to our NATO troop policies. To reduce NATO troops is a serious matter indeed.

We have also got to think of what this troop increase would mean in terms of increased taxes, the balance of payments picture, inflation, gold, and the general economic picture.

We should study moving away from the geographic approach of Vietnam strategy to a demographic approach.

On the negotiation front, I wish we had a formula to bring about a peaceful settlement soon. We do not. The negotiation track is quite bleak at the current time....

* * *

Washington, March 5, 1968.

[...]

The President: It ... appears we are about to make a rather basic change in the strategy of this war, if:

- we tell the ARVN to do more fighting.
- we tell them we will give 20,000 men; no more.
- we tell them we will do no more until they do more.
- we tell them we will be prepared to make additional troop contributions but not unless they "get with it."

I frankly doubt you will get much out of them unless they have a good coach, the right plays, and the best equipment.

Secretary Rusk: Let's put on a massive helicopter program. We always can use them. There is substantial demand for their use as civilian evacuation. They will be put to good use, no matter what the number....

The President: Yes. Let's also give the South Vietnamese the best equipment we can.... The hawks want the others to put up or shut up.

Document Analysis

This document records conversations between President Johnson and his advisors on March 4 and 5, 1968. During the first meeting on March 4, the advisors present the president with their written proposals. Evidence of this written document appears as Clark Clifford verbally summarizes the proposals: "We recommend in this paper that you meet the requirement for only those forces that may be needed to deal with any exigencies of the next 3–4 months" [emphasis added]. The advantages of using meeting notes as a primary document can be shown by looking at this document in contrast with the written document that the advisors handed their boss on March 4, 1968. The written document would offer the reader a more detailed and comprehensive look at the proposals. On the other hand, it is possible to glean from these meeting notes a summary of the proposals by their chief architects, multiple perspectives exposing the various roles of the different interlocutors, a close look at the functioning of the Johnson administration, and the president's role among his advisors.

The perspectives of the different presidential advisors formulating this proposal covered a wide spectrum. Clark Clifford expresses the differences among them: "Of course, if we had to vote on sending the straight 200,000 men or no men, we would come out all over the lot … we would be split all over the place." Yet the document is far from a cacophony of varying opinions. Throughout the March 4 meeting (the bulk of the document,) President Johnson takes on the role of questioner. He is receiving the proposal for the first time and limits his contributions to several telling questions. As for the advisors, they were not forced to vote yes or no on sending the 200,000 men as in Clifford's hypothetical, and these meetings were not the time for airing their disagreements. (The speakers put on a united front while presenting their proposals to the president, almost exclusively adopting the pronoun "we" to express the proposal.)

Despite the united front, different roles for the different interlocutors can be discerned. On March 4, 1968, Clark Clifford had been on the job for less than a week, yet he speaks the majority of the dialogue. After Clifford summarizes the plan, the president asks some specific questions; given their technical nature, they are fielded by the military brass Earle Wheeler and Paul Nitze. In a respite after one of these answers, Secretary of State Dean Rusk speaks up. He begins by stating the gravity of the situation, citing the "implications for all of our society." This may be a reference to President Johnson's domestic achievements and legacy. The shorter text from the March 5 meeting shows Rusk in a slightly different role. In this meeting, the president does the majority of the talking, and Rusk chimes in with an idea to help the president develop his thoughts.

Like Rusk, the President takes on two different roles in the two meetings. After introducing the March 4 meeting, he assumes the role of questioner. Yet the text of his questions exposes his position. His first question, "Westmoreland is asking for 200,000 men, and you are recommending 20,000 or so?" registers surprise. The later technical questions display his concern for details.

In the March 5 meeting, he muses aloud about how to put the proposals into place. Secretary Rusk turns the president's sports analogy into a "massive helicopter program." This suggestion and the president's response offer glimpses of future US policy, as well as other forces at work within this policymaking enterprise.

Essential Themes

The perspectives of the different speakers form, together, a critique of previous US policy. Clark Clifford succinctly summarizes the sentiment: "We are not convinced that our present policy will bring us to that objective [a viable South Vietnam which can live in peace]." He later uses colorful metaphors to reiterate this point: "We seem to have a sinkhole… I am not sure we can ever find our way out if we continue to shovel men into Vietnam." This skepticism toward prior policy can usefully be read alongside McNamara's sentiments from the previous year (see "No Attractive Course of Action" in the present volume) and against the CIA report from the previous month (see "The Tet Offensive: A CIA Assessment"). As well as a critique of past tactics, the document's occurrence at a crossroads of US policy offers glimpses into the major change in strategy to come. The March 5 meeting, in particular, showcases the imminent increase in the role of helicopters and the switch to local South Vietnamese troops. The latter process, called "Vietnamization," would be one of the strategies associated with the coming Nixon administration.

—*Anthony Vivian*

Bibliography and Additional Reading

Barrett, David M. *Uncertain Warriors: Lyndon Johnson and His Vietnam Advisors.* Lawrence, KS: U of Kansas P, 1993. Print.

Goodwin, Doris Kearns. *Lyndon Johnson and the American Dream.* New York: St. Martin's Press, 1991. Print.

Herring, George C. *LBJ and Vietnam: A Different Kind of War.* Austin, TX: U of Texas P, 1994. Print.

VanDeMark, Brian. *Into the Quagmire: Lyndon Johnson and the Escalation of the Vietnam War.* New York: Oxford U P, 1995. Print.

■ Testimony regarding the My Lai Massacre

Date: August-September 1969; November-December 1970
Author: Herbert L. Carter; Robert Maples; Dennis Conti; Aubrey Daniels; George Latimer; Richard Kay
Genre: testimony

Summary Overview

On March 16, 1968, Charlie Company (First Battalion, 20th Infantry Regiment, 11th Infantry Brigade, 23rd Infantry Division) got summoned to My Lai to counteract Viet Cong activity in the area. By day's end, members of the unit had slaughtered hundreds of South Vietnamese civilians. More than a year passed before the US Army began an extensive investigation, at which point Herbert L. Carter's testimony was collected. When news of the events broke in late 1969, the reports shocked the international community and further depleted support for the war among the American public. The US government charged Lieutenant William L. Calley with six counts of premeditated murder. At his trial in late 1970 and early 1971, Robert Maples and Dennis Conti gave their testimonies. Although Calley was found guilty and given a life sentence, he was later released, having served only four months in prison. The massacre had a lasting effect on the American public, bringing the violence of the war into public view and support for the war to a new low.

Defining Moment

American support for the war in Vietnam was already low and on the decline. As early as March 1967, Secretary of Defense Robert McNamara observed that the war was "unpopular" and "becoming increasingly unpopular as it escalates." One year later, North Vietnamese and Viet Cong forces launched the massive Tet Offensive. Although the assault failed to obtain its military objectives, support for the war in the United States continued to decline.

The My Lai Massacre occurred in the wake of the Tet Offensive. On March 16, 1968, American troops from Charlie Company slaughtered hundreds of unarmed and innocent South Vietnamese citizens—in-

cluding women and children. Officer Hugh Thompson, a helicopter pilot, witnessed part of the massacre and saved several civilians. He reported what he saw, but the follow-up investigation was cursory and dismissed his allegations. Another soldier, Ron Ridenhour, heard rumors of the massacre and began to collect evidence, mainly eyewitness testimonies. A little over a year after the massacre, he sent his findings to thirty Washington power brokers, including President Richard Nixon. His informal investigation prompted the Army's formal one, during which the testimony from Herbert L. Carter was collected. The Army decided to charge Lieutenant William Calley with six counts of premeditated murder. During Calley's trial in late 1970 and early 1971, both Robert Maples and Dennis Conti gave testimony as witnesses for the prosecution.

Out of the fourteen men court-martialed for their participation in the killings, Lieutenant Calley was the only one convicted. He was sentenced to life, but after a national backlash at his conviction, he ended up serving only four months. There were many reasons why Americans protested his conviction; among the most prominent was the thought that he was being used as a scapegoat for the crimes of many. Although the backlash illustrated the complexity of American public opinion, the aftermath of the My Lai Massacre brought the harsh realities and brutal violence of war to American living rooms like no other event during the Vietnam War and ultimately diminished support for the war.

Author Biography

In these testimonies, several people appear in different roles. Herbert L. Carter, Robert Maples, and Dennis Conti were GI's on the ground who witnessed the My Lai Massacre. Carter served as a 'tunnel rat,' a position specializing in subterranean search-and-destroy missions. Maples and Conti were a machine gunner and grenadier, respectively. Aubrey Daniels led the prosecution for the US government against William Calley, securing the only conviction in the proceedings. After President Richard Nixon reduced Calley's sentence, Daniels sent a letter to Nixon protesting this decision. George Latimer led Calley's defense team, which included, among others, Richard Kay.

HISTORICAL DOCUMENT

[PFC Herbert L. Carter, from Wabash County, Indiana, describes atrocities committed at My Lai]

We were picked up by helicopters at LZ Dottie early in the morning, and we were flown to My Lai. We landed outside the village in a dry rice paddy. There was no resistance from the village. There was no armed enemy in the village. We formed a line outside the village.

The first killing was an old man in a field outside the village who said some greeting in Vietnamese and waved his arms at us. Someone—either Medina or Calley—said to kill him and a big heavyset white fellow killed the man. I do not know the name of the man who shot this Vietnamese. This was the first murder.

Just after the man killed the Vietnamese, a woman came out of the village and someone knocked her down and Medina shot her with his M16 rifle. I was fifty or sixty feet from him and saw this. There was no reason to shoot this girl. Mitchell, Conti, Meadlo, Stanley, and the rest of the squad and the command group must have seen this. It was pure out-and-out murder.

Then our squad entered the village. We were making sure no one escaped from the village. Seventy-five or a hundred yards inside the village we came to where the soldiers had collected fifteen or more Vietnamese men, women, and children in a group. Medina said, "Kill everybody. Leave no one standing." Wood was there with an M60 machine gun and, at Medina's orders, he fired into the people. Sgt. Mitchell was there at this time and fired into the people with his M16 rifle, also. Widmer was there and fired into the group, and after they were down on the ground, Widmer passed among them and finished them off with his M16 rifle. Medina himself did not fire into this group.

Just after this shooting, Medina stopped a seventeen-or eighteen-year-old man with a water buffalo. Medina said for the boy to make a run for it—he tried to get him to run—but the boy wouldn't run, so Medina shot him with his M16 rifle and killed him. The command group was there. I was seventy-five or eighty feet away at the time and saw it plainly. There were some demolition men there, too, and they would be able to testify about this. I don't know any other witnesses to this murder. Medina killed the buffalo, too....

We went on through the village. Meadlo shot a Vietnamese and asked me to help him throw the man in the well. I refused and Meadlo had Carney help him throw the man in the well. I saw this murder with my own eyes and know that there was no reason to soot the man. I also know from the wounds that the man was dead.

Also in the village the soldiers had rounded up a group of people. Meadlo was guarding them. There were some other soldiers with Meadlo. Calley came up and said that he wanted them all killed. I was right there within a few feet when he said this. There were about twenty-five people in this group. Calley said, "When I walk away, I want them all killed." Meadlo and Widmer fired into this group with his M16 on automatic fire. Cowan was there and fired into the people too, but I don't think he wanted to do it. There were others firing into this group, but I don't remember who. Calley had two Vietnamese with him at this time and he killed them, too, by shooting them with his M16 rifle on automatic fire. I didn't want to get involved and I walked away. There was no reason for this killing. These were mainly women and children and a few old men. They weren't trying to escape or attack or anything. It was murder.

A woman came out of a hut with a baby in her arms and she was crying. She was crying because her little boy had been in front of her hut and between the well and the hut someone had killed the child by shooting it. She came out of the hut with her baby and Midmer shot her with an M16 and she fell. When she fell, she dropped the baby and then Widmer opened up on the baby with his M16 and killed the baby, too.

I also saw another woman come out of a hut and Calley grabbed her by the hair and shot her with a caliber .45 pistol. He held her by the hair for a minute and then let go and she fell to the ground. Some enlisted man standing there said, "Well, she'll be in the big rice paddy in the sky."

Robert Maples, Witness for the Prosecution
Direct examination by Aubrey Daniels for the prosecution:

A: We were grabbing up people. We went into hooches, got some of the people there and shot at them. One woman come up and showed me her arm, where she had been shot. She was elderly. I couldn't see how old she was. The guys pushed these people up on the trail, a few women, kids. We just moved through the village. We came to this hold or ditch or something. I was with Bergthold. Calley was there at the ditch and he asked Stanley to interpret for him. We came up. They had people standing by the hold. Calley and Meadlo were firing at the people. They were firing into the hole. I saw Meadlo firing into the hole.

Q: Where was Lieutenant Calley?
A: There. Firing.

Q: Where was his weapon?
A: Pointing into the hole.

Q: Did you have any conversation with Lieutenant Calley at that ditch?
A: Yes

Q: What did he say?
A: He asked me to use my machine gun.

Q: At the ditch?
A: Yes.

Q: What did you say?
A: I refused.

Cross examination by George Latimer:

Q: Were they firing single shot or automatic?
A: I haven't any idea. Meadlo and Lieutenant Calley was both firing into that hole. I saw people go into that hole and no one come out. That's all I know.

Q: Well, you've changed your testimony, haven't you? Didn't you tell the Peers committee in January, 1970 that you never saw Calley pushing people into that hole?
A: I never paid it no mind. I just remembered now. I haven't changed my testimony. I remember Calley was pushing people into that hole. Over a period of time, you forget things then you remember.

Q And what else have you remembered that you saw?
A: I saw Meadlo crying.

Q: From seventy-five yards away?
A: Yes.

Q: You saw tears in his eyes?
A: Yes. I saw tears in Meadlo's eyes.

Q: He had on his helmet and his gear and you saw tears in his eyes?
A: Yes.

Q: Do you remember anything else?
A: No.

Q: Well, tell me, what was so remarkable about Meadlo that made you remember him?
A: He was firing and crying.

Q: He was pointing his weapon away from you and then you saw tears in his eyes?
A: Yes.

Dennis Conti, Witness for the Prosecution
Direct examination by Aubrey Daniels:

A: As I came up, he [Calley] said round up the people.

Q: What did you do?

A: So I did, rounded up the people. There were five or six, mostly women and children. They were unarmed and huddled together.

Q: "What did you do with them?
A: I brought them back to Calley on the trail. There were others there. Thirty or forty. All women and children I remember one old man. They were in their sixties to infants.

Q: What were they doing?
A: Just standing there.

Q: Who was with them?
A: The only GI I remember was Meadlo.

Q: What happened then?
A: Calley told me and Meadlo to take the people off and push them in a rice paddy. We took them out there, pushed them off the trail and made them squat down and bunch up so they couldn't get up and run. We stayed there and guarded the. At this time, I see a young child running from a hootch toward us. He seen us and he took off. I dropped my gear and checked out a hootch with a woman and a child in it. There was an old woman in a under. I took her out and put her on the ground. Then I saw a man running away. I took the other woman and child to the group. The old woman wouldn't go, so I left her there.

Q: What was Meadlo doing at this time?
A: He was guarding the people?

Q: Where was he?
A: He was standing on the village side of the people.

Q: Then what happened?
A: Lieutenant Calley came out and said take care of these people. So we said, okay, so we stood there and watched them. He went away, then he came back and said, "I thought I told you to take care of these people. We said, "We are." He said, "I mean, kill them. I was a little stunned and I didn't know what to do. He said, "Come around this side. We'll get on line and we'll fire into them." I said, "No, I've got a grenade launcher. I'll

watch the tree line. I stood behind them and they stood side by side. So they — Calley and Meadlo—got on line and fired directly into the people. There were bursts and single shots for two minutes. It was automatic. The people screamed and yelled and fell. I guess they tried to get up, too. They couldn't. That was it. They people were pretty well messed up. Lots of heads was shot off, pieces of heads and pieces of flesh flew off the sides and arms. They were all messed up. Meadlo fired a little bit and broke down. He was crying. He said he couldn't do any more. He couldn't kill any more people. He couldn't fire into the people any more. He gave me his weapon into my hands. I said I wouldn't. "If they're going to be killed, I'm not going to do it. Let Lieutenant Calley do it, I told him. So I gave Meadlo back his weapon. At that time there was only a few kids still alive Lieutenant Calley killed them one-by-one. Then I saw a group of five women and six kids—eleven in all—going to a tree line. "Get 'em! Get 'em! Kill 'em! Calley told me. I waited until they got to the line and fired off four or five grenades. I don't know what happened....

Cross examination by Richard Kay:

Q: Did you see any dead bodies at My Lai?—How many?
A: Quite a few

Q: Were they sleeping or did they appear to be dead?
A: Well, they had holes in 'em so I assumed they were dead...

Q: Were you under medical treatment that day?
A: No.

Q: Isn't it a fact that you were taking penicillin for venereal disease?
A: No. . . . Oh, yeah you're right. I was getting shots.

Q: Isn't it a fact that the medic was carrying penicillin to give you that day on the mission?
A: Yeah, I guess you're right.

Q: And weren't you under the influence of marijuana on March 16, 1968?

A: No.

Q: Didn't you smoke it the night before?

A: No.

Q: Didn't you smoke it before getting into the helicopters that morning?

A: No.

Q: Weren't you a constant marijuana smoker?

A: No.

Q: Did you ever open your pants in front of a woman in the village of My Lai?

A: No.

Q: Isn't it a fact that you were going through My Lai that day looking for women?

A: No.

Q: Didn't you carry a woman half-nude on your shoulders and throw her down and say that say was too dirty to rape? You did do that, didn't you?

A: Oh yeah, but it wasn't at My Lai....

Q: Didn't you cuss Lieutenant Calley out because he stopped you from performing a perverse, unnatural sex act at My Lai?

A: No

Q: Do you remember you went into a hootch and started to rape a woman and Lieutenant Calley told you to get out? Do you deny that occurred?

A: Yes.

Q: Didn't you go around and tell members of your platoon about the number of times you'd raped Vietnamese women?

A: No.

Q: You didn't like Lieutenant Calley, did you, Mr. Conti?

A: I didn't dislike him; I didn't like him. He was just there.

Q: As a matter of fact, you hated him didn't you?

A: No.

Q: Do you remember one night, you were on guard duty and had a M-79 and you shot all your ammunition so when it came time to go on patrol, you didn't have any ammunition left? You remember that night?

A: That's right I didn't have any ammunition left.

Q: Weren't you mad at Lieutenant Calley for reporting you?

A: I don't think so.

Q: You deny that?

A: Yes, I do.

Q: Mr. Conti, isn't it a fact that you'd like to see Lieutenant Calley hanged?

A: No.

GLOSSARY

hooch/hootch: a thatch house or "hut"

LZ: landing zone

Document Analysis

This document is made up of three different testimonies, all transcripts of oral exchanges. They come in two types: The first constitutes general testimony Herbert L. Carter gave to investigators in an interview. The other two are court transcripts from the direct and cross examination of Robert Maples and Dennis Conti. This difference in type of testimony accounts for variations in structure and content. In the latter two, the lawyers speak as interlocutors, and their motives can be discerned from their statements.

Carter's testimony stands apart from the other two in structure and content. It includes no interlocutors, but rather a continuous summary of the actions Carter had witnessed. In the latter two testimonies, the direct examination by Aubrey Daniels steers the two witnesses to a similar summary of events, but are not as long or as detailed as that of Carter. Although some themes extend across all three testimonies (see "essential themes" below), the differences are significant. For example, Carter repeatedly calls the killings "murder." He establishes his perspective with his frequent use of that word. The word does not appear in the two formal court testimonies, where its use would likely be more limited.

In the latter two documents, the lawyers' motives can be discerned from their statements. Both Maples and Conti are witnesses for the prosecution. Daniels' aims to guide his witnesses into a descriptive account of the events that both incriminates Calley and attempts to depict the brutality of that day. The defense team attempts to discredit the two witnesses in different ways. George Latimer accuses Maples of changing his testimony: "Well, you've changed your testimony, haven't you? Didn't you tell the Peers committee in January, 1970 that you never saw Calley pushing people into that hole?" Maples counters Latimer's assertion with another detail that he did not include in his former testimony, arguing that "you forget things then you remember."

On the other hand, the defense attempts to discredit Conti by smearing his character. By his fourth question, Richard Kay demonstrates an aggression that is palpable: "Isn't it a fact that you were taking penicillin for venereal disease?" The question is not really about Conti's conditions or about medical treatments that might prevent him from being a capable witness; rather, it is intended to smear his character and reveal libertine sexual behavior. Though Conti assents to this loaded question, he refuses two later accusations. Kay accuses

him of being a "constant marijuana smoker" and a rapist. Both accusations are intended to blacken Conti's character, and the latter provides a motive for Conti to resent Calley. According to Kay's vivid questioning, Calley "stopped [Conti] from performing a perverse, unnatural sex act at My Lai," and Conti therefore resented Calley.

One of the defense's main arguments was that Calley simply followed orders. This should be considered in light of the fact that each of these three witnesses refused orders to some degree. Many participants in the massacre did not testify out of fear of incriminating themselves; therefore, it should come as no surprise that the ones who did testify were those more resistant to the killings. Only Carter's testimony includes no sign of his refusal, but later in the sequence of events he shot himself in the foot (literally) in order to be removed from the situation. His account of events should be considered in light of this indirect refusal to participate in the events. The other two testimonies show direct evidence of the witnesses' refusals. In direct examination, Maples bluntly states "I refused." Conti first establishes his separation from Calley by explaining how he misunderstood Calley's order to "take care of these people." Later in his testimony, he cites his weapon, a grenade launcher, as a reason to watch the tree line instead of firing into innocent civilians. However, this plan falters when some civilians escape toward the tree line and Calley orders Conti to kill them. He hesitates but no longer refuses.

Essential Themes

The scene, obviously, is one of aggression, confusion, death, and horror at what was taking place. Any number of emotional signatures can be found in the events at My Lai, and a number of these signatures carry over (albeit in subdued fashion) in the soldiers' accounts.

The question of whether the shooters' weapons were set to automatic appears in all three testimonies. George Latimer prods Robert Maples with a question about this detail, which Maples says he does not remember. In the testimonies of Herbert L. Carter and Conti, the witnesses freely offer the information that the shooters were firing with their weapons set to automatic. They emphasize this fact to show the shooters' eagerness to shoot and inexactness in aiming.

Gender functions the same way in different situations throughout the three testimonies. All the speakers are men, but women play a central role in the accounts of the massacres. In every testimony, women, sometimes in conjunction with children, appear in the narrative as victims. Their gender establishes their status as noncombatants, and the witnesses sometimes emphasize their gender to underscore the heinousness of the killings. The only other appearance of women in the testimonies comes in Richard Kay's cross examination of Dennis Conti. They again play the role of victims as Kay accuses Conti of rape.

—Anthony Vivian

Bibliography and Additional Reading

Allison, William Thomas. *My Lai: An American Atrocity in the Vietnam War.* Baltimore, MD: Johns Hopkins UP, 2012. Print.

Bilton, Michael & Kevin Sim. *Four Hours in My Lai.* New York: Penguin, 2003. Print.

Hersh, Seymour M. *Cover-Up.* New York: Random House, 1972. Print.

_____. *My Lai 4: A Report on the Massacre and Its Aftermath.* New York: Random House, 1970. Print.

■ President Johnson on Limiting the War

Date: March 31, 1968
Author: Lyndon B. Johnson
Genre: speech

Summary Overview

President Lyndon B. Johnson's nationally televised speech of March 31, 1968, included two major announcements: his decision to curtail the bombing campaign over North Vietnam as a way to induce the North Vietnamese into engaging in peace talks and his decision not to seek reelection as president. Both decisions are practically buried in the lengthy presentation, especially the latter announcement, which came in the penultimate paragraph, with little preparation. It marked a precipitous fall for a politician who, just four years earlier, had been elected in a landslide of historic proportions.

Defining Moment

Multiple contexts came together in President Johnson's March 31 speech, encompassing both the war in Vietnam and politics at home. Johnson had always wanted to be remembered as a great president based on his domestic policies, a program that he had termed the Great Society. He became closely identified with the Vietnam War, which he viewed as a threat to that domestic legacy. He feared that defeat in Vietnam would undermine political support for the Great Society. His decisions to escalate had been motivated by that fear as much as by events on the battlefield.

Until 1968, the escalation of the war, not the prospect of defeat, roiled US politics and fueled the antiwar movement. Then came the Viet Cong's Tet Offensive of January–February 1968, which undermined public faith in the official narrative of how well the war was going. (This was compounded by the Pentagon's confusing analysis that the offensive had backfired, resulting in the decimation of the Viet Cong, but also that US military leaders would now need 205,000 more troops.) On March 26, the "Wise Men," a team of elder statesmen that Johnson consulted, changed their previously optimistic view of the war's prospects, determining that it was time to move toward disengagement. Turmoil

extended into the president's party. Senator Eugene McCarthy (D-MN), whom Johnson had considered as a possible running mate in 1964, challenged him for the Democratic nomination on an antiwar platform. Although Johnson defeated McCarthy in the New Hampshire primary, the outcome was close enough (49.4 percent to 42.4 percent) to be a humiliation for an incumbent president. Moreover, Johnson was trailing in the polls for the next primary, Wisconsin's, scheduled for April 2. Senator Robert Kennedy (D-NY), encouraged by these results, joined the race within days. At the same time that the war was dividing the Democratic Party, segregationist Southern Democrats were reacting to Johnson's civil rights agenda by rallying around Governor George Wallace (D-GA), who was running for president as an independent.

Also, unknown to the public at the time, Johnson's health was deteriorating. It was not certain that he would live through another term, and he had struggled with the idea of announcing his retirement during his State of the Union address in January. He had already fulfilled his domestic agenda, and he may have concluded that he had become controversial enough that stepping down was the surest way to secure his domestic legacy. The war in Vietnam clearly was not going well, but if nothing else, he could structure his exit in such a way that he left the scene as a peacemaker. This he sought to do in his March 31 speech. Still, the announcement that he would not seek reelection took the public by surprise. Johnson eventually endorsed Vice President Hubert Humphrey, who had not challenged him before his decision to retire from office, but only after Humphrey agreed to continue Johnson's policies. Humphrey was nominated at the Democratic National Convention in August, but then distanced himself from the war starting in late September. Johnson continued to voice support for him, but only as a Democrat and the candidate most likely to sustain the Great Society, without reference to Vietnam.

Author Biography

Lyndon Baines Johnson was born on Aug. 27, 1908, in Stonewall, Texas. He was elected to the US House of Representatives (1937–49) and to the US Senate (1949–61), where he served as Senate majority leader for six years. After unsuccessfully seeking the Democratic nomination for president in 1960 (the first Southerner to make such as attempt since the Civil War), he served as John F. Kennedy's running mate and vice president (1961–63). He succeeded to the presidency upon Kennedy's assassination on November 22, 1963 and was reelected in 1964 in a landslide. Johnson had been a New Deal Democrat in the House, developed a more conservative reputation in the Senate (which he viewed as necessary to win state-wide elections in Texas) and was a noted liberal in the White House. As president, he prioritized civil rights legislation, federal aid to education, and a "War on Poverty," but he also drew the country into the Vietnam War. He acquired a legendary reputation for passing legislation, but this owed as much to the dramatic way in which he came to office, the existing support in Congress for his legislative agenda, and the 2–1 Democratic majorities in both houses (in 1965–66) as it did to Johnson's personal political skills. Johnson was known as LBJ, following the tradition of Democratic presidents Franklin Delano Roosevelt (FDR) and Kennedy (JFK). He died on Jan. 22, 1973, just four years and two days after leaving office.

HISTORICAL DOCUMENT

Good evening, my fellow Americans:

Tonight I want to speak to you of peace in Vietnam and Southeast Asia.

No other question so preoccupies our people. No other dream so absorbs the 250 million human beings who live in that part of the world. No other goal motivates American policy in Southeast Asia.

For years, representatives of our Government and others have traveled the world-seeking to find a basis for peace talks.

Since last September, they have carried the offer that I made public at San Antonio. That offer was this:

That the United States would stop its bombardment of North Vietnam when that would lead promptly to productive discussions-and that we would assume that North Vietnam would not take military advantage of our restraint.

Hanoi denounced this offer, both privately and publicly. Even while the search for peace was going on, North Vietnam rushed their preparations for a savage assault on the people, the government, and the allies of South Vietnam.

Their attack—during the Tet holidays—failed to achieve its principal objectives.

It did not collapse the elected government of South Vietnam or shatter its army—as the Communists had hoped.

It did not produce a "general uprising" among the people of the cities as they had predicted.

The Communists were unable to maintain control of any of the more than 30 cities that they attacked. And they took very heavy casualties.

But they did compel the South Vietnamese and their allies to move certain forces from the countryside into the cities.

They caused widespread disruption and suffering. Their attacks, and the battles that followed, made refugees of half a million human beings.

The Communists may renew their attack any day.

They are, it appears, trying to make 1968 the year of decision in South Vietnam—the year that brings, if not final victory or defeat, at least a turning point in the struggle. This much is clear:

If they do mount another round of heavy attacks, they will not succeed in destroying the fighting power of South Vietnam and its allies.

But tragically, this is also clear: Many men—on both sides of the struggle—will be lost. A nation that has already suffered 20 years of warfare will suffer once again. Armies on both sides will take new casualties. And the war will go on.

There is no need for this to be so.

There is no need to delay the talks that could bring an end to this long and this bloody war.

Tonight, I renew the offer I made last August—to stop the bombardment of North Vietnam. We ask that talks begin promptly, that they be serious talks on the substance of peace. We assume that during those talks Hanoi will not take advantage of our restraint.

We are prepared to move immediately toward peace through negotiations.

So, tonight, in the hope that this action will lead to early talks, I am taking the first step to deescalate the conflict. We are reducing—substantially reducing—the present level of hostilities.

And we are doing so unilaterally, and at once.

Tonight, I have ordered our aircraft and our naval vessels to make no attacks on North Vietnam, except in the area north of the demilitarized zone where the continuing enemy buildup directly threatens allied forward positions and where the movements of their troops and supplies are clearly related to that threat.

The area in which we are stopping our attacks includes almost 90 percent of North Vietnam's population, and most of its territory. Thus there will be no attacks around the principal populated areas, or in the food-producing areas of North Vietnam.

Even this very limited bombing of the North could come to an early end—if our restraint is matched by restraint in Hanoi. But I cannot in good conscience stop all bombing so long as to do so would immediately and directly endanger the lives of our men and our allies. Whether a complete bombing halt becomes possible in the future will be determined by events.

Our purpose in this action is to bring about a reduction in the level of violence that now exists.

It is to save the lives of brave men—and to save the lives of innocent women and children. It is to permit the contending forces to move closer to a political settlement.

And tonight, I call upon the United Kingdom and I call upon the Soviet Union—as cochairmen of the Geneva Conferences, and as permanent members of the United Nations Security Council—to do all they can to move from the unilateral act of deescalation that I have just announced toward genuine peace in Southeast Asia.

Now, as in the past, the United States is ready to send its representatives to any forum, at any time, to discuss the means of bringing this ugly war to an end.

I am designating one of our most distinguished Americans, Ambassador Averell Harriman, as my personal representative for such talks. In addition, I have asked Ambassador Llewellyn Thompson, who returned from Moscow for consultation, to be available to join Ambassador Harriman at Geneva or any other suitable place—just as soon as Hanoi agrees to a conference.

I call upon President Ho Chi Minh to respond positively, and favorably, to this new step toward peace.

But if peace does not come now through negotiations, it will come when Hanoi understands that our common resolve is unshakable, and our common strength is invincible.

Tonight, we and the other allied nations are contributing 600,000 fighting men to assist 700,000 South Vietnamese troops in defending their little country.

Our presence there has always rested on this basic belief: The main burden of preserving their freedom must be carried out by them—by the South Vietnamese themselves.

We and our allies can only help to provide a shield behind which the people of South Vietnam can survive and can grow and develop. On their efforts—on their determination and resourcefulness—the outcome will ultimately depend.

That small, beleaguered nation has suffered terrible punishment for more than 20 years.

I pay tribute once again tonight to the great courage and endurance of its people. South Vietnam supports armed forces tonight of almost 700,000 men—and I call your attention to the fact that this is the equivalent of more than 10 million in our own population. Its people maintain their firm determination to be free of domination by the North.

There has been substantial progress, I think, in building a durable government during these last 3 years. The South Vietnam of 1965 could not have survived the enemy's Tet offensive of 1968. The elected government of South Vietnam survived that attack—and is rapidly repairing the devastation that it wrought.

The South Vietnamese know that further efforts are going to be required:

- to expand their own armed forces,
- to move back into the countryside as quickly as possible,
- to increase their taxes,
- to select the very best men that they have for civil and military responsibility,
- to achieve a new unity within their constitutional government, and
- to include in the national effort all those groups who wish to preserve South Vietnam's control over its own destiny.

Last week President Thiêu ordered the mobilization of 135,000 additional South Vietnamese. He plans to reach—as soon as possible—a total military strength of more than 800,000 men.

To achieve this, the Government of South Vietnam started the drafting of 19-year-olds on March 1st. On May 1st, the Government will begin the drafting of 18-year-olds.

Last month, 10,000 men volunteered for military service—that was two and a half times the number of volunteers during the same month last year. Since the middle of January, more than 48,000 South Vietnamese have joined the armed forces—and nearly half of them volunteered to do so.

All men in the South Vietnamese armed forces have had their tours of duty extended for the duration of the war, and reserves are now being called up for immediate active duty.

President Thiêu told his people last week: "We must make greater efforts and accept more sacrifices because, as I have said many times, this is our country. The existence of our nation is at stake, and this is mainly a Vietnamese responsibility."

He warned his people that a major national effort is required to root out corruption and incompetence at all levels of government.

We applaud this evidence of determination on the part of South Vietnam. Our first priority will be to support their effort.

We shall accelerate the reequipment of South Vietnam's armed forces—in order to meet the enemy's increased firepower. This will enable them progressively to undertake a larger share of combat operations against the Communist invaders.

On many occasions I have told the American people that we would send to Vietnam those forces that are required to accomplish our mission there. So, with that as our guide, we have previously authorized a force level of approximately 525,000.

Some weeks ago—to help meet the enemy's new offensive—we sent to Vietnam about 11,000 additional Marine and airborne troops. They were deployed by air in 48 hours, on an emergency basis. But the artillery, tank, aircraft, medical, and other units that were needed to work with and to support these infantry troops in combat could not then accompany them by air on that short notice.

In order that these forces may reach maximum combat effectiveness, the Joint Chiefs of Staff have recommended to me that we should prepare to send—during the next 5 months—support troops totaling approximately 13,500 men.

A portion of these men will be made available from our active forces. The balance will come from reserve component units which will be called up for service.

The actions that we have taken since the beginning of the year

- to reequip the South Vietnamese forces,
- to meet our responsibilities in Korea, as well as our responsibilities in Vietnam,
- to meet price increases and the cost of activating and deploying reserve forces,
- to replace helicopters and provide the other military supplies we need, all of these actions are going to require additional expenditures.

The tentative estimate of those additional expenditures is $2.5 billion in this fiscal year, and $2.6 billion in the next fiscal year.

These projected increases in expenditures for our national security will bring into sharper focus the Nation's need for immediate action: action to protect the prosperity of the American people and to protect the strength and the stability of our American dollar.

On many occasions I have pointed out that, without a tax bill or decreased expenditures, next year's deficit would again be around $20 billion. I have emphasized the need to set strict priorities in our spending. I have stressed that failure to act and to act promptly and decisively would raise very strong doubts throughout the world about America's willingness to keep its financial house in order.

Yet Congress has not acted. And tonight we face the sharpest financial threat in the postwar era—a threat to the dollar's role as the keystone of international trade and finance in the world.

Last week, at the monetary conference in Stockholm, the major industrial countries decided to take a big step toward creating a new international monetary asset that will strengthen the international monetary system. I am very proud of the very able work done by Secretary Fowler and Chairman Martin of the Federal Reserve Board.

But to make this system work the United States just must bring its balance of payments to—or very close to—equilibrium. We must have a responsible fiscal policy in this country. The passage of a tax bill now, together with expenditure control that the Congress may desire and dictate, is absolutely necessary to protect this Nation's security, to continue our prosperity, and to meet the needs of our people.

What is at stake is 7 years of unparalleled prosperity. In those 7 years, the real income of the average American, after taxes, rose by almost 30 percent—a gain as large as that of the entire preceding 19 years.

So the steps that we must take to convince the world are exactly the steps we must take to sustain our own economic strength here at home. In the past 8 months, prices and interest rates have risen because of our inaction.

We must, therefore, now do everything we can to move from debate to action—from talking to voting. There is, I believe—I hope there is—in both Houses of the Congress—a growing sense of urgency that this situation just must be acted upon and must be corrected.

My budget in January was, we thought, a tight one. It fully reflected our evaluation of most of the demanding needs of this Nation.

But in these budgetary matters, the President does not decide alone. The Congress has the power and the duty to determine appropriations and taxes.

The Congress is now considering our proposals and they are considering reductions in the budget that we submitted.

As part of a program of fiscal restraint that includes the tax surcharge, I shall approve appropriate reductions in the January budget when and if Congress so decides that that should be done.

One thing is unmistakably clear, however: Our deficit just must be reduced. Failure to act could bring on conditions that would strike hardest at those people that all of us are trying so hard to help.

These times call for prudence in this land of plenty. I believe that we have the character to provide it, and tonight I plead with the Congress and with the people to act promptly to serve the national interest, and thereby serve all of our people.

Now let me give you my estimate of the chances for peace:

- the peace that will one day stop the bloodshed in South Vietnam,
- that will permit all the Vietnamese people to rebuild and develop their land,
- that will permit us to turn more fully to our own tasks here at home.

I cannot promise that the initiative that I have announced tonight will be completely successful in achieving peace any more than the 30 others that we have undertaken and agreed to in recent years.

But it is our fervent hope that North Vietnam, after years of fighting that have left the issue unresolved, will now cease its efforts to achieve a military victory and will join with us in moving toward the peace table.

And there may come a time when South Vietnamese—on both sides—are able to work out a way to settle their own differences by free political choice rather than by war.

As Hanoi considers its course, it should be in no doubt of our intentions. It must not miscalculate the pressures within our democracy in this election year.

We have no intention of widening this war.

But the United States will never accept a fake solution to this long and arduous struggle and call it peace.

No one can foretell the precise terms of an eventual settlement.

Our objective in South Vietnam has never been the annihilation of the enemy. It has been to bring about a recognition in Hanoi that its objective—taking over the South by force—could not be achieved.

We think that peace can be based on the Geneva Accords of 1954—under political conditions that permit the South Vietnamese—all the South Vietnamese—to chart their course free of any outside domination or interference, from us or from anyone else.

So tonight I reaffirm the pledge that we made at Manila—that we are prepared to withdraw our forces from South Vietnam as the other side withdraws its forces to the north, stops the infiltration, and the level of violence thus subsides.

Our goal of peace and self-determination in Vietnam is directly related to the future of all of Southeast Asia—where much has happened to inspire confidence during the past 10 years. We have done all that we knew how to do to contribute and to help build that confidence.

A number of its nations have shown what can be accomplished under conditions of security. Since 1966, Indonesia, the fifth largest nation in all the world, with a population of more than 100 million people, has had a government that is dedicated to peace with its neighbors and improved conditions for its own people. Political and economic cooperation between nations has grown rapidly.

I think every American can take a great deal of pride in the role that we have played in bringing this about in Southeast Asia. We can rightly judge—as responsible Southeast Asians themselves do—that the progress of the past 3 years would have been far less likely—if not completely impossible—if America's sons and others had not made their stand in Vietnam.

At Johns Hopkins University, about 3 years ago, I announced that the United States would take part in the great work of developing Southeast Asia, including the Mekong Valley, for all the people of that region. Our determination to help build a better land-a better land for men on both sides of the present conflict—has not diminished in the least. Indeed, the ravages of war, I think, have made it more urgent than ever.

So, I repeat on behalf of the United States again tonight what I said at Johns Hopkins—that North Vietnam could take its place in this common effort just as soon as peace comes.

Over time, a wider framework of peace and security in Southeast Asia may become possible. The new cooperation of the nations of the area could be a foundation-stone. Certainly friendship with the nations of such a Southeast Asia is what the United States seeks—and that is all that the United States seeks.

One day, my fellow citizens, there will be peace in Southeast Asia.

It will come because the people of Southeast Asia want it—those whose armies are at war tonight, and those who, though threatened, have thus far been spared.

Peace will come because Asians were willing to work for it—and to sacrifice for it—and to die by the thousands for it.

But let it never be forgotten: Peace will come also because America sent her sons to help secure it.

It has not been easy—far from it. During the past 4-1/2 years, it has been my fate and my responsibility to be Commander in Chief. I have lived—daily and nightly—with the cost of this war. I know the pain that it has inflicted. I know, perhaps better than anyone, the misgivings that it has aroused.

Throughout this entire, long period, I have been sustained by a single principle: that what we are doing now, in Vietnam, is vital not only to the security of Southeast Asia, but it is vital to the security of every American.

Surely we have treaties which we must respect. Surely we have commitments that we are going to keep. Resolutions of the Congress testify to the need to resist aggression in the world and in Southeast Asia.

But the heart of our involvement in South Vietnam—under three different presidents, three separate administrations—has always been America's own security.

And the larger purpose of our involvement has always been to help the nations of Southeast Asia become independent and stand alone, self-sustaining, as members of a great world community—at peace with themselves, and at peace with all others.

With such an Asia, our country—and the world—will be far more secure than it is tonight.

I believe that a peaceful Asia is far nearer to reality because of what America has done in Vietnam. I believe that the men who endure the dangers of battle—fighting there for us tonight—are helping the entire world avoid far greater conflicts, far wider wars, far more destruction, than this one.

The peace that will bring them home someday will come. Tonight I have offered the first in what I hope will be a series of mutual moves toward peace.

I pray that it will not be rejected by the leaders of North Vietnam. I pray that they will accept it as a means by which the sacrifices of their own people may be ended. And I ask your help and your support, my fellow citizens, for this effort to reach across the battlefield toward an early peace.

Finally, my fellow Americans, let me say this:

Of those to whom much is given, much is asked. I cannot say and no man could say that no more will be asked of us.

Yet, I believe that now, no less than when the decade began, this generation of Americans is willing to "pay any price, bear any burden, meet any hardship, support any friend, oppose any foe to assure the survival and the success of liberty."

Since those words were spoken by John F. Kennedy, the people of America have kept that compact with mankind's noblest cause.

And we shall continue to keep it.

Yet, I believe that we must always be mindful of this one thing, whatever the trials and the tests ahead. The ultimate strength of our country and our cause will lie not in powerful weapons or infinite resources or boundless wealth, but will lie in the unity of our people.

This I believe very deeply.

Throughout my entire public career I have followed the personal philosophy that I am a free man, an American, a public servant, and a member of my party, in that order always and only.

For 37 years in the service of our Nation, first as a Congressman, as a Senator, and as Vice President, and now as your President, I have put the unity of the people first. I have put it ahead of any divisive partisanship.

And in these times as in times before, it is true that a house divided against itself by the spirit of faction, of party, of region, of religion, of race, is a house that cannot stand.

There is division in the American house now. There is divisiveness among us all tonight. And holding the trust that is mine, as President of all the people, I cannot disregard the peril to the progress of the American people and the hope and the prospect of peace for all peoples.

So, I would ask all Americans, whatever their personal interests or concern, to guard against divisiveness and all its ugly consequences.

Fifty-two months and 10 days ago, in a moment of tragedy and trauma, the duties of this office fell upon me. I asked then for your help and God's, that we might continue America on its course, binding up our wounds, healing our history, moving forward in new unity, to clear the American agenda and to keep the American commitment for all of our people.

United we have kept that commitment. United we have enlarged that commitment.

Through all time to come, I think America will be a stronger nation, a more just society, and a land of greater opportunity and fulfillment because of what we have all done together in these years of unparalleled achievement.

Our reward will come in the life of freedom, peace, and hope that our children will enjoy through ages ahead.

What we won when all of our people united just must not now be lost in suspicion, distrust, selfishness, and politics among any of our people.

Believing this as I do, I have concluded that I should not permit the Presidency to become involved in the partisan divisions that are developing in this political year.

With America's sons in the fields far away, with America's future under challenge right here at home, with our hopes and the world's hopes for peace in the balance every day, I do not believe that I should devote an hour or a day of my time to any personal partisan causes or to any duties other than the awesome duties of this office—the Presidency of your country.

Accordingly, I shall not seek, and I will not accept, the nomination of my party for another term as your President.

But let men everywhere know, however, that a strong, a confident, and a vigilant America stands ready tonight to seek an honorable peace—and stands ready tonight to defend an honored cause—whatever the price, whatever the burden, whatever the sacrifice that duty may require.

Thank you for listening. Good night and God bless all of you.

Document Analysis

The administration was divided over whether outcome of the Tet Offensive represented a breakthrough to be exploited militarily, through yet another troop escalation, or an opportunity to pursue peace talks and a negotiated settlement. Secretary of Defense Robert McNamara, who had gradually turned against the war, resigned at the end of February and was replaced by Clark Clifford. Clifford, who came into office supporting the war, turned against it in a matter of weeks, having concluded that the military was unable to justify its latest troop request. In Clifford's view, escalation would result only in renewed stalemate at a higher level of violence. On the other hand, Secretary of State Dean Rusk and National Security Adviser Walt W. Rostow were convinced that conditions increasingly favored the United States. Johnson typically refused to accept either argument fully. He generally responded to their appeals with compromises and halfway measures. The March 31 speech represents one such compromise. At the same time, in announcing his resignation, he stresses that he would be able to negotiate and pursue the war without having to yield to electoral considerations.

Essential Themes

The top theme in the speech is peace, or rather the prospect of peace, in Vietnam, but it was to be a peace in which the United States still expected to achieve all its objectives. Johnson had made various quiet offers to halt the bombing of North Vietnam and one public offer in a speech in San Antonio in September 1967, but he had conditioned these offers on the other side's engaging in productive peace talks and not taking advantage of US restraint on the battlefield. Hanoi had refused, and the half of Johnson's advisers were skeptical of the idea anyway. At the same time, Johnson stressed that the war was going well and that the nation could afford to pursue both the war in Vietnam and his Great Society program at home. His initial response to the Tet Offensive had been to strengthen his commitment to the ongoing course in Vietnam with allusions to the lessons of Munich and the Domino Theory. In the March 31 speech, however, he did not allude to Munich or the Domino Theory, and his call for higher taxes was the first suggestion that scarce resources would force him to make difficult choices.

The new strategy would be to fight and negotiate simultaneously. In his March 31 speech, Johnson again spoke of halting the bombing in return for meaningful negotiations and for not taking advantage of US restraint, but this time, he did not make them preconditions. He curtailed the bombing immediately and unilaterally. (Bombing was halted north of the twentieth parallel, with the theory that the area south of that line was actively being used to supply communist forces in South Vietnam.) He also offered to send representatives "to any forum, at any time" for talks. He noted that the US objectives in Vietnam were not to annihilate North Vietnam, but to create conditions in which South Vietnam could live in peace without outside domination or interference, adding that the United States would be willing to provide economic assistance to the whole of Southeast Asia after the war ended. (This, however, ignored Hanoi's contention that there was only one Vietnam and that its artificial division into two was itself an artefact of outside domination and interference.) At the same time, Johnson announced that he was sending more troops to South Vietnam, although not nearly as many as the Pentagon had requested. The United States intensified air and ground operations against communist forces within South Vietnam to maintain pressure on Hanoi to make concessions.

By stressing the pro-peace element of his position—in effect, the position of McCarthy and Kennedy—Johnson may have hoped to undermine their chances for the nomination and make it harder for them to attack his policies or to attack Humphrey for defending his legacy. He also implied that the two were divisive partisans indifferent to America's best interests, while he stated explicitly that he was putting the "unity of the people" above partisan interests.

Hanoi agreed to negotiations, which began in May. In October 1968, after Hanoi had agreed to allow Saigon (hitherto dismissed as a US puppet) to participate in the talks—and at a time when the US military position on the ground was improving—Johnson agreed to a complete halt of the bombing of North Vietnam (although the bombing of supply routes through Laos was intensified). The Saigon government, however, delayed and obstructed. President Nguyen Van Thiêu feared that the Johnson administration intended to abandon him and hoped to get more solid support from a Republican administration. (It later emerged that Republican presidential candidate Richard M. Nixon secretly encouraged him to stall the talks.) Indeed, even as the talks proceeded, the Johnson administration remained divided on goals, whether to seek the survival of a viable, independent South Vietnam or simply to extract the United States from its quagmire. In any event, the talks made little progress. Both Hanoi and Washington resisted making concessions, each in the apparent belief that the other was on the verge of capitulation.

—Scott C. Monje, PhD

Bibliography and Additional Reading

Berman, Larry. *Lyndon Johnson's War: The Road to Stalemate in Vietnam.* New York: W. W. Norton, 1989. Print.

Busby, Horace. *The Thirty-First of March: Lyndon Johnson's Final Days in Office.* New York: Farrar, Straus, and Giroux, 2005. Print.

Herring, George C. *LBJ and Vietnam: A Different Kind of War.* Austin, TX: University of Texas Press, 1994. Print.

Jamieson, Patrick E. "Seeing the Lyndon B. Johnson Presidency through the March 31, 1968, Withdrawal Speech." *Presidential Studies Quarterly* 29.1 (March 1999): 134–49. Print.

Warner, Geoffrey. "Lyndon Johnson's War? Part 2: From Escalation to Negotiation." *International Affairs* 81.1 (January 2005): 187–215. Print.

THE ANTIWAR MOVEMENT

Opposition to the Vietnam War began slowly, mainly among religious objectors and peace advocates, but it eventually became widespread. The most public forms of activism were mass demonstrations, collective acts of civil disobedience, and the general expansion of countercultural practices. The locus classicus of the movement was the college campus, where opponents were motivated both by the pressures of the draft and by philosophical (and ideological) misgivings regarding the war and the government's role in it. Increasingly, the official line in the war began to be questioned, including by war veterans. The Vietnam Veterans Against the War helped to "mainstream" antiwar activism, and that organization and a variety of others worked to spread antiwar information and agitation. The Students for a Democratic Society (SDS) was perhaps the best known radical group of the era. Although influential through most of the 1960s, SDS would eventually splinter into extremist camps. More mundane was the effort to get the work done through electoral and legislative politics, but that too proved modestly successful as time passed and opposition to the war grew. By 1970, in the wake of President Richard Nixon's expansion of the war into Cambodia, antiwar sentiment had become pervasive. Yet even then, there also undoubtedly remained something of a "silent majority"—or a "silent half," at least—who supported both the government and the war. As with no other conflict before or since in the modern era, Vietnam split the nation and left a deep scar in the American consciousness.

■ Call for a March on Washington

Date: early 1965
Author(s): Students for a Democratic Society (SDS)
Genre: broadside; political tract

Summary Overview

The document examined here is a call to arms, of sorts, urging students of the United States to stand up against the government in order to exert pressure and bring an end to the US military presence in Vietnam. Sponsored by the radical political group Students for a Democratic Society (SDS), this leaflet expresses its authors' disapproval of the military action in South Vietnam and lists various points of contention and justifications for opposing the war during this turbulent period of American history. Its contents cover economic, social, and political subjects. The march being called for was one of the first in a long line of such demonstrations designed to protest American involvement in Southeast Asia in the 1960s and early 1970s. Such marches took place in Washington, DC, and elsewhere, but the marches at the Capitol were by far the largest and garnered the most attention.

The audience for this announcement, as noted in its opening paragraphs, is American university students. This generation of students would soon come to be known for its engagement in social and political activism, particularly concerning the Vietnam War. Appealing to this group directly, the SDS announcement advocates that each person seek to change the world around him or her in order to make it a better place. The authors considered it unacceptable to remain silent in the face of something, such as a war, with which one disagreed. The SDS wanted to mobilize the power of the population of students in order to create change in the world. The fact that students were generally of draft age (albeit typically exempt during their years of study) made them particularly aware of the hard realities of combat service in Vietnam. Still, many of them also opposed the war on philosophical grounds.

Defining Moment

The announcement for this march came at a time when tensions in the United States had begun to reach a breaking point. At least one march in protest of the war had already occurred (as evidenced by the phrase "this latest march" in the leaflet), and the April 17 march and others like it would follow in the years to come. Such acts demonstrated the growing frustration with the situation in Vietnam and the lack of a clear end for US involvement in the conflict. At this point, the United States (along with the United Nations) had been engaged in South Vietnam for almost ten years, but had directly engaged in combat operations for less than a year (following the Gulf of Tonkin Resolution of August 1964). With the increasing military activities in the country, however, a small number of people—particularly students—had started to become less supportive of their government and the military. Protests, such as this one, became more common as the numbers of casualties and other costs of the war continued to rise.

Author Biography

The Students for a Democratic Society (SDS) began in 1960 as an organization focused on addressing poverty through community organizing and political action. It quickly evolved, however, into a group opposed to the war in Vietnam, the draft, and social and political injustice. The group was student-based and student-run and had its own manifesto and agenda, concerning both domestic and international affairs. It sought, through its actions, to provide a radical critique of the status quo in areas such as racial discrimination, use of nuclear technology, and economic inequality. It became increasingly radicalized in subsequent years and lost much of its following among students and outside sympathizers. By 1969, SDS had fractured into the radical Weather Underground (eventually, the Weathermen) faction and a neo-Maoist group. During its short lifetime, however, it was at the forefront of New Left politics in the United States.

HISTORICAL DOCUMENT

[c. early 1965]

A CALL TO ALL STUDENTS TO March on Washington to end the war in Vietnam

April 17, 1965

THOSE WHO SAY, "GET OUT OF VIETNAM!"

The purpose of this pre-Easter March is to influence the Administration to halt United States participation in the war of aggression in South Vietnam. As you can see from the reproduction, this March will consist of a picket line in front of the White House, a march along the Mall to the Capitol where an attempt will be made to present a statement to the Congress, and a meeting to be addressed by, among others, Senator Ernest Gruening of Alaska and journalist I. F. Stone.

This latest March on Washington is sponsored by the Students for a Democratic Society (SDS). Organized some 60 years ago, it was first known as the Intercollegiate Socialist Society. This organization hopes to develop a grass-roots movement to alter society in the United States and recently announced that it has approximately 1,400 members in 41 campuses and cities, most of which are in the Eastern part of the United States.

The current war in Vietnam is being waged in behalf of a succession of unpopular South Vietnamese dictatorships, not in behalf of freedom. No American-supported South Vietnamese regime in the past few years has gained the support of its people, for the simple reason that the people overwhelmingly want peace, self-determination, and the opportunity for development. American prosecution of the war has deprived them of all three.

- The war is fundamental a civil war, waged by South Vietnamese against their government; it is not a "war of aggression." Military assistance from North Vietnam and China has been minimal; most guerrilla weapons are home made or are captured American arms. The areas of strongest guerrilla control are not the areas adjacent to North Vietnam. And the people could not and cannot be isolated from the guerrillas by forced settlement in "strategic hamlets"; again and again Government military attacks fail because the people tip off the guerrillas; the people and the guerrillas are inseparable. Each repressive Government policy, each napalm bomb, each instance of torture, creates more guerrillas. Further, what foreign weapons the guerrillas have obtained are small arms, and are no match for the bombers and helicopters operated by the Americans. The U.S. government is the only foreign government that has sent major weapons to Vietnam.

- It is a losing war. Well over half of the area of South Vietnam is already governed by the National Liberation Front—the political arm of the "VietCong." In the guerrillas the peasants see relief from dictatorial Government agents; from the United States they get napalm, the jellied gasoline that burns into the flesh. The highly touted "counter-insurgency" the U.S. is applying in its "pilot project war" is only new weaponry, which cannot substitute for popular government. Thousands of Government troops have defected — the traditional signal of a losing counter-guerrilla war. How many more lives must be lost before the Johnson Administration accepts the foregone conclusion?

- It is a self-defeating war. If the U.S. objective is to guarantee self-determination in South Vietnam, that objective is far better served by allowing the South Vietnamese to choose their own government — something provided for by the 1954 Geneva Agreement but sabotaged in 1956 by the American-supported dictator Ngo Dinh Diem and never allowed since. The Diem government that invited U.S. intervention was thus illegitimate, having violated the agreement that established it. The Vietnamese, North and South, have no taste for Chinese domination— these two countries have fought one another for over a thousand years. Moreover, South Vietnam is not a "domino"—the "threat" to it is internal, not Chinese, and the greater threat to stability in other Southeast Asian countries is U.S.-inspired provocation of China, not China's own plans.

- It is a dangerous war. Every passing month of hostilities increases the risk of America escalating and widening the war. Since the '50s U.S.-trained South Vietnamese commando teams have been penetrating North Vietnam, considerably provoking the North Vietnamese. We all know of the presence of American destroyers in the Tonkin Gulf, a body of water surrounded on three sides by North Vietnamese and Chinese territory. How calm would the United States be if Cuban commandos were being sent into Florida, and Chinese ships were "guarding" Cape Cod Bay?

- It is a war never declared by Congress, although it costs almost two million dollars a day and has cost billions of dollars since the U.S. began its involvement. The facts of the war have been systematically concealed by the U.S. government for years, making it appear as if those expenditures have been helping the Vietnamese people. These factors erode the honesty and decency of American political life, and make democracy at home impossible. We are outraged that two million dollars a day is expended for a war on the poor in Vietnam, while government financing is so desperately needed to abolish poverty at home. What kind of America is it whose response to poverty and oppression in South Vietnam is napalm and defoliation, whose response to poverty and oppression in Mississippi is . . . silence?

- It is a hideously immoral war. America is committing pointless murder.

But the signs are plain that America are increasingly disaffected by this state of affairs. To draw together, express, and enlarge the number of these voices of protest, and to make this sentiment visible, Students for a Democratic Society (SDS) is calling for a MARCH ON WASHINGTON TO END THE WAR IN VIETNAM.

We urge the participation of all students who agree with us that the war in Vietnam injures both Vietnamese and Americans, and should be stopped.

The March, to be held on Saturday, April 17, 1965, will include a picketing of the White House, a march down the Mall to the Capitol Building to present a statement to Congress, and a meeting with both student and adult speakers. Senator Ernest Gruening of Alaska and journalist I. F. Stone have already agreed to address the body.

Thousands of us can be heard. We dare not remain silent.

GLOSSARY

guerrilla: a member of a band of soldiers that uses unconventional tactics

the Mall: the National Mall in Washington, DC, a large, grass-covered area, lined by several of the Smithsonian Institution's museums and the National Gallery of Art; it is punctuated by the Washington Monument on one end and the Capitol and its reflecting pool on the other.

defoliation: the elimination of vegetation to gain access to an area; in Vietnam, US forces employed a defoliant called Agent Orange that proved to have lasting toxic effects

Document Analysis

The main objections of the SDS to "the war of aggression in South Vietnam" concern social justice factors, economic factors, and the meaning of freedom in South Vietnam. As shown in the first and second bullet points, the SDS does not find the Vietnam conflict to be one that requires outside, especially American, interference. As they say, it is a civil war. This is one point of view, one not held by a wide sector of society at the time, but it bears noting. The group is calling its audience's attention to an important question: does the United States have the right to interfere in South Vietnam's political affairs—its struggle toward self-determination—especially when so many of Vietnam's own people, in the form of the Viet Cong (communist opposition), are fighting against US forces? The SDS, of course, answers this question with an emphatic no. The group considered American involvement unlawful and morally reprehensible. It also regarded the American government as dishonest and deceptive in its dealings with both the Vietnamese and the American public.

The leaflet also touches on economic considerations—specifically, the financial cost of a conflict not declared as a full-scale war through an act of Congress (save via the Tonkin Gulf Resolution). They observe that great sums of money were being spent on a foreign military action, while many of the socioeconomic problems existing in the United States continued to go unchecked. If poverty and inequality are rampant, the authors argue, why not deal with those domestic issues first, before undertaking a risky foreign venture? There are human costs, too, in such a conflict. The SDS deems the many Vietnamese and American lives lost in the war not only unnecessary, but a crime against humanity. Given the use of chemical weapons, including napalm and Agent Orange, one should understand that far more damage was being done than aid was being rendered.

The document presents a number of pointed questions to its readers. One matter it takes up is the concept of freedom and what freedom means to people in the United States and those in a foreign country. The SDS states that self-determination is the only way for a country to manage its own affairs. No dictators chosen by outside powers and hated by the people should be permitted to thrive. No government hiding its actions and involved in a sea of corruption should be supported by the United States, certainly not militarily. The SDS, in other words, seeks to promote the democratic ideal, as was befitting the group's name. The tone of the document, however, makes it clear that the SDS's efforts were directed toward potentially radical solutions. Although calling on students to march, carry signs, and speak, the SDS authors note that stopping the war was imperative. The implication is that a peaceful demonstration could possibly evolve, at some point, into a more energetic form of protest.

Essential Themes

The Vietnam War and the marches and protests against it left a lasting impression on the American psyche and on the world as a whole. As this SDS leaflet notes, it seemed a "losing war" to many, even at this early stage, and one that its opponents held to be "immoral." The fear of communism and the government's reaction to that fear had split the American populace. Much of the leaflet's rhetoric is meant to persuade students who were on the fence about the war or did not pay it much heed, to wise up and recognize what crimes were being committed in their name. While not all of the antiwar protests of the era provide positive memories for the majority of Americans, they did play an important role in communicating the complexity of the conflict and the moral dilemmas that arise in such situations. Does the United States have a right to enter a foreign country and work to prop up a despised government, or does such action violate the democratic ideal? Is it acceptable to sacrifice great amounts of blood and money in pursuit of a program to defeat communism wherever it takes hold? The April 1965 March on Washington proved to be a significant affair, attracting some 15,000 protesters. Later events continued to draw large crowds of activists and the curious.

As the concluding lines of the leaflet show, when a group works together in a concerted effort, "Thousands of us can be heard." Thus, in the short-term, antiwar protesters tried to end the war—without doing so directly. Yet thousands of protests since have been founded on a similar premise—that and the notion that "we dare not remain silent." Although the SDS fractured and soon disappeared, many of its former members and those participating in its demonstrations remained active in progressive politics or pursued careers in the areas of social justice and community organizing.

—Anna Accettola, MA
Michael Shally-Jensen, PhD

Bibliography and Additional Reading

"The Antiwar Movement." *Ushistory.org.* Independence Hall Association, 2014. Web. <http://www.ushistory.org/us/55d.asp>.

DeBenedetti, Charles & Charles Chatfield. *An American Ordeal: The Antiwar Movement of the Vietnam Era.* Syracuse, NY: Syracuse UP, 1990. Print.

McCormick, Anita Louise. *The Vietnam Antiwar Movement in American History.* Berkeley Heights, NJ: Enslow, 2000. Print.

Sale, Kirkpatrick. *SDS: The Rise and Development of the Students for a Democratic Society.* New York: Random House, 1973. Print.

Shafer, D. Michael. *The Legacy: The Vietnam War in the American Imagination.* Boston: Beacon, 1990. Print.

■ Protest Speech by Paul Potter

Date: April 17, 1965
Author: Paul Potter
Genre: speech; political tract; address

Summary Overview

This document is a speech given at a 1965 march on Washington, DC, at the dawn of the antiwar movement. The speech protests not only the Vietnam War, but also the entire governmental and social system that allowed or fostered such a military conflict. With an audience made up largely of students and members of the Students for a Democratic Society (SDS), Paul Potter, president of the SDS, spoke with passion and enthusiasm, calling for broader changes than just an end to the war. He and his followers wanted to change society and the world to realize peace, justice, and equality. The SDS was just one of the many groups working against the war, but it became one of the most influential, hosting several marches and spreading its message to many and varied groups of people.

Defining Moment

Paul Potter's speech was given at a crucial moment in terms of American participation in the Vietnam War. The United States had been involved in Vietnam for nearly a decade—though only recently had it taken to the battlefield—and the antiwar movement was beginning to gear up. Students for a Democratic Society, led at this time by Potter, was gaining a following and speaking out against the war and the government and its leaders. The SDS and many other Americans believed that the United States had no place to intervene so decisively in another country's affairs. Beyond simply protesting the war, the SDS demanded that the United States turn its attention inward and focus on the major problems in American society, including poverty and racial discrimination.

Delivered at the Washington Monument, following hours of protests outside the White House, the speech inflamed the passions of its listeners and affirmed the reasons why they had gathered there together. The audience of the speech was primarily SDS members and like-minded protesters, but, as Potter himself states, they crossed race, religion, and socioeconomic boundaries in a rare show of mutual interest and support. Collectively, the audience was not simply an antiwar group but one intent on making sweeping changes to government, politics, social organization, and economic realities in the United States and the rest of the world. Although the SDS eventually splintered into smaller factions at the end of the 1960s, their goals were held up by many as ideals throughout the Vietnam era.

Author Biography

Paul Potter was born in 1939 in Illinois and attended Oberlin College. Besides being president of SDS, he was also a founding member and spent many years working within SDS and with other political groups seeking an end to the Vietnam War. In 1971, he wrote a book, *A Name for Ourselves,* about his experiences and his ideas during the SDS years and after. He was married in 1972 and had two children. He continued his work in politics, albeit through more conventional political campaigns and ballot initiatives. Potter died in 1984 at his home in New Mexico. He is still honored for his work and activism today.

HISTORICAL DOCUMENT

Most of us grew up thinking that the United States was a strong but humble nation, that involved itself in world affairs only reluctantly, that respected the integrity of other nations and other systems, and that engaged in wars only as a last resort. This was a nation with no large standing army, with no design for external conquest, that sought primarily the opportunity to develop its own resources and its own mode of living. If at some point we began to hear vague and disturbing things about what this country had done in Latin America, China, Spain and other places, we somehow remained confident about the basic integrity of this nation's foreign policy. The Cold War with all of its neat categories and black and white descriptions did much to assure us that what we had been taught to believe was true.

But in recent years, the withdrawal from the hysteria of the Cold War era and the development of a more aggressive, activist foreign policy have done much to force many of us to rethink attitudes that were deep and basic sentiments about our country. The incredible war in Vietnam has provided the razor, the terrifying sharp cutting edge that has finally severed the last vestige of illusion that morality and democracy are the guiding principles of American foreign policy. The saccharine self righteous moralism that promises the Vietnamese a billion dollars of economic aid at the very moment we are delivering billions for economic and social destruction and political repression is rapidly losing what power it might ever have had to reassure us about the decency of our foreign policy. The further we explore the reality of what this country is doing and planning in Vietnam the more we are driven toward the conclusion of Senator Morse that the United States may well be the greatest threat to peace in the world today. That is a terrible and bitter insight for people who grew up as we did—and our revulsion at that insight, our refusal to accept it as inevitable or necessary, is one of the reasons that so many people have come here today.

The President says that we are defending freedom in Vietnam. Whose freedom? Not the freedom of the Vietnamese. The first act of the first dictator, Diem, the United States installed in Vietnam, was to systematically begin the persecution of all political opposition, non Communist as well as Communist. The first American military supplies were not used to fight Communist insurgents; they were used to control, imprison or kill any who sought something better for Vietnam than the personal aggrandizement, political corruption and the profiteering of the Diem regime. The elite of the forces that we have trained and equipped are still used to control political unrest in Saigon and defend the latest dictator from the people.

And yet in a world where dictatorships are so commonplace and popular control of government so rare, people become callous to the misery that is implied by dictatorial power. The rationalizations that are used to defend political despotism have been drummed into us so long that we have somehow become numb to the possibility that some¬thing else might exist. And it is only the kind of terror we see now in Vietnam that awakens conscience and reminds us that there is something deep in us that cries out against dictatorial suppression.

The pattern of repression and destruction that we have developed and justified in the war is so thorough that it can only be called cultural genocide. I am not simply talking about napalm or gas or crop destruction or torture, hurled indiscriminately on women and children, insurgent and neutral, upon the first suspicion of rebel activity. That in itself is horrendous and incredible beyond belief. But it is only part of a larger pattern of destruction to the very fabric of the country. We have uprooted the people from the land and imprisoned them in concentration camps called "sunrise villages." Through conscription and direct political intervention and control, we have destroyed local customs and traditions, trampled upon those things of value which give dignity and purpose to life.

What is left to the people of Vietnam after 20 years of war? What part of themselves and their own lives will those who survive be able to salvage from the wreckage of their country or build on the "peace" and "security" our Great Society offers them in reward for their allegiance? How can anyone be surprised that people who have had total war waged on themselves and their culture rebel in increasing numbers against that tyranny? What other course is available? And still our only response to rebellion is more vigorous repression, more merciless opposition to the social and cultural institutions which sustain dignity and the will to resist.

Not even the President can say that this is a war to defend the freedom of the Vietnamese people. Perhaps what the President means when he speaks of freedom is the freedom of the American people.

What in fact has the war done for freedom in America? It has led to even more vigorous governmental efforts to control information, manipulate the press and pressure and persuade the public through distorted or downright dishonest documents such as the White Paper on Vietnam. It has led to the confiscation of films and other anti war material and the vigorous harassment by the FBI of some of the people who have been most outspokenly active in their criticism of the war. As the war escalates and the administration seeks more actively to gain support for any initiative it may choose to take, there has been the beginnings of a war psychology unlike anything that has burdened this country since the 1950s. How much more of Mr. Johnson's freedom can we stand? How much freedom will be left in this country if there is a major war in Asia? By what weird logic can it be said that the freedom of one people can only be maintained by crushing another?

In many ways this is an unusual march because the large majority of people here are not involved in a peace movement as their primary basis of concern. What is exciting about the participants in this march is that so many of us view ourselves consciously as participants as well in a movement to build a more decent society. There are students here who have been involved in protests over the quality and kind of education they are receiving in growingly bureaucratized, depersonalized institutions called universities; there are Negroes from Mississippi and Alabama who are struggling against the tyranny and repression of those states; there are poor people here—Negro and white—from Northern urban areas who are attempting to build movements that abolish poverty and secure democracy; there are faculty who are beginning to question the relevance of their institutions to the critical problems facing the society. Where will these people and the movements they are a part of be if the President is allowed to expand the war in Asia? What happens to the hopeful beginnings of expressed discontent that are trying to shift American attention to long neglected internal priorities of shared abundance, democracy and decency at home when those priorities have to compete with the all consuming priorities and psychology of a war against an enemy thousands of miles away?

The President mocks freedom if he insists that the war in Vietnam is a defense of American freedom. Perhaps the only freedom that this war protects is the freedom of the war-hawks in the Pentagon and the State Department to experiment with counter insurgency and guerrilla warfare in Vietnam.

Vietnam, we may say, is a laboratory ran by a new breed of gamesmen who approach war as a kind of rational exercise in international power politics. It is the testing ground and staging area for a new American response to the social revolution that is sweeping through the impoverished downtrodden areas of the world. It is the beginning of the American counter revolution, and so far no one—none of us—not the *NY Times*, nor 17 Neutral Nations, nor dozens of worried allies, nor the United States Congress have been able to interfere with the freedom of the President and the Pentagon to carry out that experiment.

Thus the war in Vietnam has only dramatized the demand of ordinary people to have some opportunity to make their own lives, and of their unwillingness, even under incredible odds, to give up the struggle against external domination. We are told, however, that the struggle can be legitimately suppressed since it might lead to the development of a Communist system, and before that ultimate menace all criticism is supposed to melt.

This is a critical point and there are several things that must be said here—not by way of celebration, but because I think they are the truth. First, if this country were serious about giving the people of Vietnam some alternative to a Communist social revolution, that opportunity was sacrificed in 1954 when we helped to install Diem and his repression of non Communist movements. There is no indication that we were serious about that goal—that we were ever willing to contemplate the risks of allowing the Vietnamese to choose their own destinies. Second, those people who insist now that Vietnam can be neutralized are for the most part looking for a sugar coating to cover the bitter bill. We must accept the consequences that calling for an end of the war in Vietnam is in fact allowing for the likelihood that a Vietnam without war will be a self styled Communist Vietnam. Third, this country must come to understand that creation of a Communist country in the world today is not an ultimate defeat. If people are given the opportunity to choose their own lives it is likely that some of them will choose what we have called "Communist systems." We are not powerless in that situation. Recent years have finally and indisputably broken the myth that the Communist world is monolithic and have conclusively shown that American power can be significant in aiding countries dominated by greater powers to become more independent and self determined. And yet the war that we are creating and escalating in Southeast Asia is rapidly eroding the base of independence of North Vietnam as it is forced to turn to China and the Soviet Union, involving them in the war and involving itself in the compromises that that implies. Fourth, I must say to you that I would rather see Vietnam Communist than see it under continuous subjugation of the ruin that American domination has brought.

But the war goes on; the freedom to conduct that war depends on the dehumanization not only of Vietnamese people but of Americans as well; it depends on the construction of a system of premises and thinking that insulates the President and his advisers thoroughly and completely from the human consequences of the decisions they make. I do not believe that the President or Mr. Rusk or Mr. McNamara or even McGeorge Bundy are particularly evil men. If asked to throw napalm on the back of a ten year old child they would shrink in horror—but their decisions have led to mutilation and death of thousands and thousands of people.

What kind of system is it that allows good men to make those kinds of decisions? What kind of system is it that justifies the United States or any country seizing the destinies of the Vietnamese people and using them callously for its own purpose? What kind of system is it that disenfranchises people in the South, leaves millions upon millions of people throughout the country impoverished and excluded from the mainstream and promise of American society, that creates faceless and terrible bureaucracies and makes those the place where people spend their lives and do their work, that consistently puts material values before human values—and still persists in calling itself free and still persists in finding itself fit to police the world? What place is there for ordinary men in that system and how are they to control it, make it bend itself to their wills rather than bending them to its?

We must name that system. We must name it, describe it, analyze it, understand it and change it. For it is only when that system is changed and brought under control that there can be any hope for stopping the forces that create a war in Vietnam today or a murder in the South tomorrow or all the incalculable, innumerable more subtle atrocities that are worked on people all over—all the time.

How do you stop a war then? If the war has its roots deep in the institutions of American society, how do you stop it? Do you march to Washington? Is that enough? Who will hear us? How can you make the decision makers hear us, insulated as they are, if they cannot hear the screams of a little girl burnt by napalm?

I believe that the administration is serious about expanding the war in Asia. The question is whether the people here are as serious about ending it. I wonder what it means for each of us to say we want to end the war in Vietnam—whether, if we accept the full meaning of that statement and the gravity of the situation, we can simply leave the march and go back to the routines of a society that acts as if it were not in the midst of a grave crisis. Maybe we, like the President, are insulated from the consequences of our own decision to end the war. Maybe we have yet really to listen to the screams of a burning child and decide that we cannot go back to whatever it is we did before today until that war has ended.

There is no simple plan, no scheme or gimmick that can be proposed here. There is no simple way to attack something that is deeply rooted in the society. If the people of this country are to end the war in Vietnam, and to change the institutions which create it, then the people of this country must create a massive social movement—and if that can be built around the issue of Vietnam then that is what we must do.

By a social movement I mean more than petitions or letters of protest, or tacit support of dissident Congressmen; I mean people who are willing to change their lives, who are willing to challenge the system, to take the problem of change seriously. By a social movement I mean an effort that is powerful enough to make the country understand that our problems are not in Vietnam, or China or Brazil or outer space or at the bottom of the ocean, but are here in the United States. What we must do is begin to build a democratic and humane society in which Vietnams are unthinkable, in which human life and initiative are precious. The reason there are twenty thousand people here today and not a hundred or none at all is because five years ago in the South students began to build a social movement to change the system. The reason there are poor people, Negro and white, housewives, faculty members, and many others here in Washington is because that movement has grown and spread and changed and reached out as an expression of the broad concerns of people throughout the society. The reason the war and the system it represents will be stopped, if it is stopped before it destroys all of us, will be because the movement has become strong enough to exact change in the society. Twenty thousand people, the people here, if they were serious, if they were willing to break out of their isolation and to accept the consequences of a decision to end the war and commit themselves to building a movement wherever they are and in whatever way they effectively can, would be, I'm convinced, enough.

To build a movement rather than a protest or some series of protests, to break out of our insulations and accept the consequences of our decisions, in effect to change our lives, means that we can open ourselves to the reactions of a society that believes that it is moral and just, that we open ourselves to libeling and persecution, that we dare to be really seen as wrong in a society that doesn't tolerate fundamental challenges.

It means that we desert the security of our riches and reach out to people who are tied to the mythology of American power and make them part of our movement.

We must reach out to every organization and individual in the country and make them part of our movement.

But that means that we build a movement that works not simply in Washington but in communities and with the problems that face people throughout the society. That means that we build a movement that understands Vietnam in all its horror as but a symptom of a deeper malaise, that we build a movement that makes possible the implementation of the values that would have prevented Vietnam, a movement based on the integrity of man and a belief in man's capacity to tolerate all the weird formulations of society that men may choose to strive for; a movement that will build on the new and creative forms of protest that are beginning to emerge, such as the teach in, and extend their efforts and intensify them; that we will build a movement that will find ways to support the increasing numbers of young men who are unwilling to and will not fight in Vietnam; a movement that will not tolerate the escalation or prolongation of this war but will, if necessary, respond to the administration war effort with massive civil disobedience¬ all over the country, that will wrench the country into a confrontation with the issues of the war; a movement that must of necessity reach out to all these people in Vietnam or elsewhere who are struggling to find decency and control for their lives.

For in a strange way the people of Vietnam and the people on this demonstration are united in much more than a common concern that the war be ended. In both countries there are people struggling to build a movement that has the power to change their condition. The system that frustrates these movements is the same. All our lives, our destinies, our very hopes to live, depend on our ability to overcome that system.

GLOSSARY

disenfranchise: to deprive someone of their right to citizenship, the right to vote, or other privileges

malaise: a condition of general weakness or discomfort; a vague or unfocused feeling; lethargy

monolithic: consisting of one piece; solid; unbroken; characterized by massiveness, total uniformity, rigidity, etc.

napalm: a jellylike substance which is highly flammable and explosive, used in bombs

GLOSSARY CONTINUED

saccharine: similar to sugar; cloyingly agreeable or ingratiating

war-hawk: one who favors war and pushes for its beginning or continuation

Document Analysis

This address, officially titled "Naming the System," was an inspiring speech to its audience, designed to specify the ways in which the US government had let down its citizens. No longer was America an isolationist, or non-interventionist country; rather, now it was one that readily got involved in foreign affairs. The idea of "Naming the System" was intended to show how the American system of government and its involvement in international affairs had changed in recent decades and what effect those changes had had in terms of the ideal of freedom, both in the United States and throughout the world.

As Potter notes, "the development of a more aggressive, activist foreign policy" is something that came about after World War II. Prior to that, the United States maintained a largely non-interventionist stance with respect to other countries, except in a few cases, such as the Spanish-American War, when the United States sought to gain control of the Philippines. But after World War II, America became more interested in attempting to improve or alter foreign governments for the benefit of the United States. It is the building of this interventionist ideology that Potter criticizes. He and his audience believed that the United States had no right to involve itself militarily in foreign conflicts, such as the one raging in Vietnam, or to act as a kind of police officer for the world. Interventionism was especially galling since there were so many issues at home that needed attention, including poverty and racially-motivated violence and discrimination.

Additionally, Potter provides a critique of the state of freedom, both inside and outside of America. What does freedom mean in the context of the 1960s? Potter denies flatly that the Vietnam War was "a war to defend the freedom of the Vietnamese people," nor does he see the war as expanding freedom in the United States. America, in its attempt to promote freedom in another country, had damaged both that country and its own citizens. The Vietnamese had been terribly brutalized by both their enemies and their allies in the guise of fostering freedom. It is true that a fear of communism prevailed in the United States at the time period, but that did not mean, in Potter's view and in the eyes of many others, that the United States could install an anticommunist dictator, hated by his own people.

Essential Themes

In the short term, the speaker's outcry against the Vietnam War and American participation in it served to rally the other antiwar activists. Potter and others like him were not content to allow the US government to do whatever it wanted, especially when its actions flew in the face of American ideals. Peacefully, with marches and rallies, as well as violently, with fires and explosions, antiwar and social reform activists in the 1960s made themselves heard.

In the longer term, many of the questions that Potter raised still go unanswered. What does freedom mean in the modern world? How has it changed in recent decades? Can American citizens maintain their freedoms when the government is engaged in violent activities abroad? In a world where laws have to be passed to keep governmental agencies from collecting data on the nation's citizens, free of the constraints of a warrant, what does freedom mean? Paul Potter was not protesting just the Vietnam War; he was protesting a change in worldview that he found dangerous and immoral.

—*Anna Accettola, MA*

Bibliography and Additional Reading

Anderson, Terry H. *The Movement and the Sixties*. New York: Oxford UP, 1996. Print.

Dancis, Bruce. *Resister: A Story of Protest and Prison during the Vietnam War*. Ithaca: Cornell UP, 2014. Print.

"Paul Potter." *50th Anniversary Conference—A New Insurgency: The Port Huron Statement in Its Time and*

Ours. University of Michigan, n.d. Web. <https://www.lsa.umich.edu/phs>.

Potter, Paul. *A Name for Ourselves; Feelings about Authentic Identity, Love, Intuitive Politics,* Us. Boston: Little, Brown, 1971. Print.

Rudd, Mark. *Underground: My Life with SDS and the Weathermen*. New York: William Morrow, 2009. Print.

■ Message from Ho Chi Minh

Date: December 23, 1966
Author: Ho Chi Minh
Genre: address; letter

Summary Overview

On December 23, 1966, Ho Chi Minh, the president of the Democratic Republic of Vietnam (DRV, or North Vietnam), sent a short message to the American people to provide his interpretation of the ongoing conflict between his nation and its ally, the National Liberation Front (NLF), on the one hand, and the United States and its ally, the Republic of Vietnam (RVN, or South Vietnam), on the other. By the end of 1966, hundreds of thousands of American soldiers were stationed in South Vietnam. As well, Rolling Thunder, the American bombing campaign, had been attacking targets in the North and the South for almost two years.

Ho's message emphasized the cruel nature of the American war effort. He condemned the American use of napalm, toxic gas, and fragmentation bombs, all of which resulted in the destruction of many towns and the deaths of thousands of people. He made it clear, however, that he did not blame the American people for the devastation. In fact, he even noted that American soldiers were also victims of American foreign policy. He held President Lyndon Johnson as solely responsible for the continuation of the war. By differentiating between the American people and their government, Ho sought to divide Americans and encourage them to resist their president's aggressive policies.

Defining the Moment

At first glance, Ho Chi Minh's message to the American people seems odd, given that his nation was at war with the United States. However, Ho had some familiarity with the United States and had previously appealed to America for support. He had actually lived in Harlem in 1912–1913. As the Allied powers negotiated an end to World War I at the Paris Peace Conference in 1919, Ho hoped to meet President Woodrow Wilson and secure his support for national self-determination for Vietnam. He not only failed to secure a meeting, but was dismayed to learn that Wilson would not support Vietnamese independence.

Similarly, when Japan surrendered in August 1945 and World War II ended, Ho announced Vietnam's independence from French colonial rule in front of thousands of cheering supporters on September 2, 1945. In a blatant appeal for American support, Ho repeatedly referred to the American Declaration of Independence in hopes that the United States would endorse Vietnamese independence and prevent the return of the French. The United States, however, chose to support French political control of Vietnam. Ho's appeal in 1967 to the American people was not a novel tactic.

The appeal in 1967 was different because North Vietnam and the United States were engaged in an ongoing war. Beginning in 1954, when the French lost control of their colonies in Southeast Asia, the United States supported several anticommunist regimes in South Vietnam with substantial aid. Between 1965 and 1966, the American role in the conflict escalated significantly. By the end of 1966, there were 385,000 American soldiers in the South. Additionally, as Ho noted, Rolling Thunder, the American bombing campaign, had bombed enemy targets in the North and the South for nearly two years, including 79,000 sorties in 1966 alone.

Ho was trying to communicate to the American people that the US government was responsible for the escalation of the conflict, not North Vietnam. He emphasized the devastating effect which the war, especially Rolling Thunder, was having on all Vietnamese. As well, because of the American government's escalation, hundreds of thousands of American soldiers had been sent to Vietnam and might be killed. In a final attack on the Johnson administration, Ho charged it had shown no interest in peace negotiations.

Author Biography

Born Nguyen Sinh Cung in 1890 in the province of Nghe An in what was then French Indochina, Ho left Vietnam in 1911 seeking adventure aboard a French merchant steamboat. He ended up in France and joined the French Socialist Party at the beginning of World War I. In 1919, at the Paris Peace Conference, he failed to secure Woodrow Wilson's support for Vietnamese self-determination. Embittered by the rejection, Ho helped form the French Communist Party in 1920. During the 1920s and 1930s, Ho traveled back and forth between the Soviet Union, China, Thailand, and Vietnam.

When Japan occupied Vietnam in 1941, Ho secretly reentered Vietnam and formed the Viet Minh to resist Japanese control. When Japan surrendered, Ho, as the leader of the Viet Minh, announced Vietnam's independence to a throng of cheering supporters on September 2, 1945. However, with American support, France regained control of French Indochina. In 1946, the First Indochina War broke out, pitting the Viet Minh against France. In 1954, after the French defeat at Dien Bien Phu, France lost its colonies. The Geneva Accords established two separate states, with the northern state, the Democratic Republic of Vietnam, controlled by Ho Chi Minh. He would remain president of the DRV until his death in 1969.

HISTORICAL DOCUMENT

On the occasion of the New Year, I would like to convey to the American people cordial wishes for peace and happiness.

The Vietnamese and American peoples should have lived in peace and friendship. But the U.S. Government has brazenly sent over 400,000 troops along with thousands of aircraft and hundreds of Warships to wage aggression on Vietnam. Night and day it has used napalm bombs, toxic gas, fragmentation bombs and other modern weapons to massacre our people, not sparing even old persons, women and children, it has burnt down or destroyed villages and towns and perpetrated extremely savage crimes. Of late, U.S. aircraft have repeatedly bombed Hanoi, our beloved capital.

It is because of the criminal war unleashed by the U.S. Government that hundreds of thousands of young Americans have been drafted and sent to a useless death for from then homeland, on the Vietnamese battlefield. In hundreds of thousands of American families, parents have lost their sons, and wives their husbands.

Nevertheless, the U.S. Government has continually clamoured about "peace negotiations" in an attempt to deceive the American and world peoples. In fact, it is daily expanding the war. The U.S. Government wrongly believes that with brutal force it could compel our people to surrender. But the Vietnamese people will never submit. We love peace, but it must be genuine peace in independence and freedom. For independence and freedom, the Vietnamese people are determined to fight the U.S. aggressors through to complete victory, whatever the hardships and sacrifices may be.

Who has caused these sufferings and mournings to the Vietnamese and American people? It is the U.S. rulers. The American people have realized this truth. More and more Americans are valiantly standing up in a vigorous struggle, demanding that the American Government respect the Constitution and the honour of the United States, stop the war of aggression in Vietnam and bring home all U.S. troops. I warmly welcome your just struggle and thank you for your support to the Vietnamese people's patriotic fight. I sincerely wish the American people many big successes in their struggle for peace, democracy and happiness.

Document Analysis

Ho Chi Minh's message was an obvious attempt to influence American public opinion. He made it clear to his American readers that he bore no ill will for Americans and did not hold them responsible for the war. Instead, he placed blame solely on President Lyndon Johnson's administration, whose actions were neither in the best interest of the American people, nor the Vietnamese. Were it not for the actions of the American government, Vietnam and the United States would almost certainly have enjoyed a friendly and mutually beneficial relationship.

Ho denounced American military strategy during the war. He strongly condemned the use of "napalm bombs, toxic gas, fragmentation bombs and other modern weapons" which "massacre our people, not sparing even old persons, women and children, it has burnt down or destroyed villages and towns and perpetrated extremely savage crimes." This was intended to make Americans feel guilty about the harm their government had caused.

In a pointed appeal to the American people, he pointed out the potentially deadly effect that the war might have on young American men. Many of the young men sent to Vietnam would die a "useless death" causing considerable grief for their families.

He also addressed the claims of the Johnson administration that peace negotiations were forthcoming. The Johnson administration was not serious about negotiations and, in fact, was planning to escalate the war under the false premise that more troops and resources would force the DRV to surrender. Ho assured the American people that his government would never abandon its fight whatever the cost. If American officials claimed otherwise, they were lying

To show that his assessment was not bizarre, Ho noted that many Americans had already begun "demanding that the American government respect the Constitution and the honour of the United States, stop the war of aggression in Vietnam and bring home all U.S. troops." He encouraged other Americans to join the movement to end the war in Vietnam.

Essential Themes

In his December 23, 1966 message to the American people, Ho Chi Minh hoped to speak directly to them without interference from the Johnson administration. At this point in the conflict, hundreds of thousands of American soldiers were fighting communist forces, and the Rolling Thunder bombing campaign was nearly two years old. The Johnson administration had fully committed itself to the war. Ho's message suggested that the American people were not fully aware of the American military effort and were certainly not in full support of American military intervention. Ho sought to give the impression that he was providing an accurate account of American actions in Vietnam, which the Johnson administration had not done.

Ho told the American people that there was no reason why the DRV and the United States could not live in peace and harmony. He and his people allegedly had no animosity for the American people. The American government was the primary impediment to peace. The American military strategy, notably the Rolling Thunder campaign, was killing innocent Vietnamese for no purpose. The war had led to the transport of American soldiers halfway across the world to die for no justifiable reason.

An obvious motivation for Ho's message was to destroy the Johnson administration's claims that it sought peace negotiations and that military victory was at hand. Ho made it clear that the DRV would fight until it unified the two Vietnams and achieved total national independence. Ho's depiction of the DRV's policy was accurate. The United States continued to bomb targets in the north and south, the number of American soldiers in Vietnam increased, and the war expanded beyond the borders of Vietnam. Yet the DRV remained resolute in its demand for reunification and complete independence even after Ho's death in 1969. The South Vietnamese government would collapse on April 30, 1975, and a unified and independent Vietnam would emerge under the direction of DRV leaders.

—Gerald F. Goodwin, PhD

Bibliography and Additional Reading

Brocheux, Pierre. *Ho Chi Minh: A Biography.* New York: Cambridge University Press, 2007. Print.

Duiker, William J. *Ho Chi Minh: A Life.* New York: Hachette Books, 2000. Print.

Halberstam, David. *Ho.* Lanham, MD: Rowman & Littlefield Publishers, 2007. Print.

Karnow, Stanley. *Vietnam: A History.* New York: Penguin Books, 1991. Print

■ Martin Luther King, Jr.: "Beyond Vietnam"

Date: April 4, 1967
Author: Martin Luther King, Jr.
Genre: sermon; speech

Summary

Dr. Martin Luther King, Jr. was easily the most celebrated civil rights leader of the 1960s, but his concerns about American society were not limited to domestic issues. He also had strong opinions about American foreign policy, particularly the ever-growing involvement of the United States in the Vietnam conflict. A committed pacifist, King had deep reservations about the war from its beginnings. However, he largely kept these criticisms to himself until April 4, 1967, when he publicly announced his opposition to the Vietnam War in a sermon delivered at the Riverside Church in New York City. Because he was the most influential civil rights leader of the era, King's opposition to the Vietnam War had significant implications for the civil rights movement, its relationship with Lyndon Johnson's administration, and the antiwar movement in general. His sermon suggested that the civil rights movement should not limit itself to domestic issues, created a permanent rift with the Johnson administration, and expanded support for the antiwar movement.

Defining Moment

Without a doubt the most significant domestic issue of the 1960s was the civil rights movement, while the most significant foreign policy issue was the Vietnam War. These two issues are often treated separately, but King's "Beyond Vietnam" argued that civil rights and the Vietnam War were not necessarily unrelated.

As a Christian pacifist and advocate of nonviolent resistance, King had always privately opposed the Vietnam War; however, like the majority of other civil rights leaders, he feared an antiwar stance would alienate President Johnson from supporting civil rights legislation. As well, King believed Johnson's pledge that he would seek peace negotiations with the Democratic Republic of Vietnam (DRV, or North Vietnam) as soon as possible.

King was hardly alone. The Urban League, the National Association for the Advancement of Colored People (NAACP), and the Student Nonviolent Coordinating Committee (SNCC) supported Johnson's policies on Vietnam or avoided taking a position on the war. However, as early as 1966, the leaders of the Congress of Racial Equality (CORE) and the SNCC openly expressed opposition to the war.

King recognized that there was a deep and significant fissure forming in the civil rights movement over the war, and he feared the conflict's continuation would lead to a permanent division in the movement. Equally significant, as the war continued and American involvement escalated, King became alarmed by the large number of black soldiers being killed. Understandably, he believed that these men should have been in the United States fighting for their civil rights. He also recognized that the war was distracting the Johnson administration from achieving its domestic goals, both the Great Society and equality for blacks. For all these reasons, King decided to announce publicly his opposition to the Vietnam War in a sermon at the Riverside Church on April 4, 1967.

Biography

Born on January 15, 1929 in Atlanta, Martin Luther King, Jr. followed in the footsteps of his father, becoming a Baptist minister after receiving a doctorate in theology from Boston University in 1955. King gained national attention for his involvement in the Montgomery Bus Boycott that same year. In 1957, King helped form the Southern Christian Leadership Conference (SCLC), an organization he would lead for the next eleven years. In 1963, King helped launch a collective movement of boycotts, demonstrations, and protests in the Deep South, most notably in Birmingham, Alabama. These events and King's "Letter from Birmingham Jail" brought national attention to the civil rights movement and his leadership. To pressure President John F. Kennedy to support civil rights legislation, King and hundreds of thousands of supporters gathered around the Lincoln Memorial in Washington, DC, where King delivered his famous "I Have a Dream" speech on August 28, 1963. King sought to galvanize public support for the Civil Rights Act of 1964, which ended legally required public segregation, and the Voting Rights Act of 1965, which ensured and protected African Americans' right to vote. King's activism expanded beyond civil rights to economic advancement for blacks. On April 4, 1967 he publically expressed his opposition to the Vietnam War. Tragically, he was assassinated by James Earl Ray exactly one year later in Memphis, Tennessee.

HISTORICAL DOCUMENT

Mr. Chairman, ladies and gentlemen, I need not pause to say how very delighted I am to be here tonight, and how very delighted I am to see you expressing your concern about the issues that will be discussed tonight by turning out in such large numbers. I also want to say that I consider it a great honor to share this program with Dr. Bennett, Dr. Commager, and Rabbi Heschel, some of the most distinguished leaders and personalities of our nation. And of course it's always good to come back to Riverside Church. Over the last eight years, I have had the privilege of preaching here almost every year in that period, and it's always a rich and rewarding experience to come to this great church and this great pulpit.

I come to this great magnificent house of worship tonight because my conscience leaves me no other choice. I join you in this meeting because I am in deepest agreement with the aims and work of the organization that brought us together: Clergy and Laymen Concerned About Vietnam. The recent statement of your executive committee are the sentiments of my own heart, and I found myself in full accord when I read its opening lines: "A time comes when silence is betrayal." That time has come for us in relation to Vietnam.

The truth of these words is beyond doubt, but the mission to which they call us is a most difficult one. Even when pressed by the demands of inner truth, men do not easily assume the task of opposing their government's policy, especially in time of war. Nor does the human spirit move without great difficulty against all the apathy of conformist thought within one's own bosom and in the surrounding world. Moreover, when the issues at hand seem as perplexing as they often do in the case of this dreadful conflict, we are always on the verge of being mesmerized by uncertainty. But we must move on.

Some of us who have already begun to break the silence of the night have found that the calling to speak is often a vocation of agony, but we must speak. We must speak with all the humility that is appropriate to our limited vision, but we must speak. And we must rejoice as well, for surely this is the first time in our nation's history that a significant number of its religious leaders have chosen to move beyond the prophesying of smooth patriotism to the high grounds of a firm dissent based upon the mandates of conscience and the reading of history. Perhaps a new spirit is rising among us. If it is, let us trace its movement, and pray that our inner being may be sensitive to its guidance. For we are deeply in need of a new way beyond the darkness that seems so close around us.

Over the past two years, as I have moved to break the betrayal of my own silences and to speak from the burnings of my own heart, as I have called for radical departures from the destruction of Vietnam, many persons have questioned me about the wisdom of my path. At the heart of their concerns, this query has often loomed large and loud: "Why are you speaking about the war, Dr. King? Why are you joining the voices of dissent?" "Peace and civil rights don't mix," they say. "Aren't you hurting the cause of your people?" they ask. And when I hear them, though I often understand the source of their concern, I am nevertheless greatly saddened, for such questions mean that the inquirers have not really known me, my commitment, or my calling. Indeed, their questions suggest that they do not know the world in which they live. In the light of such tragic misunderstanding, I deem it of signal importance to state clearly, and I trust concisely, why I believe that the path from Dexter Avenue Baptist Church—the church in Montgomery, Alabama, where I began my pastorate—leads clearly to this sanctuary tonight.

I come to this platform tonight to make a passionate plea to my beloved nation. This speech is not addressed to Hanoi or to the National Liberation Front. It is not addressed to China or to Russia. Nor is it an attempt to overlook the ambiguity of the total situation and the need for a collective solution to the tragedy of Vietnam. Neither is it an attempt to make North Vietnam or the National Liberation Front paragons of virtue, nor to overlook the role they must play in the successful resolution of the problem. While they both may have justifiable reasons to be suspicious of the good faith of the United States, life and history give eloquent testimony to the fact that conflicts are never resolved without trustful give and take on both sides. Tonight, however, I wish not to speak with Hanoi and the National Liberation Front, but rather to my fellow Americans.

Since I am a preacher by calling, I suppose it is not surprising that I have seven major reasons for bringing Vietnam into the field of my moral vision. There is at the outset a very obvious and almost facile connection between the war in Vietnam and the struggle I and others have been waging in America. A few years ago there was a shining moment in that struggle. It seemed as if there was a real promise of hope for the poor, both black and white, through the poverty program. There were experiments, hopes, new beginnings. Then came the buildup in Vietnam, and I watched this program broken and eviscerated as if it were some idle political plaything on a society gone mad on war. And I knew that America would never invest the necessary funds or energies in rehabilitation of its poor so long as adventures like Vietnam continued to draw men and skills and money like some demonic, destructive suction tube. So I was increasingly compelled to see the war as an enemy of the poor and to attack it as such.

Perhaps a more tragic recognition of reality took place when it became clear to me that the war was doing far more than devastating the hopes of the poor at home. It was sending their sons and their brothers and their husbands to fight and to die in extraordinarily high proportions relative to the rest of the population. We were taking the black young men who had been crippled by our society and sending them eight thousand miles away to guarantee liberties in Southeast Asia which they had not found in southwest Georgia and East Harlem. So we have been repeatedly faced with the cruel irony of watching Negro and white boys on TV screens as they kill and die together for a nation that has been unable to seat them together in the same schools. So we watch them in brutal solidarity burning the huts of a poor village, but we realize that they would hardly live on the same block in Chicago. I could not be silent in the face of such cruel manipulation of the poor.

My third reason moves to an even deeper level of awareness, for it grows out of my experience in the ghettos of the North over the last three years, especially the last three summers. As I have walked among the desperate, rejected, and angry young men, I have told them that Molotov cocktails and rifles would not solve their problems. I have tried to offer them my deepest compassion while maintaining my conviction that social change comes most meaningfully through nonviolent action. But they asked, and rightly so, "What about Vietnam?" They asked if our own nation wasn't using massive doses of violence to solve its problems, to bring about the changes it wanted. Their questions hit home, and I knew that I could never again raise my voice against the violence of the oppressed in the ghettos without having first spoken clearly to the greatest purveyor of violence in the world today: my own government. For the sake of those boys, for the sake of this government, for the sake of the hundreds of thousands trembling under our violence, I cannot be silent.

For those who ask the question, "Aren't you a civil rights leader?" and thereby mean to exclude me from the movement for peace, I have this further answer. In 1957, when a group of us formed the Southern Christian Leadership Conference, we chose as our motto: "To save the soul of America." We were convinced that we could not limit our vision to certain rights for black people, but instead affirmed the conviction that America would never be free or saved from itself until the descendants of its slaves were loosed completely from the shackles they still wear. In a way we were agreeing with Langston Hughes, that black bard from Harlem, who had written earlier:

O, yes, I say it plain,
America never was America to me,

And yet I swear this oath—
America will be!

Now it should be incandescently clear that no one who has any concern for the integrity and life of America today can ignore the present war. If America's soul becomes totally poisoned, part of the autopsy must read "Vietnam." It can never be saved so long as it destroys the hopes of men the world over. So it is that those of us who are yet determined that "America will be" are led down the path of protest and dissent, working for the health of our land.

As if the weight of such a commitment to the life and health of America were not enough, another burden of responsibility was placed upon me in 1954. And I cannot forget that the Nobel Peace Prize was also a commission, a commission to work harder than I had ever worked before for the brotherhood of man. This is a calling that takes me beyond national allegiances.

But even if it were not present, I would yet have to live with the meaning of my commitment to the ministry of Jesus Christ. To me, the relationship of this ministry to the making of peace is so obvious that I sometimes marvel at those who ask me why I am speaking against the war. Could it be that they do not know that the Good News was meant for all men—for communist and capitalist, for their children and ours, for black and for white, for revolutionary and conservative? Have they forgotten that my ministry is in obedience to the one who loved his enemies so fully that he died for them? What then can I say to the Vietcong or to Castro or to Mao as a faithful minister of this one? Can I threaten them with death or must I not share with them my life?

Finally, as I try to explain for you and for myself the road that leads from Montgomery to this place, I would have offered all that was most valid if I simply said that I must be true to my conviction that I share with all men the calling to be a son of the living God. Beyond the calling of race or nation or creed is this vocation of sonship and brotherhood. Because I believe that the Father is deeply concerned, especially for His suffering and helpless and outcast children, I come tonight to speak for them. This I believe to be the privilege and the burden of all of us who deem ourselves bound by allegiances and loyalties which are broader and deeper than nationalism

and which go beyond our nation's self-defined goals and positions. We are called to speak for the weak, for the voiceless, for the victims of our nation, for those it calls "enemy," for no document from human hands can make these humans any less our brothers.

And as I ponder the madness of Vietnam and search within myself for ways to understand and respond in compassion, my mind goes constantly to the people of that peninsula. I speak now not of the soldiers of each side, not of the ideologies of the Liberation Front, not of the junta in Saigon, but simply of the people who have been living under the curse of war for almost three continuous decades now. I think of them, too, because it is clear to me that there will be no meaningful solution there until some attempt is made to know them and hear their broken cries.

They must see Americans as strange liberators. The Vietnamese people proclaimed their own independence in 1954—in 1945 rather—after a combined French and Japanese occupation and before the communist revolution in China. They were led by Ho Chi Minh. Even though they quoted the American Declaration of Independence in their own document of freedom, we refused to recognize them. Instead, we decided to support France in its reconquest of her former colony. Our government felt then that the Vietnamese people were not ready for independence, and we again fell victim to the deadly Western arrogance that has poisoned the international atmosphere for so long. With that tragic decision we rejected a revolutionary government seeking self-determination and a government that had been established not by China—for whom the Vietnamese have no great love—but by clearly indigenous forces that included some communists. For the peasants this new government meant real land reform, one of the most important needs in their lives.

For nine years following 1945 we denied the people of Vietnam the right of independence. For nine years we vigorously supported the French in their abortive effort to recolonize Vietnam. Before the end of the war we were meeting eighty percent of the French war costs. Even before the French were defeated at Dien Bien Phu, they began to despair of their reckless action, but we did not. We encouraged them with our huge financial and military supplies to continue the war even after they had lost the will. Soon we would be paying almost the full costs of this tragic attempt at recolonization.

After the French were defeated, it looked as if independence and land reform would come again through the Geneva Agreement. But instead there came the United States, determined that Ho should not unify the temporarily divided nation, and the peasants watched again as we supported one of the most vicious modern dictators, our chosen man, Premier Diem. The peasants watched and cringed and Diem ruthlessly rooted out all opposition, supported their extortionist landlords, and refused even to discuss reunification with the North. The peasants watched as all of this was presided over by United States influence and then by increasing numbers of United States troops who came to help quell the insurgency that Diem's methods had aroused. When Diem was overthrown they may have been happy, but the long line of military dictators seemed to offer no real change, especially in terms of their need for land and peace.

The only change came from America as we increased our troop commitments in support of governments which were singularly corrupt, inept, and without popular support. All the while the people read our leaflets and received the regular promises of peace and democracy and land reform. Now they languish under our bombs and consider us, not their fellow Vietnamese, the real enemy. They move sadly and apathetically as we herd them off the land of their fathers into concentration camps where minimal social needs are rarely met. They know they must move on or be destroyed by our bombs.

So they go, primarily women and children and the aged. They watch as we poison their water, as we kill a million acres of their crops. They must weep as the bulldozers roar through their areas preparing to destroy the precious trees. They wander into the hospitals with at least twenty casualties from American firepower for one Vietcong-inflicted injury. So far we may have killed a million of them, mostly children. They wander into the towns and see thousands of the children, homeless, without clothes, running in packs on the streets like animals. They see the children degraded by our soldiers as they beg for food. They see the children selling their sisters to our soldiers, soliciting for their mothers.

What do the peasants think as we ally ourselves with the landlords and as we refuse to put any action into our many words concerning land reform? What do they think as we test out our latest weapons on them, just as the Germans tested out new medicine and new tortures in the concentration camps of Europe? Where are the roots of the independent Vietnam we claim to be building? Is it among these voiceless ones?

We have destroyed their two most cherished institutions: the family and the village. We have destroyed their land and their crops. We have cooperated in the crushing of the nation's only noncommunist revolutionary political force, the unified Buddhist Church. We have supported the enemies of the peasants of Saigon. We have corrupted their women and children and killed their men.

Now there is little left to build on, save bitterness. Soon the only solid physical foundations remaining will be found at our military bases and in the concrete of the concentration camps we call "fortified hamlets." The peasants may well wonder if we plan to build our new Vietnam on such grounds as these. Could we blame them for such thoughts? We must speak for them and raise the questions they cannot raise. These, too, are our brothers.

Perhaps a more difficult but no less necessary task is to speak for those who have been designated as our enemies. What of the National Liberation Front, that strangely anonymous group we call "VC" or "communists"? What must they think of the United States of America when they realize that we permitted the repression and cruelty of Diem, which helped to bring them into being as a resistance group in the South? What do they think of our condoning the violence which led to their own taking up of arms? How can they believe in our integrity when now we speak of "aggression from the North" as if there was nothing more essential to the war? How can they trust us when now we charge them with violence after the murderous reign of Diem and charge them with violence while we pour every new weapon of death into their land? Surely we must understand their feelings, even if we do not condone their actions. Surely we must see that the men we supported pressed them to their violence. Surely we must see that our own computerized plans of destruction simply dwarf their greatest acts.

How do they judge us when our officials know that their membership is less than twenty-five percent communist, and yet insist on giving them the blanket name? What must they be thinking when they know that we are aware of their control of major sections of Vietnam, and yet we appear ready to allow national elections in which this highly organized political parallel government will not have a part? They ask how we can speak of free elections when the Saigon press is censored and controlled by the military junta. And they are surely right to wonder what kind of new government we plan to help form without them, the only real party in real touch with the peasants. They question our political goals and they deny the reality of a peace settlement from which they will be excluded. Their questions are frighteningly relevant. Is our nation planning to build on political myth again, and then shore it up upon the power of a new violence?

Here is the true meaning and value of compassion and nonviolence, when it helps us to see the enemy's point of view, to hear his questions, to know his assessment of ourselves. For from his view we may indeed see the basic weaknesses of our own condition, and if we are mature, we may learn and grow and profit from the wisdom of the brothers who are called the opposition.

So, too, with Hanoi. In the North, where our bombs now pummel the land, and our mines endanger the waterways, we are met by a deep but understandable mistrust. To speak for them is to explain this lack of confidence in Western worlds, and especially their distrust of American intentions now. In Hanoi are the men who led this nation to independence against the Japanese and the French, the men who sought membership in the French Commonwealth and were betrayed by the weakness of Paris and the willfulness of the colonial armies. It was they who led a second struggle against French domination at tremendous costs, and then were persuaded to give up the land they controlled between the thirteenth and seventeenth parallel as a temporary measure at Geneva. After 1954 they watched us conspire with Diem to prevent elections which could have surely brought Ho Chi Minh to power over a unified Vietnam, and they realized they had been betrayed again. When we ask why they do not leap to negotiate, these things must be considered.

Also, it must be clear that the leaders of Hanoi considered the presence of American troops in support of the Diem regime to have been the initial military breach of the Geneva Agreement concerning foreign troops. They remind us that they did not begin to send troops in large numbers and even supplies into the South until American forces had moved into the tens of thousands.

Hanoi remembers how our leaders refused to tell us the truth about the earlier North Vietnamese overtures for peace, how the president claimed that none existed when they had clearly been made. Ho Chi Minh has watched as America has spoken of peace and built up its forces, and now he has surely heard the increasing international rumors of American plans for an invasion of the north. He knows the bombing and shelling and mining we are doing are part of traditional pre-invasion strategy. Perhaps only his sense of humor and of irony can save him when he hears the most powerful nation of the world speaking of aggression as it drops thousands of bombs on a poor, weak nation more than eight hundred, or rather, eight thousand miles away from its shores.

At this point I should make it clear that while I have tried to give a voice to the voiceless in Vietnam and to understand the arguments of those who are called "enemy," I am as deeply concerned about our own troops there as anything else. For it occurs to me that what we are submitting them to in Vietnam is not simply the brutalizing process that goes on in any war where armies face each other and seek to destroy. We are adding cynicism to the process of death, for they must know after a short period there that none of the things we claim to be fighting for are really involved. Before long they must know that their government has sent them into a struggle among Vietnamese, and the more sophisticated surely realize that we are on the side of the wealthy, and the secure, while we create a hell for the poor.

Surely this madness must cease. We must stop now. I speak as a child of God and brother to the suffering poor of Vietnam. I speak for those whose land is being laid waste, whose homes are being destroy, whose culture is being subverted. I speak for the poor in America who are paying the double price of smashed hopes at home, and dealt death and corruption in Vietnam. I speak as a citizen of the world, for the world as it stands aghast at the path we have taken. I speak as one who loves America, to the leaders of our own nation: The great initiative in this war is ours; the initiative to stop it must be ours.

This is the message of the great Buddhist leaders of Vietnam. Recently one of them wrote these words, and I quote:

Each day the war goes on the hatred increased in the hearts of the Vietnamese and in the hearts of those of humanitarian instinct. The Americans are forcing even their friends into becoming their enemies. It is curious that the Americans, who calculate so carefully on the possibilities of military victory, do not realize that in the process they are incurring deep psychological and political defeat. The image of America will never again be the image of revolution, freedom, and democracy, but the image of violence and militarism.

Unquote.

If we continue, there will be no doubt in my mind and in the mind of the world that we have no honorable intentions in Vietnam. If we do not stop our war against the people of Vietnam immediately, the world will be left with no other alternative than to see this as some horrible, clumsy, and deadly game we have decided to play. The world now demands a maturity of America that we may not be able to achieve. It demands that we admit we have been wrong from the beginning of our adventure in Vietnam, that we have been detrimental to the life of the Vietnamese people. The situation is one in which we must be ready to turn sharply from our present ways. In order to atone for our sins and errors in Vietnam, we should take the initiative in bringing a halt to this tragic war.

I would like to suggest five concrete things that our government should do to begin the long and difficult process of extricating ourselves from this nightmarish conflict:

Number one: End all bombing in North and South Vietnam.

Number two: Declare a unilateral cease-fire in the hope that such action will create the atmosphere for negotiation.

Three: Take immediate steps to prevent other battlegrounds in Southeast Asia by curtailing our military buildup in Thailand and our interference in Laos.

Four: Realistically accept the fact that the National Liberation Front has substantial support in South Vietnam and must thereby play a role in any meaningful negotiations and any future Vietnam government.

Five: Set a date that we will remove all foreign troops from Vietnam in accordance with the 1954 Geneva Agreement. [sustained applause]

Part of our ongoing [applause continues], part of our ongoing commitment might well express itself in an offer to grant asylum to any Vietnamese who fears for his life under a new regime which included the Liberation Front. Then we must make what reparations we can for the damage we have done. We must provide the medical aid that is badly needed, making it available in this country if necessary. Meanwhile [applause], meanwhile, we in the churches and synagogues have a continuing task while we urge our government to disengage itself from a disgraceful commitment. We must continue to raise our voices and our lives if our nation persists in its perverse ways in Vietnam. We must be prepared to match actions with words by seeking out every creative method of protest possible.

As we counsel young men concerning military service, we must clarify for them our nation's role in Vietnam and challenge them with the alternative of conscientious objection. [sustained applause] I am pleased to say that this is a path now chosen by more than seventy students at my own alma mater, Morehouse College, and I recommend it to all who find the American course in Vietnam a dishonorable and unjust one. [applause] Moreover, I would encourage all ministers of draft age to give up their ministerial exemptions and seek status as conscientious objectors. [applause] These are the times for real choices and not false ones. We are at the moment when our lives must be placed on the line if our nation is to survive its own folly. Every man of humane convictions must decide on the protest that best suits his convictions, but we must all protest.

Now there is something seductively tempting about stopping there and sending us all off on what in some circles has become a popular crusade against the war in Vietnam. I say we must enter that struggle, but I wish to go on now to say something even more disturbing.

The war in Vietnam is but a symptom of a far deeper malady within the American spirit, and if we ignore this sobering reality [applause], and if we ignore this sobering reality, we will find ourselves organizing "clergy and laymen concerned" committees for the next generation. They will be concerned about Guatemala and Peru. They will be concerned about Thailand and Cambodia. They will be concerned about Mozambique and South Africa. We will be marching for these and a dozen other names and attending rallies without end unless there is a significant and profound change in American life and policy. [sustained applause] So such thoughts take us beyond Vietnam, but not beyond our calling as sons of the living God.

In 1957 a sensitive American official overseas said that it seemed to him that our nation was on the wrong side of a world revolution. During the past ten years we have seen emerge a pattern of suppression which has now justified the presence of U.S. military advisors in Venezuela. This need to maintain social stability for our investments accounts for the counterrevolutionary action of American forces in Guatemala. It tells why American helicopters are being used against guerrillas in Cambodia and why American napalm and Green Beret forces have already been active against rebels in Peru.

It is with such activity that the words of the late John F. Kennedy come back to haunt us. Five years ago he said, "Those who make peaceful revolution impossible will make violent revolution inevitable." [applause] Increasingly, by choice or by accident, this is the role our nation has taken, the role of those who make peaceful revolution impossible by refusing to give up the privileges and the pleasures that come from the immense profits of overseas investments. I am convinced that if we are to get on to the right side of the world revolution, we as a nation must undergo a radical revolution of values. We must rapidly begin [applause], we must rapidly begin the shift from a thing-oriented society to a person-oriented society. When machines and computers, profit motives and property rights, are considered more important than people, the giant triplets of racism, extreme materialism, and militarism are incapable of being conquered.

A true revolution of values will soon cause us to question the fairness and justice of many of our past and present policies. On the one hand we are called to play the Good Samaritan on life's roadside, but that will be only an initial act. One day we must come to see that the whole Jericho Road must be transformed so that men and women will not be constantly beaten and robbed as they make their journey on life's highway. True compassion is more than flinging a coin to a beggar. It comes to see than an edifice which produces beggars needs restructuring. [applause]

A true revolution of values will soon look uneasily on the glaring contrast of poverty and wealth. With righteous indignation, it will look across the seas and see individual capitalists of the West investing huge sums of money in Asia, Africa, and South America, only to take the profits out with no concern for the social betterment of the countries, and say, "This is not just." It will look at our alliance with the landed gentry of South America and say, "This is not just." The Western arrogance of feeling that it has everything to teach others and nothing to learn from them is not just.

A true revolution of values will lay hand on the world order and say of war, "This way of settling differences is not just." This business of burning human beings with napalm, of filling our nation's homes with orphans and widows, of injecting poisonous drugs of hate into the veins of peoples normally humane, of sending men home from dark and bloody battlefields physically handicapped and psychologically deranged, cannot be reconciled with wisdom, justice, and love. A nation that continues year after year to spend more money on military defense than on programs of social uplift is approaching spiritual death. [sustained applause]

America, the richest and most powerful nation in the world, can well lead the way in this revolution of values. There is nothing except a tragic death wish to prevent us from reordering our priorities so that the pursuit of peace will take precedence over the pursuit of war. There is nothing to keep us from molding a recalcitrant status quo with bruised hands until we have fashioned it into a brotherhood.

This kind of positive revolution of values is our best defense against communism. [applause] War is not the answer. Communism will never be defeated by the use of atomic bombs or nuclear weapons. Let us not join those who shout war and, through their misguided passions, urge the United States to relinquish its participation in the United Nations. These are days which demand wise restraint and calm reasonableness. We must not engage in a negative anticommunism, but rather in a positive thrust for democracy [applause], realizing that our greatest defense against communism is to take offensive action in behalf of justice. We must with positive action seek to remove those conditions of poverty, insecurity, and injustice, which are the fertile soil in which the seed of communism grows and develops.

These are revolutionary times. All over the globe men are revolting against old systems of exploitation and oppression, and out of the wounds of a frail world, new systems of justice and equality are being born. The shirtless and barefoot people of the land are rising up as never before. The people who sat in darkness have seen a great light. We in the West must support these revolutions.

It is a sad fact that because of comfort, complacency, a morbid fear of communism, and our proneness to adjust to injustice, the Western nations that initiated so much of the revolutionary spirit of the modern world have now become the arch antirevolutionaries. This has driven many to feel that only Marxism has a revolutionary spirit. Therefore, communism is a judgment against our failure to make democracy real and follow through on the revolutions that we initiated. Our only hope today lies in our ability to recapture the revolutionary spirit and go out into a sometimes hostile world declaring eternal hostility to poverty, racism, and militarism. With this powerful commitment we shall boldly challenge the status quo and unjust mores, and thereby speed the day when "every valley shall be exalted, and every mountain and hill shall be made low [Audience:] (Yes); the crooked shall be made straight, and the rough places plain."

A genuine revolution of values means in the final analysis that our loyalties must become ecumenical rather than sectional. Every nation must now develop an overriding loyalty to mankind as a whole in order to preserve the best in their individual societies.

This call for a worldwide fellowship that lifts neighborly concern beyond one's tribe, race, class, and nation is in reality a call for an all-embracing and unconditional love for all mankind. This oft misunderstood, this oft misinterpreted concept, so readily dismissed by the Nietzsches of the world as a weak and cowardly force, has now become an absolute necessity for the survival of man. When I speak of love I am not speaking of some sentimental and weak response. I'm not speaking of that force which is just emotional bosh. I am speaking of that force which all of the great religions have seen as the supreme unifying principle of life. Love is somehow the key that unlocks the door which leads to ultimate reality. This Hindu-Muslim-Christian-Jewish-Buddhist belief about ultimate reality is beautifully summed up in the first epistle of Saint John: "Let us love one another (Yes), for love is God. (Yes) And every one that loveth is born of God and knoweth God. He that loveth not knoweth not God, for God is love. . . . If we love one another, God dwelleth in us and his love is perfected in us." Let us hope that this spirit will become the order of the day.

We can no longer afford to worship the god of hate or bow before the altar of retaliation. The oceans of history are made turbulent by the ever-rising tides of hate. History is cluttered with the wreckage of nations and individuals that pursued this self-defeating path of hate. As Arnold Toynbee says: "Love is the ultimate force that makes for the saving choice of life and good against the damning choice of death and evil. Therefore the first hope in our inventory must be the hope that love is going to have the last word." Unquote.

We are now faced with the fact, my friends, that tomorrow is today. We are confronted with the fierce urgency of now. In this unfolding conundrum of life and history, there is such a thing as being too late. Procrastination is still the thief of time. Life often leaves us standing bare, naked, and dejected with a lost opportunity. The tide in the affairs of men does not remain at flood—it ebbs. We may cry out desperately for time to pause in her passage, but time is adamant to every plea and rushes on. Over the bleached bones and jumbled residues of numerous civilizations are written the pathetic words, "Too late." There is an invisible book of life that faithfully records our vigilance or our neglect. Omar

Khayyam is right: "The moving finger writes, and having writ moves on."

We still have a choice today: nonviolent coexistence or violent coannihilation. We must move past indecision to action. We must find new ways to speak for peace in Vietnam and justice throughout the developing world, a world that borders on our doors. If we do not act, we shall surely be dragged down the long, dark, and shameful corridors of time reserved for those who possess power without compassion, might without morality, and strength without sight.

Now let us begin. Now let us rededicate ourselves to the long and bitter, but beautiful, struggle for a new world. This is the calling of the sons of God, and our brothers wait eagerly for our response. Shall we say the odds are too great? Shall we tell them the struggle is too hard? Will our message be that the forces of American life militate against their arrival as full men, and we send our deepest regrets? Or will there be another message— of longing, of hope, of solidarity with their yearnings, of commitment to their cause, whatever the cost? The choice is ours, and though we might prefer it otherwise, we must choose in this crucial moment of human history.

As that noble bard of yesterday, James Russell Lowell, eloquently stated:

> Once to every man and nation comes a
> moment do decide,

In the strife of truth and Falsehood, for the good or evil side;

Some great cause, God's new Messiah offering each the bloom or blight,

And the choice goes by forever 'twixt that darkness and that light.

Though the cause of evil prosper, yet 'tis truth alone is strong

Though her portions be the scaffold, and upon the throne be wrong

Yet that scaffold sways the future, and behind the dim unknown

Standeth God within the shadow, keeping watch above his own.

And if we will only make the right choice, we will be able to transform this pending cosmic elegy into a creative psalm of peace. If we will make the right choice, we will be able to transform the jangling discords of our world into a beautiful symphony of brotherhood. If we will but make the right choice, we will be able to speed up the day, all over America and all over the world, when justice will roll down like waters, and righteousness like a mighty stream. [sustained applause]

Document Analysis

On April 4, 1967, Dr. Martin Luther King, Jr. declared his opposition to the Vietnam War in a sermon known as "Beyond Vietnam" at the Riverside Church in New York City. King sought to explain how and why he had reached an antiwar position and how his antiwar views related to the larger civil rights movement.

His address began by noting that many people had questioned why he would speak out against the war when it seemingly had little to do with the civil rights movement and could, in fact, alienate supporters in Lyndon Johnson's administration. King challenged the notion that the two issues were unrelated. The Vietnam War drew significant money, resources, and manpower away from civil rights causes. Additionally, King rec-

ognized an enormous irony: the draft sent thousands of African Americans to Vietnam to protect the rights and freedoms of the Vietnamese when African Americans did not enjoy equal rights in their own country. He maintained that he "could not be silent in the face of such cruel manipulation of the poor."

King's position as a Christian minister, advocate of nonviolence, and winner of the Nobel Peace Prize, also clearly led him to oppose the war on moral and religious grounds. King argued that his religious and moral beliefs required him to "speak for the weak, for the voiceless, for the victims of our nation" and even "for those it calls 'enemy.'"

He reminded his audience that the United States had long opposed Vietnamese self-determination by first ignoring Ho Chi Minh's Declaration of Independence in 1945, then supporting French colonial rule from 1946–1954, and finally supporting the division of the nation and the rule of various South Vietnamese autocrats. While the American government had promised the Vietnamese people peace and prosperity, they had broken both promises. King asserted, "We have destroyed their two most cherished institutions: the family and the village. We have destroyed their land and their crops....We have corrupted their women and children and killed their men." To King, it was not surprising that many Vietnamese did not support the American presence. He reminded his audience that even many American soldiers had come to understand the immoral nature of the conflict.

King maintained that the only way "to atone for our sins and errors in Vietnam" was to end American participation in the war. The United States should immediately end all bombing campaigns in North and South Vietnam, establish a unilateral cease-fire, push for an end to fighting in Laos and the rest of Southeast Asia, accept that the National Liberation Front (NLF) had support in South Vietnam, include them in any negotiations to end the war, and commit to removing all American troops from Vietnam as outlined in the 1954 Geneva Agreement.

King concluded that American actions in Vietnam were part of a larger foreign policy problem. He maintained that, under the guise of Cold War defense, the United States had continually intervened in the affairs of other nations. He called on the American people to make a new commitment to a "revolution of values," which included "eternal hostility to poverty, racism, and militarism." Embracing these principles was the only way of creating a more just and fair world.

Essential Themes

King's Riverside Church sermon was a significant departure for him in many respects. Prior to April 4, 1967 most Americans, regardless of race, viewed King primarily as a civil rights leader. Even those who supported the black struggle for civil rights expected King to speak about issues relating to civil rights and racial discrimination, but little else. However, King had always held strong opinions about the Vietnam War and American foreign policy in general, but he kept those views largely private. In speaking out against the war, he expanded his own role from that of a civil rights leader solely focused on domestic issues to one who felt a responsibility to speak out on issues of conscience. In voicing his opposition to the war publicly, King also pointed out that the Vietnam War and the battle for civil rights were not mutually exclusive issues. His speech focused on the negative effects which the Vietnam War was having on African Americans and the civil rights movement more generally.

King's condemnation of the Vietnam War was very controversial, and the reactions to his sermon reflected these divisions. King's address caused a permanent rupture to the civil rights coalition he had formed with the Johnson administration, an alliance that had accomplished such significant victories as the Civil Rights Act of 1964 and the Voting Rights Act of 1965. In the first few years of the war, King had hesitated to speak out against it because he feared damaging this alliance. His "Beyond Vietnam" sermon revealed that condemnation of the war had become more important to him than unequivocal support for the Johnson administration. King clearly felt that his responsibilities as a civil rights leader and minister required him to speak out against the war.

Reactions were also mixed among African Americans. Many civil rights leaders, including influential members of the NAACP and SCLC, condemned his remarks on the Vietnam War. They argued that his energies were better served by focusing on civil rights and not foreign policy issues. They also feared, as King had, that his criticisms of the war would destroy the positive relationship they had with the Johnson administration. Others responded more favorably to King's sermon. Almost overnight, many African Americans came to see King as the representative of the African American antiwar movement. Many liberal whites who had supported programs to end poverty and to attain civil rights for blacks were persuaded by King's sermon that the Vietnam War was severely weakening the possibility of achieving the domestic goals they sought.

—*Gerald F. Goodwin, PhD*

Bibliography and Additional Reading

Garrow, David. *Bearing the Cross: Martin Luther King, Jr., and the Southern Christian Leadership Conference.* New York: William Morrow, 2004. Print.

Eldridge, Lawrence Allen. *Chronicles of a Two-Front War: Civil Rights and Vietnam in the African American Press.* Columbia, Missouri: University of Missouri Press, 2011. Print.

Lucks, Daniel S. *Selma to Saigon: The Civil Rights Movement and the Vietnam War*. Lexington, Kentucky: The University Press of Kentucky, 2004. Print.

Westheider, James E. *The African-American Experience in Vietnam: Brothers in Arms*. Lanham, MD: Rowman and Littlefield Publishers, 2007. Print.

■ An Antidraft Call to Action

Date: 1967
Author: Anonymous
Genre: petition; political tract; address

Summary Overview

The document reprinted here is a petition addressed mainly to young men of draft age during the Vietnam War. It was intended to call potential draftees and citizens not only to protest, but to refuse the military draft. It outlines, in several numbered points, why the war in Vietnam could be considered illegal and immoral and why, therefore, it was appropriate to refuse to be a part of it. The document does not only call for people to speak up or to march as a means of demonstrating their opinion, but rather to actively go against the federal code in defying the requirement of military service. The actions proposed in the petition were illegal at the time, and anyone carrying them out could be, and usually was, prosecuted in a court of law by the United States government. The petition outlines ethical and moral objections to the Vietnam War that many of the war's opponents agreed with.

Defining Moment

This document was printed at a time when the war in Vietnam and the corresponding protests at home were increasing dramatically. More and more young men were needed to fight in Southeast Asia, and more and more people rebelled against conscription and the war in general. The draft laws required that any American male citizen between the age of 18 and 26 register and hold a draft card so that he could be selected, according to date of birth, to serve up to four years in the military. Avoiding registration, disregarding one's draft status, or fleeing military service if selected, were illegal acts and subject to a variety of punishments. Before 1967, there had been a few ways in which a person could legally avoid serving, but by the time the following call for resistance was printed, federal regulations had tightened,

significantly limiting those options. For example, college-aged students who planned to go on to graduate school could no longer claim exempt status on the basis of their educational path.

As this petition shows, many opponents began to believe that the draft during the Vietnam years was an abuse of power because it forced young men to fight in a war that was widely considered illegal and immoral. The perceived illegal role of the United States in the conflict in Southeast Asia lay at the heart of the antidraft movement and was pivotal to many of the antiwar protests taking place at this time. The petition is a well organized, well argued example of a statement by one of these protest groups—in this case, professors from all around the country. The document outlines the main issues arising from the Vietnam War and how potential draftees could address them.

Author Biography

This petition was put together in response to one of a number of changes to the United States' policy on draft exemptions, most of which narrowed the number of young men who could be exempted from service. A group of professors decided to speak out against this change. Named the University Committee on War and Peace, this "faculty antiwar group"—as the University of Pennsylvania newspaper *The Daily Pennsylvanian* called them—visited academic institutions as far apart as the University of California, Santa Barbara, and Harvard University in Massachusetts, bringing together students and professors to resist the draft and work toward a peaceful resolution of the war. The group worked to collect the draft card of any student who turned one in and to publicize the message that the act sent.

HISTORICAL DOCUMENT

To the young men of America, to the whole of the American people, and to all men of goodwill everywhere:

1. An ever growing number of young American men are finding that the American war in Vietnam so outrages their deepest moral and religious sense that they cannot contribute to it in any way. We share their moral outrage.

2. We further believe that the war is unconstitutional and illegal. Congress has not declared a war as required by the Constitution. Moreover, under the Constitution, treaties signed by the President and ratified by the Senate have the same force as the Constitution itself. The Charter of the United Nations is such a treaty. The Charter specifically obligates the United States to refrain from force or the threat of force in international relations. It requires member states to exhaust every peaceful means of settling disputes and to submit disputes which cannot be settled peacefully to the Security Council. The United States has systematically violated all of these Charter provisions for thirteen years.

3. Moreover, this war violates international agreements, treaties and principles of law which the United States Government has solemnly endorsed. The combat role of the United States troops in Vietnam violates the Geneva Accords of 1954 which our government pledged to support but has since subverted. The destruction of rice, crops and livestock; the burning and bulldozing of entire villages consisting exclusively of civilian structures; the interning of civilian non-combatants in concentration camps; the summary executions of civilians in captured villages who could not produce satisfactory evidence of their loyalties or did not wish to be removed to concentration camps; the slaughter of peasants who dared to stand up in their fields and shake their fists at American helicopters; these are all actions of the kind which the United States and the other victorious powers of World War II declared to be crimes against humanity for which individuals were to be held personally responsible even when acting under the orders of their governments and for which Germans were sentenced at Nuremberg to long prison terms and death. The pro-

hibition of such acts as war crimes was incorporated in treaty law by the Geneva Conventions of 1949, ratified by the United States. These are commitments to other countries and to Mankind, and they would claim our allegiance even if Congress should declare war.

4. We also believe it is an unconstitutional denial of religious liberty and equal protection of the laws to withhold draft exemption from men whose religious or profound philosophical beliefs are opposed to what in the Western religious tradition have been long known as unjust wars.

5. Therefore, we believe on all these grounds that every free man has a legal right and a moral duty to exert every effort to end this war, to avoid collusion with it, and to encourage others to do the same. Young men in the armed forces or threatened with the draft face the most excruciating choices. For them various forms of resistance risk separation from their families and their country, destruction of their careers, loss of their freedom and loss of their lives. Each must choose the course of resistance dictated by his conscience and circumstances. Among those already in the armed forces some are refusing to obey specific illegal and immoral orders, some are attempting to educate their fellow servicemen on the murderous and barbarous nature of the war some are absenting themselves without official leave. Among those not in the armed forces some are applying for status as conscientious objectors to American aggression in Vietnam, some are refusing to be inducted. Among both groups, some are resisting openly and paying a heavy penalty, some are organizing more resistance within the United States and some have sought sanctuary in other countries.

6. We believe that each of these forms of resistance against illegitimate authority is courageous and justified. Many of us believe that open resistance to the war and the draft is the course of action most likely to strengthen the moral resolve with which all of us can oppose the war and most likely to bring an end to the war.

7. We will continue to lend our support to those who undertake resistance to this war. We will raise funds to organize draft resistance unions, to supply legal defense and bail, to support families and otherwise aid resistance to the war in whatever ways may seem appropriate.

8. We firmly believe that our statement is the sort of speech that under the First Amendment must be free, and that the actions we will undertake are as legal as is the war resistance of the young men themselves. But we recognize that the courts may find otherwise, and that if so we might all be liable to prosecution and severe pun-ishment. In any case, we feel that we cannot shrink from fulfilling our responsibilities to the youth whom many of us teach, to the country whose freedom we cherish, and to the ancient traditions of religion and philosophy which we strive to preserve in this generation.

9. We call upon all men of good will to join us in this confrontation with immoral authority. Especially we call upon the universities to fulfill their mission of enlighten-ment and religious organizations to honor their heritage of brotherhood. Now is the time to resist.

GLOSSARY

draft: military conscription

conscientious objector: one who refuses to take up weapons in a military conflict or to serve in the military because of religious or moral objections

Document Analysis

This document is a petition, officially called "A Call to Resist Illegitimate Authority," that circulated around many colleges and appealed directly to potential draft-ees—that is, young men between the ages of 18 and 26. The document focuses on two main issues: the im-morality and illegality of the Vietnam conflict and the tension between guaranteed First Amendment rights and federal laws concerning draft service. By outlining personal freedoms and perceived illegal actions by the American government, the petition presents a many-layered picture of why this group was protesting the Vietnam War and why the collection and destruction of draft cards was central to its purpose.

The first major focus of the petition is the legality of the conflict and the personal morality of those drafted into service. As the petition states (in points two and three), those who signed their name to the petition did so to indicate that they no longer agreed that the Unit-ed States was acting in a legal manner and in accord with the regulations set down by the United Nations and the Geneva Convention. The authors go so far as to compare the leaders and some of the soldiers with Nazi war criminals who were tried after World War II in the Nuremberg trials. Such strong statements demonstrate the contempt with which the authors held the US gov-ernment and its involvement in Vietnam. They desire to have nothing to do with the conflict and encourage oth-ers to stand against it, too. They also state quite force-fully that the war as immoral, especially when it forces young men who object to the violence to participate in it. The authors believe that those who disapprove of the war on moral grounds should be exempt from service.

A second major focus is the tension between the pe-titioners' First Amendment rights and the legal rami-fications of not adhering to laws regarding the draft. While the ability to protest and speak out about a war deemed unjust and illegal is protected by the First Amendment (freedom of speech), the active avoidance of service as mandated by the government is punish-able under federal law. The petition goes beyond simple objection to the laws covering the draft; it also calls on its readers to engage in acts of civil disobedience. In this case, such disobedience most often occurred when faculty members of the University Committee on War and Peace collected the draft cards of participating students and burned or otherwise destroyed them. For that reason, many of the authors and signatories were punished for their involvement. In the eyes of the law, they had crossed the line between speaking and acting in defense of their beliefs.

Essential Themes

The most enduring legacy of the document, and others like it, is the attention that came to be paid to the act of forcing young men (and women) to be soldiers. The draft was ended in 1973, and, today, the United States has an entirely voluntary military force. This change is partially owing to the decreased need for massive troop numbers in today's military and partially due to the increase in voluntary servicemen and servicewomen. But it is also partially owing to the very vocal, and occasionally violent, reaction to the draft during the 1960s and early 1970s. Some 210,000 Americans are thought to have evaded the draft then, 30,000 of them leaving the country to do so. Since that time, there has been a heightened awareness of the inequalities of the draft—most draftees tend to come from poor or working-class communities—just as there has been an increased awareness and respect for religious and moral objections to participating in combat.

Another legacy of the document, and those like it, is the continuing debate about the boundaries of freedom of speech and the First Amendment. What constitutes acceptable public protest, and when do matters shade into illegal actions? The limiting of draft exemptions provoked many citizens to take actions—burning draft cards and fleeing the country—that were considered illegal. The US Supreme Court, in *United States v. O'Brien* (1968), ruled that draft card burning was illegal; the decision was roundly criticized by legal experts. As a point of comparison, burning an American flag was also then illegal; yet that act was later labeled a form of free speech by the Supreme Court.

A related question is this: if a person considers the government's authority regarding a foreign war to be suspect or illegal, is not civil disobedience all that remains? How does a person or a group find an acceptable balance between individual ideals and the legal constraints of the situation? These types of questions continue to be a focus for activists of all types. The Vietnam War was not the first time that such questions were raised, but it was one of the most notable of such times in US history.

—*Anna Accettola, MA*

Bibliography and Additional Reading

Berrigan, Daniel, Robin Anderson, & James L. Marsh. *The Trial of the Catonsville Nine*. New York: Fordham University Press, 2004. Print.

Foley, Michael Stewart. *Confronting the War Machine: Draft Resistance during the Vietnam War*. Chapel Hill, NC: University of North Carolina Press, 2003. Print.

Kaye, David. "April Is a Big Antiwar Month on Campus and in Nation." *The Daily Pennsylvanian* [Philadelphia] 2 Apr. 1968, 84th ed.: 1, 4. Print.

Kent, Stephen A. *From Slogans to Mantras: Social Protest and Religious Conversion in the Late Vietnam War Era*. Syracuse, NY: Syracuse University Press, 2001. Print.

Useem, Michael. *Conscription, Protest, and Social Conflict: the Life and Death of a Draft Resistance Movement*. New York: Wiley-Interscience, 1973. Web.

■ An Unwinnable War

Date: February 8, 1968
Author: Robert F. Kennedy
Genre: speech; address

Summary Overview

On February 8, 1968 Senator Robert F. Kennedy of New York announced his opposition to the Vietnam War during a speech in Chicago. His speech occurred as American soldiers and soldiers of the Republic of Vietnam (RVN, or South Vietnam) were fighting to dislodge communist forces that had seized military bases and cities in the RVN during the Tet Offensive. He provided a critical assessment of the American military intervention in Vietnam, arguing that the war was having a devastating effect on both the Vietnamese and Americans. He argued that the Tet Offensive proved once and for all that the war was unwinnable. The only sensible course was to withdraw all American forces from Vietnam. An influential member of the Democratic Party, Kennedy's denunciation put him in direct opposition to the war policies of Democratic president Lyndon Johnson and provided him with a platform with which to seek the Democratic presidential nomination in 1968.

Defining the Moment

In many respects, Kennedy's "Unwinnable War" speech represented a dramatic shift in his views. As a close advisor to his brother, John F. Kennedy, Robert Kennedy had supported American aid to South Vietnam in the early 1960s. His support for the war continued during the first years of Lyndon Johnson's presidency, even as Johnson sent hundreds of thousands of American combat troops to fight in the south against anti-government communist forces.

Kennedy's relationship with Johnson was complex. Although Johnson appreciated Kennedy's earlier support for escalation, he was also paranoid about his potential influence. Johnson thought that Kennedy's views on Vietnam were far more hawkish than his own. He feared that if he did not aggressively fight the war, Kennedy would use it as an opportunity to criticize him, undercut his support, and improve his own popularity among democrats.

Over time, Kennedy became more critical of American involvement in the war, but he largely kept his criticisms to himself as he did not want to appear disloyal or create divisions within the Democratic Party. Kennedy's "Unwinnable War" speech was the first time he publicly called for an end to the war. His comments were largely a reaction to the Tet Offensive. For months, the Johnson administration had told the American people that the United States was winning the war and that it would be over soon. On January 30, 1968, the Vietnamese New Year, the National Liberation Front (NLF) and North Vietnamese Army (NVA) conducted a series of coordinated attacks against important and symbolic military and civilian targets throughout South Vietnam. As scenes of insurgents attacking the US embassy flashed across millions of American TV screens, any hope that the war would soon be over was permanently broken. Kennedy's speech was meant to address this new and troubling reality. His criticisms of the war were likely shared by many Americans listening who had similarly concluded that the events of the past days had proven once and for all that the Vietnam War was in fact an unwinnable war.

Biography

Born in Brookline, Massachusetts on November 20, 1925, Robert F. Kennedy was not only the brother of President John F. Kennedy, but also an influential political actor in his own right. After military service in

World War II, Kennedy earned a law degree from the University of Virginia and served as council for several congressional committees during the 1950s. When his older brother was elected president in 1960, Kennedy was appointed attorney general of the United States. He was one of his brother's closest advisors and, as attorney general, played an instrumental role in determining the Kennedy administration's response to the civil rights movement. In 1964, Kennedy was elected to the US Senate. He had long had reservations about Johnson's policy in Vietnam, but after the Tet Offensive began in late January 1968, he publicly expressed his opposition to the war. On March 31, 1968, he announced his candidacy for the Democratic presidential nomination. After winning several state Democratic primaries, he was assassinated by Sirhan Sirhan in Los Angeles on June 5, 1968.

HISTORICAL DOCUMENT

Our enemy, savagely striking at will across all of South Vietnam, has finally shattered the mask of official illusion with which we have concealed our true circumstances, even from ourselves. But a short time ago we were serene in our reports and predictions of progress.

The Vietcong will probably withdraw from the cities, as they were forced to withdraw from the American Embassy. Thousands of them will be dead.

But they will, nevertheless, have demonstrated that no part or person of South Vietnam is secure from their attacks: neither district capitals nor American bases, neither the peasant in his rice paddy nor the commanding general of our own great forces.

No one can predict the exact shape or outcome of the battles now in progress, in Saigon or at Khesanh. Let us pray that we will succeed at the lowest possible cost to our young men.

But whatever their outcome, the events of the last two weeks have taught us something. For the sake of those young Americans who are fighting today, if for no other reason, the time has come to take a new look at the war in Vietnam, not by cursing the past but by using it to illuminate the future.

And the first and necessary step is to face the facts. It is to seek out the austere and painful reality of Vietnam, freed from wishful thinking, false hopes and sentimental dreams. It is to rid ourselves of the "good company," of those illusions which have lured us into the deepening swamp of Vietnam.

We must, first of all, rid ourselves of the illusion that the events of the past two weeks represent some sort of victory. That is not so.

It is said the Vietcong will not be able to hold the cities. This is probably true. But they have demonstrated despite all our reports of progress, of government strength and enemy weakness, that half a million American soldiers with 700,000 Vietnamese allies, with total command of the air, total command of the sea, backed by huge resources and the most modern weapons, are unable to secure even a single city from the attacks of an enemy whose total strength is about 250,000. . . .

For years we have been told that the measure of our success and progress in Vietnam was increasing security and control for the population. Now we have seen that none of the population is secure and no area is under sure control.

Four years ago when we only had about 30,000 troops in Vietnam, the Vietcong were unable to mount the assaults on cities they have now conducted against our enormous forces. At one time a suggestion that we protect enclaves was derided. Now there are no protected enclaves.

This has not happened because our men are not brave or effective, because they are. It is because we have misconceived the nature of the war: It is because we have sought to resolve by military might a conflict whose issue depends upon the will and conviction of the South Vietnamese people. It is like sending a lion to halt an epidemic of jungle rot.

This misconception rests on a second illusion—the illusion that we can win a war which the South Vietnamese cannot win for themselves.

You cannot expect people to risk their lives and endure hardship unless they have a stake in their own society. They must have a clear sense of identification with their own government, a belief they are participating in a cause worth fighting for.

People will not fight to line the pockets of generals or swell the bank accounts of the wealthy. They are far more likely to close their eyes and shut their doors in the face of their government—even as they did last week.

More than any election, more than any proud boast, that single fact reveals the truth. We have an ally in name only. We support a government without supporters. Without the efforts of American arms that government would not last a day.

The third illusion is that the unswerving pursuit of military victory, whatever its cost, is in the interest of either ourselves or the people of Vietnam.

For the people of Vietnam, the last three years have meant little but horror. Their tiny land has been devastated by a weight of bombs and shells greater than Nazi Germany knew in the Second World War.

We have dropped 12 tons of bombs for every square mile in North and South Vietnam. Whole provinces have been substantially destroyed. More than two million South Vietnamese are now homeless refugees.

Imagine the impact in our own country if an equivalent number—over 25 million Americans—were wandering homeless or interned in refugee camps, and millions more refugees were being created as New York and Chicago, Washington and Boston, were being destroyed by a war raging in their streets.

Whatever the outcome of these battles, it is the people we seek to defend who are the greatest losers.

Nor does it serve the interests of America to fight this war as if moral standards could be subordinated to immediate necessities. Last week, a Vietcong suspect was turned over to the chief of the Vietnamese Security Services, who executed him on the spot—a flat violation of the Geneva Convention on the Rules of War.

The photograph of the execution was on front pages all around the world—leading our best and oldest friends to ask, more in sorrow than in anger, what has happened to America?

The fourth illusion is that the American national interest is identical with—or should be subordinated to—the selfish interest of an incompetent military regime.

We are told, of course, that the battle for South Vietnam is in reality a struggle for 250 million Asians—the beginning of a Great Society for all of Asia. But this is pretension.

We can and should offer reasonable assistance to Asia; but we cannot build a Great Society there if we cannot build one in our own country. We cannot speak extravagantly of a struggle for 250 million Asians, when a struggle for 15 million in one Asian country so strains our forces, that another Asian country, a fourth-rate power which we have already once defeated in battle, dares to seize an American ship and hold and humiliate her crew.

The fifth illusion is that this war can be settled in our own way and in our own time on our own terms. Such a settlement is the privilege of the triumphant: of those who crush their enemies in battle or wear away their will to fight.

We have not done this, nor is there any prospect we will achieve such a victory.

Unable to defeat our enemy or break his will—at least without a huge, long and ever more costly effort—we must actively seek a peaceful settlement. We can no longer harden our terms every time Hanoi indicates it may be prepared to negotiate; and we must be willing to foresee a settlement which will give the Vietcong a chance to participate in the political life of the country.

These are some of the illusions which may be discarded if the events of last week are to prove not simply a tragedy, but a lesson: a lesson which carries with it some basic truths.

First, that a total military victory is not within sight or around the corner; that, in fact, it is probably beyond our grasp; and that the effort to win such a victory will only result in the further slaughter of thousands of innocent and helpless people—a slaughter which will forever rest on our national conscience.

Second, that the pursuit of such a victory is not necessary to our national interest, and is even damaging that interest.

Third, that the progress we have claimed toward increasing our control over the country and the security of the population is largely illusory.

Fourth, that the central battle in this war cannot be measured by body counts or bomb damage, but by the extent to which the people of South Vietnam act on a sense of common purpose and hope with those that govern them.

Fifth, that the current regime in Saigon is unwilling or incapable of being an effective ally in the war against the Communists.

Sixth, that a political compromise is not just the best path to peace, but the only path, and we must show as much willingness to risk some of our prestige for peace as to risk the lives of young men in war.

Seventh, that the escalation policy in Vietnam, far from strengthening and consolidating international resistance to aggression, is injuring our country through the world, reducing the faith of other peoples in our wisdom and purpose and weakening the world's resolve to stand together for freedom and peace.

Eighth, that the best way to save our most precious stake in Vietnam—the lives of our soldiers—is to stop the enlargement of the war, and that the best way to end casualties is to end the war.

Ninth, that our nation must be told the truth about this war, in all its terrible reality, both because it is right—

and because only in this way can any Administration rally the public confidence and unity for the shadowed days which lie ahead.

No war has ever demanded more bravery from our people and our Government—not just bravery under fire or the bravery to make sacrifices—but the bravery to discard the comfort of illusion—to do away with false hopes and alluring promises.

Reality is grim and painful. But it is only a remote echo of the anguish toward which a policy founded on illusion is surely taking us.

This is a great nation and a strong people. Any who seek to comfort rather than speak plainly, reassure rather than instruct, promise satisfaction rather than reveal frustration—they deny that greatness and drain that strength. For today as it was in the beginning, it is the truth that makes us free.

Document Analysis

As American and Army of the Republic of Vietnam (ARVN) forces continued to battle communist forces throughout South Vietnam, Kennedy declared his opposition to the Vietnam War in a speech in Chicago on February 8, 1968. Kennedy justified his opposition, arguing that the war did not serve the interests of either the Vietnamese or the American people and was unwinnable. He also noted that the Johnson administration had purposely misled the American people about the true nature and status of the war.

Clearly, the Tet Offensive loomed large in his thinking. He maintained that the attacks had "shattered the mask of official illusion" that American forces were winning the war and that it would soon be over. He noted that while the NLF's immediate goal of overthrowing the South Vietnamese government would fail, thousands of American soldiers would ultimately be killed in the process. The Tet Offensive also proved that the Johnson administration's claim that communist forces were near defeat was nothing more than an illusion. The simple fact that the NLF was able to conduct coordinated attacks throughout the South was proof that "no part or person of South Vietnam is secure from their attacks: neither district capitals nor Ameri-

can bases, neither the peasant in his rice paddy nor the commanding general of our own great forces."

In Kennedy's estimation, the only way forward was to accept the reality of the war. First and foremost, the offensive proved once and for all that despite having more than half a million American soldiers in Vietnam, supported by 700,000 allied ARVN soldiers with the most modern weaponry and total control of the air and sea, communist forces could not be prevented from attacking nearly every city and important military installation in South Vietnam simultaneously. In the past, Johnson's administration had justified the need for more American forces in Vietnam with the argument that they were needed to control enemy forces and maintain security. Kennedy claimed that the recent offensive proved that no quantity of soldiers and resources would be enough to secure these goals.

Kennedy maintained that victory depended "upon the will and conviction of the South Vietnamese people." Yet they were largely led by corrupt military officials, whose dedication to popular rule was tenuous at best and whose primary concern was making money. Many Vietnamese had little confidence in their officials and, therefore, little interest in defending the country they represented. Additionally, American bombing campaigns had done little to gain support from Vietnamese civilians especially as thousands were killed or injured. The South had more than 2 million refugees as a result of the bombing.

Equally important, the war not only placed American soldiers in the difficult position of fighting, and even dying, for a corrupt regime, it also diverted American resources from more pressing domestic needs. Kennedy noted that "we cannot build a Great Society there if we cannot build one in our own country." Even at the international level, Kennedy maintained that continued escalation of the war damaged American standing abroad, "reducing the faith of other peoples in our wisdom and purpose and weakening the world's resolve to stand together for freedom and peace."

Kennedy concluded that the only sensible reaction to the realities of the Vietnam War was to seek a peaceful settlement with the Democratic Republic of Vietnam (DRV, or North Vietnam) and the NLF. He believed that a peace settlement was the only way to avoid continued suffering and the only way for the Johnson administration to regain the trust and confidence of the American people.

Essential Themes

Robert F. Kennedy served as an influential advisor during his brother's presidency. During this time he expressed support for American intervention in Vietnam, a position which he maintained during the first years of Johnson's presidency. By late 1967, Kennedy had become increasingly skeptical about American involvement in Vietnam, but he hesitated to express these views publicly for fear of appearing disloyal to the president. However, the Tet Offensive permanently destroyed Kennedy's confidence that the war could be won in a timely matter. In his mind, the fact that the Vietnamese communist forces could conduct such a significant military attack meant that the war was unwinnable. Thus, Kennedy's "Unwinnable War" speech

represented a significant shift in how he viewed American military intervention. It also led a significant break in his relationship with Johnson's administration.

Kennedy's speech established his reputation as an antiwar politician. Overnight, he became the most prominent antiwar politician. In the months before the Tet Offensive antiwar Democrats had tried unsuccessfully to convince Kennedy to run against Johnson in the 1968 Democratic nomination race. When he turned them down, they turned to Senator Eugene McCarthy of Minnesota. Quite unexpectedly, McCarthy came close to defeating Johnson in the New Hampshire primary on March 12, 1968. This close election motivated Kennedy to announce his entry into the race. Influenced at least in part by the entry of such a formidable candidate, Johnson announced on March 31 that he would not be seeking the Democratic nomination. After winning the California primary in early June, Kennedy established himself as a major contender for the nomination. However, his journey to the presidency was cut short when he was assassinated on June 5, 1968.

—Gerald F. Goodwin, PhD

Bibliography and Additional Reading

Clarke, Thurston. *The Last Campaign: Robert F. Kennedy and 82 Days That Inspired America*. New York: Henry Holt and Company, 2008. Print.

Moss, George Donelson. *Vietnam: An American Ordeal*. Upper Saddle River, New Jersey: Pearson Prentice Hall, 2006. Print.

Oberdorfer, Don. *Tet!: The Turning Point in the Vietnam War*. Baltimore, MD: Johns Hopkins UP, 2001. Print.

Small, Melvin. *Antiwarriors: The Vietnam War and the Battle for America's Hearts and Minds*. Lanham, MD: Rowman & Littlefield Publishers, 2002. Vietnam: America in the War Years Ser. Print.

■ "We are Mired in Stalemate"

Date: February 27, 1968
Author: Walter Cronkite
Genre: editorial

Summary Overview

Walter Cronkite was the news anchor of the *CBS Evening News with Walter Cronkite* and known as "the most trusted man in America." In the 1960s, television news consisted primarily of half-hour evening news programs by the three networks, CBS, NBC and ABC. After 1965, network coverage of the war increased and the Vietnam War became known as the "Television War." The networks tended to convey the US military's optimistic assessments of the war until the 1968 Tet Offensive, in which the Viet Cong guerrillas and North Vietnam Army (NVA) launched a massive surprise attack on South Vietnam's cities and provincial capitals, previously considered secure areas. Although US and South Vietnamese forces ultimately drove communist forces from the cities and inflicted huge casualties upon them, the Tet Offensive undermined the US military's claims that victory was near and led many Americans to conclude the war could not be won. Due to the impact the Tet Offensive had on US public opinion, it is considered the turning point of the war. Cronkite was shocked by the scale of the Tet Offensive and decided to go to South Vietnam to try to make an accurate assessment of the war. *Report from Vietnam* showed Cronkite's interviews with both generals and front-line soldiers. Cronkite ended the special report with a brief editorial in which he concluded the US was "mired in stalemate" and that the only way out was negotiations. By concluding the war could not be won, Cronkite brought his immense prestige to the growing calls for US withdrawal from Vietnam and helped make criticism of the war more acceptable to mainstream Americans.

Defining Moment

During the 1960s, Walter Cronkite and his prime competitors, Chet Huntley and David Brinkley of NBC's *Huntley-Brinkley Report*, were widely admired as authoritative and objective national figures. The personal bond between Cronkite and the American public was cemented on the day of President John F. Kennedy's assassination, November 22, 1963, when Cronkite famously removed his glasses and, visibly shaken, reported that President Kennedy had died from his gun shot wounds in Dallas.

Beginning in 1965, television news was increasingly dominated by reports from South Vietnam. The networks tended to reflect the American public's early support for the war and faith in the military. Cronkite, a member of the WWII generation, shared many Americans' faith in US institutions.

The Tet Offensive, which began on January, 30, 1968, shook Cronkite's confidence in the military's positive assessment of the war. Tet is a Lunar New Year holiday lasting several days. During the war, Tet was usually accompanied by a general cease fire. In 1968, however, the Viet Cong guerrillas and the NVA used the cease fire to launch a massive surprise offensive across South Vietnam, targeting its cities and provincial capitals, both US and South Vietnamese military strongholds. During the Tet Offensive, the war moved from patrols and firefights in the mountains, jungles, and rice paddies to fierce urban warfare. The Viet Cong and NVA hoped to hold the cities; however, the US and South Vietnamese militaries employed massive firepower to slowly dislodge them.

Despite General William Westmoreland's assertion that Tet was a victory, the images of Viet Cong guerrillas in once secure cities, including the grounds of the US embassy in Saigon, caught all by surprise and convinced many Americans that the war was not being won. Still, it was difficult for many Americans to question the once-revered US military or to oppose an American war. The antiwar movement had grown, but even in early 1968, many Americans considered the antiwar movement outside the mainstream and unpatriotic.

Cronkite left his studio anchor desk to journey to South Vietnam in February 1968 with a small news team to learn for himself what was really going on. Cronkite reported from the ruins of Saigon and from the front-lines in Hue. He attempted to reach Khe Sanh, the besieged US military base in the mountains of western South Vietnam, but was unable to get through. (US marines would eventually break the siege.) His reporting from South Vietnam appeared on a special 30-minute broadcast *Report from Vietnam*. At the conclusion, Cronkite gave a brief editorial from his desk in New York. In the editorial, Cronkite gave a carefully crafted assessment of the war and concluded the United States was "mired in stalemate." Cronkite argued the only way to end the war was negotiations with the enemy.

Cronkite's editorial helped legitimize dissent on the war. The editorial was a powerful symbol that opposing the war was no longer just the province of campus radicals and pacifist churches, but could be as mainstream as Walter Cronkite himself.

Author Biography

Walter Leland Cronkite, Jr. was born on November 4, 1916 in St. Joseph, Missouri. He was raised in Houston, Texas, and attended the University of Texas at Austin where he worked on the school paper. Cronkite went on to become a United Press (UP) reporter and flew with US bomber missions over Europe during World War II as well as reported from the Battle of the Bulge. During the 1950s, Cronkite worked for CBS television and become famous for his political convention coverage. He hosted a historical re-enactment program *You Are There* from 1953–1957. From 1962–1981, he was the anchor of *The CBS Evening News with Walter Cronkite*. Cronkite died on July 17, 2009.

HISTORICAL DOCUMENT

These ruins are in Saigon, capital and largest city of South Vietnam. They are left here by an act of war, Vietnamese against Vietnamese. Hundreds died here. Here in these ruins can be seen physical evidence of the Vietcong's Tet Offensive, but far less tangible is what those ruins mean, and like everything else in this burned and blasted and weary land, they mean success or setback, victory or defeat, depending upon whom you talk to.

There are doubts about the measure of success or setback, but even more, there are doubts about the exact measure of the disaster itself. All that is known with certainty is that on the first two nights of the Tet Lunar New Year, the Vietcong and North Vietnamese Regular Forces, violating the truce agreed on for that holiday, struck across the entire length of South Vietnam, hitting the largest 35 cities, towns, and provincial capitals. How many died and how much damage was done, however, are still but approximations, despite the official figures.

The very preciseness of the figures brings them under suspicion. Anyone who has wandered through these ruins knows than an exact count is impossible. Why, just a short while ago a little old man came and told us that two VC were buried in a hastily dug grave up at the end of the block. Had they been counted? And what about these ruins? Have they gone through all of them for buried civilians and soldiers? And what about those 14 VC we found in the courtyard behind the post office at Hue? Had they been counted and tabulated? They certainly hadn't been buried. We came to Vietnam to try to determine what all this means to the future of the war here. We talked to officials, top officials, civilian and military, Vietnamese and American. We toured damaged areas like this, and refugee centers. We paid a visit to the Battle at Hue, and to the men manning northernmost provinces, where the next big communist offensive is expected. All of this is the subject of our report.

We came to Vietnam to try to determine what all this means to the future of the war here. We talked to officials, top officials, civilian and military, Vietnamese and American. We toured damaged areas like this, and refugee centers. We paid a visit to the Battle at Hue, and to the men manning northernmost provinces, where the next big communist offensive is expected. All of this is the subject of our report....

Tonight, back in more familiar surroundings in New York, we'd like to sum up our findings in Vietnam, an analysis that must be speculative, personal, subjective. Who won and who lost in the great Tet offensive against the cities? I'm not sure. The Vietcong did not win by a knockout, but neither did we. The referees of history may make it a draw. Another standoff may be coming in the big battles expected south of the Demilitarized Zone. Khesanh could well fall, with a terrible loss in American lives, prestige and morale, and this is a tragedy of our stubbornness there; but the bastion no longer is a key to the rest of the northern regions, and it is doubtful that the American forces can be defeated across the breadth of the DMZ with any substantial loss of ground. Another standoff. On the political front, past performance gives no confidence that the Vietnamese government can cope with its problems, now compounded by the attack on the cities. It may not fall, it may hold on, but it probably won't show the dynamic qualities demanded of this young nation. Another standoff.

We have been too often disappointed by the optimism of the American leaders, both in Vietnam and Washington, to have faith any longer in the silver linings they find in the darkest clouds. They may be right, that Hanoi's winter-spring offensive has been forced by the Communist realization that they could not win the longer war of attrition, and that the Communists hope that any success in the offensive will improve their position for eventual negotiations. It would improve their posi-

tion, and it would also require our realization, that we should have had all along, that any negotiations must be that—negotiations, not the dictation of peace terms. For it seems now more certain than ever that the bloody experience of Vietnam is to end in a stalemate. This summer's almost certain standoff will either end in real give-and-take negotiations or terrible escalation; and for every means we have to escalate, the enemy can match us, and that applies to invasion of the North, the use of nuclear weapons, or the mere commitment of one hundred, or two hundred, or three hundred thousand more American troops to the battle. And with each escalation, the world comes closer to the brink of cosmic disaster.

To say that we are closer to victory today is to believe, in the face of the evidence, the optimists who have been wrong in the past. To suggest we are on the edge of defeat is to yield to unreasonable pessimism. To say that we are mired in stalemate seems the only realistic, yet unsatisfactory, conclusion. On the off chance that military and political analysts are right, in the next few months we must test the enemy's intentions, in case this is indeed his last big gasp before negotiations. But it is increasingly clear to this reporter that the only rational way out then will be to negotiate, not as victors, but as an honorable people who lived up to their pledge to defend democracy, and did the best they could.

This is Walter Cronkite. Good night.

Document Analysis

The document begins with Cronkite's introduction to *Report from Vietnam*, and the section after the ellipses is his famous editorial, which concludes the special, back in his New York studio. The introduction sets the stage for his conclusion that the war cannot be won. He is standing among the ruins of Saigon in the wake of brutal and destructive fighting, describing South Vietnam as a "burned and blasted and weary land…." Much of the US military's assessment of the war's progress was done in statistics, especially official "body counts" of the killed. Cronkite challenges the reliability of official US military statistics by questioning whether the many dead bodies he encountered were counted in official tallies: "The very preciseness of the figures brings them under suspicion…. An exact count is impossible."

In the editorial, Cronkite qualifies his conclusions by stating "an analysis must be speculative, personal,

subjective." As for who won the Tet Offensive, Cronkite states, "I'm not sure." This cautious approach sets Cronkite apart from the confident proclamations of success by the US military and the impassioned denunciations of the war by much of the antiwar movement. It is Cronkite's very caution that makes his conclusions so powerful. Cronkite declares that the war is a "standoff." He states, "To say we are mired in stalemate seems the only realistic, yet unsatisfactory conclusion." He anticipates the arguments of war hawks calling for further military escalation by declaring the communists could match each US move right up to and including the use of nuclear weapons (possessed by North Vietnam's backers, the Soviet Union and People's Republic of China).

Cronkite positions himself between the optimists who find "silver linings … in the darkest clouds" and the "unreasonable pessimism" of those who say the US is "on the edge of defeat…" He concludes that "… it is increasingly clear to this reporter that the only rational way out then will be to negotiate, not as victors, but as an honorable people who lived up to their pledge to defend democracy, and did the best they could." Cronkite thus builds slowly to his conclusion by steering a middle course throughout his editorial. America is not winning or losing, but stuck in a stalemate. He doesn't condemn America's motives in waging the war, unlike much of the antiwar movement, but he challenges the idea that the war can be won. He calls neither for escalation nor retreat, but negotiations.

Essential Themes

Walter Cronkite's editorial was a significant statement against the ongoing US war in Vietnam. It has come to symbolize the impact of the Tet Offensive on American public opinion, when many realized the enemy was far from defeated. While some, like General William Westmoreland, have argued Tet was a huge defeat of the communists and, with further escalation, the US could have won the war, most historians agree with Cronkite's conclusion that Tet revealed a war "mired in stalemate." Historians differ over the editorial's impact. Some regard it as a bellwether of changing US opinion, whereas others argue for its direct and widespread impact.

Historian Douglas Brinkley, in his biography *Cronkite*, describes the editorial as the equivalent of an earthquake, calling it "seismic" (Brinkley 379). President Lyndon B. Johnson's press secretary, George Christian, later quoted the president as saying, "If I've lost Cronkite, I've lost the country." Christian's later accounts backtracked from that statement, but whatever President Johnson may have said, there is no doubt he was well aware of Cronkite's editorial and that it was a sign that Middle America's support for the war was waning.

—*Robert Surbrug, PhD*

Bibliography and Additional Readings

Brinkley, Douglas. *Cronkite*. New York: HarperCollins P, 2012. Print.

Cronkite, Walter. *A Reporter's Life*. New York: Ballantine Books, 1997. Print.

Kurlansky, Mark. *1968: The Year that Rocked the World*. New York: Ballantine P, 2004. Print.

Vietnam War with Walter Cronkite. Nar. Walter Cronkite. Marathon Music and Video, 2003. Documentary.

Weathermen Manifesto

Date: June 18, 1969
Authors: John Jacobs; Karin Asbley; Bill Ayers; Bernadine Dohrn; Jeff Jones; Gerry Long; Howie Machtinger; Jim Mellen; Terry Robbins; Mark Rudd; Steve Tappis.
Genre: political tract

Summary Overview

Students for a Democratic Society (SDS) was founded in 1960 and became the largest campus group of the New Left. In its early years, SDS identified with the nonviolent civil rights movement and organized around the issues of racism, student rights, and poverty. After 1965, SDS focused on opposing the escalating war in Vietnam. SDS's actions evolved from legal protests of the war to forms of militant resistance, such as building occupations and confrontations with police. By 1969, a faction of SDS concluded that protest and resistance had accomplished little and only revolution could bring about change. This faction named itself the "Weathermen" (although it included men and women), took over SDS in 1969, and issued its "Weathermen Manifesto." In the early 1970s, the Weathermen went underground and carried out a series of bombings to protest the war, racism, and state repression.

Defining Moment

SDS's actions evolved in the late 1960s from legal protests and teach-ins to acts of resistance. Examples included the building occupation at the University of Wisconsin, Madison in 1967 to demonstrate against Dow Chemical Company, manufacturer of napalm, and the Columbia Student Uprising in 1968 to protest university racism and complicity in the war. In both actions, hundreds of students were beaten by police and arrested. By 1969, a faction of SDS concluded only a revolution could bring about an end to war and racism. In June, this faction took over SDS after a divisive national meeting in Chicago.

They called themselves "Weatherman" (but became known as the "Weathermen") after a line from a Bob Dylan song, "You don't need a weatherman to know which way the wind blows." The idea was that the Weathermen were pointing in the direction of the revolutionary winds blowing across America.

The Weathermen issued their manifesto on June 18, 1969. In it, they argued that student radicals must ally themselves with third world revolutionaries, such as those in Vietnam and Cuba, in the fight against US imperialism. White radicals needed to follow the lead of African Americans, the most oppressed people in America, and therefore the most revolutionary group. The manifesto also described America's culturally rebellious youth as ripe for revolution.

The Weathermen's first major action was billed as "the Days of Rage," a destructive rampage through the wealthy neighborhoods of Chicago, where a few hundred Weathermen engaged in vandalism and street battles with police and were arrested.

In early 1970, the Weathermen decided to go underground (that is, into hiding) and renamed themselves the "Weather Underground Organization." Henceforth, the organization would not number more than fifty members. Throughout the early 1970s, the Weather Underground carried out bombings of buildings they associated with the war and racism. These included a bombing of the Capitol building in 1971 and of the Pentagon in 1972. These bombings tended to destroy small sections of these buildings and were responsible for no loss of life. However, in the spring of 1970, three Weathermen were killed when a bomb they were preparing to detonate at a military dance at Fort Dix, NJ, accidentally exploded in a Greenwich Village townhouse. By 1970, members of the Weathermen joined Black Panthers on the FBI's Ten Most Wanted List.

Author Biography

John Jacobs, known as "JJ," is considered the primary author of the Weathermen Manifesto. Raised in Connecticut, Jacobs, along with his close friend, Mark Rudd, was one of the major leaders of the Colombia Student Uprising in the spring of 1968. He was expelled from the Weathermen in 1970 over ideological differences. Jacobs went underground to hide from the FBI during the 1970s and held odd jobs until his death from cancer in 1997.

HISTORICAL DOCUMENT

The very first question people in this country must ask in considering the question of revolution is where they stand in relation to the United States as an oppressor nation, and where they stand in relation to the masses of people throughout the world whom US imperialism is oppressing. . . .

It is in this context that we must examine the revolutionary struggles in the United States. We are within the heartland of a world-wide monster, a country so rich from its world-wide plunder that even the crumbs doled out to the enslaved masses within its borders provide for material existence very much above the conditions of the masses of people of the world. The US empire, as world-wide system, channels wealth, based upon the labor and resources of the rest of the world, into the United States. The relative affluence existing in the United States is directly dependent upon the labor and natural resources of the Vietnamese, the Angolans, the Bolivians and the rest of the peoples of the Third World. All of the United Airlines Astrojets, all of the Holiday Inns, all of Hertz's automobiles, your television set, car and wardrobe already belong, to a large degree, to the people of the rest of the world. . . .

The goal is the destruction of US imperialism and the achievement of a classless world: world communism. Winning state power in the US will occur as a result of the military forces of the US overextending themselves around the world and being defeated piecemeal; struggle within the US will be a vital part of this process, but when the revolution triumphs in the US it will have been made by the people of the whole world. For socialism to be defined in national terms within so extreme and historical an oppressor nation as this is only imperialist national chauvinism on the part of the "movement."

In this context, why an emphasis on youth? Why should young people be willing to fight on the side of Third World peoples? . . .

As imperialism struggles to hold together this decaying, social fabric, it inevitably resorts to brute force and authoritarian ideology. People, especially young people, more and more find themselves in the iron grip of authoritarian institutions. Reaction against the pigs or teachers in the schools, welfare pigs or the army is generalizable and extends beyond the particular repressive institution to the society and the State as a whole. The legitimacy of the State is called into question for the first time in at least 20 years, and the antiauthoritarianism which characterizes the youth rebellion turns into rejection of the State, a refusal to be socialized into American society. Kids used to try to beat the system from inside the army or from inside the schools; now they desert from the army and burn down the schools. . . .

The struggle of black people—as a colony—is for self-determination, freedom, and liberation from US imperialism. Because blacks have been oppressed and held in an inferior social position as a people, they have a right to decide, organize and act on their common destiny as a people apart from white interference. Black self-determination does not simply apply to determination of their collective political destiny at some future time. It is directly tied to the fact that because all blacks experience oppression in a form that no whites do, no whites are in a position to fully understand and test from their own practice the real situation black people face and the necessary response to it. This is why it is necessary for black people to organize separately and determine their actions separately at each stage of the struggle. . . .

In general, young people have less stake in a society (no family, fewer debts, etc.), are more open to new ideas (they have not been brainwashed for so long or so well), and are therefore more able and willing to move in a revolutionary direction. Specifically in America, young people have grown up experiencing the crises in imperialism. They have grown up along with a developing black liberation movement, with the liberation of

Cuba, the fights for independence in Africa and the war in Vietnam....

This crisis in imperialism affects all parts of the society. America has had to militarize to protect and expand its empire; hence the high draft calls and the creation of a standing army of three and a half million, an army which still has been unable to win in Vietnam. Further, the huge defense expenditures—required for the defense of the empire and at the same time a way of making increasing profits for the defense industries—have gone hand in hand with the urban crisis around welfare, the hospitals, the schools, housing, air and water pollution. The State cannot provide the services it has been forced to assume responsibility for, and needs to increase taxes and to pay its growing debts while it cuts services and uses the pigs to repress protest. The private sector of the economy can't provide jobs, particularly unskilled jobs. The expansion of the defense and education industries by the State since World War II is in part an attempt to pick up the slack, though the inability to provide decent wages and working conditions for "public" jobs is more and more a problem....

...the war against Vietnam is not "the heroic war against the Nazis"; it's the big lie, with napalm burning through everything we had heard this country stood for. Kids begin to ask questions: Where is the Free World— And who do the pigs protect at home? ...

A revolution is a war; when the Movement in this country can defend itself militarily against total repression it will be part of the revolutionary war.

This will require a cadre organization, effective secrecy, self-reliance among the cadres, and an integrated relationship with the active mass-based Movement. To win a war with an enemy as highly organized and centralized as the imperialists will require a (clandestine) organization of revolutionaries, having also a unified "general staff"; that is, combined at some point with discipline under one centralized leadership. Because war is political, political tasks—the international communist revolution—must guide it. Therefore the centralized organization of revolutionaries must be a political organization as well as military, what is generally called a "Marxist-Leninist" party.

GLOSSARY

cadre: disciplined members of a tight-knit revolutionary organization

chauvinism: a prejudiced devotion to one's own group

Marxist-Leninism: Karl Marx's philosophy as interpreted by Vladimir Lenin and the Russian Bolsheviks emphasizing the need for a disciplined, vanguard political organization to lead a workers' revolution

"pigs": a term of derision used by many radicals and hippies in the Vietnam War era to refer to police and sometimes to any supporters of "the Establishment"

Document Analysis

The Weathermen Manifesto views the United States through the ideological lens of Marxism-Leninism as an imperialist, capitalist, and militaristic power that enriches its ruling class through exploitation of poor, nonwhite majorities around the world. Racism, poverty, and the war in Vietnam are seen as inevitable expressions of this imperialist system, which cannot be changed through reform, but only world-wide revolution. The authors condemn liberalism and pacifism as dead ends. White radicals must ally themselves with revolutionary forces in the third world, like the Viet Cong, and domestically with Black Nationalist groups, like the Black Panthers.

There are a few keys in this document to understanding why some middle-class white college students became so radicalized and ultimately resorted to violence. Many of these activists had grown up in the post-World

War II era when America was celebrated as a beacon of freedom and democracy. In the 1960s, the ugliness of American racism and the brutality of Vietnam, often conveyed through television, highlighted the gap between America's high ideals and the often harsh reality. This resulted in a progressive disillusionment with America and ultimately the conclusion that America was the exact opposite of what they had been led to believe, in the words of the manifesto, "a world-wide monster." A line that captures this disillusionment is "Vietnam is not 'the heroic war against the Nazis'; it's the big lie, with napalm burning through everything we had heard this country stood for."

The other key is the document's emphasis on African Americans and other oppressed non-white peoples. Throughout the 1960s, these white activists saw blacks arrested, beaten, shot, and jailed for seeking freedom. This induced a sense of guilt among many white radicals and a belief that to prove their commitment, they must be willing to put their own sheltered lives on the line. As the authors declare, "blacks experience oppression in a form that no whites do…" and thus whites cannot lead but only follow African American revolutionaries. They also state that America's "affluence… is directly dependent upon the labor and natural resources … of the Third World." Thus, the Weathermen reject their middle-class, white privilege to make common cause with the oppressed of the third world in fighting for "a classless world: world communism."

One area where the Weathermen broke with other ideological revolutionary groups was the role they ascribe to youth caught up in the social rebellion of the hippie counterculture. Many student radicals held hippies in disdain for focusing on lifestyle, music, and drugs rather than active politics, but the Weathermen see these alienated youth as ripe for recruitment into the revolution.

Essential Themes

Early SDS had rejected rigid ideologies for a generalized search for democratic ideals and lives of personal authenticity. By 1969, however, SDS had become radicalized in the face of the war and worsening racial unrest. Members of different factions of SDS looked for a roadmap to revolution in the ideologies of Marx, Lenin, Mao, Castro, and other communist revolutionaries. This led to bitter ideological debates that ultimately fragmented SDS and ended with the Weathermen taking over the organization.

The Weathermen saw themselves as a tight-knit revolutionary organization modeled on groups like the Viet Cong. This caused them to go underground in 1970 and carry out a series of bombings. Ironically, going underground cut them off from the very mass movement they hoped to lead, especially during the campus uprisings in May 1970 in the wake of the US invasion of Cambodia.

As the war slowly wound down for the US, the revolutionary visions of 1968–1970 waned and new movements, such as feminism, environmentalism, and the gay liberation movement, emerged as the vanguard of social change. The Weathermen, now the Weather Underground Organization, were joined by other guerrilla groups, like the Symbionese Liberation Army, which kidnapped newspaper heiress Patty Hearst in 1974, and the Black Liberation Army, which killed several police officers. These violent groups—many would call them terrorists—ultimately effected little change in America. They had adopted third world models of revolutionary organization, which were never adaptable to the realities of an advanced industrial nation like the United States. Nevertheless, groups like the Weathermen stand as an enduring testimony of the extremes to which many idealistic young Americans were driven by the unrelenting war in Vietnam and the bitter struggle for racial equality.

—*Robert Surbrug, PhD*

Bibliography and Additional Readings

Berger, Dan. *The Weather Underground and the Politics of Solidarity.* Oakland, CA: AK P, 2006. Print.

Burrough, Bryan. *Days of Rage: America's Radical Underground, the FBI, and the Forgotten Age of Revolutionary Violence.* New York: Penguin P, 2015. Print.

Gitlin, Todd. *Sixties: Years of Hope, Days of Rage.* New York: Bantam, 1987. Print.

Jacobs, Ron. *The Way the Wind Blew: A History of the Weather Underground.* New York: Verso, 1997. Print.

Sale, Kirkpatrick. *SDS.* New York: Random House, 1973. Print.

Varon, Jeremy. *Bringing the War Home: The Weather Underground, the Red Army Faction, and the Revolutionary Violence in the 1960s and 1970s.* Berkeley and Los Angeles: U of California P, 2004. Print.

![header bar]

■ George McGovern Urges an End to the War

Date: September 1, 1970
Author: George McGovern
Genre: speech; address

Summary Overview

Before introducing the McGovern-Hatfield Amendment on the Senate floor, Senator George McGovern of South Dakota provided a stinging indictment not only of the Vietnam War, but also of the Senate, which had allowed the war to continue for years. In blunt terms, McGovern criticized his fellow senators for not having the courage to speak out against the war and thereby allowing thousands of Americans to be injured or killed in Vietnam. He maintained that the Senate had essentially ceded all foreign policy decisions to President Richard Nixon. McGovern's amendment would provide an opportunity for his fellow senators to redeem themselves by cutting off all funding for the war. It would also require Nixon to withdraw all American soldiers from Vietnam by the end of 1971. By voting in favor of the amendment, the Senate could not only alter American policy in Vietnam, it could also place significant restrictions on the executive branch and reassert congressional influence over the conduct of the war and American foreign policy in general.

Defining Moment

On September 1, 1970 George McGovern introduced the McGovern-Hatfield Amendment to an appropriations bill funding military operations in Vietnam. McGovern was a longtime critic of American involvement in Vietnam. In a September 24, 1963 speech in the Senate, he declared that American intervention in Southeast Asia was a failure. Despite his reservations, on August 10, 1964, McGovern voted in favor of the Gulf of Tonkin Resolution, which authorized President Lyndon Johnson to use military force in Vietnam. McGovern became increasingly disillusioned as American military involvement escalated, but he initially hesitated to criticize Johnson publicly because he feared alienating him, and he hoped that Johnson would initiate peace negotiations. By 1966, he had broken completely with the Johnson administration over Vietnam

policy. McGovern's credentials as an antiwar stalwart in Congress only grew when he ran for the Democratic nomination for president in 1968 on a platform calling for an end to American military intervention. Although he did not win the nomination, his national profile grew considerably—which likely emboldened him to continue his antiwar advocacy.

McGovern introduced the McGovern-Hatfield Amendment in reaction to President Richard Nixon's decision to expand the war into Cambodia. On April 30, 1970, Nixon announced that he had ordered American forces to attack two major North Vietnamese Army (NVA) military bases in Cambodian territory. From a military standpoint, the Cambodian incursion was somewhat successful, but the expansion of the war into a previously neutral country reenergized the antiwar movement at home. On May 4, 1970, during a protest at Kent State University, National Guardsmen fired indiscriminately into a crowd, killing four and wounding nine. In reaction to the events at Kent State, protests erupted around the country.

The Cambodian incursion and the subsequent domestic reaction to it likely encouraged McGovern to ramp up his criticisms of the Vietnam War and especially Nixon's handling of the conflict. These events also emboldened McGovern and Republican Senator Mark Hatfield of Oregon to challenge directly Nixon's presidential authority by attempting to cut off all military funding for the war.

Biography

George McGovern was born in Avon, South Dakota, on July 19, 1922. Shortly after the Japanese attack on Pearl Harbor, McGovern enlisted in the military. Beginning in 1944, he flew thirty-five air missions over Austria, Czechoslovakia, Germany, Hungary, Italy, and Poland. McGovern's military service and, particularly, the devastation he witnessed in Europe during the war would have a profound effect on his view of the Vietnam War. A South Dakota Democrat, McGovern was elected to the House of Representatives in 1952 and won a seat in the US Senate in 1962. During the Vietnam War, he became a leading antiwar activist. In 1970, he introduced the Hatfield-McGovern Amendment, which sought the complete withdrawal of American troops from Vietnam by the end of 1971. Although the amendment failed, it emboldened McGovern to run for the Democratic nomination for president in 1972. He won his party's nomination in large part because of his antiwar stance. McGovern was defeated handily by Richard Nixon in the 1972 election, but he remained in the Senate until 1981.

HISTORICAL DOCUMENT

McGovern's remarks on Senate Floor, *Sept. 1, 1970.*

Every Senator in this chamber is partly responsible for sending 50,000 young Americans to an early grave. This chamber reeks of blood. Every Senator here is partly responsible for that human wreckage at Walter Reed and Bethesda Naval and all across our land—young men without legs, or arms, or genitals, or faces or hopes. There are not very many of these blasted and broken boys who think this war is a glorious adventure. Do not talk to them about bugging out, or national honor or courage. It does not take any courage at all for a congressman, or a senator, or a president to wrap himself in the flag and say we are staying in Vietnam, because it is not our blood that is being shed. But we are responsible for those young men and their lives and their hopes. And if we do not end this damnable war those young men will someday curse us for our pitiful willingness to let the Executive carry the burden that the Constitution places on us.

Text of McGovern-Hatfield Amendment.

McGovern–Hatfield Amendment, H.R. 17123

(a) In accordance with public statements of policy by the President, no funds authorized by this or any other act may be obligated or expended to maintain a troop level of more than 280,000 armed forces of the United States in Vietnam after April 30, 1971.

(b) After April 30, 1971, funds herein authorized or hereafter appropriated may be expended in connection with activities of American Armed Forces in and over Indochina only to accomplish the following objectives:

1. the orderly termination of military operations there and the safe and systematic withdrawal of remaining armed forces by December 31, 1971;
2. to secure the release of prisoners of war;
3. the provision of asylum for Vietnamese who might be physically endangered by withdrawal of American forces; and
4. to provide assistance to the Republic of Vietnam consistent with the foregoing objectives; provided however, that if the President while giving effect to the foregoing paragraphs of this section, finds in meeting the termination date that members of the American armed forces are exposed to unanticipated clear and present danger, he may suspend the application of paragraph 2(a) for a period not to exceed 60 days and shall inform the Congress forthwith of his findings; and within 10 days following application of the suspension the President may submit recommendations, including (if necessary) a new date applicable to subsection b(1) for Congressional approval.

Document Analysis

On September 1, 1970, Senator George McGovern introduced the McGovern-Hatfield Amendment accompanied by a number of blunt criticisms of the Senate and its role in President Nixon's failed Vietnam policies. McGovern intended to provide the Senate with an opportunity to take responsibility for their previously poor decisions and bring an end to the Vietnam War by cutting off funding and requiring that all troops be removed from Vietnam by the end of 1971.

McGovern began his speech on the Senate floor on September 1, 1970 by urging an end to the Vietnam

War noting that every single senator in the chamber was partly responsible for leading "50,000 young Americans to an early grave" in Vietnam. He was likely making reference to the Gulf of Tonkin Resolution, which the Senate approved by a vote of 88–2. His comments suggest that he was willing to bear some personal responsibility for the war, as he voted in favor of the Gulf of Tonkin Resolution.

McGovern argued that senators, elected officials, had a responsibility to their constituents, but many had failed to represent them by continuing to support the war. As a result, thousands had been killed in Vietnam and many more lay injured "without legs, or arms, or genitals, or faces or hopes" in military hospitals. He sternly pointed out that American soldiers had the most to lose if the conflict continued. Yet many senators and other supporters of Richard Nixon's policies continued to wrap themselves "in the flag and say we are staying in Vietnam." In a savage aside, he added "it is not our blood that is being shed." McGovern suggested that the only way to serve properly the interests of the soldiers fighting the war was to vote to end the war. It was also the only way to save the reputation of the Senate.

After his remarks, McGovern introduced the McGovern-Hatfield Amendment to an appropriations bill funding military operations in Vietnam. The amendment sought to establish an overall timeline for the removal of all American forces and thereby end American participation in the war. The amendment stated that after April 30, 1971, Congress would forbid any more soldiers from being sent to Vietnam unless they were helping to "secure the release of prisoners of war," or the removal of Vietnamese who might be endangered by American withdrawal. Most importantly, the amendment called for "the orderly termination of military operations there and the safe and systematic withdrawal of remaining armed forces by December 31, 1971."

Essential Themes

Senator McGovern's remarks and the McGovern-Hatfield Amendment had several purposes. In scathing terms, McGovern attacked his fellow senators for allowing President Nixon to determine American policy in Vietnam without any Senate input. As a result, the executive branch had been allowed unilaterally to decide policy in the Vietnam War resulting in the deaths of tens of thousands of American soldiers. The Senate bore some responsibility for these deaths.

Most importantly, the amendment sought to end direct American involvement in the Vietnam War. However, it also sought to reclaim Congressional influence over American policy in Vietnam and issue a strong rebuke to the Nixon administration. The amendment was introduced within the context of the American invasion of Cambodia, which Nixon had ordered solely on his own authority. By introducing the amendment, McGovern sought to demonstrate that Nixon's solo decision would precipitate congressional reaction. The amendment failed by a vote of 55–39, but it did provide a warning to Nixon that he faced growing congressional opposition. It also gave antiwar forces, inside and outside Congress, a new potential tactic.

On a personal level, the amendment raised McGovern's national profile and established him as one of the most outspoken and influential antiwar politicians. McGovern's criticism of the war and the Nixon administration positioned him perfectly to run for the Democratic presidential nomination in 1972. He won the nomination in large part because of support from antiwar Democrats, who made up a sizable portion of the party. Nixon would win the presidential election of 1972 in a landslide, but McGovern's antiwar activism, highlighted by his 1970 remarks, forced Nixon to take additional steps to end the war in 1972, which might not have happened had the Democratic Party nominated a more centrist candidate.

—Gerald F. Goodwin, PhD

Bibliography and Additional Reading

Ambrose, Stephen E. *The Wild Blue: The Men and Boys Who Flew the B-24s Over Germany 1944–45*. New York: Simon & Schuster, 2002. Print.

Berman, Larry. *No Peace No Honor: Nixon, Kissinger, and Betrayal in Vietnam*. New York: Simon & Schuster, 2001. Print.

Mann, Robert. *A Grand Delusion: America's Descent Into Vietnam*. New York: Basic Books, 2002. Print.

Small, Melvin. *Antiwarriors: The Vietnam War and the Battle for America's Hearts and Minds*. Lanham, MD: SR Books, 2002. Vietnam: America in the War Years Ser. Print.

■ *Report of the President's Commission on Campus Unrest,* with Response from President Nixon

Date(s): October 1970 (report); December 12, 1970 (letter)
Genre: report
Author(s): William W. Scranton (commission chair); Richard M. Nixon (president)

Summary Overview

Campus protests against the Vietnam War had been growing in size and militancy since 1965. In the spring of 1970, it appeared that campus unrest might have been dying down as a result of President Richard M. Nixon's "Vietnamization" policy, which began a gradual reduction in US troops in South Vietnam. On April 30, 1970, Nixon announced an invasion into Cambodia to wipe out communist bases near South Vietnam's border. The Cambodian incursion set off the largest wave of student protest of the Vietnam War. The campus unrest that followed included a national student strike and shooting deaths of students at Kent State and Jackson State universities. In response, President Nixon established "The President's Commission on Campus Unrest," chaired by former Pennsylvania governor William W. Scranton (Republican), to investigate the student protests and authorities' responses to them. The commission issued its *Report of the President's Commission on Campus Unrest* the following fall.

Defining Moment

By the spring of 1970, the phased-withdrawal of US troops from Vietnam was proceeding on schedule and antiwar protests appeared to dwindle. On April 30, 1970, however, President Nixon announced the incursion of US and South Vietnamese troops into Cambodia to wipe out North Vietnamese Army and Viet Cong military "sanctuaries." The expansion of the war into an officially neutral nation at a time when many believed the war was winding down unleashed a torrent of criticism and an eruption of campus protest, both peaceful and violent.

On Friday, May 1, Kent State students in downtown Kent, Ohio, engaged in widespread acts of vandalism in response to the Cambodian invasion, including breaking shop windows, setting bonfires in the streets, and throwing bottles at police cars. The next evening, a group of campus radicals set fire to the ROTC building, which they saw as a symbol of the war. A detachment of the Ohio National Guard, exhausted from extended duty due to a violent Teamsters strike, was called in and occupied the Kent State campus. Ohio governor James Rhodes gave a press conference from Kent on May 3 in which he denounced the students as "worse than the brown shirts [Nazis] and the communist element and also the night riders [KKK] …"

On Monday, May 4, the National Guard attempted to break up a peaceful rally scheduled for noon, which provoked rock throwing from a group of students. Many students remained peaceful or were mere spectators, while others simply made their way to class. However, more militant students engaged in running battles with the Guardsmen, each group tossing tear-gas canisters back and forth. Eventually, the besieged Guard unit took position on a hill and fired into a crowd of students, killing four and wounding nine.

Following the Kent State shootings, many local residents said that they regretted the National Guard did not shoot more students, and Nixon referred to student protestors as "the bums blowing up the campuses." The nation's polarization over the war and the antiwar protests hardened. On May 9, New York City was the scene of the "Hard Hat Riot," in which hundreds of American, flag-waving construction workers attacked peaceful antiwar protestors in front of City Hall.

The killings at Kent State triggered a nationwide student strike, the largest in US history, in which more than 500 campuses were shut down. Then, on May 14, at Jackson State, a mostly African American university, Mississippi State Police responded to violent protests over Cambodia and local racial issues by firing a barrage of over sixty rounds into a female dormitory, killing two black male students who had retreated there.

In response to the campus uprisings, President Nixon appointed a commission headed by former Pennsylvania governor William W. Scranton, to investigate the protests and especially the killings at Kent State and Jackson State. The commission conducted numerous interviews, reviewed police and FBI reports, and examined photographs and film pertaining to the killings. The following October, it issued *The Report of the President's Commission on Campus Unrest.* The report described the war as the main source of student anger, condemned students who resorted to violence, and strongly criticized the use of live ammunition at Kent State and Jackson State.

Author Biography

William Warren Scranton was born on July 19, 1917 in Madison, Connecticut, to a wealthy Pennsylvania family. He graduated from Yale in 1939 and attended Yale Law School. Scranton served in a non-combat role in the Army Air Force (USAAF) during World War II. Scranton practiced law in Pennsylvania until being appointed briefly as an assistant to Secretary of State Christian Herter by President Dwight D. Eisenhower in 1959. He was elected to Congress from a Pennsylvania district in 1960 and went on to win the Pennsylvania governorship in 1962 as a moderate Republic, serving until 1967. Scranton made a brief run for the Republican nomination for president in 1964. Scranton undertook several diplomatic missions for different presidents over his life time and served as United Nations ambassador under President Gerald R. Ford in 1976–7. Scranton passed away at the age of 96 on July 28, 2013.

HISTORICAL DOCUMENT

The conduct of many students and nonstudent protesters at Kent State on the first four days of May 1970 was plainly intolerable. We have said in our report, and we repeat: Violence by students on or off the campus can never be justified by any grievance, philosophy, or political idea. There can be no sanctuary or immunity from prosecution on the campus. Criminal acts by students must be treated as such wherever they occur and whatever their purpose. Those who wrought havoc on the town of Kent, those who burned the ROTC building, those who attacked and stoned National Guardsmen, and all those who urged them on and applauded their deeds share the responsibility for the deaths and injuries of May 4.

The widespread student opposition to the Cambodian action and their general resentment of the National Guardsmen's presence on the campus cannot justify the violent and irresponsible actions of many students during the long weekend. The Cambodian invasion defined a watershed in the attitude of Kent students toward American policy in the Indochina war.

Kent State had experienced no major turmoil during the preceding year, and no disturbances comparable in scope to the events of May had ever occurred on the campus. Some students thought the Cambodian action was an unacceptable contradiction of the announced policy of gradual withdrawal from Vietnam, or that the action constituted invasion of a neutral country, or that it would prolong rather than shorten the war. Opposition to the war appears to have been the principal issue around which students rallied during the first two days of May.

Thereafter, the presence of the National Guard on campus was the focus of discontent. The Guard's presence appears to have been the main attraction and the main issue for most students who came to the May 4 rally. For students deeply opposed to the war, the Guard was a living symbol of the military system they opposed. For other students, the Guard was an outsider on their campus, prohibiting all their rallies, even peaceful ones, ordering them about, and tear gassing them when they refused to obey.

The May 4 rally began as a peaceful assembly on the Commons—the traditional site of student assemblies. Even if the Guard had authority to prohibit a peaceful gathering—a question that is at least debatable—the decision to disperse the noon rally was a serious error. The timing and manner of the dispersal were disastrous. Many students were legitimately in the area as they went to and from class. The rally was held during the crowded noontime luncheon period. The rally was peaceful, and there was no apparent impending violence. Only when the Guard attempted to disperse the rally did some students react violently.

Under these circumstances, the Guard's decision to march through the crowd for hundreds of yards up and down a hill was highly questionable. The crowd simply swirled around them and reformed again after they had passed. The Guard found itself on a football practice field far removed from its supply base and running out of tear gas. Guardsmen had been subjected to harassment and assault, were hot and tired, and felt dangerously vulnerable by the time they returned to the top of Blanket Hill. When they confronted the students, it was only too easy for a single shot to trigger a general fusillade.

Many students considered the Guard's march from the ROTC ruins across the Commons up Blanket Hill, down to the football practice field, and back to Blanket Hill as a kind of charade. Tear gas canisters were tossed back and forth to the cheers of the crowd, many of whom acted as if they were watching a game.

Lt. Alexander D. Stevenson, a platoon leader of Troop G, described the crowd in these words:

"At the time of the firing, the crowd was acting like this whole thing was a circus. The crowd must have thought that the National Guard was harmless. They were having fun with the Guard. The circus was in town."

The actions of some students were violent and criminal and those of some others were dangerous, reckless, and irresponsible. The indiscriminate firing of rifles into a crowd of students and the deaths that followed were unnecessary, unwarranted, and inexcusable.

The National Guardsmen on the Kent State campus were armed with loaded M-1 rifles, high-velocity weapons with a horizontal range of almost two miles. As they confronted the students, all that stood between a guardsman and firing was the flick of a thumb on the safety mechanism, and the pull of an index finger on the trigger. When firing began, the toll taken by these lethal weapons was disastrous.

The Guard fired amidst great turmoil and confusion, engendered in part by their own activities. But the guardsmen should not have been able to kill so easily in the first place. The general issuance of loaded weapons to law enforcement officers engaged in controlling disorders is never justified except in the case of armed resis-

tance that trained sniper teams are unable to handle. This was not the case at Kent State, yet each guardsman carried a loaded M-1 rifle.

This lesson is not new. The National Advisory Commission on Civil Disorders and the guidelines of the Department of the Army set it out explicitly.

No one would have died at Kent State if this lesson had been learned by the Ohio National Guard. Even if the guardsmen faced danger, it was not a danger that called for lethal force. The 61 shots by 28 guardsmen certainly cannot be justified. Apparently, no order to fire was given, and there was inadequate fire control discipline on Blanket Hill. The Kent State tragedy must mark the last time that, as a matter of course, loaded rifles are issued to guardsmen confronting student demonstrators. Our entire report attempts to define the lessons of Kent State, lessons that the Guard, police, students, faculty, administrators, government at all levels, and the American people must learn-and begin, at once, to act upon. We commend it to their attention.

* * *

Pres. Richard Nixon's Letter to the Chairman, President's Commission on Campus Unrest, on the Commission's Report.

December 12, 1970

Dear Bill:

As you will recall, when you submitted the major report of the Commission on Campus Unrest on September 26, I was leaving for Europe. Even though I did not have time to study the document then, I wanted it released. For it is as much or more addressed to students, professors and academic administrators, and to the public generally, as to the Federal Government. The new academic year was beginning, and there was good reason to hope your report could help set the tone for the year.

I have now had the opportunity to study the report, along with your other findings, including the survey results released November 5. I should like to state formally at this time what I stated informally in September. You, the members of the Commission, and its staff have my personal thanks for the considerable time and energy you invested in this task.

Publication of the document causes us to reflect again on the importance of higher education in our national life. A greater proportion of Americans now enjoy the opportunity for advanced education than has ever been reached by any people in history.

At the same time that we have asked our colleges and universities to educate increasing numbers of Americans, we have asked them to assume other burdens along the frontiers of our society's endeavors. Our entire society benefits from their free pursuit of the truth. As our colleges and universities celebrate the life of the mind and the advancement of knowledge, they simultaneously provide invaluable assistance to the countless tasks which our people undertake. Because we entrust our institutions of higher learning with all these tasks, we are immeasurably in their debt.

Yet today these institutions are in danger of losing their health and vitality as centers of learning. Thus, your emphatic condemnation and rejection of the use of violence as a means of effecting change—on or off campus is welcome.

Your firm position that the Government itself cannot, and should not, assume responsibility for maintaining order on campus is also welcome. In my ninth week in office, I wrote that the policy of this administration was to avoid direct involvement of the Federal Government in the institutional affairs of a college campus. Academic freedom is the cornerstone of the American educational system. Consistent with that belief, I have opposed Federal legislation that would terminate institutional aid to colleges where disruption or violence occurs. Nothing would deliver greater power into the hands of the militant few than Federal attempts to punish institutions for the deeds of a minority.

Responsibility for maintaining a peaceful and open climate for learning in an academic community does not rest with the Federal Government it rests squarely with the members of that academic community themselves.

In your report you have clearly avoided the cliché that the only way to end campus violence is to solve once and for all the social problems that beset our nation. That thought parallels my own—expressed last September—in a speech at Kansas State University: To attempt to

blame Government for all the woes of the university is rather the fashion these days. But, really, it is to seek an excuse, not a reason, for their troubles.

... If the war were to end today, if the environment were cleaned up tomorrow morning, and all the other problems for which Government has the responsibility were solved tomorrow afternoon—the moral and spiritual crisis in the universities would still exist.

Removing the causes of legitimate dissent has in my lifetime been one of the constant endeavors of the American Government. It remains the business of this administration. Though optimistic about our capacities to redress just grievances, I am not so utopian as to believe all will be redressed in this administration, or even in our lifetime. And so, in this democratic society, we shall always have and shall always need dissent.

Because the American college is the seedbed of so much of that dissent; because the American university has such a vital role to play in educating future leaders to find the answers we did not—the universities must be protected; they must be preserved.

As high officials in this administration have already noted, your studies of the history of student protest provide us with a valuable perspective. First, they reflect the complex nature of the causes of student unrest. Secondly, they remind us that student disruption is not a problem confined to this administration, or to this past decade, or even to this society alone. Every free society on earth—to one degree or another—faces similar crises on its campuses.

One point of departure I would draw to your analysis of the "youth culture." I have seen personally thousands, indeed tens of thousands, of young people who do not in the slightest conform to the predominant description of students and young people in this report. I believe your survey corroborates my observation.

Perhaps there is considerable truth in the contention that just as the "youth culture" you describe has adherents in our generation, so also, the traditional culture of American life has millions of adherents within the younger generation—and neither generation is monolithic. The new generation contains alienated young men of passion and idealism who march in protest against our efforts in southeast Asia; it also contains young men of passion and idealism willing to risk their lives in an effort to rescue a handful of comrades-in-arms in a North Vietnamese prison camp.

One cannot draw up an indictment of an entire generation—young or old just as one cannot draw an indictment of one segment or race of our diverse people. History has surely taught us the falseness and injustice of that.

This younger generation which contains the tiny minority of violence prone that you rightly condemn, contains as well millions of others; students, soldiers and workers, the vast majority of whom represent the hope of this country.

The call for tolerance expressed in your report echoes sentiments of my own; again expressed at Kansas State:

Those decencies, those self-restraints, those patterns of mutual respect for the rights and feelings of one another, the willingness to listen to somebody else, without trying to shout him down, those patterns of mutual respect for the rights and the feelings of one another—these are what we must preserve if freedom itself is to be preserved.

The ideas of the younger generation, the individuals within the younger generation, must not be condemned by anyone out of hand on the irrelevant grounds of the cut of their clothes or the length of their hair. But also, young people must make corresponding efforts to recognize that the achievements of their parents' generation—the ending of the depression without resort to the odious alternative of dictatorship, the defeat of totalitarian imperialism across two oceans, the tremendous strides of the last two decades toward full citizenship for all Americans; the containment of new aggression abroad, and the provision of more abundance and more freedom for more people than in any other society on Earth—these are not the achievements of a generation of men and women lacking either in idealism or courage, or greatness.

Too often, age is made an artificial barrier between Americans. When it is, it should be ignored or swept aside. No generation holds a monopoly on wisdom or virtue—and each generation has made or will make historic contributions to the greatness and goodness of America.

In these times, one cannot often enough emphasize the need for individual responsibility and individual accountability. That is one of the basic underpinnings

of a democratic system. And society cannot abide, cannot accept, the cynical contention of those who absolve themselves of responsibility for disruptive and violent actions—on the grounds that society somehow has not measured up to their ideals.

Responsibility for disruption of a university campus rests squarely on the shoulders of the disrupters—and those among their elders in the faculty and the larger community who encourage or condone disruption.

Students must indeed accept responsibility for presenting valid ideas in a reasonable and persuasive manner. By being self-critical, responsive to legitimate grievances, and ready to change, colleges and universities can remove conditions that give rise to student protest● Law enforcement officers should use only the minimum force necessary in dealing with disorders when they arise. A human life—the life of a student, soldier, or police officer—is a precious thing, and the taking of a life can be justified only as a necessary and last resort.

The recommendations you make for university reform are properly the concern of the campus community, and I will comment on them only to this extent.

Your reassertion of the truth that colleges and universities are first and foremost centers of teaching and learning, research and scholarship—not political instrumentalities—is timely. A thought drawn from the writings of Professor Kenneth Keniston is worth repeating: The main task of the university is to maintain a climate in which, among other things, the critical spirit can flourish. If individual universities as organizations were to align themselves officially with specifically political positions, their ability to defend the critical function would be undermined. Acting as a lobby or pressure group for some particular judgment or proposal, a university in effect closes its doors to those whose critical sense leads them to disagree.

On the other hand, political involvement of the members of the university community is quite another matter. They enjoy the identical rights of political action as all Americans; and, like other Americans they should be encouraged to exercise those rights.

Students comprise four percent of the national population. They have the right to be heard—both collectively and as individuals.

Yet, no single group within a democratic society has a superior right to be heeded; and no single group has the fight to use physical coercion, disruption or violence to achieve its political end or social objectives. The legitimacy and justice of causes should be judged on forcefulness of the reason and logic and evidence marshalled in its behalf not on the forcefulness of the tactics employed to advance it. As often as not, the raucous voice of dissent can be wrong—and the quiet voice of disagreement can be right.

If there is an area in which I would wish that the report could be expanded, it would be through addition of an analysis of that great majority of colleges and universities-subject to identical internal pressures, subject to the same outside cultural and political forces—where students, faculties and administrators have guided their institutions, with the maintenance of academic freedom and a minimum of disruption and disorder, through the troubled times of the last decade. There is much to be praised and emulated in these private and public institutions. There is much we can learn from these educators and their successes.

The recommendations you make to universities for controlling disorders will have value for them but they are properly the concern of the campus community and I will not comment on them here.

Your call for responsiveness in our colleges and universities needs constantly to be underscored. Just as they should be responsive to legitimate demands and grievances of students and faculties; so also, they have an obligation to be responsive to the hard-working men and women, who may never have had an opportunity for a college education—but whose tax dollars helped enable them to become the great institutions they are today.

You point out the enormous influence the Federal Government has on higher education. As I stated in my Message on Higher Education sent to the Congress in March, 1970:

> For three decades now the Federal Government has been hiring universities to do work it wanted done. In far the greatest measure, this work has been in the national interest, and the Nation is in the debt of those universities that have so brilliantly performed it. But the time has come for the Federal Government to help academic communities to pursue excellence and reform in fields of their own choosing as well, and by means of their own choice.

I take it your analysis would very much support the establishment of a National Foundation for Higher Education which I have proposed for the purpose of moving away from narrowly defined categorical aid programs which, whatever their original intent, have increasingly come to be seen as restrictive and undesirable.

I welcome the Commission's support of the student aid provisions of the Higher Education Opportunity Act of 1970, which was proposed in my message. If enacted, this proposal would profoundly change the access of low-income students to higher education. It is a fundamental social reform long past due. Again, I refer to the March 1970 Message: No qualified student who wants to go to college should be barred by lack of money. That has long been a great American goal; I propose that we achieve it now.

Something is basically unequal about opportunity for higher education when a young person whose family earns more than $15,000 a year is nine times more likely to attend college than a young person whose family earns less than $3,000.

The chapter on the Black Student Movement is a useful statement in this context; and one I read with interest. You point out that while Black College enrollment has doubled in recent years, contrary to widespread impressions, the proportion of Black students to white students who attend college has not substantially increased. I share the Commission's concern over this. Our student assistance proposals will provide benefits to cover one million additional students besides those now receiving aid, and many of these will be Black and Spanish-surnamed. In addition, before the start of this academic year, we directed an additional $30 million to the traditionally Black colleges, bringing their share of Federal aid to education to 3 percent where they enroll but 2 percent of the nation's college students.

You have made a number of specific recommendations to the Federal Government. I have asked my cabinet to review these recommendations and to report their views directly to me. Secretary Laird is reviewing the suggestions and recommendations pertaining to the National Guard and the Reserve Officer Training Corps. Attorney General Mitchell is reviewing the many suggestions pertaining to law enforcement activities within his jurisdiction and the special reports on Kent State and Jackson State. Secretaries Hodgson and Richardson are reviewing the recommendations for expanding opportunities for youth employment and social participation.

In the final section on the role of the Government in relation to campus unrest you have addressed yourself to the proper role of the Presidency in attempting to heal the divisive wounds which have from time to time been visible in this nation. Both of us, I am sure, regret the distorted press accounts of this section of the report.

Throughout my public life I have come to know the immense moral authority of the Presidency. During these past twenty-two months I have tried to exercise that authority to bring an end to violence and bitterness; and I have sought to use the power of this office to advance the cause of peace abroad and social justice at home. These are matters upon which every President answers daily to his conscience and quadrennially to his judge—the American people.

On the matter of campus disorders, I have already addressed myself at length and in depth to this critical subject—as a private citizen and as President. Few domestic issues have consumed more of my attention, interest and concern while in office. The appointment of this Presidential commission to study the matter is but one measure of that concern.

In dealing with the issues of importance to students enumerated by the Commission, this administration has sought to terminate poverty through a national Family Assistance Program; we have sought to expand educational opportunity for all our young people through a revised student assistance program; we are seeking to equalize—and one day remove—the burdens of the draft upon young people; we are making strides in equal employment opportunity; we have made new advances against America's ancient injustice—discrimination. We have reordered the nation's priorities. We have redirected American foreign policy. We have diminished America's involvement in the Asian war and sought to end that war in a way that will justify the sacrifices of this generation

of young Americans, and prevent similar sacrifices by their younger brothers of the next generation.

We have sought to bring Americans together in national agreements, by a national commitment to the basic underlying principles of a free society—to new recognition of the fundamental truth that the preservation of a democratic system of government is far more important than any single immediate reform that could conceivably issue from that system.

The task of the Presidency is to respect the opinions of the electorate, to seek the truth, and to lead the nation. Thus, for example, I would have to say that an effort "to convince all Americans of the need to confront candidly the serious and continuing problems of the nation," is a matter far more complex than might at first seem the case. That complexity begins with the fact that there are widely divergent views within our society as to just what our problems are. The views implicit in the Commission's report range from observations that would doubtless be accepted by a great portion of the nation to conclusions that may be shared by only a small minority. This does not make any of them wrong, or right. Nor should the Commission have refrained from expressing them. To the contrary: I said on the occasion of receiving the report that I was sure it would be controversial given the moment and importance of the issue.

Every President in our lifetime has taken office with large segments of our people in vigorous opposition to his person, his policies, and his programs. That opposition is an inevitable but natural barrier to the capacity of a President to lead all the people in the direction and to the goals he deems right and fitting for the nation.

Those in opposition to a President's foreign or domestic policies have a right to make that opposition known through every legitimate means in a democratic system. But no minority, no matter how united, how vocal, or how articulate, has veto power over a President's decision to do what he believes is right in the nation's interest.

With regard to the setting of national priorities, and the allocation of national resources, the views of students and all citizens, and the suggestions of your Commission are welcome—but final determination in these matters must rightly rest with the elected representatives of all the American people. The thought of Dr. Sidney Hook is here appropriate: The history of American higher education is a history of change. Violence has never played an appreciable role in that history. It need not play a role today if it is recognized that the primary function of higher education is the quest for knowledge, wisdom and vision, not the conquest of political power; that the university is not responsible for the existence of war, poverty and other evils; and that the solution of these and allied problems lies in the hands of the democratic citizenry and not of a privileged elite.

Moral authority in a great and diverse nation such as ours does not reside in the Presidency alone. There are thousands upon thousands of individuals—clergy, teachers, public officials, scholars, writers—to whom segments of the nation look for moral, intellectual and political leadership.

Over the decade of disorders just ended some of these leaders of the national community have spoken or acted with forthrightness and courage, on and off the campus, unequivocally condemning violence and disruption as instruments of change and reaffirming the principles upon which continuance of a free society depends.

High in that category I would place the Vice President of the United States. History will look favorably I believe upon these men and women. It may well look severely upon those others—on and off campus—who for whatever reason refused or failed to speak out forthrightly against the inequities visited upon the academic community.

Yet I think we can all agree that the task of the nation, no less than that of the higher education community, is to regain its strength and its confidence, and to retain its independence. There is no higher priority in the concerns of the national government.

The work of the Commission has expanded our understanding of what has been happening. Other individuals have also thought deeply on the same subject. I have received reports and letters from many of them and I expect to consider these informed views and to share them with others who share our concern for higher education. As the survival and strength of our public and private educational institutions is so critical to our national future, necessary public and political discussion of the issue will surely continue—and indeed be advanced by your report.

I commend it particularly to the consideration of the White House Conference on Youth, because the report is the concern of all young people, not just students alone.

Quite beyond our agreements and differences, I write to assure you that the report is now receiving and will continue to receive the closest attention within the administration. I trust this will be true in the nation at large.

With personal regards,
Sincerely,

RICHARD NIXON

[Honorable William W. Scranton, 704 Northeastern National Bank Building, Scranton, Pennsylvania 18503]

Document Analysis

The "President's Commission on Campus Unrest Conclusions regarding Kent State University 1970" seeks to give a balanced report that attributes some blame to the provocations of violent protestors, but places more blame on tactical errors and the use of live ammunition by the National Guard. The report states categorically, "Violence by students on or off the campus can never be justified by any grievance, philosophy, or political idea." On the other hand, it declares that the National Guard's "decision to disperse the [peaceful] noon rally was a serious error." The report is especially critical of the Guardsmen having live ammunition in their rifles, stating, "The general issuance of loaded weapons to law enforcement officers engaged in controlling disorders is never justified except in the case of armed resistance...."

Although Scranton and his fellow commissioners condemn student violence, they defend peaceful protest and show sympathy for the students' concerns. Scranton writes, "For students deeply opposed to the war, the Guard was a living symbol of the military system they opposed. For other students, the Guard was an outsider on their campus, prohibiting all their rallies, even peaceful ones, ordering them about, and tear gassing them when they refused to obey."

The written response of President Richard Nixon to William Scranton's report is marked by its single-minded focus on "youth culture" and what was often described at the time as "the generation gap." Nixon praises Scranton for criticizing student radicals, stating, "your emphatic condemnation and rejection of the use of violence as a means of effecting change—on or off campus is welcome." Biographers often depict Nixon as particularly concerned with the growing number of young people in revolt against traditional American culture and institutions. This is evident in Nixon's defensive, but accurate, assertion that "the traditional culture of American life has millions of adherents within the younger generation."

What is most notable in the president's response is what it does not mention. There is little mention of the war or the decision to send troops into Cambodia. And there is practically no acknowledgement of one of the commission's main conclusions: namely, that the National Guard should not have had loaded weapons and that, as a national policy, neither the police nor the National Guard should respond to campus unrest with bullets. For Nixon, the main issue is not lethal failures by the authorities, but rather the generational tensions that were so palpable in 1970.

Essential Themes

The President's Commission on Campus Unrest was one of four major commissions in the decade ending in 1970. The first was "The President's Commission on the Status of Women," chaired by Eleanor Roosevelt, which documented major gender discrimination in American society in its 1963 report. The second and most controversial was the "President's Commission on the Assassination of President Kennedy," headed by Supreme Court Justice Earl Warren. The Warren Report of 1964 famously concluded that Lee Harvey Oswald had acted alone, a conclusion that would be challenged by numerous conspiracy theorists over the decades.

The third was the "The National Advisory Commission on Civil Disorders" on the urban riots/rebellions during the 1967 "Long Hot Summer" and headed by Illinois governor Otto Kerner (Democrat). The Kerner Report's conclusion that America had moved toward "two societies, one black, one white—separate and unequal" is often cited even today.

The last was the Scranton Commission's investigation of campus unrest. Each of these commissions was headed by a respected, mainstream political figure and sought to include representatives of different groups. In the case of the Scranton Commission, these included representatives of universities, law enforcement, and a student member.

Of the three commissions, the President's Commission on Campus Unrest is the least remembered today. Nevertheless, the Scranton Report is a significant examination of a divisive time in American history and its conclusions represent a generally thoughtful appraisal of the May 1970 campus unrest that some historians consider the final paroxysm of national protest against the war in Vietnam.

—*Robert Surbrug, PhD*

Bibliography and Additional Readings

Kent State: The Day the War Came Home. Dir. Chris Triffo. Single Spark Pictures, 2000. Documentary.

Michener, James. *Kent State: What Happened and Why*. New York: Random House, 1971. Print.

Perlstein, Rick. *Nixonland: The Rise of a President and the Fracturing of America*. New York: Scribner, 2008. Print.

Report of the President's Commission on Campus Unrest ("Scranton Commission"). Washington, DC: US Government Printing Office, 1970. Print and Web.

■ John Kerry's Testimony before the Senate Foreign Relations Committee

Date: April 22, 1971
Author: John Kerry
Genre: testimony

Summary Overview

On April 22, 1971, John Kerry, a decorated Vietnam veteran, testified before the Senate Foreign Relations Committee not only about some of his own experiences as a soldier in Vietnam, but also about the experiences of some of his fellow soldiers. Representing the Vietnam Veterans Against the War (VVAW), Kerry provided a veteran's antiwar perspective on the war and thus brought greater attention to this viewpoint. Kerry's testimony focused in large part on the experiences of soldiers who had testified a month earlier during the "Winter Soldier" investigations. According to these accounts, many American soldiers either witnessed or participated in war crimes against the Vietnamese, including murder, rape, and torture. While government officials claimed that the United States needed to be in Vietnam to protect the Vietnamese from communism, in reality, according to Kerry, their presence brought death and hardship to the Vietnamese and pain and guilt to American soldiers. He concluded that the only way to ease the pain and suffering of the Vietnamese and American soldiers was to end the war and pull American troops out of Vietnam.

Defining the Moment

When John Kerry testified before the Senate Foreign Relations Committee in April 1971, he did not do so just as a concerned citizen, but rather as a Vietnam veteran and representative of the VVAW. Vietnam veterans had a long, significant involvement in the antiwar movement. As the largest Vietnam veteran organization during this period, the VVAW was at the forefront of the veteran antiwar movement. On April 15, 1967, Vietnam veteran Jan Barry carried a banner reading "Vietnam Veterans Against the War" during Mobilization to End the War protests in New York City. After the protest, Barry and five friends formed the VVAW.

As the war continued, the VVAW's size and influence grew significantly. In September 1970, the VVAW conducted its first national demonstration called Operation Rapid American Withdrawal (RAW), which consisted of between 100 and 200 Vietnam veterans marching from Morristown, New Jersey, to Valley Forge, Pennsylvania, retracing the steps taken by Revolutionary Army soldiers during the American Revolution.

From January 31 to February 2, 1971, the VVAW conducted a series of hearings known as the "Winter Soldier" investigations in Detroit. During the hearings, at least 100 Vietnam veterans revealed gruesome incidents of rape, torture, and murder, which they had either witnessed or participated in during their service in Vietnam. The testimony of these soldiers was meant to show that because wartime atrocities against the Vietnamese were not rare, but common and widespread, the war needed to end. The hearings garnered little media attention, but they did embolden the VVAW to confront Congress in a more direct manner. Between April 19 and 23 at least a few thousand VVAW members converged on Washington, DC, to conduct a series of protests known collectively as Dewey Canyon III. As part of these protests, Kerry testified before the Senate Foreign Relations Committee. The incidents revealed in the "Winter Soldier" investigations formed the core of Kerry's testimony

At the same time, hundreds of VVAW members met with their elected representatives to discuss their opposition to the war. The week's events culminated with a march to the Capitol. Here, at least 600 veterans, many of them dressed in their uniforms and battle fatigues, threw their discharge papers, and the medals and ribbons they had earned in Vietnam onto the Capitol steps.

Biography

John Kerry was born December 11, 1943 in Denver, Colorado. After graduating from Yale University in 1966, Kerry enlisted in the US Navy. In 1968, he was sent to Vietnam, where he commanded patrol boats and earned a Bronze Star, Silver Star, and three Purple Hearts. Returning to the United States, Kerry became disenchanted with the Vietnam War and joined the VVAW. Kerry participated in the "Winter Soldier" investigations and the Dewey Canyon III protests. After practicing law for a number of years, Kerry was elected lieutenant governor of Massachusetts in 1982. Two years later, he was elected to the United States Senate. During his time in the Senate, Kerry was instrumental in normalizing relations between the United States and Vietnam. The Democratic Party nominated him for the presidency in 2004, but he lost to incumbent president George W. Bush. In February 2013, he was appointed secretary of state by President Barack Obama.

HISTORICAL DOCUMENT

Mr. Kerry: I would like to talk, representing all those veterans, and say that several months ago in Detroit, we had an investigation at which over 150 honorably discharged and many very highly decorated veterans testified to war crimes committed in Southeast Asia, not isolated incidents but crimes committed on a day-to-day basis with the full awareness of officers at all levels of command.

It is impossible to describe to you exactly what did happen in Detroit, the emotions in the room, the feelings of the men who were reliving their experiences in Vietnam, but they did. They relived the absolute horror of what this country, in a sense, made them do.

They told the stories at times they had personally raped, cut off ears, cut off heads, tape wires from portable telephones to human genitals and turned up the power, cut off limbs, blown up bodies, randomly shot at civilians, razed villages in fashion reminiscent of Genghis Khan, shot cattle and dogs for fun, poisoned food stocks, and generally ravaged the country side of South Vietnam in addition to the normal ravage of war, and the normal and very particular ravaging which is done by the applied bombing power of this country.

We call this investigation the "Winter Soldier Investigation." The term "Winter Soldier" is a play on words of Thomas Paine in 1776 when he spoke of the Sunshine Patriot and summertime soldiers who deserted at Valley Forge because the going was rough.

We who have come here to Washington have come here because we feel we have to be winter soldiers now. We could come back to this country; we could be quiet; we could hold our silence; we could not tell what went on in Vietnam, but we feel because of what threatens this country, the fact that the crimes threaten it, no reds, and not redcoats but the crimes which we are committing that threaten it, that we have to speak out.

I would like to talk to you a little bit about what the result is of the feelings these men carry with them after coming back from Vietnam. The country doesn't know it yet, but it has created a monster, a monster in the form of millions of men who have been taught to deal and to trade in violence, and who are given the chance to die for the biggest nothing in history; men who have returned with a sense of anger and a sense of betrayal which no one has yet grasped.

As a veteran and one who feels this anger, I would like to talk about it. We are angry because we feel we have been used in the worst fashion by the administration of this country.

In 1970 at West Point, Vice President Agnew said "some glamorize the criminal misfits of society while our best men die in Asian rice paddies to preserve the freedom which most of those misfits abuse" and this was used as a rallying point for our effort in Vietnam.

But for us, as boys in Asia, whom the country was supposed to support, his statement is a terrible distortion from which we can only draw a very deep sense of revulsion. Hence the anger of some of the men who are here in Washington today. It is a distortion because we in no way consider ourselves the best men of this country, because those he calls misfits were standing up for us in a way that nobody else in this country dared to, because so many who have died would have returned to this country to join the misfits in their efforts to ask for an immediate withdrawal from South Vietnam, because so many of those best men have returned as quadriplegics and amputees, and they lie forgotten in Veterans' Administration hospitals in this country which fly the flag which so many have chosen as their own personal symbol. And we cannot consider ourselves America's best men when we are ashamed of and hated what we were called on to do in Southeast Asia.

In our opinion, and from our experience, there is nothing in South Vietnam, nothing which could happen that realistically threatens the United States of America. And to attempt to justify the loss of one American life in Vietnam, Cambodia or Laos by linking such loss to the preservation of freedom, which those misfits supposedly abuse, is to use the height of criminal hypocrisy, and it is that kind of hypocrisy which we feel has torn this country apart.

We are probably much more angry than that and I don't want to go into the foreign policy aspects because I am outclassed here. I know that all of you talk about every possible alternative of getting out of Vietnam. We understand that. We know you have considered the seriousness of the aspects to the utmost level and I am not going to try to deal on that, but I want to relate to you the feeling that many of the men who have returned to this country express because we are probably angriest about all that we were told about Vietnam and about the mystical war against communism.

We found that not only was it a civil war, an effort by a people who had for years been seeking their liberation from any colonial influence whatsoever, but also we found that the Vietnamese whom we had enthusiastically molded after our own image were hard put to take up the fight against the threat we were supposedly saving them from.

We found most people didn't even know the difference between communism and democracy. They only wanted to work in rice paddies without helicopters strafing them and bombs with napalm burning their villages and tearing their country apart. They wanted everything to do with the war, particularly with this foreign presence of the United States of America, to leave them alone in peace, and they practiced the art of survival by siding with which ever military force was present at a particular time, be it Vietcong, North Vietnamese, or American.

We found also that all too often American men were dying in those rice paddies for want of support from their allies. We saw first hand how money from American taxes was used for a corrupt dictatorial regime. We saw that many people in this country had a one-sided idea of who was kept free by our flag, as blacks provided the highest percentage of casualties. We saw Vietnam ravaged equally by American bombs as well as by search and destroy missions, as well as by Vietcong terrorism, and yet we listened while this country tried to blame all of the havoc on the Vietcong.

We rationalized destroying villages in order to save them. We saw America lose her sense of morality as she accepted very coolly a My Lai and refused to give up the image of American soldiers who hand out chocolate bars and chewing gum.

We learned the meaning of free fire zones, shooting anything that moves, and we watched while America placed a cheapness on the lives of Orientals.

We watched the U.S. falsification of body counts, in fact the glorification of body counts. We listened while month after month we were told the back of the enemy was about to break. We fought using weapons against "oriental human beings," with quotation marks around that. We fought using weapons against those people which I do not believe this country would dream of using were we fighting in the European theater or let us say a non-third-world people theater, and so we watched while men charged up hills because a general said that hill has to be taken, and after losing one platoon or two platoons they marched away to leave the high for the reoccupation by the North Vietnamese because we watched pride allow the most unimportant of battles to be blown into extravaganzas, because we couldn't lose, and we couldn't retreat, and because it didn't matter how many American bodies were lost to prove that point. And so there were Hamburger Hills and Khe Sanhs and Hill 881's and Fire Base 6's and so many others.

Now we are told that the men who fought there must watch quietly while American lives are lost so that we can exercise the incredible arrogance of Vietnamizing the Vietnamese. Each day... (Applause)

The Chairman: I hope you won't interrupt. He is making a very significant statement. Let him proceed.

Mr. Kerry: Each day to facilitate the process by which the United States washes her hands of Vietnam someone has to give up his life so that the United States doesn't have to admit something that the entire world already knows, so that we can't say that we have made a mistake. Someone has to dies so that President Nixon won't be, and these are his words, "the first President to lose a war."

We are asking Americans to think about that because how do you ask a man to be the last man to dies in Vietnam? How do ask a man to be the last man to die for a mistake? But we are trying to do that, and we are doing it with thousands of rationalizations, and if you read carefully the President's last speech to the people of this country, you can see that he says, and says clearly: But the issue, gentlemen, the issue is communism, and the question is whether or not we will leave that country to the communists or whether or not we will try to give it hope to be a free people. But the point is they are not a free people now under us. They are not a free people, and we cannot fight communism all over the world, and I think we should have learned that lesson by now.

But the problem of veterans goes beyond this personal problem, because you think about a poster in this country with a picture of Uncle Sam and the picture says "I want you." And a young man comes out of high school and says, "That is fine. I am going to serve my country." And he goes to Vietnam and he shoots and he kills and he does his job or maybe he doesn't kill, maybe he just goes and he comes back, and when he gets back to this country he finds that he isn't really wanted, because the largest unemployment figure in the country—it varies depending on who you get it from, the VA Administration 15 percent, various other sources 22 percent. But the largest corps of unemployed in this country are veterans of this war, and of those veterans 33 percent of the unemployed are black. That means 1 out of every 10 of the Nation's unemployed is a veteran of Vietnam.

The hospitals across the country won't, or can't meet their demands. It is not a question of not trying. They don't have the appropriations. A man recently died after he had a tracheotomy in California, not because of the operation but because there weren't enough personnel to clean the mucous out of his tube and he suffocated to death.

Another young man just died in a New York VA hospital the other day. A friend of mine was lying in a bed two beds away and tried to help him, but he couldn't. He rang a bell and there was nobody there to service that man and so he died of convulsions.

I understand 57 percent of all those entering the VA hospitals talk about suicide. Some 27 percent have tried, and they try because they come back to this country and they have to face what they did in Vietnam, and then they come back and find the indifference of a country that doesn't really care, that doesn't really care.

Suddenly we are faced with a very sickening situation in this country, because there is no moral indignation and, if there is, it comes from people who are almost exhausted by their past indignations, and I know that many of them are sitting in front of me. The country seems to have lain down and shrugged off something as serious as Laos, just as we calmly shrugged off the loss of 700,000 lives in Pakistan, the so-called greatest disaster of all times.

But we are here as veterans to say we think we are in the midst of the greatest disaster of all times now because they are still dying over there, and not just Americans, Vietnamese, and we are rationalizing leaving that country so that those people can go on killing each other for years to come.

Americans seems to have accepted the idea that the war is winding down, at least for Americans, and they have also allowed the bodies which were once used by a President for statistics to prove that we were winning that war, to be used as evidence against a man who followed orders and who interpreted those orders no differently than hundreds of other men in Vietnam.

We veterans can only look with amazement on the fact that this country has been unable to see there is absolutely no difference between ground troops and a helicopter crew, and yet people have accepted a differentiation fed them by the administration.

No ground troops are in Laos, so it is all right to kill Laotians by remote control. But believe me the helicopter crews fill the same body bags and they wreak the same kind of damage on the Vietnamese and Laotian countryside as anybody else, and the President is talking about allowing that to go on for many years to come. One can only ask if we will really be satisfied only when the troops march into Hanoi.

We are asking here in Washington for some action, action from the Congress of the United States of America which has the power to raise and maintain armies, and which by the Constitution also has the power to declare war.

We have come here, not to the President, because we believe that this body can be responsive to the will of the people, and we believe that the will of the people says that we should be out of Vietnam now.

We are here in Washington also to say that the problem of this war is not just a question of war and diplomacy. It is part and parcel of everything that we are trying as human beings to communicate to people in this country, the question of racism, which is rampant in the military, and so many other questions also, the use of weapons, the hypocrisy in our taking umbrage in the Geneva Conventions and using that as justification for a continuation of this war, when we are more guilty than any other body of violations of those Geneva Conventions, in the use of free fire zones, harassment interdiction fire, search and destroy missions, the bombings, the torture of prisoners, the killing of prisoners, accepted policy by many units in South Vietnam. That is what we are trying to say. It is party and parcel of everything.

An American Indian friend of mine who lives in the Indian Nation at Alcatraz put it to me very succinctly. He told me how as a boy on an Indian reservation he had watched television and he used to cheer the cowboys when they came in and shot the Indians, and then suddenly one day he stopped in Vietnam and he said "My God, I am doing to these people the very same thing that was done to my people." And he stopped. And that is what we are trying to say, that we think this thing has to end.

We are also here to ask, and we are here to ask vehemently, where are the leaders of our country? Where is the leadership? We are here to ask where are McNamara, Rostow, Bundy, Gilpatric and so many others. Where are they now that we, the men whom they sent off to war, have returned? These are commanders who have deserted their troops, and there is no more serious crime in the law of war. The Army says they never leave their wounded.

The Marines say they never leave even their dead. These men have left all the casualties and retreated behind a pious shield of public rectitude. They have left the real stuff of their reputation bleaching behind them in the sun in this country.

Finally, this administration has done us the ultimate dishonor. They have attempted to disown us and the sacrifice we made for this country. In their blindness and fear they have tried to deny that we are veterans or that we served in Nam. We do not need their testimony. Our own scars and stumps of limbs are witnesses enough for others and for ourselves.

We wish that a merciful God could wipe away our own memories of that service as easily as this administration has wiped their memories of us. But all that they have done and all that they can do by this denial is to make more clear than ever our own determination to undertake one last mission, to search out and destroy the last vestige of this barbarous war, to pacify our own hearts, to conquer the hate and the fear that have driven this country these last 10 years and more and so when, in 30 years from now, our brothers go down the street without a leg, without an arm or a face, and small boys ask why, we will be able to say "Vietnam" and not mean a desert, not a filthy obscene memory but mean instead the pace where America finally turned and where soldiers like us helped it in the turning. Thank you. (Applause)

The Chairman: Mr. Kerry, it is quite evident from that demonstration that you are speaking not only for yourself but for all your associates, as you properly said in the beginning. You said you wished to communicate. I can't imagine anyone communicating more eloquently than you did. I think it is extremely helpful and beneficial to the committee and the country to have you make such a statement. You said you had been awake all night. I can see that you spent that time very well indeed. (Laughter)

Perhaps that was the better part, better that you should be awake than otherwise.

You have said that the question before this committee and the Congress is really how to end the war. The resolutions about which we have been hearing testimony during the past several days, the sponsors of which are some members of this committee, are seeking the most practical way that we can find and, I believe, to do it at the earliest opportunity that we can. That is the purpose of these hearing and that is why you were brought here.

You have been very eloquent about the reasons why we should proceed as quickly as possible. Are you familiar with some of the proposals before this committee?

Mr. Kerry: Yes, I am, Senator.

The Chairman: Do you support or do you have any particular views about any one of them you wish to give the committee?

Mr. Kerry: My feeling, Senator, is undoubtedly this Congress, and I don't mean to sound pessimistic, but I do not believe that this Congress will, in fact, end the war as we would like to, which is immediately and unilaterally and, therefore, if I were to speak I would say we would set a date and the date obviously would be the earliest possible date. But I would like to say, in answering that, that I do not believe it is necessary to stall any longer. I have been to Paris. I have talked with both delegations at the peace talks, that is to say the Democratic Republic of Vietnam and the Provisional Revolutionary Government and of all eight of Madam Binh's points it has been stated time and time again, and was stated by Senator Vance Hartke when he returned from Paris, and it has been stated by many other officials of this Government, if the United States were to set a date for withdrawal the prisoners of war would be returned.

I think this negates very clearly the argument of the President that we have to maintain a presence in Vietnam, to use as a negotiating block for the return of those prisoners. The setting of a date will accomplish that.

As to the argument concerning the danger to our troops were we to withdraw or state that we would, they have also said many times in conjunction with that statement that all of our troops, the moment we set a date, will be given safe conduct out of South Vietnam. The only other important point is that we allow the South Vietnamese people to determine their own figure and that ostensibly is what we have been fighting for anyway.

I would, therefore, submit that the most expedient means of getting out of South Vietnam would be for the President of the United States to declare a cease-fire, to stop this blind commitment to a dictatorial regime, the Thiêu-Ky-Khiem regime, accept a coalition regime which would represent all the political forces of the country which is in fact what a representative government is supposed to do and which is in fact what this Government here in this country purports to do, and pull the troops out without losing one more American, and still further without losing the South Vietnamese.

Senator Symington: Thank you, Mr. Chairman.

Mr. Kerry, please move your microphone. You have a Silver Star; have you not?

Mr. Kerry: Yes, I do.

Senator Symington: And a Purple Heart?

Mr. Kerry: Yes, I do.

Senator Symington: How many clusters?

Mr. Kerry: Two clusters.

Senator Symington: So you have been wounded three times.

Mr. Kerry: Yes, sir.

Senator Symington: I have no further questions, Mr. Chairman.

The Chairman: Senator Aiken. (Applause)

Senator Aiken: Mr. Kerry, the Defense Department seems to feel that if we set a definite date for withdrawal when our forces get down to a certain level, they would be seriously in danger by the North Vietnamese and the Vietcong. Do you believe that the North Vietnamese would undertake to prevent our withdrawal from the country and attack the troops that remain there?

Mr. Kerry: Well, Senator, if I may answer you directly, I believe we are running that danger with the present course of withdrawal because the President has neglected to state to this country exactly what his response will be when we have reached the point that we do have, let us say, 50,000 support troops in Vietnam.

Senator Aiken: I am not telling you what I think. I am telling what the Department says.

Mr. Kerry: Yes, sir; I understand that.

Senator Aiken: Do you believe the North Vietnamese would seriously undertake to impede our complete withdrawal?

Mr. Kerry: No, I do not believe that the North Vietnamese would and it has been clearly indicated at the Paris peace talks they would not.

Senator Aiken: Do you think they might help carry the bags for us? (Laughter)

Mr. Kerry: I would say they would be more prone to do that then the Army of the South Vietnamese. (Laughter) (Applause)

Senator Aiken: I think your answer is ahead of my question. (Laughter)

—

Senator Aiken: But what I would like to know now is if we, as we complete our withdrawal and, say, get down to 10,000, 20,000, 30,000 or even 50,000 troops there, would there be any effort on the part of the South Vietnamese government of the South Vietnamese army, in your opinion, to impede their withdrawal?

Mr. Kerry: No; I don't think so, Senator.

Senator Aiken: I don't see why North Vietnam should object.

Mr. Kerry: I don't for the simple reason, I used to talk with officers about their—we asked them, and one officer took great pleasure in playing with me in the sense that he would say, "Well, you know you American, you come over here for 1 year and you can afford, you know, you go to Hong Kong for R. & R. and if you are a good boy you get another R. & R. or something you know. You can afford to charge bunkers, but I have to try and be here for 30 years and stay alive." And I think that that really is the governing principle by which those people are now living and have been allowed to live because of our mistake. So that when we in fact state, let us say, that we will have a cease-fire or have a coalition government, most of the 2 million men you often hear quoted under arms, most of whom are regional popular reconnaissance forces, which is to say militia, and a very poor militia at that, will simply lay down their arms, if they haven't done so already, and not fight. And I think you will find they will respond to whatever government evolves which answer their needs, and those needs quite simply are to be fed, to bury their dead in plots where their ancestors lived, to be allowed to extend their culture, to try and exist as human beings. And I think that is what will happen.

I can cite many, many instances, sir, as in combat when these men refused to fight with us, when they shot with their guns over tin this area like this and their heads turned facing the other way. When we were taken under fire we Americans, supposedly fighting with them, and pinned down in a ditch, and I was in the Navy and this was pretty unconventional, but when we were pinned down in a ditch recovering bodies or something and they refused to come in and help us, point blank refused. I don't believe they want to fight, sir.

Senator Aiken: Do you think we are under obligation to furnish them with extensive economic assistance?

Mr. Kerry: Yes, sir. I think we have a very definite obligation to make extensive reparations to the people of Indochina.

—

Senator Pell: Wouldn't you agree with me though that what he did in herding old men, women and children into a trench and then shooting them was a little bit beyond the perimeter of even what has been going on in this war and that that action should be discouraged. There are other actions not that extreme that have gone on and have been permitted. If we had not taken action or cognizance of it, it would have been even worse. It would have indicated we encouraged this kind of action.

Mr. Kerry: My feeling, Senator, on Lieutenant Calley is what he did quite obviously was a horrible, horrible, horrible thing and I have no bone to pick with the fact that he was prosecuted. But I think that in this question you have to separate guilt from responsibility, and I think clearly the responsibility for what has happened there lies elsewhere.

I think it lies with the men who designed free fire zones. I think it lies with the men who encourage body counts. I think it lies in large part with this country, which allows a young child before he reaches the age of 14 to see 12,500 deaths on television, which glorifies the John Wayne syndrome, which puts out fighting man comic books on the stands, which allows us in training to do calisthenics to four counts, on the fourth count of which we stand up and shout "kill" in unison, which has posters in barracks in this country with a crucified Vietnamese, blood on him, and underneath it says "kill the gook," and I think that clearly the responsibility for all of this is what has produced this horrible aberration.

Now, I think if you are going to try Lieutenant Calley then you must at the same time, if this country is going to demand respect for the law, you must at the same time try all those other people who have responsibility, and any aversion that we may have to the verdict as veterans is not to say that Calley should be freed, not to say that he is innocent, but to say that you can't just take him alone.

Document Analysis

On April 22, 1971, John Kerry, representing the VVAW, provided testimony to the Senate Foreign Relations Committee about the nature of the Vietnam War. Kerry provided an intensely critical assessment of the war, arguing that it had caused irreparable harm to both the Vietnamese and American soldiers. Kerry maintained that the only way to relieve the continued suffering of both groups was to end American participation in the war.

Kerry's testimony began by referencing the "Winter Soldier" investigation during which 150 honorably discharged and decorated veterans testified to war crimes they committed or witnessed in Vietnam. He recalled that veterans "relived the absolute horror of what this country, in a sense, made them do" including incidents of torture, rape, and murder. Many Vietnam veterans were not only deeply dismayed by their participation in such an immoral war, but also by their country, which sent them to Vietnam under false pretenses. He proclaimed, "The country doesn't know it yet, but it has created a monster, a monster in the form of millions of men who have been taught to deal and to trade in violence, and who are given the chance to die for the biggest nothing in history." After spending only a short time in Vietnam, most soldiers came away realizing that the conflict was actually a civil war, which didn't require American intervention. Additionally, most Vietnamese just wanted to be left "alone in peace."

Kerry was particular critical of the American military strategy in Vietnam, which treated Vietnamese lives as expendable. He expressed doubts that the United States would have conducted free fire zones, search and destroy missions, used napalm, or conducted indiscriminate bombings if the war had been waged against whites in Europe. Additionally, Kerry claimed that American soldiers were continually forced to engage in missions that had little strategic military purpose other than confirming that American soldiers shouldn't lose or retreat.

Kerry criticized the administration of President Richard Nixon for refusing to acknowledge something that most Americans realized—the war couldn't be won. Officials continued to send troops to Vietnam under the illusion that things might improve. Nixon's refusal to accept reality led to an expansion of the war and continued casualties. This led Kerry famously to question, "How do you ask a man to be the last man to die in Vietnam? How do you ask a man to be the last man to die for a mistake?"

Kerry concluded by reminding members of the Senate that they had the ability to alter American policy in Vietnam. He encouraged his listeners to do everything in their power to end the war unilaterally and immediately. During the question and answer section that followed his testimony, Kerry elaborated that the United States should immediately declare a cease-fire; accept a coalition government in Vietnam, which would represent various political views; and pull all American troops out of Vietnam.

Essential Themes

Kerry's testimony regarding the prevalence of wartime atrocities in Vietnam had an impact in a number of areas. On a personal level, it placed Kerry in the public spotlight for the first time in his life and, to some extent, was the beginning of his long career in national politics. More significantly, Kerry's testimony engendered greater attention for opponents of the war, particularly veterans. By speaking directly to an influential Senate committee, Kerry was able to present the experiences of soldiers who had served in Vietnam as well as explain why many veterans had moved to an antiwar stance. It also provided Kerry and the VVAW with an opportunity to present their case for an end to the war directly to an influential committee.

Kerry was not only speaking to members of the Senate, but also to the American people. The VVAW had been disheartened to some extent when the media barely covered the "Winter Soldier" investigations a few months earlier. Kerry's testimony provided him with a major forum to present the VVAW's position on the war directly to the American people, including many veterans who might share their views. Perhaps not surprisingly, in the aftermath of Kerry's testimony and Dewey Canyon III, VVAW's membership increased to more than 20,000.

Because he was a Vietnam veteran, Kerry's opinions about the war proved difficult for officials to ignore. Pro-war politicians were accustomed to dismissing antiwar protestors as hippies and naïve college students with simplistic and uniformed opinions about the true nature of the war, but this was difficult to do with Kerry and the VVAW. Not surprisingly, officials in Nixon's administration worried about the VVAW's potential influence and did their best to discredit them by incorrectly claiming that many of the VVAW were not actually veterans. It is true that the Dewey Canyon III protests represented the height of the VVAW's influence, but Kerry's testimony helped the VVAW to remain an important organization in the antiwar movement for the remainder of the war.

—*Gerald F. Goodwin, PhD*

Biography and Additional Reading

Brinkley, Douglas. *Tour of Duty: John Kerry and the Vietnam War.* New York: HarperCollins, 2009. Print.

Cortright, David. *Soldiers in Revolt: GI Resistance During the Vietnam War.* Chicago: Haymarket Books, 2005. Print.

Moser, Richard. *The New Winter Soldiers: GI and Veteran Dissent During the Vietnam Era.* New Brunswick, NJ: Rutgers University Press, 1996. Print.

Small, Melvin. *Antiwarriors: The Vietnam War and the Battle For America's Hearts and Minds.* Lanham, MD: Rowman & Littlefield Publishers, 2002. Vietnam: America in the War Years Ser. Print.

Nixon's War

By the time Richard Nixon came to office in January 1969, peace talks between North and South Vietnam (and the United States) had already opened in Paris. Both sides were weary after the battles of Tet—and at home, in the case of the US government—and North Vietnam was seeking relief from the bombing. Nixon had campaigned on the rhetoric of ending the war in an honorable way, and when the peace talks failed to advance he took the first step in that direction: a plan for phased withdrawals of US forces under a policy of "Vietnamization" of the war. At the same time, Nixon increased assistance to the government of Nguyen Van Thiêu and expanded military training programs in South Vietnam.

All of this may or may not have proved fruitful on its own, but to hedge his bets Nixon also undertook an expansion of the war into Cambodia, where North Vietnamese supply lines fed opposition forces in the south. Worse, he hid this fact from the public—and even sections of his own administration—until the spring of 1970, when he announced that the Cambodia operation would be expanded further still. This news unleashed a storm of protest in the United States and led to violent confrontations on some college campuses, including Kent State and Jackson State universities, where National Guard and police units killed and injured a number of students. Congress reacted by pushing for a timetable for ending military operations in Cambodia and Vietnam and by repealing the Tonkin Gulf Resolution, which had authorized the use of "all necessary measures" to defend US interests in the region. Additional blows to the Pentagon and the administration came when news broke, in late 1969, about the 1968 killing of civilians by a US Army platoon operating in My Lai; and when *The New York Times* began publishing, in the summer of 1971, a secret government report on military matters in Southeast Asia that came to be known as the Pentagon Papers. With these disclosures, the public began to lose any lingering conviction that precious American values were at stake in the war and started to believe instead that the United States had made a mistake in getting involved in Vietnam in the first place.

Capitalizing on the weak support for the war in the United States, in the spring of 1972 North Vietnam launched a massive attack on the South. Nixon, refusing to back down, reacted by returning to bombing campaigns in the North, mining a northern harbor (where Russian supplies arrived), and expanding air operations in the South. After several more months of war, peace negotiations were resumed in October 1972. Much diplomatic back and forth, including many close calls, ensued. Indeed, as late as December 1972 Nixon was re-launching bomb attacks on the North—only one month before a somewhat unconvincing peace settlement was finally reached in Paris.

■ Conversation between Presidents Nixon and Thiêu

Date: June 8, 1969
Author(s): Richard M. Nixon; Nguyen Van Thiêu; Henry Kissinger; Nguyen Phu Duc
Genre: discussion; meeting minutes

Summary Overview

Midway Atoll was the scene for two very important moments in United States history. It served as the location for both an important US naval victory in World War II over the Japanese in 1942 and also as the setting for the first official meeting between President Nixon and President Thiêu of South Vietnam in 1969. This memorandum reports the discussion between Nixon and Thiêu from the American perspective. In this conversation, Nixon and Thiêu discussed a radical change in US policy toward Vietnam since the 1964 Gulf of Tonkin Resolution, which gave the president authority to use whatever means he deemed necessary for the security of Southeast Asia. The United States would begin "phased withdrawals" of armed forces, but still provide support to South Vietnam through funds and advisors. Nixon subsequently called this process "Vietnamization." The United States thus appeared to be faithful in promoting security in South Vietnam and in honoring domestic voices calling for the end of foreign military engagement.

Defining Moment

Support for the Vietnam War in the United States began to dramatically decrease in 1968 as no ostensible progress had been made in checking the advance of the North Vietnamese. At the start of the year, the North Vietnamese violated the truce to launch a surprise campaign, known as the Tet Offensive, which targeted military and civilian centers in South Vietnam. Both sides suffered tremendous casualties; the Tet Offensive also created thousands of new South Vietnamese refugees and crippled infrastructure. Faith in President Lyndon Johnson's leadership was another casualty of the Tet Offensive. Recognizing that his supporters had vanished, Johnson declined to run for reelection at the end of March.

Richard Nixon urged a more subtle approach to Vietnam in his 1968 presidential campaign, one that

he hoped would satisfy both proponents and opponents of the war. In order to become president and enact his plan, Nixon needed the South Vietnamese to refrain from any hasty agreements in the peace talks. In speeches, Nixon painted the Democratic opponent Hubert Humphrey, the current vice president under Johnson, as sabotaging American interests by favoring compromise with the communists in North Vietnam. In reality, Nixon used Kissinger as his foreign envoy and Anna Chennault, a Chinese American citizen-diplomat, to convince President Thiêu in Saigon to delay the peace talks. A Nixon presidency, Thiêu was told, would result in a better bargain for South Vietnam.

Nixon's gambit paid off: in November 1968, President Thiêu announced that he opposed negotiations and the cessation of bombings over North Vietnam. Shortly thereafter, Nixon won the presidential election. However, President Thiêu and his government were left with some anxieties. Thiêu was uneasy because the United States had already abandoned his predecessor, Ngo Dinh Diem, to a coup (and assassination) in 1964. The South Vietnamese government questioned, too, how much US military intelligence knew about the Tet Offensive before it began; divided US advice concerning negotiations from both American political parties during an election year increased their insecurities. This memorandum records how presidents Nixon and Thiêu confirmed their alliance to the world in their first official meeting at Midway.

Author Biography

Richard M. Nixon won the United States presidency in 1968 on the promise that he had a plan to end the Vietnam War. As National Security Advisor, Henry Kissinger worked with the president on this plan. The two men spent the next four years publically and privately working on an end to the conflict in a way that preserved US credibility. Kissinger eventually received the Nobel Peace Prize in 1973 for his work in creating the Paris Peace Accords, although the provisions of this agreement had little effect in creating lasting peace. Nixon was credited with drawing down US participation in the war at the same time that he ramped up bombing and seemingly prolonged the war.

Nguyen Van Thiêu attended school in France before returning to Vietnam. Once there, he served briefly in the predominantly communist Viet Minh. Thiêu switched his allegiance to the French-backed army, continued to serve once the French withdrew, and eventually was part of a military junta in 1963 that overthrew President Ngo Dinh Diem. In 1967, Thiêu won the election to become the president of the Republic of Vietnam despite widespread claims of election rigging. Allegations of corruption and complacency tarnished Thiêu's tenure as president. Shortly before the fall of Saigon, Thiêu fled to Britain. Nguyen Phu Duc was the special assistant to the president in South Vietnam; he participated in many of the tense peace talks with Kissinger.

HISTORICAL DOCUMENT

Memorandum of Conversation
Midway Island, *June 8, 1969.*

PRESENT
- President Nixon
- President Thiêu
- Henry Kissinger
- Nguyen Phu Duc

President Nixon began the meeting by stressing that he preferred to have private talks. He assured President Thiêu that what he would say would be in confidence. They could agree on that.

President Thiêu said that speculation as to differences between them is untrue; that he was very glad to have this opportunity to talk with the President.

President Nixon stated that the press is trying to drive a wedge between the two Presidents with respect to reports about American pressure. Unless President Thiêu heard something from him directly, he should disregard it. There is currently a lot of speculation regarding American pressures for a coalition government and it is entirely unfounded. (The President called on Henry Kissinger to confirm that fact.) The President gave a general appraisal of the situation, stating that the war in Vietnam concerns not only Vietnam but the entire Pacific. The people of South Vietnam, however, have the greatest stake. If the peace is inadequate, there will be repercussions all over Asia. There can be no reward for those engaged in aggression. At the same time, self-determination is not only in the Vietnamese interest, but in the American interest as well. It would improve the prospects of peace throughout the Pacific.

The President mentioned that we have a difficult political problem in the U.S. and that he appreciated Saigon's understanding for his domestic problems. At the same time, he understood President Thiêu's problems. It is not our wish for President Thiêu to get too far ahead and wind up with no country to lead. President Nixon described the Congressional situation and the importance of the 1970 elections. The U.S. domestic situation is a weapon in the war. (At this point the President asked Henry Kissinger to explain the Cambodian strikes.)

President Thiêu felt that the intentions of the enemy are crucial; the issue is the spread of Communism. Any false peace will affect all of Asia. Both the Vietnamese people and the world need peace. He recognized the U.S. desire for peace. He knew that the U.S. had no desire to occupy Vietnam but that its sole objective was to achieve peace. The Vietnamese should be reasonable and must consider not only Vietnamese opinions but those of the U.S. as well. The war in Vietnam is not a military one and neither side can win militarily. Therefore, there must be a reasonable compromise. President Thiêu understood the difficulties of the President with a large army abroad incurring constant casualties. He felt that his country must make progress in order to help us to withdraw.

Thiêu stated that Hanoi deliberately creates a deadlock in Paris and attacks the GVN as the chief obstacle to peace. The Communists are weaker, but Hanoi can continue the war at a reduced rate of casualties for many years. Hence, a negotiated peace is essential. Thiêu said he was trying to make progress in winning the political war. Even if Hanoi continues the war, the GVN will win the population.

The President next turned to the subject of troop replacements. Thiêu stated that troop replacements, if not handled carefully, could be misunderstood by the North Vietnamese and their allies. He pointed out that we have kept saying the war is going better. We must now prove it; it is important for both U.S. and Vietnamese opinion. Even though the war is going on, we must use the troop replacement to fight Communist propaganda.

By July 15, Thiêu said, it should be possible to phase out one-third of the Third Marine Division and six battalions from the Delta. At the same time, he wanted to emphasize a difference of opinion with General Abrams. His aim was to extend administrative control over 100% of the population next year. Therefore, the regional and popular forces are crucial. As they improve, they can replace mobile U.S. forces and ARVN combat divisions. The regional and popular forces can free regular forces to fight a mobile war. This was better than building up new combat divisions.

President Nixon said that we have confused the press by not denying any conflict between us. It would be obvious after today that no conflict existed. The two Presidents then discussed plans for the communiqué.

Turning to the negotiations, President Nixon asked how we should respond to Le Duc Tho's proposal for bilateral talks.

President Thiêu misunderstood the President's question about the Tho proposal and said the GVN would object to any U.S. attempt to talk to the NLF. After Mr. Kissinger clarified the issue, President Thiêu said that he agrees to bilateral talks unless the U.S. tries to settle directly with the NLF. The United States should introduce the military subject and listen to the political projections of the other side. Before replying, the GVN would have to be fully consulted.

President Nixon asked several questions regarding Vietnamese political institutions, commenting that Thiêu knew his people and required timing. He emphasized that there was no wedge between the U.S. and GVN nor between Thiêu and his people.

Break for Lunch

Thiêu asked about how we should respond to Communist strategy in Paris. President Nixon replied that we should not seem overanxious.

Thiêu asked about military operations. President Nixon said he thought the Communists were suffering badly and intelligence indicated there was very little in the pipeline to the South from Hanoi. Thiêu felt that the reason for the latest attacks was to maintain an impression of strength for the Communist world conference and to bring pressure on U.S. public opinion. The Communists faced a dilemma: they wanted to economize their human resources but also wished to maintain U.S. casualties. Thus they continue the tactics of pressure. The Communists pretend that the current deadlock is our fault. The only way to overcome this strategy is to set a deadline. Hanoi knows that delay is to their advantage. Thiêu suggested we make our most conciliatory proposal and then establish a deadline for a response, so that time does not work for the other side.

President Nixon asked whether Thiêu planned to go on in his political program from his March 25 speech. Thiêu replied that we must not be put into the position of always making new proposals. At some early point, we must state (a) that the U.S. and Saigon agree, and (b) that our proposals are as far as we can go. President Thiêu stated that he did not want to be pushed from one position to another—as was the case with the shape-of-the-table issue. If he could have the assurance that we would back some set of Saigon proposals, he was certain that we could work out a common position. But he did not want to have an escalation of proposals. Hanoi tended to take 15 small concessions and parlay them into one major concession.

Thiêu asked for assurances that we would not use every concession by the GVN as a signal for new demands. There must be an end to it. Mr. Kissinger asked, "But how do you play the political game?" Thiêu replied that if there were a withdrawal of forces and an end of terrorism, the GVN could consider the NLF as another party in elections. If the NLF wants guarantees, the GVN was ready to discuss it with them in generous terms. Thiêu said he was ready to accept an international body. It could not interfere in the GVN's area of sovereignty but it could organize and supervise elections. The GVN was willing to accept as many as 10,000 international inspectors and frontier guards. He was prepared to implement free choice and self-determination; in other words, a free vote and free candidature. Thiêu felt that everyone was aware that political competition was inevitable.

President Nixon urged Thiêu to do everything possible and asked if it would be any help to him if we provided a political organizer. The U.S. had done this with Magsaysay and it had been helpful. It is up to President Thiêu if he wants this kind of assistance. Thiêu responded that more support for cadres was necessary.

President Nixon mentioned that Hanoi has never had real elections and is thus employing a double standard. Thiêu pointed out that 56% of those "elected" in North Vietnam were women. This shows the magnitude of their manpower problem. He reiterated that there would be elections after the withdrawal of non-South Vietnamese forces. Thiêu was prepared for good international supervision—even without troops.

President Nixon wondered whether the GVN could siphon off the political forces in the center to weaken the Viet Cong. Thiêu responded that when we have a common position on our side, we can have a united front. What made the middle ground in Saigon so uncertain was the fear that the U.S. would withdraw support. Hence, many politicians were holding themselves available for a coalition government with the NLF.

President Nixon asked why not a united front now; the GVN is going to win and that is a great asset. Thiêu stated very frankly that there was a sagging of spirit in Saigon. Many still believe that the Viet Cong can have political concessions. The intellectuals are waiting for political concessions imposed on Saigon by the U.S. They were encouraged in this by loose statements from U.S. cabinet members. Mr. Duc interjected that the Saigon population was very worried.

President Thiêu asked what had been meant by local elections in the early drafts of the President's May 14 speech. The President replied that he meant that elections could be held in provinces where ceasefires had been arranged. Thiêu said that this was an interesting possibility.

President Nixon said that the fact that the people in Saigon were jittery worried him. Thiêu returned to his view that territorial forces had to be strengthened. General Abrams wants to train divisions. Thiêu wants to train 130,000 Regional Forces and Popular Forces. Abrams doubts the manpower resources are available. Thiêu thinks it easier to form RF and PF than regular forces. If the GVN has more RF and PF, it can phase out combat divisions. Thiêu wants the U.S. to reconsider his plan regarding the RF and PF, and for someone to talk to General Abrams.

President Nixon mentioned the stories in the press about the poor performance of the 5th and 18th Divisions. Thiêu said it is a question of leadership. President Nixon recalled the story of when General Pershing's desire to attack was thwarted by a classmate who said the morale of his divisions was shot. Pershing replied, your morale is shot and fired him. There are no tired divisions, only tired commanders.

GLOSSARY

GVN: Government of the Republic of Vietnam (South Vietnam)

NLF: National Liberation Front, the political arm of the Viet Cong in North Vietnam

ARVN: the Army of the Republic of Vietnam (South Vietnam), included the PF (Popular Forces) and RF (Regional Forces)

Document Analysis

The purpose of the meeting between the President Nixon and President Thiêu on Midway Island was to clarify what US de-escalation meant for South Vietnamese self-determination. After all, Nixon won the presidency by promising the American public that he would shift from the old policy of bombardment in Vietnam. What did this mean for the safety of President Thiêu's government? Soon after the conversation that this memorandum records, Nixon and Thiêu released a joint communiqué that announced American troop withdrawals publicly. Written from the US perspective, this memorandum verifies the communiqué released following the meeting that stated the United States and South Vietnam were still united. The United States would support South Vietnamese military and political decisions, but would not be chiefly responsible for them, a policy also known as the Nixon Doctrine.

The meeting begins with both sides assuring the other that they have similar interests and ought to present a united front. Nixon first tells Thiêu "self-determination is not only in the Vietnamese interest, but in the American interest as well." Thiêu ought not heed reports claiming that there were differences between their administrations. Nixon's success at home is connected to Thiêu's survival: "U.S. domestic situation is a weapon in the war." In turn, Thiêu assures Nixon that he "understood the difficulties of the President with a large army abroad" and he is aware that the US is not trying to replace South Vietnamese sovereignty with its own agenda.

Although both presidents reassured one another of their support, this memorandum also shows that Thiêu was hopeful that Vietnamization was not simply US abandonment. Military control, in Thiêu's perspective, had to support political control. South Vietnam needed to make progress in order to facilitate US withdrawal, and Thiêu could not affirm yet that his country was able to defend itself alone. The progress of the South Vietnamese army and the withdrawal of US forces needed to happen on a schedule that both countries agreed upon. The success of Vietnamization relied on this cooperation, yet Thiêu already shows that he has a difference of opinion with General Creighton Abrams, US commander of military operations in Vietnam. Thiêu wanted to focus on regional and popular forces in the country side rather than regular combat troops so he could "extend administrative control over 100% of the population."

The US and South Vietnam also needed to agree on free elections. When Nixon questions Thiêu about elections, the South Vietnamese president quickly assures him that a free state needs political competition. Thiêu reiterates, however, that success will come from full support. "When we have a common position on our side," says Thiêu, "we can have a united front." Saigon could not be united if the US was not united: "the fear that the U.S. would withdraw support" caused consternation in Saigon. In order to prove to Thiêu that

Vietnamization is not abandonment, Nixon quotes from General Pershing, an exemplary commander in the US military: "there are no tired divisions, only tired commanders." Nixon's use of a paradigm of heroic leadership supports the premise that he considered the policy of de-escalation part of an honorable system of foreign policy.

Essential Themes

The end of hostilities in World War II was also the end of a certain type of war. A war of ideologies took over in its place. Although the communist threat consumed American minds and politics in the 1950s and 60s, actual confrontation only occurred by proxy wars. Each side in the tense Cold War supported smaller-scale combat in developing nations as a way to check the other side's global hegemony. This memorandum traces the plans of Nixon and Thiêu to thwart North Vietnam ideologically.

Instead of staging large battles, United States administrations, starting with Eisenhower, placed emphasis on small-unit action, gathering intelligence, and pacification. President Johnson's administration seemed to stray from this policy: there were increased draft quotas and major bombings over North Vietnam during 1964–1968. Nixon's administration returned, at least ostensibly, to the idea of pacification. Phased American troop withdrawals from Vietnam would place greater combat responsibility on the South Vietnamese; the Americans could return to fighting by proxy and provide only money and equipment. The meeting between Presidents Nixon and Thiêu at Midway Atoll in June 1969 set the framework for this process, later known as Vietnamization (also as de-Americanization).

The key component to Vietnamization's success had to be a united front between the two allies against their enemy. Inability to compromise with the North proved fatal to the success of Vietnamization. Ideology could not be inflexible in this new warfare. The Nixon administration needed more unconditional support from the American public than it had in order to implement its designs; an ineffectual government in Saigon did not have the popular support to manage the defense of its own independence without significant American military support. North Vietnam, however, had a dedicated communist foundation.

Regardless, the central tenants of Vietnamization have survived well into the 2000s. United States' involvement in Latin America and the Middle East shows remarkable similarities to the ideas propagated during Nixon's administration. Similar to Nixon's situation in Vietnam, the United States has found it difficult to wage a successful ideological war without grassroots support.

—Ashleigh Fata, MA

Bibliography and Additional Reading

Karnow, Stanley. *Vietnam: A History.* New York: Penguin, 1991. Print.

Kimball, Jeffrey P. *Nixon's Vietnam War.* Lawrence, KS: U of Kansas, 1998. Print.

Kissinger, Henry. *Ending the Vietnam War: A History of America's Involvement in and Extrication from the Vietnam War.* New York: Simon & Schuster, 2003. Print.

Nguyen, Phu Duc, & Arthur J. Dommen. *The Viet-Nam Peace Negotiations: Saigon's Side of the Story.* Christiansburg, VA: Dalley Book Service, 2005. Print.

■ Henry Kissinger to Nixon

Date: September 10, 1969
Author: Henry Kissinger
Genre: memorandum

Summary Overview

President Nixon began phased withdrawals of American armed forces in 1969; South Vietnam needed to assume responsibility for its defense in a process called "Vietnamization." As national security advisor, Henry Kissinger worked with Nixon in the goal of preserving the United States' credibility as a military giant in global leadership, while satisfying the antiwar proponents who called for withdrawal. However, Kissinger noted in this private memorandum from Nixon's first year as president that the present US plan for de-escalating the war and winning was too optimistic. Domestic political divisions and corruption in South Vietnam were providing the North Vietnamese ample opportunities to entrench themselves in their positions. Kissinger recognized that there was no middle ground in American policy: unilateral withdrawal meant defeat; continued military operations could preserve the South Vietnamese government only if President Nguyen Van Thiêu improved it. Kissinger's early concerns in this memorandum would prove true by 1975, when North Vietnam captured Saigon.

Defining Moment

In 1968, Richard Nixon portrayed himself as a candidate with a plan for negotiating "peace with honor" in the Vietnam War. Not only would Nixon bring the troops home, but he would also keep US promises to their South Vietnamese allies to preserve their sovereignty. The idea to have "phased withdrawals" of US armed forces did not begin with Nixon, but it would be inextricably tied to his administration under the name "Vietnamization." Compared to policy after the Gulf of Tonkin Resolution in 1964, the United States would take a less active role in preserving Southeast Asian peace.

Henry Kissinger, an academic and defense strategist until Nixon's presidency, was essential to this new state of US policy. Even before Nixon appointed Kissinger

the national security advisor, the intellectual German immigrant wrote articles in the journal Foreign Affairs about how a government's interests justified the means used to accomplish those interests. Kissinger was willing to use this philosophy before Nixon was sworn in as president. In an event known as the "Chennault Affair," Kissinger and Nixon cooperated in legally dubious contact with President Thiêu in South Vietnam: if Thiêu delayed peace negotiations with the North Vietnamese, the Nixon administration would negotiate better concessions for South Vietnam. The counterpoint to Kissinger's pragmatic philosophy, however, was a willingness to abandon allies after they became a liability. In this private memorandum to the president, Kissinger illustrates all the features that would define the Nixon administration in subsequent years: a disdain for the antiwar movement, pessimism, and pragmatism.

This memorandum is an outline of the dangerous political game that the Nixon administration needed to play domestically and globally. Antiwar protestors are sentimental opponents in this scheme, and the North Vietnamese are cunning manipulators, who knew that they could exploit South Vietnam's overdependence on United States armed forces. Time was on the side of the Politburo, the collective leadership that replaced Ho Chi Minh after his death on September 2, 1969. Kissinger's memo late in 1969 is proof that he had significantly tempered his expectations that American diplomacy could accomplish a victorious peace quickly. As early as Nixon's first year, Kissinger doubts that Vietnamization will provide the leverage he needed in negotiations.

Author Biography

Henry Kissinger came from a family of immigrant Jews who escaped Nazi Germany in 1938. As a private in World War II, Kissinger entered politics when he administered the city of Krefeld. After the war, Kissinger attended Harvard and received his PhD in political science in 1954. He would go on to assemble a network of contacts in the US government, while also publishing frequently. Kissinger's *Nuclear Weapons and Foreign Policy* was a bestseller in 1958; the book established his credentials as a respectable defense specialist. The Harvard intellectual became an important figure in the Nixon administration. As national security advisor, Kissinger made changes to the National Security Council system that made Kissinger the principal foreign policy advisor to the president. Both Nixon and Kissinger subscribed to a realist ideology: they believed strongly in the importance and maintenance of power at any cost in domestic and foreign relations. Despite charges of being a courtier, chameleon, and flatterer, Kissinger has remained an important and visible figure in American foreign policy for decades after the Vietnam War.

HISTORICAL DOCUMENT

SUBJECT
Our Present Course on Vietnam

I have become deeply concerned about our present course on Vietnam. This memorandum is to inform you of the reasons for my concern. It does not discuss alternative courses of action, but is provided for your background consideration. You know my recommendations.

While time acts against both us and our enemy, it runs more quickly against our strategy than against theirs. This pessimistic view is based on my view of Hanoi's strategy and the probable success of the various elements of our own.

I. U.S. Strategy

In effect, we are attempting to solve the problem of Vietnam on three highly interrelated fronts: (1) within the U.S., (2) in Vietnam, and (3) through diplomacy. To achieve our basic goals through diplomacy, we must be reasonably successful on both of the other two fronts.

a. U.S.
The pressure of public opinion on you to resolve the war quickly will increase—and I believe increase greatly—during the coming months. While polls may show that large numbers of Americans now are satisfied with the Administration's handling of the war, the elements of an evaporation of this support are clearly present. The plans for student demonstrations in October are well known, and while many Americans will oppose the students' activities, they will also be reminded of their own opposition to the continuation of the war. As mentioned below, I do not believe that "Vietnamization" can significantly reduce the pressures for an end to the war, and may, in fact, increase them after a certain point. Particularly significant is the clear opposition of many "moderate" leaders of opinion, particularly in the press and in the East (e.g., Life Magazine). The result of the recrudescence of intense public concern must be to polarize public opinion. You will then be somewhat in the same position as was President Johnson, although the substance of your position will be different. You will be caught between the Hawks and the Doves.

The effect of these public pressures on the U.S. Government will be to accentuate the internal divisiveness that has already become apparent to the public and Hanoi. Statements by government officials which attempt to assuage the Hawks or Doves will serve to confuse Hanoi but also to confirm it in its course of waiting us out.

b. Vietnam
Three elements on the Vietnam front must be considered—(1) our efforts to "win the war" through military operations and pacification, (2) "Vietnamization," and (3) the political position of the GVN.

(1) I do not believe that with our current plans we can win the war within two years, although our success or failure in hurting the enemy remains very important.

(2) "Vietnamization" must be considered both with regard to its prospects for allowing us to turn the war over to the Vietnamese, and with regard to its effect on Hanoi and U.S. public opinion. I am not optimistic about the

ability of the South Vietnamese armed forces to assume a larger part of the burden than current MACV plans allow. These plans, however, call for a thirty-month period in which to turn the burden of the war over to the GVN. I do not believe we have this much time.

In addition, "Vietnamization" will run into increasingly serious problems as we proceed down its path.

- Withdrawal of U.S. troops will become like salted peanuts to the American public: The more U.S. troops come home, the more will be demanded. This could eventually result, in effect, in demands for unilateral withdrawal—perhaps within a year.
- The more troops are withdrawn, the more Hanoi will be encouraged—they are the last people we will be able to fool about the ability of the South Vietnamese to take over from us. They have the option of attacking GVN forces to embarrass us throughout the process or of waiting until we have largely withdrawn before doing so (probably after a period of higher infiltration).
- Each U.S. soldier that is withdrawn will be relatively more important to the effort in the south, as he will represent a higher percentage of U.S. forces than did his predecessor. (We need not, of course, continue to withdraw combat troops but can emphasize support troops in the next increments withdrawn. Sooner or later, however, we must be getting at the guts of our operations there.)
- It will become harder and harder to maintain the morale of those who remain, not to speak of their mothers.
- "Vietnamization" may not lead to reduction in U.S. casualties until its final stages, as our casualty rate may be unrelated to the total number of American troops in South Vietnam. To kill about 150 U.S. soldiers a week, the enemy needs to attack only a small portion of our forces.
- "Vietnamization" depends on broadening the GVN, and Thiêu's new government is not significantly broader than the old (see below). The best way to broaden the GVN would be to create the impression that the Saigon government is winning or at least permanent. The more uncertainty there is about the outcome of the war, the less the prospect for "Vietnamization."

(3) We face a dilemma with the GVN: The present GVN cannot go much farther towards a political settlement without seriously endangering its own existence; but at the same time, it has not gone far enough to make such a settlement likely.

Thiêu's failure to "broaden" his government is disturbing, but not because he failed to include a greater variety of Saigon's Tea House politicians. It is disturbing because these politicians clearly do not believe that Thiêu and his government represent much hope for future power, and because the new government does not offer much of a bridge to neutralist figures who could play a role in a future settlement. This is not to mention his general failure to build up political strength in non-Catholic villages. In addition, as U.S. troops are withdrawn, Thiêu becomes more dependent on the political support of the South Vietnamese military.

c. Diplomatic Front

There is not therefore enough of a prospect of progress in Vietnam to persuade Hanoi to make real concessions in Paris. Their intransigence is also based on their estimate of growing U.S. domestic opposition to our Vietnam policies. It looks as though they are prepared to try to wait us out.

II. Hanoi's Strategy

There is no doubt that the enemy has been hurt by allied military actions in the South, and is not capable of maintaining the initiative on a sustained basis there. Statistics on enemy-initiated activities, as well as some of Giap's recent statements, indicate a conscious decision by Hanoi to settle down to a strategy of "protracted warfare." This apparently consists of small unit actions with "high point" flurries of activity, and emphasis on inflicting U.S. casualties (particularly through rocket and mortar attacks). This pattern of actions seems clearly to indicate a low-cost strategy aimed at producing a psychological, rather than military, defeat for the U.S.

This view of their strategy is supported by our estimates of enemy infiltration. They could infiltrate more men, according to intelligence estimates, despite growing domestic difficulties. The only logical reason for their not having done so is that more men were not needed in the pipeline—at least for a few months—to support a lower-cost strategy of protracted warfare. It seems most unlikely that they are attempting to "signal" to us a desire for a de facto mutual withdrawal, although this cannot be discounted. There is no diplomatic sign of this—except in Xuan Thuy's linkage of points two and three of the PRG program— and I do not believe they trust us enough to "withdraw" a larger percentage of their men than we have of ours, as they would be doing.

Hanoi's adoption of a strategy designed to wait us out fits both with its doctrine of how to fight a revolutionary war and with its expectations about increasingly significant problems for the U.S.

III. Conclusion

In brief, I do not believe we can make enough evident progress in Vietnam to hold the line within the U.S. (and the U.S. Government), and Hanoi has adopted a strategy which it should be able to maintain for some time—barring some break like Sino-Soviet hostilities. Hence my growing concern.

GLOSSARY

GVN: Government of the Republic of Vietnam (South Vietnam)

MACV: US Military Assistance Command, Vietnam, a group overseeing advisory and assistance efforts in Vietnam

PRG: Provisional Revolutionary Government, an underground government opposed to President Thiêu in South Vietnam

Document Analysis

In this memo, Kissinger illustrates to the president that Vietnamization is an idealistic and likely unsuccessful program for ending the Vietnam War. These doubts were a rationale for the president to delay an immediate unilateral withdrawal from Vietnam in 1969: South Vietnam simply was not ready to defend itself. Kissinger divides his concerns into three interrelated topics: domestic divisions, problems within the power structure in Saigon, and Hanoi's advantages. Kissinger wanted to chasten any optimistic notions the president had of a quick solution to the war through de-escalation and diplomacy. This memo also foreshadows Nixon's significant compromises with Soviet Russia and China in 1972. From the beginning of Nixon's first term, Kissinger advocated a multifaceted approach to a conflict his predecessors tried to solve only by military force.

First, Kissinger points out that Vietnamization will not mend the division between pro- and anti-war contingents in the US government ("the Hawks and the Doves"). It was very possible for Nixon to suffer the same backlash of public opinion that destroyed the public's faith in his predecessor's administration. Instead of addressing that the crisis of faith originated in sentiment, Kissinger compares this desire for troop withdrawal to a trivial craving for unhealthy food. He says, "withdrawal of U.S. troops will become like salted peanuts to the American public." Opponents have used such statements to condemn brutal pragmatics of Nixonian foreign policy.

Next, statements about Saigon's efficacy reveal Kissinger's political philosophy further. For Kissinger, utility and expediency are more important than ethics. Vietnamization was only the appearance of a united front, as the Presidents Nixon and Thiêu wanted to portray between their countries. Kissinger characterizes Thiêu's government (GVN) as a series of "failures" and "disturbing" in its lack of action. Yet, Kissinger does not advise abandoning Thiêu to his fate: supporting an ally, even if he is a poor leader, is more important for US diplomacy than self-determination for Vietnam.

Finally, Kissinger addresses the enemy's strategy. The war is "psychological, rather than military." Bombings were only useful as long as the enemy did not have a more powerful communist ally. The third and last part of Kissinger's memo advises Nixon that he needs to recover their ideological losses on the ideological front of the Vietnam War for an effective diplomacy strategy. Kissinger's statement that "barring some break like-Sino-Soviet hostilities" is prescient for this ideological combat. Tensions ran high between Soviet Russia and China already, and Nixon would use this as leverage when he reopened contact with Chairman Mao in 1972. As a result of cooling relations with Hanoi's former supporters, Kissinger was able to finalize the Paris Peace Accords soon thereafter.

At no point in this memo does Kissinger express a positive belief that the United States can maintain both the moral high ground and victory in Vietnam. This memo exemplifies the early pessimism about the war that would eventually devolve into the "decent interval" practice. Diplomacy, for Kissinger, was a waiting game: either for the enemy to give in, or for the home front to forget about the losses it suffered.

Essential Themes

It is difficult to avoid psychologizing the national security advisor when examining the ideas he promoted in Nixon's government. As a result, opinions about Kissinger span a spectrum from "hero" to "war criminal." As well, the divisiveness between the growing voice of the American media and the revelation of White House secret memoranda served only to heighten the disjunction between Kissinger's realist ideology at a time when the United States wanted to portray itself as ideologically superior. The crisis of faith in American leadership did not begin with Kissinger and Nixon, but their partnership provided the most evidence for pessimists.

In Kissinger's "salted peanuts" memorandum, however, there is a clear impression that the men in the executive branch recognized the difficulty of maintaining the moral high ground in a proxy war. "Vietnamization" seemed like the ethical compromise for the United States against an unethical enemy. In theory, extricating American soldiers and assisting the South Vietnamese government to support its own defense

was morally expedient: Vietnamization allowed the Nixon administration to protect its interests at home and abroad. Kissinger's pessimism regarding the "ethical solution" to the Vietnam War would play out in the increasingly manipulative and secret strategies of the executive branch. Covert bombings over Cambodia and Laos were already occurring at the time of this memorandum; the United States had to ease relations with Russia and China three years later in order to gain some leverage over Hanoi in the stalemate negotiations in Paris. Although Kissinger's dedication to *realpolitik* in diplomacy seemed effective on paper, it showed an inability to comprehend the reality of human behavior in war: Americans would not tolerate deception from their leaders, and many in South Vietnam did not favor the government in Saigon.

Parallels been the Vietnam War and the Iraq conflict in the early 2000s were inescapable, in part because Kissinger continued his participation in White House affairs after Nixon. The advice that troop withdrawals would become like "salted peanuts" has been used, as it was in the 1970s, to increase bipartisan conflict in the United States at the expense of human suffering abroad.

—Ashleigh Fata, MA

Bibliography and Additional Reading

Dallek, Robert. *Nixon and Kissinger: Partners in Power.* New York: HarperCollins Pub., 2007. Print.

Karnow, Stanley. *Vietnam: A History.* New York: Penguin, 1991. Print.

Kimball, Jeffrey P. *Nixon's Vietnam War.* Lawrence, KS: U of Kansas, 1998. Print.

Kissinger, Henry & Clare Boothe Luce. *White House Years.* Boston: Little, Brown, 1979. Print.

Prados, John. "Kissinger's 'Salted Peanuts' and the Iraq War." *National Security Archive.* National Security Archive & George Washington University, 2006. Web. <http://nsarchive.gwu.edu/news/20061001/>.

■ Nixon on the "Silent Majority" and "Vietnamization"

Date: November 03, 1969
Author: Richard M. Nixon
Genre: speech

Summary Overview

In his speech of November 3, 1969, President Richard M. Nixon introduced a new phrase, "silent majority," and a new policy, termed "Vietnamization." He distinguished the silent majority, the people that he believed supported his policies, from the "vocal minority" of antiwar protesters. Vietnamization involved shifting more of the burden of fighting the war from US troops to a larger and better trained and equipped South Vietnamese army, which would eventually permit the United States to withdraw. These terms served to frame the subsequent debate in America about the Vietnam War.

Defining Moment

Denouncing those who advocated walking away from the nation's commitments, Nixon pledged during the campaign that he could achieve "an honorable peace" in Vietnam. (The standard phrase later became "peace with honor.") In speeches and public statements he generally assumed hardline positions on Vietnam, but he took a different line in private sessions with liberal reporters and newspaper editors. The public came to believe that he had a "secret plan to end the war," although he did not use that terminology. The phrase was introduced by a reporter who was trying to summarize the candidate's vague and contradictory claims regarding the possibility of a quick victory. Still, Nixon never explicitly disowned the phrase.

Nixon's actual plans focused more on reducing the United States' direct role in the war so as to minimize domestic opposition to it. Eventually this would involve continuation of the negotiations with North Vietnam initiated by President Lyndon B. Johnson, coercive military actions to compel the North Vietnamese to make concessions in the peace talks (which was also consistent with the Johnson administration), the improved equipment and training of the South Vietnamese army (the Army of the Republic of Vietnam, or ARVN), and periodic announcements of unilateral US troop withdrawals accompanied by positive reports on how the war was proceeding. This is not to say that Nixon would have rejected an acceptable settlement, but that he was prepared to continue the war in other ways if a settlement was not reached. Perceptions also mattered. In August, North Vietnamese leader Ho Chi Minh responded to a US negotiating proposal in a manner that he may have considered a serious counteroffer, but which Nixon considered an outright rejection.

In internal discussions, the notion of shifting the major burden of ground combat to ARVN was initially referred to as "de-Americanizing" the war. Eventually, the accepted term was Vietnamization. National Security Adviser Henry Kissinger was skeptical of Vietnamization and warned that pressure to resolve the war quickly would increase if Vietnamization failed to reduce US casualties.

In the summer of 1969, as Nixon was sending secret envoys to meet with the North Vietnamese, he also had plans drawn up for a "savage blow" against North Vietnam. The White House called the operation Duck Hook, while at the US command in Saigon it was known as Pruning Knife. Elements of the plan included heavy conventional bombing (532 sorties a day), the mining of harbors (in Cambodia, too, for good measure), and a ground invasion across the Demilitarized Zone (DMZ) that separated North and South Vietnam. At least some consideration was given to the use of tactical nuclear weapons. The onslaught would occur in intervals of four days, with every fifth day off to give Hanoi a chance to respond, until North Vietnam agreed to negotiate seriously. A presidential speech announcing the offensive was drafted in September. ("It is my duty to tell you tonight of a major decision in our quest for an honorable peace in Vietnam.") Without revealing details, Nixon conveyed threats of severe military action in early November if Hanoi was not forthcoming in negotiations.

Nixon finally decided against Duck Hook/Pruning Knife on November 1. The secretaries of state and defense and members of the National Security Council staff had opposed it all along, saying it would prolong the war rather than end it; that the North Vietnamese and the Viet Cong had not been intimidated by the threats; that it would not change the military situation within South Vietnam; that it would further fuel the antiwar movement at home; that it would elicit adverse reactions from the Soviet Union, China, and Europe; and that Hanoi would never believe that it was intended to encourage negotiations. Nixon and Kissinger later expressed regret for not following through on the plan.

The "moratorium" on the war—a peace demonstration that brought hundreds of thousands of protesters onto the streets of Washington on October 15—helped seal the fate of Duck Hook/Pruning Knife. Nixon concluded that the show of domestic opposition undercut the credibility of the ultimatum. An even larger demonstration was planned for mid-November, and launching this offensive immediately before it could have had unpredictable results. The president also allowed that the death of Ho Chi Minh in September might open new possibilities for negotiation.

Thus the circumstances for Nixon's November 3 speech were set. In it, he set out to dampen antiwar sentiment and mobilize his supporters. By revealing the existence of "subterranean" support for his policies, he would seek to undermine resistance to his policies in the bureaucracy and in the nation as a whole.

Author Biography

Richard Milhous Nixon was born on Jan. 9, 1913, in Yorba Linda, California, and was raised as a Quaker. He graduated from Whittier College (1934) and Duke University Law School (1937), served as an officer in the US Navy in World War II, and was elected by California to the House of Representatives in 1946. Nixon joined the House Un-American Activities Committee and gained a national reputation for his investigation of Alger Hiss, whom he accused of espionage for the Soviet Union. He won election to the Senate in 1950 and developed a reputation as a staunch anticommunist crusader ("red-baiter"). Representing the conservative wing of the Republican Party, Nixon was selected as Dwight D. Eisenhower's running mate and served as vice president (1953–61). Selected as his party's presidential nominee in 1960, he lost narrowly to John F. Kennedy. In 1962, he lost the election for governor of California and temporarily retired from politics. Returning to the political scene, he was elected president in 1968, after campaigning on a promise to end the war in Vietnam and to restore law and order after years of political turmoil, protests, and race riots. Despite his anticommunist reputation, he sought to improve relations with the Soviet Union and China, in part, but not entirely, to help extricate the United States from Vietnam. Reelected in 1972 in a landslide, he became, in 1974, the first president in US history to resign in disgrace, as a result of the Watergate affair. Nixon died on April 22, 1994.

HISTORICAL DOCUMENT

Good evening, my fellow Americans.

Tonight I want to talk to you on a subject of deep concern to all Americans and to many people in all parts of the world—the war in Vietnam.

I believe that one of the reasons for the deep division about Vietnam is that many Americans have lost confidence in what their Government has told them about our policy. The American people cannot and should not be asked to support a policy which involves the overriding issues of war and peace unless they know the truth about that policy.

Tonight, therefore, I would like to answer some of the questions that I know are on the minds of many of you listening to me.

How and why did America get involved in Vietnam in the first place? How has this administration changed the policy of the previous administration? What has really happened in the negotiations in Paris and on the battlefront in Vietnam? What choices do we have if we are to end the war? What are the prospects for peace? Now, let me begin by describing the situation I found when I was inaugurated on January 20:

- The war had been going on for 4 years. 1,000 Americans had been killed in action.
- The training program for the South Vietnamese was behind schedule. 540,000 Americans were in Vietnam with no plans to reduce the number.
- No progress had been made at the negotiations in Paris and the United States had not put forth a comprehensive peace proposal.
- The war was causing deep division at home and criticism from many of our friends as well as our enemies abroad.

In view of these circumstances there were some who urged that I end the war at once by ordering the immediate withdrawal of all American forces.

From a political standpoint this would have been a popular and easy course to follow. After all, we became involved in the war while my predecessor was in office. I could blame the defeat which would be the result of my action on him and come out as the peacemaker. Some put it to me quite bluntly: This was the only way to avoid allowing Johnson's war to become Nixon's war.

But I had a greater obligation than to think only of the years of my administration and of the next election. I had to think of the effect of my decision on the next generation and on the future of peace and freedom in America and in the world.

Let us all understand that the question before us is not whether some Americans are for peace and some Americans are against peace. The question at issue is not whether Johnson's war becomes Nixon's war.

The great question is: How can we win America's peace?

Well, let us turn now to the fundamental issue. Why and how did the United States become involved in Vietnam in the first place? Fifteen years ago North Vietnam, with the logistical support of Communist China and the Soviet Union, launched a campaign to impose a Communist government on South Vietnam by instigating and supporting a revolution.

In response to the request of the Government of South Vietnam, President Eisenhower sent economic aid and military equipment to assist the people of South Vietnam in their efforts to prevent a Communist takeover. Seven years ago, President Kennedy sent 16,000 military personnel to Vietnam as combat advisers. Four years ago, President Johnson sent American combat forces to South Vietnam.

Now, many believe that President Johnson's decision to send American combat forces to South Vietnam was wrong. And many others—I among them—have been strongly critical of the way the war has been conducted.

But the question facing us today is: Now that we are in the war, what is the best way to end it?

In January I could only conclude that the precipitate withdrawal of American forces from Vietnam would be a disaster not only for South Vietnam but for the United States and for the cause of peace.

For the South Vietnamese, our precipitate withdrawal would inevitably allow the Communists to repeat the massacres which followed their takeover in the North 15 years before; They then murdered more than 50,000 people and hundreds of thousands more died in slave labor camps.

We saw a prelude of what would happen in South Vietnam when the Communists entered the city of Hue last year. During their brief rule there, there was a bloody reign of terror in which 3,000 civilians were clubbed, shot to death, and buried in mass graves.

With the sudden collapse of our support, these atrocities of Hue would become the nightmare of the entire nation—and particularly for the million and a half Catholic refugees who fled to South Vietnam when the Communists took over in the North.

For the United States, this first defeat in our Nation's history would result in a collapse of confidence in American leadership, not only in Asia but throughout the world.

Three American Presidents have recognized the great stakes involved in Vietnam and understood what had to be done.

In 1963, President Kennedy, with his characteristic eloquence and clarity, said:

> ... we want to see a stable government there, carrying on a struggle to maintain its national independence. We believe strongly in that. We are not going to withdraw from that effort. In my opinion, for us to withdraw from that effort would mean

a collapse not only of South VietNam, but Southeast Asia. So we are going to stay there.

President Eisenhower and President Johnson expressed the same conclusion during their terms of office.

For the future of peace, precipitate withdrawal would thus be a disaster of immense magnitude.

A nation cannot remain great if it betrays its allies and lets down its friends.

Our defeat and humiliation in South Vietnam without question would promote recklessness in the councils of those great powers who have not yet abandoned their goals of world conquest.

This would spark violence wherever our commitments help maintain the peace—in the Middle East, in Berlin, eventually even in the Western Hemisphere.

Ultimately, this would cost more lives.

It would not bring peace; it would bring more war.

For these reasons, I rejected the recommendation that I should end the war by immediately withdrawing all of our forces. I chose instead to change American policy on both the negotiating front and battlefront. In order to end a war fought on many fronts, I initiated a pursuit for peace on many fronts. In a television speech on May 14, in a speech before the United Nations, and on a number of other occasions I set forth our peace proposals in great detail.

We have offered the complete withdrawal of all outside forces within 1 year.

We have proposed a cease-fire under international supervision.

We have offered free elections under international supervision with the Communists participating in the organization and conduct of the elections as an organized political force. And the Saigon Government has pledged to accept the result of the elections.

We have not put forth our proposals on a take-it-or-leave-it basis. We have indicated that we are willing to discuss the proposals that have been put forth by the other side. We have declared that anything is negotiable except the right of the people of South Vietnam to determine their own future. At the Paris peace conference,

Ambassador Lodge has demonstrated our flexibility and good faith in 40 public meetings.

Hanoi has refused even to discuss our proposals. They demand our unconditional acceptance of their terms, which are that we withdraw all American forces immediately and unconditionally and that we overthrow the Government of South Vietnam as we leave.

We have not limited our peace initiatives to public forums and public statements. I recognized, in January, that a long and bitter war like this usually cannot be settled in a public forum. That is why in addition to the public statements and negotiation I have explored every possible private avenue that might lead to a settlement.

Tonight I am taking the unprecedented step of disclosing to you some of our other initiatives for peace—initiatives we undertook privately and secretly because we thought we thereby might open a door which publicly would be closed.

I did not wait for my inauguration to begin my quest for peace.

Soon after my election, through an individual who is directly in contact on a personal basis with the leaders of North Vietnam, I made two private offers for a rapid, comprehensive settlement. Hanoi's replies called in effect for our surrender before negotiations.

Since the Soviet Union furnishes most of the military equipment for North Vietnam, Secretary of State Rogers, my Assistant for National Security Affairs, Dr. Kissinger, Ambassador Lodge, and I, personally, have met on a number of occasions with representatives of the Soviet Government to enlist their assistance in getting meaningful negotiations started. In addition, we have had extended discussions directed toward that same end with representatives of other governments which have diplomatic relations with North Vietnam. None of these initiatives have to date produced results.

In mid-July, I became convinced that it was necessary to make a major move to break the deadlock in the Paris talks. I spoke directly in this office, where I am now sitting, with an individual who had known Ho Chi Minh on a personal basis for 25 years. Through him I sent a letter to Ho Chi Minh. I did this outside of the usual diplomatic channels with the hope that with the necessity of making statements for propaganda removed, there might be constructive progress toward bringing the war to an end. Let me read from this letter to you now:

Dear Mr. President:

I realize that it is difficult to communicate meaningfully across the gulf of four years of war. But precisely because of this gulf, I wanted to take this opportunity to reaffirm in all solemnity my desire to work for a just peace. I deeply believe that the war in Vietnam has gone on too long and delay in bringing it to an end can benefit no one—least of all the people of Vietnam.

The time has come to move forward at the conference table toward an early resolution of this tragic war. You will find us forthcoming and open-minded in a common effort to bring the blessings of peace to the brave people of Vietnam. Let history record that at this critical juncture, both sides turned their face toward peace rather than toward conflict and war.

I received Ho Chi Minh's reply on August 30, 3 days before his death. It simply reiterated the public position North Vietnam had taken at Paris and flatly rejected my initiative.

The full text of both letters is being released to the press.

In addition to the public meetings that I have referred to, Ambassador Lodge has met with Vietnam's chief negotiator in Paris in 11 private sessions.

We have taken other significant initiatives which must remain secret to keep open some channels of communication which may still prove to be productive.

But the effect of all the public, private, and secret negotiations which have been undertaken since the bombing halt a year ago and since this administration came into office on January 20, can be summed up in one sentence: No progress whatever has been made except agreement on the shape of the bargaining table.

Well now, who is at fault?

It has become clear that the obstacle in negotiating an end to the war is not the President of the United States. It is not the South Vietnamese Government.

The obstacle is the other side's absolute refusal to show the least willingness to join us in seeking a just peace. And it will not do so while it is convinced that all it has to do is to wait for our next concession, and our next concession after that one, until it gets everything it wants.

There can now be no longer any question that progress in negotiation depends only on Hanoi's deciding to negotiate, to negotiate seriously.

I realize that this report on our efforts on the diplomatic front is discouraging to the American people, but the American people are entitled to know the truth—the bad news as well as the good news—where the lives of our young men are involved.

Now let me turn, however, to a more encouraging report on another front.

At the time we launched our search for peace I recognized we might not succeed in bringing an end to the war through negotiation. I, therefore, put into effect another plan to bring peace—a plan which will bring the war to an end regardless of what happens on the negotiating front.

It is in line with a major shift in U.S. foreign policy which I described in my press conference at Guam on July 25. Let me briefly explain what has been described as the Nixon Doctrine—a policy which not only will help end the war in Vietnam, but which is an essential element of our program to prevent future Vietnams.

We Americans are a do-it-yourself people. We are an impatient people. Instead of teaching someone else to do a job, we like to do it ourselves. And this trait has been carried over into our foreign policy In Korea and again in Vietnam, the United States furnished most of the money, most of the arms, and most of the men to help the people of those countries defend their freedom against Communist aggression.

Before any American troops were committed to Vietnam, a leader of another Asian country expressed this opinion to me when I was traveling in Asia as a private citizen. He said: "When you are trying to assist another nation defend its freedom, U.S. policy should be to help them fight the war but not to fight the war for them."

Well, in accordance with this wise counsel, I laid down in Guam three principles as guidelines for future American policy toward Asia:

- First, the United States will keep all of its treaty commitments.
- Second, we shall provide a shield if a nuclear power threatens the freedom of a nation allied with US or of a nation whose survival we consider vital to our security.
- Third, in cases involving other types of aggression, we shall furnish military and economic assistance when requested in accordance with our treaty commitments. But we shall look to the nation directly threatened to assume the primary responsibility of providing the manpower for its defense.

After I announced this policy, I found that the leaders of the Philippines, Thailand, Vietnam, South Korea, and other nations which might be threatened by Communist aggression, welcomed this new direction in American foreign policy.

The defense of freedom is everybody's business—not just America's business. And it is particularly the responsibility of the people whose freedom is threatened. In the previous administration, we Americanized the war in Vietnam. In this administration, we are Vietnamizing the search for peace.

The policy of the previous administration not only resulted in our assuming the primary responsibility for fighting the war, but even more significantly did not adequately stress the goal of strengthening the South Vietnamese so that they could defend themselves when we left.

The Vietnamization plan was launched following Secretary Laird's visit to Vietnam in March. Under the plan, I ordered first a substantial increase in the training and equipment of South Vietnamese forces.

In July, on my visit to Vietnam, I changed General Abrams' orders so that they were consistent with the objectives of our new policies. Under the new orders, the primary mission of our troops is to enable the South Vietnamese forces to assume the full responsibility for the security of South Vietnam.

Our air operations have been reduced by over 20 percent.

And now we have begun to see the results of this long overdue change in American policy in Vietnam.

After 5 years of Americans going into Vietnam, we are finally bringing American men home. By December 15, over 60,000 men will have been withdrawn from South Vietnam, including 20 percent of all of our combat forces.

The South Vietnamese have continued to gain in strength. As a result they have been able to take over combat responsibilities from our American troops.

Two other significant developments have occurred since this administration took office.

- Enemy infiltration, infiltration which is essential if they are to launch a major attack, over the last 3 months is less than 20 percent of what it was over the same period last year.
- Most important—United States casualties have declined during the last 2 months to the lowest point in 3 years.

Let me now turn to our program for the future.

We have adopted a plan which we have worked out in cooperation with the South Vietnamese for the complete withdrawal of all U.S. combat ground forces, and their replacement by South Vietnamese forces on an orderly scheduled timetable. This withdrawal will be made from strength and not from weakness. As South Vietnamese forces become stronger, the rate of American withdrawal can become greater.

I have not and do not intend to announce the timetable for our program. And there are obvious reasons for this decision which I am sure you will understand. As I have indicated on several occasions, the rate of withdrawal will depend on developments on three fronts.

One of these is the progress which can be or might be made in a Paris talks. An announcement of a fixed timetable for our withdrawal would completely remove any incentive for the enemy to negotiate an agreement. They would simply wait until our forces had withdrawn and then move in.

The other two factors on which we will base our withdrawal decisions are the level of enemy activity and the progress of the training programs of the South

Vietnamese forces. And I am glad to able to report tonight progress on both of these fronts has been greater than we anticipated when we started the program in June for withdrawal. As a result, our timetable for withdrawal is more optimistic now than when we made our first estimates in June. Now, this clearly demonstrates why it is not wise to be frozen in on a fixed timetable.

We must retain the flexibility to base each withdrawal decision on the situation as it is at that time rather than on estimates that are no longer valid.

Along with this optimistic estimate, I must—in all candor—leave one note of caution. If the level of enemy activity significantly increases we might have to adjust our timetable accordingly.

However, I want the record to be completely clear on one point.

At the time of the bombing halt just a year ago, there was some confusion as to whether there was an understanding on the part of the enemy that if we stopped the bombing of North Vietnam they would stop the shelling of cities in South Vietnam. I want to be sure that there is no misunderstanding on the part of the enemy with regard to our withdrawal program.

We have noted the reduced level of infiltration, the reduction of our casualties, and are basing our withdrawal decisions partially on those factors. If the level of infiltration or our casualties increase while we are trying to scale down the fighting, it will be the result of a conscious decision by the enemy.

Hanoi could make no greater mistake than to assume that an increase in violence will be to its advantage. If I conclude that increased enemy action jeopardizes our remaining forces in Vietnam, I shall not hesitate to take strong and effective measures to deal with that situation.

This is not a threat. This is a statement of policy, which as Commander in Chief of our Armed Forces, I am making in meeting my responsibility for the protection of American fighting men wherever they may be.

My fellow Americans, I am sure you can recognize from what I have said that we really only have two choices open to us if we want to end this war.

- I can order an immediate, precipitate withdrawal of all Americans from Vietnam without regard to the effects of that action.

- Or we can persist in our search for a just peace through a negotiated settlement if possible, or through continued implementation of our plan for Vietnamization if necessary, a plan in which we will withdraw all of our forces from Vietnam on a schedule in accordance with our program, as the South Vietnamese become strong enough to defend their own freedom.

I have chosen this second course. It is not the easy way. It is the right way.

It is a plan which will end the war and serve the cause of peace—not just in Vietnam but in the Pacific and in the world.

In speaking of the consequences of a precipitate withdrawal, I mentioned that our allies would lose confidence in America.

Far more dangerous, we would lose confidence in ourselves. Oh, the immediate reaction would be a sense of relief that our men were coming home. But as we saw the consequences of what we had done, inevitable remorse and divisive recrimination would scar our spirit as a people.

We have faced other crises in our history and have become stronger by rejecting the easy way out and taking the right way in meeting our challenges. Our greatness as a nation has been our capacity to do what had to be done when we knew our course was right.

I recognize that some of my fellow citizens disagree with the plan for peace I have chosen. Honest and patriotic Americans have reached different conclusions as to how peace should be achieved.

In San Francisco a few weeks ago, I saw demonstrators carrying signs reading: "Lose in Vietnam, bring the boys home."

Well, one of the strengths of our free society is that any American has a right to reach that conclusion and to advocate that point of view. But as President of the United States, I would be untrue to my oath of office if I allowed the policy of this Nation to be dictated by the minority who hold that point of view and who try to impose it on the Nation by mounting demonstrations in the street.

For almost 200 years, the policy of this Nation has been made under our Constitution by those leaders in the Congress and the White House elected by all of the people. If a vocal minority, however fervent its cause, prevails over reason and the will of the majority, this Nation has no future as a free society.

And now I would like to address a word, if I may, to the young people of this Nation who are particularly concerned, and I understand why they are concerned, about this war.

I respect your idealism. I share your concern for peace. I want peace as much as you do. There are powerful personal reasons I want to end this war. This week I will have to sign 83 letters to mothers, fathers, wives, and loved ones of men who have given their lives for America in Vietnam. It is very little satisfaction to me that this is only one-third as many letters as I signed the first week in office. There is nothing I want more than to see the day come when I do not have to write any of those letters.

I want to end the war to save the lives of those brave young men in Vietnam.

But I want to end it in a way which will increase the chance that their younger brothers and their sons will not have to fight in some future Vietnam someplace in the world.

And I want to end the war for another reason. I want to end it so that the energy and dedication of you, our young people, now too often directed into bitter hatred against those responsible for the war, can be turned to the great challenges of peace, a better life for all Americans, a better life for all people on this earth.

I have chosen a plan for peace. I believe it will succeed.

If it does succeed, what the critics say now won't matter. If it does not succeed, anything I say then won't matter.

I know it may not be fashionable to speak of patriotism or national destiny these days. But I feel it is appropriate to do so on this occasion.

Two hundred years ago this Nation was weak and poor. But even then, America was the hope of millions in the world. Today we have become the strongest and richest nation in the world. And the wheel of destiny has turned so that any hope the world has for the survival of peace and freedom will be determined by whether the American people have the moral stamina and the courage to meet the challenge of free world leadership.

Let historians not record that when America was the most powerful nation in the world we passed on the other side of the road and allowed the last hopes for peace and freedom of millions of people to be suffocated by the forces of totalitarianism.

And so tonight—to you, the great silent majority of my fellow Americans—I ask for your support.

I pledged in my campaign for the Presidency to end the war in a way that we could win the peace. I have initiated a plan of action which will enable me to keep that pledge.

The more support I can have from the American people, the sooner that pledge can be redeemed; for the more divided we are at home, the less likely the enemy is to negotiate at Paris.

Let us be united for peace. Let us also be united against defeat. Because let us understand: North Vietnam cannot defeat or humiliate the United States. Only Americans can do that.

Fifty years ago, in this room and at this very desk, President Woodrow Wilson spoke words which caught the imagination of a war-weary world. He said: "This is the war to end war." His dream for peace after World War I was shattered on the hard realities of great power politics and Woodrow Wilson died a broken man.

Tonight I do not tell you that the war in Vietnam is the war to end wars. But I do say this: I have initiated a plan which will end this war in a way that will bring us closer to that great goal to which Woodrow Wilson and every American President in our history has been dedicated—the goal of a just and lasting peace.

As President I hold the responsibility for choosing the best path to that goal and then leading the Nation along it. I pledge to you tonight that I shall meet this responsibility with all of the strength and wisdom I can command in accordance with our hopes, mindful of your concerns, sustained by your prayers.

Thank you and goodnight.

Document Analysis

The day after his speech a number of municipal and state elections were held in which Republican and other conservative candidates did well. Nixon pointed to this as evidence that the silent majority of Americans supported him and his policies. This was, in Nixon's view, one of the rare speeches that change the course of history.

The White House received 50,000 telegrams and 30,000 letters praising the speech. An overnight poll showed support for his Vietnam policy rising to 77 percent after the speech, from 58 percent before. This was the highest rating that Nixon would receive during his first term for his handling of the war. It was not entirely a coincidence. The Nixon White House had an unprecedented apparatus for measuring and influencing public opinion, which involved both in-house and commercial polling operations. In addition to keeping close track of trends in opinion, the administration would propose "loaded" questions in order to boost favorable responses. (A 1970 survey allegedly intended to gauge the public reaction to the Cambodia incursion asked, "Do you support the president's action to end the war in Vietnam, to avoid getting into a war in Cambodia, to protect U.S. troops?") In this case, the administration sought to preempt opinion in a variety of ways. For instance, the White House—according to court testimony thirty years later, in 1999, by former Nixon aide Alexander Butterworth—solicited positive letters and telegrams from labor unions, the Veterans of Foreign Wars, the American Legion, Air Force retirees, governors, and state Republican chairmen. (Butterworth described the response as "contrived" but sincere.) White House chief of staff (and former advertising executive) H. R. Haldeman reported in his diary that, on the night of the speech, the president ordered him to "get 100 vicious dirty calls to *New York Times* and *Washington Post* about their editorials (even though no idea what they'll be)." Nixon always assumed the press would be negative.

The polling surge, however, was short lived, lasting about two weeks. So was the mail campaign. Three weeks after the speech, the number of antiwar letters to the White House outnumbered supportive letters once again.

Essential Themes

In mid-October, when Nixon sat down to write the first draft his November 3 speech, he started with a note to himself. He scrawled across the top of his note pad: "Don't Get Rattled—Don't Waver—Don't React."

The speech began with Nixon's assertion that he was interested in peace, but specified that he intended to "win" the peace. After briefly reviewing the origins of the war in a manner that overlooked any US responsibility, he detailed reasons why the United States had to stay in the war. ("For the future of peace, precipitate withdrawal would thus be a disaster of immense magnitude. . . . It would not bring peace; it would bring more war.") And, to be sure, exiting an ongoing war without strongly adverse consequences is not a simple matter.

Nixon outlined the conciliatory steps that he was prepared to take and his willingness to discuss the other side's proposals, attributing the failure to make progress fully to the North Vietnamese. At that point, he shifted the discussion to the policy of Vietnamization, which he described as an aspect of the Nixon Doctrine (or Guam Doctrine), which he had first proclaimed on the island of Guam on July 25, 1969. The Nixon Doctrine was a plan to minimize US intervention in the developing world by building up local allies ("pillars of stability") to defend themselves and to police their own respective regions with the support of the United States. Thus the United States would arm, train, and equip the military forces of South Vietnam so that they could fight their own battles. This would permit the United States to initiate a gradual withdrawal of its forces, a process that had already begun. Eventually, he said, all US forces would be removed "on an orderly scheduled timetable," although he did indicate the length of that timetable. The timing would be tied to conditions on the ground: the strength of ARVN, the reduction in US casualties, and the level of infiltration of enemy forces into South Vietnam. With his plan, he offered something both to those who did not want to give up on the Vietnam War and to those who wanted more than anything to leave the war behind.

Finally, contrasting his proposal to a hasty and calamitous abandoning of an ally, he distinguished between the "vocal minority" of Americans who protested the war and demanded an immediate exit and the "great silent majority" who supported his approach, whom he identified with reason, and upon whose political support he would rely. At the same time, he saw in this division (but mostly in the war's opponents) grave threats not only to the war effort, but to the future of the United States itself. ("If a vocal minority, however fervent its cause, prevails over reason and the will of the majority, this Nation has no future as a free society. . . . North Vietnam cannot defeat or humiliate the United States. Only Americans can do that.")

—*Scott C. Monje, PhD*

Bibliography and Additional Reading

Berman, Larry. *No Peace, No Honor: Nixon, Kissinger, and Betrayal in Vietnam.* New York: Free Press, 2001. Print.

Campbell, Karlyn Kohrs. *The Great Silent Majority: Nixon's 1969 Speech on Vietnamization.* College Station, TX: Texas A&M University Press, 2014. Print.

Haldeman, H. R. *The Haldeman Diaries: Inside the Nixon White House.* New York: Putnam's, 1994. Print.

Katz, Andrew Z. "Public Opinion and Foreign Policy: The Nixon Administration and the Pursuit of Peace with Honor in Vietnam." *Presidential Studies Quarterly* 27.3 (Summer 1997): 496–513. Print.

Kimball, Jeffrey. *Nixon's Vietnam War.* Lawrence, KS: University Press of Kansas, 1998. Print.

Perlstein, Rick. *Nixonland: The Rise of a President and the Fracturing of America.* New York: Scribner, 2008. Print.

Rottinghaus, Brandon. "'Dear Mr. President': The Institutionalization and Politicization of Public Opinion Mail in the White House." *Political Science Quarterly* 121.3 (2006): 451–76. Print.

■ Nixon on Operations in Cambodia

Date: April 30, 1970
Genre: address
Author: Richard M. Nixon

Summary Overview

President Richard Nixon, upon assuming office in 1969, began implementing his program of "Vietnamization" in which US ground troops would be gradually withdrawn and replaced by newly trained South Vietnamese troops. In the spring of 1970, Nixon turned his attention to neutral Cambodia, where the North Vietnamese and Viet Cong had long maintained military sanctuaries on the border with South Vietnam. Nixon believed the communist presence in eastern Cambodia posed a threat to both the Cambodian government and the U.S.-backed government in South Vietnam, as well as threatened Vietnamization. Nixon made the controversial decision to order a joint US-South Vietnamese invasion of Cambodia to attempt to wipe out these communist sanctuaries. Nixon's announcement of the decision in his address to the nation on April 30, 1970 sparked the largest wave of campus protests in US history, which included the tragic shooting deaths of students at Kent State in Ohio and Jackson State in Mississippi.

Defining Moment

The 1954 Geneva Accords, which divided Vietnam into North and South pending elections (that never occurred), also established the neutrality of Cambodia. Nevertheless, during the Vietnam War the North Vietnamese and Viet Cong maintained scattered bases—"military sanctuaries"—throughout the sparsely populated and densely forested sections of eastern Cambodia, from which they could supply their forces in South Vietnam as well as carry out cross-border raids.

Cambodian leader Prince Norodom Sihanouk had to conduct a delicate balancing act to maintain Cambodia's official neutrality. Openly supporting North Vietnam could incur the anger of the United States and cause the Vietnam War to spill over into Cambodia, and challenging the North Vietnamese/Viet Cong sanctuaries might provoke the North Vietnamese into

supporting the Cambodian communist Khmer Rouge and toppling Sihanouk. Sihanouk decided to overlook the communist sanctuaries, which he felt little power to remove, while professing official neutrality.

Nixon went after these communist sanctuaries in Cambodia early in his presidency with a top secret B-52 bombing campaign called "Operation Menu." Nixon knew open military action would be regarded as a violation of Cambodia's neutrality and the Gulf of Tonkin Resolution passed by Congress in 1964, which authorized military action only in Vietnam. Furthermore, at a time when the American public believed the US was winding down its war in Vietnam, an openly acknowledged expansion of the war into Cambodia could spark massive antiwar protests.

By the spring of 1970, however, Prince Sihanouk had been overthrown by a pro-American Cambodian general named Lon Nol and the North Vietnamese fought Cambodian Army forces for the first time. Nixon and his national security advisor Henry Kissinger now made the controversial decision to order a US and South Vietnamese military incursion into Cambodia.

In his April 30, 1970 address Nixon argued these sanctuaries needed to be wiped out to protect US troops during Vietnamization and uphold America's credibility. Failure to act, Nixon declared, would make the United States appear to be a "pitiful and helpless giant." Nixon's announcement sparked a firestorm of criticism and an explosion of campus protests that culminated in the largest student strike in US history and the killings at Kent State and Jackson State. The Cambodia operation lasted until the end of June, and while successfully destroying some communist bases and ammunition depots, the North Vietnamese and Viet Cong were soon back in their sanctuaries.

Author Biography

Richard Milhous Nixon was born in Yorba Linda, California, on January 9, 1913. He attended Whittier College and Duke University Law School. During World II, Nixon served in the Navy in a non-combat role in the Pacific Theater. He was elected as a Republican to the United States House of Representatives from a California district in 1946 and to the US Senate in 1950. Nixon served as vice president under President Dwight D. Eisenhower from 1953–1961. He lost his bid for president to John F. Kennedy in 1960. In 1962, he lost a run for California governor. Nixon was elected president of the United States in 1968 and re-elected by a landslide in 1972. On August 9, 1974, amidst the Watergate scandal, Nixon became the first president in US history to resign from the presidency. Nixon died on April 22, 1994.

HISTORICAL DOCUMENT

Good evening my fellow Americans:

Ten days ago, in my report to the Nation on Vietnam, I announced a decision to withdraw an additional 150,000 Americans from Vietnam over the next year. I said then that I was making that decision despite our concern over increased enemy activity in Laos, in Cambodia, and in South Vietnam.

At that time, I warned that if I concluded that increased enemy activity in any of these areas endangered the lives of Americans remaining in Vietnam, I would not hesitate to take strong and effective measures to deal with that situation.

Despite that warning, North Vietnam has increased its military aggression in all these areas, and particularly in Cambodia.

After full consultation with the National Security Council, Ambassador Bunker, General Abrams, and my other advisers, I have concluded that the actions of the enemy in the last 10 days clearly endanger the lives of Americans who are in Vietnam now and would constitute an unacceptable risk to those who will be there after withdrawal of another 150,000.

To protect our men who are in Vietnam and to guarantee the continued success of our withdrawal and Vietnamization programs, I have concluded that the time has come for action.

Tonight, I shall describe the actions of the enemy, the actions I have ordered to deal with that situation, and the reasons for my decision.

Cambodia, a small country of 7 million people, has been a neutral nation since the Geneva agreement of 1954—an agreement, incidentally, which was signed by the Government of North Vietnam.

American policy since then has been to scrupulously respect the neutrality of the Cambodian people. We have maintained a skeleton diplomatic mission of fewer than 15 in Cambodia's capital, and that only since last August. For the previous 4 years, from 1965 to 1969, we did not have any diplomatic mission whatever in Cambodia. And for the past 5 years, we have provided no military assistance whatever and no economic assistance to Cambodia.

North Vietnam, however, has not respected that neutrality.

For the past 5 years—as indicated on this map that you see here—North Vietnam has occupied military sanctuaries all along the Cambodian frontier with South Vietnam. Some of these extend up to 20 miles into Cambodia. The sanctuaries are in red and, as you note, they are on both sides of the border. They are used for hit and run attacks on American and South Vietnamese forces in South Vietnam.

These Communist occupied territories contain major base camps, training sites, logistics facilities, weapons and ammunition factories, airstrips, and prisoner-of-war compounds.

For 5 years, neither the United States nor South Vietnam has moved against these enemy sanctuaries because we did not wish to violate the territory of a neutral nation. Even after the Vietnamese Communists began to expand these sanctuaries 4 weeks ago, we counseled patience to our South Vietnamese allies and imposed restraints on our own commanders.

In contrast to our policy, the enemy in the past 2 weeks has stepped up his guerrilla actions and he is concentrating his main forces in these sanctuaries that you see on this map where they are building up to launch massive attacks on our forces and those of South Vietnam.

North Vietnam in the last 2 weeks has stripped away all pretense of respecting the sovereignty or the neutrality of Cambodia. Thousands of their soldiers are invading the country from the sanctuaries; they are encircling the capital of Phnom Penh. Coming from these sanctuaries, as you see here, they have moved into Cambodia and are encircling the capital.

Cambodia, as a result of this, has sent out a call to the United States, to a number of other nations, for assistance. Because if this enemy effort succeeds, Cambodia would become a vast enemy staging area and a springboard for attacks on South Vietnam along 600 miles of frontier—a refuge where enemy troops could return from combat without fear of retaliation.

North Vietnamese men and supplies could then be poured into that country, jeopardizing not only the lives of our own men but the people of South Vietnam as well.

Now confronted with this situation, we have three options.

First, we can do nothing. Well, the ultimate result of that course of action is clear. Unless we indulge in wishful thinking, the lives of Americans remaining in Vietnam after our next withdrawal of 150,000 would be gravely threatened.

Let us go to the map again. Here is South Vietnam. Here is North Vietnam. North Vietnam already occupies this part of Laos. If North Vietnam also occupied this whole band in Cambodia, or the entire country, it would mean that South Vietnam was completely outflanked and the forces of Americans in this area, as well as the South Vietnamese, would be in an untenable military position.

Our second choice is to provide massive military assistance to Cambodia itself. Now unfortunately, while we deeply sympathize with the plight of 7 million Cambodians whose country is being invaded, massive amounts of military assistance could not be rapidly and effectively utilized by the small Cambodian Army against the immediate threat. With other nations, we shall do our best to provide the small arms and other equipment which the Cambodian Army of 40,000 needs and can use for its defense. But the aid we will provide will be limited to the purpose of enabling Cambodia to defend its neutrality and not for the purpose of making it an active belligerent on one side or the other.

Our third choice is to go to the heart of the trouble. That means cleaning out major North Vietnamese and Vietcong occupied territories—these sanctuaries which serve as bases for attacks on both Cambodia and American and South Vietnamese forces in South Vietnam. Some of these, incidentally, are as close to Saigon as Baltimore is to Washington. This one, for example [indicating], is called the Parrot's Beak. It is only 33 miles from Saigon.

Now faced with these three options, this is the decision I have made.

In cooperation with the armed forces of South Vietnam, attacks are being launched this week to clean out major enemy sanctuaries on the Cambodian-Vietnam border.

A major responsibility for the ground operations is being assumed by South Vietnamese forces. For example, the attacks in several areas, including the Parrot's Beak that I referred to a moment ago, are exclusively South Vietnamese ground operations under South Vietnamese command with the United States providing air and logistical support.

There is one area, however, immediately above Parrot's Beak, where I have concluded that a combined American and South Vietnamese operation is necessary.

Tonight, American and South Vietnamese units will attack the headquarters for the entire Communist military operation in South Vietnam. This key control center has been occupied by the North Vietnamese and Vietcong for 5 years in blatant violation of Cambodia's neutrality.

This is not an invasion of Cambodia. The areas in which these attacks will be launched are completely occupied and controlled by North Vietnamese forces. Our purpose is not to occupy the areas. Once enemy forces are driven out of these sanctuaries and once their military supplies are destroyed, we will withdraw.

These actions are in no way directed to the security interests of any nation. Any government that chooses to use these actions as a pretext for harming relations with the United States will be doing so on its own responsibility, and on its own initiative, and we will draw the appropriate conclusions.

Now let me give you the reasons for my decision.

A majority of the American people, a majority of you listening to me, are for the withdrawal of our forces from Vietnam. The action I have taken tonight is indispensable for the continuing success of that withdrawal program.

A majority of the American people want to end this war rather than to have it drag on interminably. The action I have taken tonight will serve that purpose.

A majority of the American people want to keep the casualties of our brave men in Vietnam at an absolute minimum. The action I take tonight is essential if we are to accomplish that goal.

We take this action not for the purpose of expanding the war into Cambodia but for the purpose of ending the war in Vietnam and winning the just peace we all desire. We have made—we will continue to make every possible effort to end this war through negotiation at the conference table rather than through more fighting on the battlefield.

Let us look again at the record. We have stopped the bombing of North Vietnam. We have cut air operations by over 20 percent. We have announced withdrawal of over 250,000 of our men. We have offered to withdraw all of our men if they will withdraw theirs. We have offered to negotiate all issues with only one condition—and that is that the future of South Vietnam be determined not by North Vietnam, and not by the United States, but by the people of South Vietnam themselves.

The answer of the enemy has been intransigence at the conference table, belligerence in Hanoi, massive military aggression in Laos and Cambodia, and stepped-up attacks in South Vietnam, designed to increase American casualties.

This attitude has become intolerable. We will not react to this threat to American lives merely by plaintive diplomatic protests. If we did, the credibility of the United States would be destroyed in every area of the world where only the power of the United States deters aggression.

Tonight, I again warn the North Vietnamese that if they continue to escalate the fighting when the United States is withdrawing its forces, I shall meet my responsibility as Commander in Chief of our Armed Forces to take the action I consider necessary to defend the security of our American men.

The action that I have announced tonight puts the leaders of North Vietnam on notice that we will be patient in working for peace; we will be conciliatory at the conference table, but we will not be humiliated. We will not be defeated. We will not allow American men by the thousands to be killed by an enemy from privileged sanctuaries.

The time came long ago to end this war through peaceful negotiations. We stand ready for those negotiations. We have made major efforts, many of which must remain secret. I say tonight: All the offers and approaches made previously remain on the conference table whenever Hanoi is ready to negotiate seriously.

But if the enemy response to our most conciliatory offers for peaceful negotiation continues to be to increase its attacks and humiliate and defeat us, we shall react accordingly.

My fellow Americans, we live in an age of anarchy, both abroad and at home. We see mindless attacks on all the great institutions which have been created by free civilizations in the last 500 years. Even here in the United States, great universities are being systematically destroyed. Small nations all over the world find themselves under attack from within and from without.

If, when the chips are down, the world's most powerful nation, the United States of America, acts like a pitiful, helpless giant, the forces of totalitarianism and anarchy will threaten free nations and free institutions throughout the world.

It is not our power but our will and character that is being tested tonight. The question all Americans must ask and answer tonight is this: Does the richest and strongest nation in the history of the world have the character to meet a direct challenge by a group which rejects every effort to win a just peace, ignores our warning, tramples on solemn agreements, violates the neutrality of an unarmed people, and uses our prisoners as hostages?

If we fail to meet this challenge, all other nations will be on notice that despite its overwhelming power the United States, when a real crisis comes, will be found wanting.

During my campaign for the Presidency, I pledged to bring Americans home from Vietnam. They are coming home.

I promised to end this war. I shall keep that promise.

I promised to win a just peace. I shall keep that promise.

We shall avoid a wider war. But we are also determined to put an end to this war.

In this room, Woodrow Wilson made the great decisions which led to victory in World War I. Franklin Roosevelt made the decisions which led to our victory in World War II. Dwight D. Eisenhower made decisions which ended the war in Korea and avoided war in the Middle East. John F. Kennedy, in his finest hour, made the great decision which removed Soviet nuclear missiles from Cuba and the Western Hemisphere.

I have noted that there has been a great deal of discussion with regard to this decision that I have made and I should point out that I do not contend that it is in the same magnitude as these decisions that I have just mentioned. But between those decisions and this decision there is a difference that is very fundamental. In those decisions, the American people were not assailed by counsels of doubt and defeat from some of the most widely known opinion leaders of the Nation.

I have noted, for example, that a Republican Senator has said that this action I have taken means that my party has lost all chance of winning the November elections. And others are saying today that this move against enemy sanctuaries will make me a one-term President.

No one is more aware than I am of the political consequences of the action I have taken. It is tempting to take the easy political path: to blame this war on previous administrations and to bring all of our men home immediately, regardless of the consequences, even though that would mean defeat for the United States; to desert 18 million South Vietnamese people, who have put their trust in us and to expose them to the same slaughter and savagery which the leaders of North Vietnam inflicted on hundreds of thousands of North Vietnamese who chose freedom when the Communists took over North Vietnam in 1954; to get peace at any price now, even though I know that a peace of humiliation for the United States would lead to a bigger war or surrender later.

I have rejected all political considerations in making this decision.

Whether my party gains in November is nothing compared to the lives of 400,000 brave Americans fighting for our country and for the cause of peace and freedom in Vietnam. Whether I may be a one-term President is insignificant compared to whether by our failure to act in this crisis the United States proves itself to be unworthy to lead the forces of freedom in this critical period in world history. I would rather be a one-term President and do what I believe is right than to be a two-term President at the cost of seeing America become a second-rate power and to see this Nation accept the first defeat in its proud 190-year history.

I realize that in this war there are honest and deep differences in this country about whether we should have become involved, that there are differences as to how the war should have been conducted. But the decision I announce tonight transcends those differences. For the lives of American men are involved. The opportunity for Americans to come home in the next 12 months is involved. The future of 18 million people in South Vietnam and 7 million people in Cambodia is involved. The possibility of winning a just peace in Vietnam and in the Pacific is at stake.

It is customary to conclude a speech from the White House by asking support for the President of the United States. Tonight, I depart from that precedent. What I ask is far more important. I ask for your support for our brave men fighting tonight halfway around the world-not for territory—not for glory—but so that their younger brothers and their sons and your sons can have a chance to grow up in a world of peace and freedom and justice.

Thank you and good night.

Document Analysis

President Richard Nixon's address announcing United States and South Vietnamese incursions into Cambodia proceeds on two levels. First, Nixon outlines the objective of the operation and lays out reasons for it that are consistent with his earlier promises to reduce US involvement in the Vietnam War. Here, Nixon argues he must temporarily expand the war in order to successfully execute Vietnamization. Second, he elevates his decision to go into Cambodia to the level of an epic struggle between freedom and the forces of "totalitarianism" and "anarchy" at home and abroad.

Nixon begins by noting his earlier announcement that 150,000 US troops would be withdrawn from South Vietnam over the next year. He states this withdrawal is threatened by the communist presence in base camps in eastern Cambodia. Only by wiping out these camps, he argues, can the US safely carry out its draw down in South Vietnam.

Nixon then asserts United States policy had been to "scrupulously respect the neutrality of the Cambodian people." Here the president is misleading the American public. Soon after assuming the presidency, Nixon had ordered the top secret "Operation Menu," which consisted of heavy bombing of communist sanctuaries in Cambodia as well as secret cross-border ground operations. These secret operations would not be revealed until 1973 amidst Congressional investigations into the Watergate scandal (some members of Congress wanted the illegal forays into Cambodia to be added to the other proposed articles of impeachment.)

Nixon puts full blame upon North Vietnam, which violated Cambodia's neutrality by setting up bases there. While correct in his description of the role of the communist sanctuaries, Nixon overstates their importance when he declares them "the headquarters for the entire Communist military operation in South Vietnam."

The most remarkable part of the address is when Nixon ties his Cambodian decision to a global struggle against totalitarianism and anarchy. Nixon links what he sees as communist aggression overseas to the antiwar movement in America, which he accuses of "systematically" destroying great universities and "institutions created by free civilizations in the last 500 years." Nixon condemns protesters in America, whom he privately blamed for constraining his latitude for action in Vietnam. In the address's most memorable line, Nixon declares, "If, when the chips are down, the world's most powerful nation, the United States of America, acts like a pitiful, helpless giant, the forces of totalitarianism and anarchy will threaten free nations and free institutions throughout the world." Here, the president, as in his "Silent Majority" speech the previous fall, is addressing those he regards as patriotic, mainstream Americans as opposed to radicals and liberals.

Nixon concludes by seeking to highlight the bravery of his decision. He compares himself to previous presidents making momentous decisions, but states that they, unlike him, were not assailed by voices of protest and doubt. He seeks to elevate the courage of his decision even more by asserting that his party may lose seats in upcoming elections and that he may be a one-term president, but he'd rather suffer the political consequences than see America reduced to a "second-rate power."

Essential Themes

Nixon argues he must order the invasion of Cambodia to safeguard America's slow withdrawal of combat troops from the war in South Vietnam. He places the blame for his action squarely on the North Vietnamese and Viet Cong. He asserts the operation will be of short duration and restricted to the limited objectives of removing Communist sanctuaries.

The decision to cross into Cambodia is linked to what the president feels is a global struggle between freedom and totalitarianism/anarchy. Nixon returns repeatedly to the theme that failure to act will result in the United States' humiliation and defeat. Note the number of times Nixon uses variations on the word "humiliation" and images of weakness and impotence in his address. Like President Lyndon B. Johnson before him, Nixon feared failure in Vietnam would spell humiliation for himself personally and the United States.

Nixon anticipates that his controversial decision to go into Cambodia will trigger condemnation and protest. Thus, Nixon portrays his decision as that of a courageous president acting alone for the good of the country despite political repercussions for himself or his party. Nevertheless, Nixon and his advisors failed to anticipate the full scale and fury of the protests his decision would spark. Within weeks, hundreds of campuses would be shut down by the largest explosion of protests throughout the whole war, and students would be shot dead at Kent State and Jackson State. And after the Cambodia operation, the communists slowly returned to their sanctuaries.

—*Robert Surbrug, PhD*

Bibliography and Additional Readings

Dallek, Robert. *Nixon and Kissinger: Partners in Power.* New York: HarperCollins P., 2007. Print.

Karnow, Stanley. *Vietnam: A History.* New York: Penguin Books, 1984. Print.

Shawcross, William, *Sideshow: Nixon, Kissinger and the Destruction of Cambodia.* New York: Simon and Schuster, 1979. Print.

Vietnam: A Television History: Episode 8, "Laos and Cambodia." Dir. Judith Vecchione, Austin Hoyt, Martin Smith, & Bruce Palling. Nar. Will Lyman. Boston: WGBH, 1983. Documentary.

Young, Marilyn B. *The Vietnam Wars, 1945–1990.* New York: HarperPerennial, 1991. Print.

■ Taped Conversation between Nixon and Kissinger

Date: August 3, 1972
Author: Richard M. Nixon, Henry Kissinger
Genre: discussion; transcript

Summary Overview

In the summer of 1972, President Nixon's mind was on his upcoming reelection. Although his public approval rating was high, Nixon still worried about his legacy. Expanded military operations in Cambodia stirred increasingly violent demonstrations at home: Nixon won no popularity contests when four students were killed during a 1970 protest at Kent State University. Additionally, decreased troop morale, desertion, and increased fragging (killing of another soldier or commander, usually by fragmentation grenade) weakened the US armed forces in Vietnam. Determined to preserve his own and the United States' prestige, Nixon and his national security advisor, Henry Kissinger, discussed their options in a private, taped meeting. The men discussed delaying the end of US involvement for a "decent interval" until a weak and corrupt government in South Vietnam could justifiably take the blame for its own downfall in the media. The revelation of this tape after the end of the war seemed to support the picture of Nixon and Kissinger as *realpolitik* strategists, who subordinated individual suffering to the needs of the state.

Defining Moment

Nixon and Kissinger inherited a difficult situation in Vietnam from their predecessors. Deception, intransigence, and stalling tactics on both sides characterized the ceasefire negotiations between Saigon and Hanoi. South Vietnam's president Nguyen Van Thiêu was subject to the United States' demands in order to maintain his government's legitimacy. Often relying on Soviet and Chinese support, North Vietnam pressed for the removal of Thiêu and the coalition government. Hanoi's proposals were unacceptable for the United States: the "leader of the free world" could not tolerate communist government after supporting their opponents for so long. At the time of this private conversation between the American president and foreign policy advisor, the United States had mediated negotiations for nearly four years.

Rather than give in to an embarrassing compromise, the Nixon administration secretly decided to stall for a "decent interval" until both the presidential election was concluded and Saigon could be blamed for its own defeat. The conversation between Nixon and Kissinger exemplifies an increasingly pragmatic and pessimistic trend in American foreign policy. South Vietnam was no longer as important to Nixon's image as it had been in Nixon's first presidential campaign. By 1972, several events complicated the status of American foreign relations. First, as part of a plan to gain leverage over the Soviets, Nixon planned a historic trip to reopen relations with communist China in February. Nixon then met with Soviet leader Leonid Brezhnev in May: the two opposed nations signed a series of agreements in a stunning moment of détente, a period of less strained political relations between the United States and Soviet Russia. Finally, an aggressive campaign designed by North Vietnam to improve their bargaining position in peace talks (the Easter Offensive) occupied American and South Vietnamese military corps from March–October 1972.

Although audiotapes of White House conversations did not begin with Nixon, his implementation of automatic voice-activated recordings was more extensive and secretive. The revelation of the scope and content on these tapes after the investigation of the Watergate scandal would inextricably link Nixon's administration to a history of secrecy and manipulation. Kissinger, too, as participant in such machinations, would tarnish his reputation as peacemaker by the information revealed in these tapes.

Author Biography

Richard M. Nixon showed himself to be a political opportunist from 1950–60 both as a member of Congress and as Eisenhower's vice president by encouraging anti-communist hysteria. Nixon returned to power with the presidency in 1968 by capitalizing on dissension among the Democrats over the unpopular Vietnam War. Citing the need to win "peace with honor" to the public, Nixon was privately intent on maintaining his own popularity and the United States' leadership at any cost. Disparities between Nixon's public promises to curb the war and covert, escalated bombing stirred US dissatisfaction. As a result, Nixon increased pressure on his advisor Kissinger to find a formula to resolve the war.

Henry Kissinger, a Jewish immigrant from Nazi Germany, served in the US military during World War II. Afterwards, he attained his PhD in political science at Harvard in 1954 and then involved himself as an advisor in several different political capacities. As Nixon's national security advisor, Kissinger conducted negotiations to reduce American involvement and end the war in Vietnam. Although Kissinger would eventually receive the Nobel Peace Prize in 1973 for his participation in the Paris Peace Accords, bombardment continued in Vietnam.

HISTORICAL DOCUMENT

President Nixon: Now, let's look at that just a moment again, think about it some more, but let's be perfectly cold-blooded about it. If you look at it from the standpoint of our game with the Soviets and the Chinese, from the standpoint of running this country, I think we could take, in my view, almost anything, frankly, that we can force on Thiêu. Almost anything. I just come down to that. You know what I mean? Because I have a feeling we would not be doing, like I feel about the Israeli, I feel that in the long run we're probably not doing them an in—uh . . . a disfavor due to the fact that I feel that the North Vietnamese are so badly hurt that the South Vietnamese are probably going to do fairly well. [Kissinger attempts to interject.] But also due to the fact—because I look at the tide of history out there—South Vietnam probably can never even survive anyway. I'm just being perfectly candid. I—

Henry A. Kissinger: In the pull-out area—

President Nixon: [Unclear] we've got to be—if we can get certain guarantees so that they aren't . . . as you know, looking at the foreign policy process, though, I mean, you've got to be—we also have to realize, Henry, that winning an election is terribly important. It's terribly important this year—but can we have a viable foreign policy if a year from now or two years from now, North Vietnam gobbles up South Vietnam? That's the real question.

Kissinger: If a year or two years from now North Vietnam gobbles up South Vietnam, we can have a viable foreign policy if it looks as if it's the result of South Vietnamese incompetence. If we now sell out in such a way that, say, within a three- to four-month period, we have pushed President Thiêu over the brink—we ourselves—I think, there is going to be—even the Chinese won't like that. I mean, they'll pay verbal—verbally, they'll like it.

President Nixon: But it'll worry them.
Kissinger: But it will worry everybody. And domestically in the long run it won't help us all that much because our opponents will say we should've done it three years ago.

President Nixon: I know.
Kissinger: So we've got to find some formula that holds the thing together a year or two, after which—after a year, Mr. President, Vietnam will be a backwater. If we settle it, say, this October, by January '74 no one will give a damn.

President Nixon: Yeah, having in mind the fact that, you know, as we all know, the—the analogy—comparison [to] Algeria is not on—is not at all for us. But on the other hand, nobody gives a goddamn about what happened to Algeria—
Kissinger: Mm-hmm.

President Nixon: —after they got out. [chuckling] You know what I mean? But Vietnam, I must say . . . Jesus, they've fought so long, dying, and now . . . I don't know.

Document Analysis

Nixon won his first presidential term by manipulating the South Vietnamese president, Thiêu, into delaying peace talk concessions in 1968; the incumbent president won his second term in part by yet again manipulating events in South Vietnam. If Kissinger could delay a resolution about a ceasefire in Vietnam until Nixon won reelection, This conversation, secretly recorded before the results of the 1972 election, shows that Kissinger and Nixon entertained notions of political expediency and fatalism in their approach to foreign affairs.

First, the conversation between the two men shows that they considered South Vietnam part of a small piece in a larger game. "Let's be perfectly cold-blooded about it," Nixon says to Kissinger. The US had been playing a game with Soviet Russia and China since the 1950s, and Thiêu was merely a pawn on whom the Americans could force "almost anything" in the negotiations. Additionally, Nixon tells Kissinger: "winning an election is terribly important," but he gives no other reason for its importance than having a "viable foreign policy." Kissinger responds that the Chinese and domestic opponents would not look favorably on them if they could blame Saigon's collapse on the Nixon administration. Absent from these remarks are the earlier rhetorical ploys about the need to win "peace with honor" and the "silent majority" who believed in the war. By a certain point, Kissinger asserts, the administration can preserve its power at Saigon's expense, and no one in the American public "will give a damn."

In addition to showing that the American government's interests justify the means, this conversation indicates that Nixon believed in a postcolonial fatalism that doomed Saigon before he came to office. The president recognizes that even though the Easter Offensive caused a great amount of damage to North Vietnam, "South Vietnam probably can never survive anyway." In the course of the conversation, Nixon mentions both the Israelis and the Algerians, two groups who were fighting or had struggled over sovereignty with different, but disastrous, results. Of course, the United States was not fighting for its own independence in Vietnam. The fact that Nixon states "nobody gives a goddamn about what happened in Algeria" connects his fatalism back again to a political philosophy that expediency was morally justified for a world superpower. The French left the Algerians to kill each other after independence; the same thing would likely happen in Vietnam. If the United States and China no longer cared about Saigon's fated

fall, then it was no longer necessary to preserve South Vietnam against its opponents.

Finally, this taped conversation is another piece of evidence that Kissinger and Nixon were anxious about the legacy the administration would leave. However, Nixon's closing words do prove that the man was capable of comprehending the scale of human suffering. "Jesus, they've fought for so long, dying, and now…I don't know," remarks Nixon. Behind the "decent interval" strategy lay not only calculated policy, but also *aporia*—doubt or puzzlement—after years of no political progress.

Essential Themes

The extent of Nixon and Kissinger's secret plans were not known until years after this conversation. The transcript of this conversation between Nixon and Kissinger supports the belief of those who criticize the Nixon administration for damaging faith in the ethics of American foreign policy. How far were US leaders willing to go without the consent of the constituents who elected them? What was the difference between a US ally and a pawn? The "decent interval" plan damaged credibility in Nixon's foreign policy program, even though it remained a popular model for presidents after him.

At the beginning of his first term, President Nixon proposed an approach to foreign policy that was called the Nixon Doctrine: the United States would use its military might only to assist in the defense of allies, not to assume the entire responsibility of the defense. Viewed positively, the Nixon Doctrine was supposed to support legitimate governments against insurrection. However, the United States continued to employ this policy to support ineffective and unpopular governments. A primary fault behind the Nixon Doctrine was an optimistic belief that the United States can apply its own systems to countries with different histories and demographics. For example, the United States refused to withdraw support from President Thiêu, who granted favors to the Catholic minority in a Buddhist country. In turn, Saigon could not maintain a strong military without a strong government. The political structure in Saigon proved to be ill-prepared to handle the organization of local defense despite years of US assistance. Once all US combat troops left, South Vietnam withstood northern assault for a little less than two years.

A critic could also view the Nixon Doctrine as a tool of imperialism that imposed US policy on foreign nationals. Nixon's concern about the Algerian analogy alludes to this negative view. France's colonialist failures in both Algeria and Vietnam were an inescapable comparison for the United States' involvement in Vietnam during the 1970s, just as the mistakes made in Vietnam would become an analogy later for the United States' intervention in the Middle East thirty years later.

—Ashleigh Fata, MA

Bibliography and Additional Reading

Greenberg, David. *Nixon's Shadow: The History of an Image.* New York: W.W. Norton, 2003. Print.

Karnow, Stanley. *Vietnam: A History.* New York: Penguin, 1991. Print.

Kimball, Jeffrey P. *Nixon's Vietnam War.* Lawrence, KS: U of Kansas, 1998. Print.

Nguyen, Phu Duc & Arthur J. Dommen. *The Viet-Nam Peace Negotiations: Saigon's Side of the Story.* Christiansburg, VA: Dalley Book Service, 2005. Print.

Snep, Frank. *Decent Interval: An Insider's Account of Saigon's Indecent End* Told by the CIA's Chief Strategy Analyst in Vietnam. New York: Random, 1977. Print.

■ President Nixon to President Thiêu

Date: January 5, 1973
Author: Richard M. Nixon
Genre: letter

Summary Overview

In a January 5, 1973 letter to Nguyen Van Thiêu, President of South Vietnam, President Richard Nixon explained his position on a number of issues emerging from peace negotiations taking place in Paris between representatives of the United States and North Vietnam. The two nations were trying to negotiate an end to the Vietnam War. It is clear from Nixon's letter that Thiêu had continually voiced concerns about the terms. Thiêu feared that the United States would sign a treaty that would not require the North to remove 150,000 of its troops from South Vietnamese territory. Nixon's letter informed Thiêu that not only was North Vietnam inflexible on the issue, but also that he would not allow Thiêu's concerns to complicate, delay, or destroy the pending peace agreement. He also flatly warned Thiêu that should he choose not to support the agreement negotiated with the North, he should expect an end to American support for his government and his country. Nixon was clearly more interested in securing an American exit from the war than defending the interests of South Vietnam.

Defining Moment

Nixon's letter to Thiêu occurred within the context of ongoing peace negotiations between the United States and North Vietnam. It reveals that considerable tension existed between Nixon and Thiêu. Beginning in late September 1972, American representatives, including National Security Advisor Henry Kissinger began negotiating with their counterparts in North Vietnam, led by Le Duc Tho to end the Vietnam War. However, reaching an agreement acceptable to all parties proved elusive, especially since the North represented the interests of the National Liberation Front (NLF; but known by this time as the Provisional Revolutionary Government, or PRG), the primary domestic opponent of South Vietnam, while the United States represented the interests of South Vietnam. The major barriers to a potential settlement were North Vietnam's insistence that Thiêu be removed from power and that his demand regarding the removal of North Vietnamese Army (NVA) soldiers from South Vietnam be ignored. Not surprisingly, talks between the two sides broke down a number of times.

Although the North Vietnamese eventually dropped their demand for Thiêu's removal, Thiêu refused to compromise, insisting that he would never support any agreement that allowed for the continued presence of NVA troops in South Vietnam. On December 18, Nixon, hoping to place pressure on the North Vietnamese government and convince Thiêu of his sincere support for the South, ordered a sustained bombing campaign of North Vietnam known as Operation Linebacker II, or the "Christmas Bombing." During the twelve-day bombing campaign, American pilots dropped 20,000 tons of explosives on North Vietnam, the most concentrated bombing campaign of the entire war.

The Christmas Bombing had considerable repercussions in the United States, particularly since Nixon had announced months earlier that peace was at hand. The response from Congress was swift. On January 2, 1973, the House Democratic Caucus voted to cut off all funds to fight the war and two days later the Senate Democratic Caucus concurred. Nixon pointed this out to Thiêu, likely to show him that congressional support for continued American assistance was all but dead.

Nonetheless, Thiêu continued to insist that he would not support any peace agreement that did not address his concerns about the presence of NVA forces. Nixon lost patience completely. His letter informed Thiêu in no uncertain terms that if he did not change his mind and support the agreement, the United States would sign the agreement anyway.

Biography

Born in Yorba Linda, California, on January 9, 1913, Richard Nixon, a California Republican, was elected to the US House of Representatives in 1946 and to the Senate in 1950. He served as vice president under Dwight D. Eisenhower for two terms (1953–1961). In the 1960 presidential election, he lost narrowly to John F. Kennedy. Promising "peace with honor" and an end to the stalemate in Vietnam, Nixon defeated Democratic candidate Hubert Humphrey for the presidency in 1968 in an amazing political comeback. Nixon's Vietnam policy was multifaceted: he wanted to train South Vietnamese soldiers so that they could replace most American military forces in Vietnam, a program called "Vietnamization." At the same time, he escalated the war by expanding bombing campaigns in Vietnam and, most controversially, into neighboring Laos and Cambodia. Nixon's administration eventually negotiated an end to the Vietnam War. On January 27, 1973 the United States and the North Vietnamese signed a peace agreement officially bringing an end to the war. Nixon resigned as president as a result of the Watergate crisis on August 9, 1974.

HISTORICAL DOCUMENT

Dear Mr. President:

This will acknowledge your letter of December 20, 1972.

There is nothing substantial that I can add to my many previous messages, including my December 17 letter, which clearly stated my opinions and intentions. With respect to the question of North Vietnamese troops, we will again present your views to the Communists as we have done vigorously at every ether opportunity in the negotiations. The result is certain to be once more the rejection of our position. We have explained to you repeatedly why we believe the problem of North Vietnamese troops is manageable under the agreement, and I see no reason to repeat all the arguments.

We will proceed next week in Paris along the lines that General Haig explained to you. Accordingly, if the North Vietnamese meet our concerns on the two outstanding substantive issues in the agreement, concerning the DMZ and type method of signing and if we can arrange acceptable supervisory machinery, we will proceed to conclude the settlement. The gravest consequence would then ensue if your government chose to reject the agreement and split off from the United States. As I said in my December 17 letter, "I am convinced that your refusal to join us would be an invitation to disaster—to the loss of all that we together have fought for over the past decade. It would be inexcusable above all because we will have lost a just and honorable alternative."

As we enter this new round of talks, I hope that our countries will now show a united front. It is imperative for our common objectives that your government take no further actions that complicate our task and would make more difficult the acceptance of the settlement by all parties. We will keep you informed of the negotiations in Paris through daily briefings of Ambassador [Pham Dang] Lam.

I can only repeat what I have so often said: The best guarantee for the survival of South Vietnam is the unity of our two countries which would be gravely jeopardized if you persist in your present course. The actions of our Congress since its return have clearly borne out the many warnings we have made.

Should you decide, as I trust you will, to go with us, you have my assurance of continued assistance in the post-settlement period and that we will respond with full force should the settlement be violated by North Vietnam. So once more I conclude with an appeal to you to close ranks with us.

Sincerely,
RICHARD NIXON

Document Analysis

President Richard Nixon's letter to Nguyen Van Thiêu, president of South Vietnam, occurred in the context of ongoing negotiations between American and North Vietnamese representatives in Paris to end the war. Nixon's letter deals almost exclusively with the details of this agreement. It reveals that Nixon and Thiêu had dramatically different expectations as to what an acceptable peace agreement should look like. Nixon clearly believed that any peace agreement, which alleviated American concerns and allowed the United States to exit the conflict was acceptable, while Thiêu wanted to make sure that the agreement adequately addressed his concerns and secured a future for his government and country.

It is clear from Nixon's letter that Thiêu was particularly concerned with the continued presence of 150,000 NVA soldiers in South Vietnamese territory, a concern that he had voiced many times. Nixon attempted to assuage Thiêu's fears by promising that "the problem of North Vietnamese troops is manageable under the agreement." Nixon clearly expected nothing less than complete support from Thiêu for the American position on any peace agreement. He warned Thiêu that "the gravest consequence would then ensue if your government chose to reject the agreement and split off from the United States." He also made it clear that the United States would sign the agreement with or without the South Vietnamese government's support.

Nixon's statements reveal how little influence Thiêu and his government had over the details and nature of the peace negotiations and agreement. This is noteworthy because the initial justification for American military intervention in Vietnam had been to ensure the survival of a non-communist government in South Vietnam. However, by 1973, the United States seemingly cared very little about South Vietnamese concerns about the peace agreement or even if the peace agreement would potentially compromise its future independence. Nixon expected South Vietnam to show a common front with the United States, warning that Thiêu must "take no further actions that complicate our task and would make more difficult the acceptance of the settlement by all parties."

Nixon's letter concluded with a promise of continued American aid for Thiêu if he supported the peace agreement, suggesting that if he chose not to support the agreement, American support would end and South Vietnam would be abandoned. However, Nixon promised to meet the North Vietnamese with military force if they chose to violate the terms of the peace agreement, a promise he nor his successors would be able to keep in 1974–1975.

Essential Themes

Nixon's frank letter to Thiêu provides a window into the complex nature of American foreign policy and the negotiations, which led to an end to American involvement in Vietnam. The letter also reveals that relations between Nixon and Thiêu's government had frayed considerably. The two governments were supposedly allies, but the letter demonstrates that the two lead-

ers' priorities and expectations regarding an acceptable peace agreement were far apart. Thiêu had long refused to support any agreement which allowed for NVA troops to remain within his nation's borders. The North Vietnamese had refused to sign any peace agreement that required them to remove their soldiers. The Christmas Bombing on December 18, 1973 was an attempt to reassure Thiêu and place more pressure on the North.

However, as Nixon's letter demonstrates, in spite of the sustained bombing of North Vietnam, Thiêu remained unwilling to support an agreement that did not require the removal of all NVA forces. Nixon, facing congressional and popular opposition to the war and influenced by his own desire to extract American forces from Vietnam, was no longer willing to humor or address Thiêu's concerns about the agreement. He bluntly warned Thiêu that if he did not support the peace agreement reached between the United States and North Vietnam, he would sign the agreement anyway. He also suggested that this would be the end of American financial support for Thiêu. Nixon's reaction demonstrates that he did not view the relationship between the United States and South Vietnam as an equal partnership. He expected Thiêu to follow his lead and sign the agreement, regardless of whether it was in Thiêu's or his country's best interests.

Not surprisingly, Nixon got his way, and on January 27, 1973, representatives from the United States, North and South Vietnam, and the Provisional Revolutionary Government signed the Paris Peace Agreement, officially "ending" the Vietnam War. The agreement did not require the removal of NVA forces, a fact that would have grave consequences for the future of South Vietnam. The Paris Peace Accords ended American military involvement in Vietnam, but it did nothing to end the war for the Vietnamese. Thiêu had good reason to fear the continued presence of 150,000 enemy soldiers in his country, as fighting resumed a short time after the Paris Peace Accords were signed. The war ended when the NVA toppled the South Vietnamese government on April 30, 1975. By this time, Nixon had already resigned, having been undone by the Watergate scandal; Gerald Ford, Nixon's successor, was unable to persuade Congress to provide further aid for South Vietnam.

—*Gerald F. Goodwin, PhD*

Bibliography and Additional Reading

Berman, Larry. *No Peace No Honor: Nixon, Kissinger, and Betrayal in Vietnam.* New York: Simon & Schuster, 2001. Print.

Kimball, Jeffrey. *Nixon's Vietnam War.* Lawrence, KS: University Press of Kansas, 1998. Print.

Hung, Nguyen Tien & Jerrold L. Schecter. *The Palace File.* New York: Harper & Row Publishers, 1986. Print.

■ The Paris Peace Accords

Date: January 27, 1973
Authors: Henry Kissinger, Le Duc Tho, et al.
Genre: treaty

Summary Overview

The signing of the Paris Accords in 1973 marked the end of almost a century of foreign intervention in Vietnam, going back to the beginning of French colonialism in the 1880s. It also marked an end to more than twenty-five years of intermittent warfare, both civil/sectarian and international, which began with the French re-entry into Vietnam in 1946 after losing the region to the Japanese in World War II. The growing antiwar segment of the American population was pleased that America's longest war to date was finally ending, and President Richard Nixon believed he was fulfilling his promises of exiting Indochina, while maintaining US global credibility.

The agreement itself deals with many of the usual issues involving the cessation of conflict between two belligerents, such as the end to bombing and the promise not to reintroduce troops. However, certain aspects of the document are unique to the American conflict in Vietnam. The latter includes issues pertaining to the continued presence of US military advisors, which had helped lead the United States into the conflict in the first place, and the very contentious issue of soldiers who had been captured or were missing in action. The document also relates, more generally, to the period's political debates over and later academic reflections on whether or not South Vietnam could have survived for long after the US exit in early 1973.

Defining Moment

Most centrally, and an issue that is somewhat debated by historians, the Paris Accords of 1973 represented the failure of the United States to solve the main dilemma faced by American presidents across three decades, from Dwight D. Eisenhower to Richard M. Nixon: how to create a viable, non-communist South Vietnam that could stand on its own. Technically, South Vietnam would survive for two more years, but the exit of the United States via the Paris Accords of 1973 sig-nified the beginning of the end for a nation that had only officially existed for less than twenty years, since the Geneva Accords of 1954. For North Vietnam and communists in South Vietnam, the 1973 agreement was an enormous step toward final fulfillment of the 1954 Geneva Accords. The latter had provided for elections in 1956, but these never occurred because President Eisenhower and the South Vietnamese leader at that time, Ngo Dinh Diem, knew that the communists would triumph electorally and unite the country under a communist government. In fact, the first article of the Accords harkens back to the idea of a unified Vietnam as envisioned in the 1954 agreement.

For many in the United States, the final agreement to end American military involvement in Vietnam came as welcome news. The conflict was (and remains) one of the most contentious issues among Americans that occurred during the 1960s. It led to massive protests, especially during the 1968 Democratic Convention in Chicago; the 1969 antiwar demonstration in Washington, DC; and the protests in reaction to President Nixon's invasion of Cambodia in 1970, which led to the shootings of students at Kent State University in Ohio and Jackson State College in Mississippi. As for President Nixon himself, he was finally delivering on promises to get the United States out of Vietnam, which he had made during the 1968 presidential campaign. Still, exiting the conflict took him four years to accomplish, in part because he wanted to achieve, as he put it, "peace with honor," by which he generally meant preserving America's international credibility throughout the exit process by leaving in place what appeared to be a functioning South Vietnam. In reality, most observers, and most historians since, did not believe that South Vietnam would last long after American forces left.

Author Biography

The main American negotiator was Nixon's national security advisor Henry Kissinger, who would also be the US secretary of state starting later in 1973. Kissinger's diplomatic activities were wide-ranging, including "shuttle diplomacy" in the Middle East and in southern Africa during the early and mid-1970s. President Nixon often worked closely with Kissinger, even bypassing the State Department, to conduct American foreign policy. Kissinger would continue as secretary of state during the administration of President Gerald Ford.

Le Duc Tho was the primary negotiator on the Vietnamese side. He was a member of the highest ruling group in the communist structure of the North Vietnamese government, the Politburo. It took years of negotiations to reach an agreement that was satisfactory, even on a temporary basis, to all the parties involved—the United States, North Vietnam, the communists in South Vietnam, and the non-communist South Vietnamese government.

As a result of the 1973 Paris Accords, both men received a Nobel Peace Prize, although Le Duc Tho refused to accept his, and critics have said that Kissinger did not deserve his based on his involvement in the war and other military actions.

HISTORICAL DOCUMENT

Article 1

.... The United States and all other countries respect the independence, sovereignty, unity, and territorial integrity of Viet-Nam as recognized by the 1954 Geneva Agreements on Viet-Nam . . .

Article 2

A cease fire shall be observed throughout South Viet-Nam as of 2400 hours G.M.T., on January 27, 1973. At the same hour, the United States will stop all its military activities against the territory of the Democratic Republic of Viet-Nam by ground, air and naval forces, wherever they may be based, and end the mining of the territorial waters, ports, harbors, and waterways of the Democratic Republic of Viet-Nam. The United States will remove, permanently deactivate or destroy all the mines in the territorial waters, ports, harbors, and waterways of North Viet-Nam as soon as this Agreement goes into effect. The complete cessation of hostilities mentioned in this Article shall be durable and without limit of time....

Article 4

The United States will not continue its military involvement or intervene in the internal affairs of South Viet-Nam.

Article 5

Within sixty days of the signing of this Agreement, there will be a total withdrawal from South Viet-Nam of troops, military advisers, and military personnel including technical military personnel and military personnel associated with the pacification program, armaments, munitions, and war material of the United States and those of the other foreign countries mentioned in Article 3(a). Advisers from the above-mentioned countries to all paramilitary organizations and the police force will also be withdrawn within the same period of time.

Article 6

The dismantlement of all military bases in South Viet-Nam of the United States and of the other foreign countries mentioned in Article 3(a) shall be completed within sixty days of the signing of this Agreement.

Article 7

From the enforcement of the cease-fire to the formation of the government provided for in Article 9(b) and 14 of this Agreement, the two South Vietnamese parties shall not accept the introduction of troops, military advisers, and military personnel including technical military personnel, armaments, munitions, and war material into South Viet-Nam....

Article 8

a. The return of captured military personnel and foreign civilians of the parties shall be carried out simultaneously with and completed not later than the same day as the troop withdrawal mentioned in Article 5. The parties shall exchange complete lists of the above-mentioned captured military personnel and foreign civilians on the day of the signing of this Agreement.

b. The Parties shall help each other to get information about those military personnel and foreign civilians of the parties missing in action, to determine the location and take care of the graves of the dead so as to facilitate the exhumation and repatriation of the remains, and to take any such other measures as may be required to get information about those still considered missing in action.

c. The question of the return of Vietnamese civilian personnel captured and detained in South Viet-Nam will be resolved by the two South Vietnamese parties on the basis of the principles of Article 21(b) of the Agreement on the Cessation of Hostilities in Viet-Nam of July 20, 1954. The two South Vietnamese parties will do so in a spirit of national reconciliation and concord, with a view to ending hatred and enmity, in order to ease suffering and to reunite families. The two South Vietnamese parties will do their utmost to resolve this question within ninety days after the cease-fire comes into effect....

Article 11

Immediately after the cease-fire, the two South Vietnamese parties will: achieve national reconciliation and concord, end hatred and enmity, prohibit all acts of reprisal and discrimination against individuals or organizations that have collaborated with one side or the other; ensure the democratic liberties of the people: personal freedom, freedom of speech, freedom of the press, freedom of meeting, freedom of organization, freedom of political activities, freedom of belief, freedom of movement, freedom of residence, freedom of work, right to property ownership, and right to free enterprise....

Chapter V The Reunification of Viet-Nam and The Relationship Between North and South Viet-Nam

Article 15

The reunification of Viet-Nam shall be carried out step by step through peaceful means on the basis of discussions and agreements between North and South Viet-Nam, without coercion or annexation by either party, and without foreign interference. The time for reunification will be agreed upon by North and South Viet-Nam. Pending reunification:

a. The military demarcation line between the two zones at the 17th parallel is only provisional and not a political or territorial boundary, as provided for in paragraph 6 of the Final Declaration of the 1954 Geneva Conference.

b. North and South Viet-Nam shall respect the Demilitarized Zone on either side of the Provisional Military Demarcation Line.

c. North and South Viet-Nam shall promptly start negotiations with a view to reestablishing normal relations in various fields. Among the questions to be negotiated are the modalities of civilian movement across the Provisional Military Demarcation Line.

d. North and South Viet-Nam shall not join any military alliance or military bloc and shall not allow foreign powers to maintain military bases, troops, military advisers, and military personnel on their respective territories, as stipulated in the 1954 Geneva Agreements on Viet-Nam....

Article 21

The United States anticipates that this Agreement will usher in an era of reconciliation with the Democratic Republic of Viet-Nam as with all the peoples of Indochina. In pursuance of its traditional policy, the United States will contribute to healing the wounds of war and to postwar reconstruction of the Democratic Republic of Viet-Nam and throughout Indochina.

Article 22

The ending of the war, the restoration of peace in Viet-Nam, and the strict implementation of this Agreement will create conditions for establishing a new, equal and mutually beneficial relationship between the United States and the Democratic Republic of Viet-Nam on the basis of respect of each other's independence and sovereignty, and non-interference in each other's internal affairs. At the same time this will ensure stable peace in Viet-Nam and contribute to the preservation of lasting peace in Indochina and Southeast Asia....

The Return of Captured Military Personnel and Foreign Civilians

Article 1

The parties signatory to the Agreement shall return the captured military personnel of the parties mentioned in Article 8(a) of the Agreement as follows: all captured military personnel of the United States and those of the other foreign countries mentioned in Article 3(a) of the Agreement shall be returned to United States authorities; all captured Vietnamese military personnel, whether belonging to regular or irregular armed forces, shall be returned to the two South Vietnamese parties; they shall be returned to that South Vietnamese party under whose command they served.

Article 2

All captured civilians who are nationals of the United States or of any other foreign countries mentioned in Article 3(a) of the Agreement shall be returned to United States authorities. All other captured foreign civilians shall be returned to the authorities of their country of nationality by any one of the parties willing and able to do so.

Article 3

The parties shall today exchange complete lists of captured persons mentioned in Articles 1 and 2 of this Protocol.

Article 4

a. The return of all captured persons mentioned in Articles 1 and 2 of this Protocol shall be completed within sixty days of the signing of the Agreement at a rate no slower than the rate of withdrawal from South Viet-Nam of United States forces and those of the other foreign countries mentioned in Article 5 of the Agreement.

b. Persons who are seriously ill, wounded or maimed, old persons and women shall be returned first. The remainder shall be returned either by returning all from one detention place after another or in order of their dates of capture, beginning with those who have been held the longest....

With Regard to Dead and Missing Persons

Article 10

a. The Four-Party Joint Military Commission shall ensure joint action by the parties in implementing Article 8 (b) of the Agreement. When the Four-Party Joint Military Commission has ended its activities, a Four-Party Joint Military team shall be maintained to carry on this task.

b. With regard to Vietnamese civilian personnel dead or missing in South Viet-Nam, the two South Vietnamese parties shall help each other to obtain information about missing persons, determine the location and take care of the graves of the dead, in a spirit of national reconciliation and concord, in keeping with the people's aspirations....

Document Analysis

While every treaty to end a conflict contains agreements to end the fighting in various ways, the Paris Accords of 1973 included many items specific to the American war in Vietnam. Even though the United States never invaded North Vietnam and fought exclusively in South Vietnam (with a brief invasion of Cambodia in 1970 and occasional bombing of both Laos and Cambodia),

US President Lyndon Johnson, and especially Nixon, had bombed North Vietnam—heavily at times—in attempts to limit the capacity of the North to aid the communist rebels in South Vietnam and sometimes, as Nixon did in December 1972, to try to jumpstart stalled negotiations. American forces had also mined one of the main harbors of North Vietnam (officially called the Democratic Republic of Vietnam) earlier in 1972, and therefore Article 2 contained language that the United States would henceforth cease this activity in addition to ending military operations in South Vietnam itself.

In addition, both sides knew that it had been the presence of US military advisors in South Vietnam, first under Eisenhower in the late 1950s and then increasing in number under President John Kennedy in the early 1960s, that had helped to lead the United States toward higher levels of American involvement, up to and including Johnson's escalation in mid-1965. Therefore, Article 5 contained clear language that not only would regular American military personnel leave Vietnam, but so too would "military advisers, and military personnel including technical military personnel and military personnel associated with the pacification program, armaments, munitions, and war material of the United States and those of the other foreign countries." Likewise, "advisors...to all paramilitary organizations and the police force" would leave forthwith. The Accords were trying to close all loopholes that would allow any reintroduction of outside armed forces.

The references to the return of prisoners, found in numerous places, were especially important for the United States, as public clamor had grown for the government to achieve the return of US troops captured by communist forces. By the end of the war in early 1973, around six hundred Americans remained in enemy hands, including more than thirty who had recently been imprisoned when shot down during Nixon's December 1972 bombing campaign of North Vietnam. All of these prisoners were returned to the United States as American forces left in early 1973, but a similar issue would linger for decades in the form of searching for Americans who were still missing in action (MIA) in the Indochina region. At the end of the war, almost 2,400 US servicemen remained unaccounted for; as of 2015, the number remains over 1,600, although the investigative work continues. As historian Gary Hess points out, while US MIA rates in earlier twentieth century wars were actually higher than in Vietnam, the issue remained influential for more than two decades in the relations between the two countries. Overall, while the Paris Accords was, in some respects, a standard treaty that included the removal of military forces, the specifics of future political developments, and language of reconciliation, the document also dealt with specifics of the American war in Vietnam, including aerial bombing of North Vietnam, the role of military advisors

during the build-up to full-fledged war, and the thorny issue of prisoners of war (POWs) and MIAs.

Essential Themes

In addition to the themes already noted above, a central debate among Americans in the 1970s and among historians since then has been over whether or not the Paris Accords had contained the necessary stipulations for South Vietnam to survive on its own after American withdrawal. As historian Gary Hess notes, in early 1973, the South Vietnamese government "could claim control over 75 percent of the territory and 85 percent of the population of South Vietnam. Its army, including reserves, totaled about one million troops, nearly 10 times the estimated strength of Viet Cong and North Vietnamese units in the South" (Hess 132). In addition, most American bases and military hardware were simply turned over to South Vietnamese forces and, as historian George Herring indicates, "the United States kept a formidable armada of naval power and airpower" in the region (Herring 287–288). Nevertheless, with fighting resuming shortly after the exit of US forces, and after a final push in the first months of 1975 by communist forces in South Vietnam, that country ceased to exist by May 1, 1975. Some, including Nixon, Kissinger, and some of the final leaders of South Vietnam, later claimed that had Congress provided the funding for South Vietnam as requested in early 1975 by President Gerald Ford (who replaced Nixon in August 1974 in the wake of the Watergate scandal), the South would not have fallen. Still, most historians argue that no matter what the actions of the United States might have been, the ongoing unpopularity of various South Vietnamese governments, the unwillingness of most units in the South Vietnamese army to fight during the final campaigns between 1973 and 1975, and the decades-old determination by communist leaders and forces to unite the nation meant that South Vietnam was doomed after early 1973.

—*Kevin Grimm, PhD*

Bibliography and Additional Reading

Herring, George C. *America's Longest War: The United States and Vietnam, 1950–1975*, 3rd edition. New York: McGraw Hill, Inc., 1996. Print.

Hess, Gary. *Vietnam and the United States: Origins and Legacy of War,* rev. ed. New York: Twayne Publishers, 1998. Print.

Phillips, Jak. "Top 10 Nobel Prize Controversies: Nobel-Winner Wrangling, Henry Kissinger." *TIME*. Time Inc., 7 Oct. 2011. Web. <http://content.time.com/time/specials/packages/article/0,28804,2096389_2096388_2096386,00.html>.

US Department of Defense. "Soldier Missing from Vietnam War Accounted For (Newton)." *Defense POW/MIA Accounting Agency.* Department of Defense, 8 Jun. 2015. Web. <http://www.dpaa.mil/NewsStories/NewsReleases/tabid/10159/Article/598458/soldier-missing-from-vietnam-war-accounted-for-newton.aspx>.

AFTERMATH

The denouement of the conflict in Vietnam was as tragic as any event in the war. Although a presumed peace had been achieved in January 1973 and the Americans had pulled out with their "honor" intact, all was not as it seemed. Almost immediately after the peace accords, South Vietnam faced renewed military challenges from the North and from its enemies in the South—as many observers had predicted would happen. The difference now was that South Vietnam was on its own. Within two years communist oppositional forces were encircling Saigon and threatening the country's survival. A request was made by President Gerald Ford for congressional authorization of additional funds, the case being made personally before Congress by Henry Kissinger. But to no avail—the request was denied. A last-ditch effort was made to remove the last Americans from the capital along with hundreds of Vietnamese who had supported the United States. It was a tense time, but in the end the US embassy was abandoned and Saigon fell to the communists. Although the Vietnamese nation was once again unified, it had been devastated by decades of war. The idea of the United States having exited the scene "with honor" seemed more dubious than ever.

Back home in the United States, however, the war was already something that most Americans were happy to forget. The need to change the narrative to something more positive soon extended to those who had evaded the draft during the war years. First, in September 1974, President Ford issued an amnesty offer to draft avoiders, allowing them to serve in alternative programs if they declared themselves; then, in January 1977, President Jimmy Carter authorized a full pardon of evaders. The move caused consternation among the war's supporters, but the general consensus was that it was the right thing to do. In addition, many came to feel that it was time to honor those who had lost their lives fighting in the war. War veteran Jan Scruggs put forth the idea of erecting a national monument. Yet, like almost everything else concerning Vietnam, that project too proved controversial. The design chosen for the memorial, created by a young Chinese American named Maya Lin, seemed too severe in the eyes of many. A compromise was agreed to that saw Lin's original monument erected along with a pair of more traditional statuary works. Over the years, however, the Vietnam Veterans Memorial came to be widely revered and today remains one of the most visited sites in Washington, D.C.

■ Plea for Emergency Aid for Saigon

Date: April 15, 1975
Author: Henry Kissinger
Genre: speech; petition

Summary Overview

Between mid-1965 and early 1973, American forces fought a full-fledged war in South Vietnam against regular North Vietnamese soldiers and communist irregular guerillas from the South. When direct combat between American and communist forces ended in March 1973 with the exit of US troops from South Vietnam, the latter country remained on the map for two more years, until April 1975. With the adoption of the Paris Peace Accords in 1973, covering the US withdrawal, vague political agreements were established among the competing forces in South Vietnam, which were supposed to be expanded and worked out in detail later. These agreements gave US president Richard Nixon and his national security advisor Henry Kissinger the ability to say that they had achieved "peace with honor" in Vietnam, and they argued that South Vietnam had a good chance to succeed as a nation in 1973. In reality, the military situation favored the communist forces. With the US public and Congress very wary of more aid to South Vietnam, when communist forces began a new offensive in early 1975, they met with unexpected success and soon threatened to take over all of South Vietnam in one campaign. In the midst of the South Vietnamese collapse, Kissinger lobbied Congress for more aid to the besieged South Vietnamese government. His speech revealed his own beliefs about the viability of the 1973 Paris Peace Accords, which he helped construct, and also provided windows into debates that have raged ever since on both the role of US credibility in leading America into the conflict and also on the actual possibility of South Vietnamese success after 1973.

Defining Moment

Kissinger's speech before the Senate Committee on Appropriations occurred in the midst of the military collapse of South Vietnam in the spring of 1975. In December 1974, communist forces had begun a hesitant offensive in the Central Highlands of South Vietnam. Unexpectedly, for both the communists and the Americans who were watching, the forces of South Vietnam rapidly disintegrated and the communists were able to continue a sustained offensive into the heart of South Vietnam. By mid-April, the complete takeover of South Vietnam by communist forces was imminent and all the major cities were either in communist hands or severely threatened.

In the middle of this chaos in South Vietnam, even as US officials prepared evacuation plans for the remaining Americans in the capital city of Saigon, Kissinger urged the US Senate to provide increased funding for the beleaguered South Vietnamese, which US president Gerald Ford had officially requested from Congress. Estimating the South Vietnamese armed forces had abandoned around $800 million worth of materiel while retreating over the last couple of months, Kissinger recognized that "the amount of military assistance the President has requested is of the same general magnitude as the value of the equipment lost," but argued that the aid would still work. Detractors, both then and since, have wondered why the United States should provide such extensive aid if previous aid and materiel had been so casually wasted (Herring 296). Kissinger's claim that the new aid would cover only "minimum requirements" to stabilize the situation in South Vietnam—and it was debated whether that would actually happen—also held the door open to requests for further high levels of aid to come. By 1975, however, the US public and most US leaders had concluded that the United States had spent enough blood and treasure in South Vietnam. Congress denied this request for more military funding.

Author Biography

Henry Kissinger was the US national security advisor, a powerful position in the US bureaucracy that was created in 1947 to fight the Cold War, from 1969 to 1975, under both Nixon and President Gerald Ford. He was also the US secretary of state from 1973 to 1977. While he served both Nixon and Carter, he is most known for his years under Nixon, during which he helped wind down American involvement in Vietnam. Alongside his North Vietnamese counterpart in negotiations, Le Duc Tho, Kissinger received the 1973 Nobel Peace Prize for the 1973 Paris Peace Accords, under which US forces left South Vietnam.

HISTORICAL DOCUMENT

The long and agonizing conflict in Indo-china has reached a tragic stage. The events of the past month have been discussed at great length before the Congress and require little additional elaboration. In Viet-Nam President Thiêu ordered a strategic withdrawal from a number of areas he regarded as militarily untenable. However, the withdrawal took place in great haste, without adequate advance planning, and with insufficient coordination. It was further complicated by a massive flow of civilian refugees seeking to escape the advancing North Vietnamese Army. Disorganization engendered confusion; fear led to panic. The results, as we all know, were tragic losses—of territory, of population, of material, and of morale.

But to fully understand what has happened, it is necessary to have an appreciation of all that went before. The North Vietnamese offensive, and the South Vietnamese response, did not come about by chance—although chance is always an element in warfare. The origins of these events are complex, and I believe it would be useful to review them briefly.

Since January 1973, Hanoi has violated—continuously, systematically, and energetically—the most fundamental provisions of the Paris agreement. It steadily increased the numbers of its troops in the South. It improved and expanded its logistics system in the South. It increased the armaments and ammunition of its forces in the South.

And as you know, it blocked all efforts to account for personnel missing in action. These are facts, and they are indisputable. All of these actions were of course in total violation of the agreement. Parallel to these efforts, Hanoi attempted—with considerable success—to immobilize the various mechanisms established by the agreement to monitor and curtail violations of the cease-fire. Thus, it assiduously prepared the way for further military actions.

South Viet-Nam's record of adherence to the agreement has not been perfect. It is, however, qualitatively and quantitatively far better than Hanoi's. South Viet-Nam did not build up its armed forces. It undertook no major offensive actions—although it traded thrusts and probes with the Communists. It cooperated fully in establishing and supporting the cease-fire control mechanisms provided for in the agreement. And it sought, as did the United States, full implementation of those provisions of the agreement calling for an accounting of soldiers missing in action.

But perhaps more relevant to an understanding of recent events are the following factors.

While North Viet-Nam had available several reserve divisions which it could commit to battle at times and places of its choosing, the South had no strategic reserves. Its forces were stretched thin, defending lines of communication and population centers throughout the country.

While North Viet-Nam, by early this year, had accumulated in South Viet-Nam enough ammunition for two years of intensive combat. South Vietnamese commanders had to ration ammunition as their stocks declined and were not replenished.

While North Viet-Nam had enough fuel in the South to operate its tanks and armored vehicles for at least 18 months. South Viet-Nam faced stringent shortages.

In sum, while Hanoi was strengthening its army in the South, the combat effectiveness of South Viet-Nam's army gradually grew weaker. While Hanoi built up its reserve divisions and accumulated ammunition, fuel, and other military supplies, U.S. aid levels to Viet-Nam were cut—first by half in 1973 and then by another third in 1974. This coincided with a worldwide inflation and a fourfold increase in fuel prices. As a result almost all of our military aid had to be devoted to ammunition and fuel. Very little was available for spare parts, and none for new equipment.

These imbalances became painfully evident when the offensive broke full force, and they contributed to the tragedy which unfolded. Moreover, the steady diminution in the resources available to the Army of South Viet-Nam unquestionably affected the morale of its officers and men. South Vietnamese units in the northern and central provinces knew full well that they faced an enemy superior both in numbers and in firepower.

They knew that reinforcements and resupply would not be forthcoming. When the fighting began they also knew, as they had begun to suspect, that the United States would not respond. I would suggest that all of these factors added significantly to the sense of helplessness, despair, and, eventually, panic which we witnessed in late March and early April.

I would add that it is both inaccurate and unfair to hold South Viet-Nam responsible for blocking progress toward a political solution to the conflict. Saigon's proposals in its conversations with PRG [Provisional Revolutionary Government] representatives in Paris were in general constructive and conciliatory. There was no progress toward a compromise political settlement because Hanoi intended that there should not be. Instead, North Viet-Nam's strategy was to lay the groundwork for an eventual military offensive, one which would either bring outright victory or at least allow Hanoi to dictate the terms of a political solution.

Neither the United States nor South Viet-Nam entered into the Paris agreement with the expectation that Hanoi would abide by it in every respect. We did believe, however, that the agreement was sufficiently equitable to both sides that its major provisions could be accepted and acted upon by Hanoi and that the contest could be shifted thereby from a military to a political track. However, our two governments also recognized that, since the agreement manifestly was not self-enforcing, Hanoi's adherence depended heavily on maintaining a military parity in South Viet-Nam. So long as North Viet-Nam confronted a strong South Vietnamese army and so long as the possibility existed of U.S. intervention to offset the strategic advantages of the North, Hanoi could be expected to forgo major military action. Both of those essential conditions were dissipated over the past

two years. Hanoi attained a clear military superiority, and it became increasingly convinced that U.S. intervention could be ruled out. It therefore returned to a military course, with the results we have seen.

The present situation in Viet-Nam is ominous. North Viet-Nam's combat forces far outnumber those of the South, and they are better armed. Perhaps more important, they enjoy a psychological momentum which can be as decisive as armaments in battle. South Viet-Nam must reorganize and reequip its forces, and it must restore the morale of its army and its people. These tasks will be difficult, and they can be performed only by the South Vietnamese. However, a successful defense will also require resources—arms, fuel, ammunition, and medical supplies—and these can come only from the United States.

Large quantities of equipment and supplies, totaling perhaps $800 million, were lost in South Viet-Nam's precipitous retreat from the northern and central areas. Much of this should not have been lost, and we regret that it happened. But South Viet-Nam is now faced with a different strategic and tactical situation and different military requirements. Although the amount of military assistance the President has requested is of the same general magnitude as the value of the equipment lost, we are not attempting simply to replace those losses. The President's request, based on General Weyand's [Gen. Frederick C. Weyand, Chief of Staff, United States Army] assessment, represents our best judgment as to what is needed now, in this new situation, to defend what is left of South Viet-Nam. Weapons, ammunition, and supplies to reequip four divisions, to form a number of ranger groups into divisional units, and to upgrade some territorial forces into infantry regiments will require some $326 million. The balance of our request is for ammunition, fuel, spare parts, and medical supplies to sustain up to 60 days of intensive combat and to pay for the cost of transporting those items. These are minimum requirements, and they are needed urgently.

The human tragedy of Viet-Nam has never been more acute than it now is. Hundreds of thousands of South Vietnamese have sought to flee Communist control and are homeless refugees. They have our compassion, and they must also have our help. Despite commendable efforts by the South Vietnamese Government, the burden of caring for these innocent victims is beyond its capacity. The United States has already done much to assist these people, but many remain without adequate food, shelter, or medical care. The President has asked that additional efforts and additional resources be devoted to this humanitarian effort. I ask that the Congress respond generously and quickly.

The objectives of the United States in this immensely difficult situation remain as they were when the Paris agreement was signed—to end the military conflict and establish conditions which will allow a fair political solution to be achieved. We believe that despite the tragic experience to date, the Paris agreement remains a valid framework within which to proceed toward such a solution. However, today, as in 1973, battlefield conditions will affect political perceptions and the outcome of negotiations. We therefore believe that in order for a political settlement to be reached which preserves any degree of self-determination for the people of South Viet-Nam, the present military situation must be stabilized. It is for these reasons that the President has asked Congress to appropriate urgently additional funds for military assistance for Viet-Nam.

I am acutely aware of the emotions aroused in this country by our long and difficult involvement in Viet-Nam. I understand what the cost has been for this nation and why frustration and anger continue to dominate our national debate. Many will argue that we have done more than enough for the Government and the people of South Viet-Nam. I do not agree with that proposition, however, nor do I believe that to review endlessly the wisdom of our original involvement serves a useful purpose now.

For despite the agony of this nation's experience in Indochina and the substantial reappraisal which has taken place concerning our proper role there, few would deny that we are still involved or that what we do—or fail to do—will still weigh heavily in the outcome. We cannot by our actions alone insure the survival of South Viet-Nam. But we can, alone, by our inaction assure its demise. The United States has no legal obligation to the Government and the people of South Viet-Nam of which

the Congress is not aware. But we do have a deep moral obligation—rooted in the history of our involvement and sustained by the continuing efforts of our friends. We cannot easily set it aside. In addition to the obvious consequences for the people of Viet-Nam, our failure to act in accordance with that obligation would inevitably influence other nations' perceptions of our constancy and our determination.

American credibility would not collapse, and American honor would not be destroyed. But both would be weakened, to the detriment of this nation and of the peaceful world order we have sought to build.

Mr. Chairman, as our Ambassador in Phnom Penh was about to be evacuated last week he received a letter from a longtime friend of the United States who has been publicly marked for execution. Let me share that letter with you:

> "Dear Excellency and Friend, I thank you very sincerely for your letter and for your offer to transport me towards freedom. I cannot, alas, leave in such a cowardly fashion. As for you, and in particular for your great country, I never believed for a moment that you would have this sentiment of abandoning a people which has chosen liberty. You have refused us your protection, and we can do nothing about it.
>
> You leave, and my wish is that you and your country will find happiness under this sky. But, mark it well, that if I shall die here on the spot and in my country that I love, it is too bad, because we all are born and must die one day."

Mr. Chairman, ladies and gentlemen, I suspect that neither Ambassador [John Gunther] Dean nor I will ever be able to forget that letter or the brave man who wrote it. Let us now, as Americans, act together to assure that we receive no more letters of this kind.

Document Analysis

Throughout the document, Kissinger largely blames two sources for the imminent defeat of South Vietnam—the North Vietnamese and American unwillingness to extend any more aid to the crumbling nation. In Kissinger's view, the 1973 Paris Peace Accords had put in place a viable path forward toward a political solution between North and South Vietnam, although most people at the time were unsure what that eventual settlement would look like. After all, the North Vietnamese and the communists in South Vietnam had long vowed to unite the country, by any means necessary, under a communist government. Therefore, most historians tend to see the aspects of the 1973 agreement that related to the political future of South Vietnam as only temporary, although Kissinger and Nixon at the time, and their supporters since, have insisted that the 1973 Accords provided a legitimate chance for South Vietnam to succeed. Therefore, he largely blamed the North Vietnamese for escalating the conflict again after 1973, stating, "It is both inaccurate and unfair to hold South Viet-Nam responsible for blocking progress toward a political solution to the conflict." He argued that North Vietnam never took the political aspects of the Paris settlement seriously and were always planning on a military takeover of the South.

Relatedly, Kissinger argues, the lack of American willingness to give South Vietnam more aid in fact encouraged North Vietnamese intransigence and spurred their military offensives, including the final one in early 1975. He argues, "So long as the possibility existed of U.S. intervention to offset the strategic advantages of the North, Hanoi could be expected to forgo major military action." Basically, for Kissinger, when it became clear that the United States would no longer support South Vietnam with new funding or more weapons, it seemed to open the door to a communist victory. In fact, dismissing the charges of others that the South Vietnamese armed forces were unwilling to fight, Kissinger finds the root cause of their retreat and disintegration in the American lack of aid. In a kind of linked effect, he argues that the lack of American aid has led to a lack of good war materiel for the South Vietnamese army, which then produced low morale because the soldiers felt unsupported and undersupplied. This low morale is said to have caused them to flee when "they faced an enemy superior both in numbers and in firepower." Thus, the aid that Kissinger is requesting would, in his assessment, allow an "end to the military conflict and [would] establish conditions which will allow a fair political solution to be achieved." In essence, renewed American aid would bolster the morale and fighting ability of the South Vietnamese forces, halt the communist advance, and shift the entire future of Vietnam back again away from the military realm to the political realm, as it had been, he believed, in early 1973.

Essential Themes

One key theme, as Kissinger, Nixon, and a few historians supportive of this view have argued, is that if the United States had shown a deeper willingness to continue the flow of military and financial aid to South Vietnam, the nation would have survived. Others, however, have countered that if an army of over half a million well-equipped and well-trained American soldiers could not win the war in the South, then additional aid between 1973 and 1975 would not have done the trick. The latter group also tends to think, contra Kissinger, that the 1973 Paris Peace Accords were largely a cover for Nixon to get the United States out of Vietnam and that there was never a very good chance, either in 1973 or earlier, that South Vietnam would remain a viable nation. (The reasons given are varied.) There is an additional debate, of course, about whether or not the war would have been won if military operations had been consistently expanded to North Vietnam and if the cost to both the Vietnamese and the United States would have been justified; but the debate about South Vietnam's chances for success after the US exit is a separate issue about which there is a general consensus—with a few dissenting opinions.

Another major theme relates to the justification for US involvement in Vietnam, going back to President John F. Kennedy, if not earlier. Near the end of the document, Kissinger argues that "American credibility…and American honor…would be weakened, to the detriment of this nation and of the peaceful world order we have sought to build." The latter part of the phrase is especially important in revealing Kissinger's thinking. Many historians agree that the primary reason the United States entered into a war in South Vietnam was that successive American presidents had promised support to that nation, and that if support was not then forthcoming, people around the world, both allies and enemies, would not take America's word at face value. Many American leaders feared that this would then encourage communist advances around the globe, in an expansive application of the domino theory, which usually formally applied only to Southeast Asia in warning of the fall to communism of Laos, Cambodia, Thailand, and other countries in the region if South Vietnam should fall. Both at the time and since then, Americans have debated whether US global credibility would actually have suffered if the United States had not fought in Vietnam, and some suggest that engaging in fighting actually had the opposite effect—namely, diminishing American credibility because the United States seemed to have made an unwise choice to fight there. Kissinger's words in April 1975 show that, almost a decade after President Lyndon Johnson escalated the American involvement in Vietnam to a full-blown war, and more than two years after the last American troops left, one of America's top leaders still believed that US credibility was on the line in South Vietnam.

—*Kevin Grimm, PhD*

Bibliography and Additional Reading

Herring, George C. *America's Longest War: The United States and Vietnam, 1950–1975*. 3rd edition. New York: McGraw Hill, Inc., 1996.

Hess, Gary. *Vietnam and the United States: Origins and Legacy of War*. Rev. Ed. New York: Twayne Publishers, 1998.

■ Pardon of Draft Evaders

Date: January 21, 1977
Author: Jimmy Carter
Genre: law

Summary Overview

Between 1940 and 1973 the Selective Service Administration oversaw the draft in the United States. During the Vietnam War, draft calls escalated dramatically, forcing numerous American males between the ages of 18 and 26 to confront the choice of going to war or finding a way out of the draft. Many middle-class men were able to avoid the draft through a variety of deferrals or by attaining a position in the National Guard. Several thousand draft resisters chose prison over going to Vietnam. Tens of thousands of those drafted chose exile. The most common destination was Canada, which had fairly liberal immigration policies and neighbored the United States. Canada has historically served as a refuge for those fleeing repression in the United States. These include about 100,000 Loyalists after the American Revolution, fugitive slaves, and Sitting Bull and his Lakota people. After the end of US military involvement in the Vietnam War, the tens of thousands of young men in exile remained one of the unresolved and controversial issues of the war. On Sept. 16, 1974, President Gerald R. Ford issued a "conditional amnesty" for draft evaders and military deserters, which featured "earned re-entry" in exchange for two years of alternative service. On January 21, 1977, President Jimmy Carter issued a broader "pardon" for all draft evaders, but not military deserters.

Defining Moment

Opposition to the draft during the Vietnam War grew dramatically as the war expanded and became more unpopular. Refusing induction carried a penalty of five years in prison and up to a $10,000 fine. Many Americans sought legal deferments or a place in the National Guard to avoid going to Vietnam, and several thousand chose to go to prison as an act of protest. But for many, the draft meant facing one of two stark choices: go to Vietnam or flee the country. Due to its geographical proximity and liberal immigration laws, the majority of those choosing flight crossed the border to Canada.

Estimates vary as to how many Americans fled to Canada, but conservative estimates are at least 50,000 and perhaps many more. Another large contingent of Americans going into Canadian exile were young women, often the wives or girlfriends of male draft evaders. Among the male exiles were several thousand military deserters, who faced even more severe punishment. Approximately 1,000 Americans chose to flee to Sweden; the majority of these were military deserters.

While some Americans sought legal "landed status" in Canada, which would entitle them to work permits, health care, and welfare benefits, others simply moved to Canada without making their American origins known. The three most common Canadian destinations were Vancouver, Toronto, and Montreal. However, due to Vancouver's stringent union work requirements and French being Montreal's official language, Toronto became the largest destination for American exiles.

Americans made up a relatively small percentage of Canada's immigrant population, but they received a great deal of attention. Many Canadians initially were hostile to these Americans, and until 1969, Canada conducted a covert policy of turning back US military deserters at the border. Many Canadians, however, felt strongly about national sovereignty and were reluctant to become policemen for the US government. Antiwar Canadians, meanwhile, formed organizations like Amex and the Toronto Anti-Draft Program to advocate for American draft evaders and help them settle into Canadian life. As the Vietnam War became more unpopular among Canadians in the late 1960s, Canada's role as a sanctuary became a point of national pride, although American draft evaders were never given any considerations not afforded to all immigrants.

Critics of draft evaders came not only from veterans and traditional Americans, but from some on the left. Students for a Democratic Society (SDS) felt the exodus to Canada deprived them of potential recruits for revolution in America, and the pacifist folk singer Joan Baez, whose husband David was in a US prison for draft resistance, told American draft evaders in the audience at a Toronto concert, "How dare you be here while my David is suffering in jail" (Hagen 27).

After US involvement in the Vietnam War ended in January 1973, tens of thousands of draft evaders remained in Canadian exile. Exiles and their supporters formed the National Coalition for Universal and Unconditional Amnesty (NCUUA) to lobby for the return of all draft evaders and military deserters. Weeks into his presidency, President Gerald Ford issued an unconditional pardon to the recently resigned President Richard Nixon for all crimes associated with the Watergate scandal. This raised the question of a pardon for draft evaders, and a week later, on September 16, 1974, Ford issued a "conditional amnesty" for draft evaders and military deserters, in which they could apply for re-entry to the United States and have charges dropped if they agreed to two years of alternative service as determined by the Selective Service Administration. The window for Ford's pardon lasted until the following spring. The majority of those choosing to participate in Ford's conditional amnesty were military deserters already serving time in US prisons.

During his campaign for the presidency, Jimmy Carter promised to issue an unconditional pardon for draft evaders, telling *Newsweek* he preferred pardon to amnesty because "Amnesty means what you did was right; pardon means what you did is forgiven" (Dickerson 159). Carter officially announced his pardon pledge before approximately 5,000 American Legion members

in Seattle on August 24, 1976. Carter's announcement was met with five minutes of booing, but nationally, Carter received credit for his courage in making the announcement before a hostile audience.

On his first day in office, Carter issued a pardon for all Vietnam draft evaders. Conservative Arizona senator Barry Goldwater denounced the pardon as "the most disgraceful thing a president has ever done" (Dickerson 162). Some on the left criticized Carter for not going further and pardoning military deserters. Passions soon subsided, however, and Carter's pardon was welcomed as a step toward healing the wounds of a deeply divisive war.

Author Biography

James Earl Carter, Jr. was born on October 1, 1929 in Plains, Georgia where he grew up. In 1943, Carter entered the Naval Academy in Annapolis, Maryland, and in 1946 married his wife Rosalynn. Carter served on submarines and, beginning in 1952, assisted Admiral Hyman Rickover in developing America's nuclear submarine force. After his service, Carter worked as a farmer and in 1962 was elected as a Democrat to the Georgia State Senate. In 1966, he lost a race for governor to segregationist Lester Maddox, but won the governorship in 1970. Carter was elected the thirty-ninth president of the United States in 1976 over incumbent Gerald Ford, but he lost his bid for re-election to Ronald Reagan in 1980. Carter's post-presidency life has involved work with Habitat for Humanity and the Carter Center, which has supported community health programs around the world. In 2002, Carter was awarded the Nobel Peace Prize.

HISTORICAL DOCUMENT

Proclamation 4483

Acting pursuant to the grant of authority in Article II, Section 2, of the Constitution of the United States. I, Jimmy Carter, President of the United States, do hereby grant a full, complete and unconditional pardon to: (1) all persons who may have committed any offense between August 4, 1964 and March 28, 1973 in violation of the Military Selective Service Act or any rule or regulation

promulgated thereunder; and (2) all persons heretofore convicted, irrespective of the date of conviction, of any offense committed between August 4, 1964 and March 28, 1973 in violation of the Military Selective Service Act, or any rule or regulation promulgated thereunder, restoring to them full political, civil and other rights.

This pardon does not apply to the following who are specifically excluded there from:

1. All persons convicted of or who may have committed any offense in violation of the Military Selective Service Act, or any rule or regulation promulgated thereunder, involving force or violence; and

2. All persons convicted of or who may have committed any offense in violation of the Military Selective Service Act, or any rule or regulation promulgated thereunder, in connection with duties or responsibilities arising out of employment as agents, officers or employees of the Military Selective Service system.

IN WITNESS WHEREOF, I have unto set my hand this 21st day of January, in the year of our Lord nineteen hundred and seventy-seven, and of the Independence of the United States of America the two hundred and first.

Executive Order 11967

The following actions shall be taken to facilitate Presidential Proclamation of Pardon of January 21, 1977:

1. The Attorney General shall cause to be dismissed with prejudice to the government all pending indictments for violations of the Military Selective Service Act alleged to have occurred between August 4, 1964 and March 28, 1973 with the exception of the following:

a. Those cases alleging acts of force or violence deemed to be serious by the Attorney General as to warrant continued prosecution; and

b. Those cases alleging acts in violation of the Military Selective Service Act by agents, employees or officers of the Selective Service System arising out of such employment.

2. The Attorney General shall terminate all investigations now pending and shall not initiate further investigations alleging violations of the Military Selective Service Act between August 4, 1964 and March 28, 1973, with the exception of the following:

a. Those cases involving allegations of force or violence deemed to be so serious by the Attorney General as to warrant continued investigation, or possible prosecution; and

b. Those cases alleging acts in violation of the Military Selective Service Act by agents, employees or officers of the Selective Service System arising out of such employment.

3. Any person who is or may be precluded from reentering the United States under 8 U.S.C. 1182(a)(22) or under any other law, by reason of having committed or apparently committed any violation of the Military Selective Service Act shall be permitted as any other alien to reenter the United States.

The Attorney General is directed to exercise his discretion under 8 U.S.C. 1182 (d)(5) or other applicable law to permit the reentry of such persons under the same terms and conditions as any other alien.

This shall not include anyone who falls into the exceptions of paragraphs 1 (a) and (b) and 2 (a) and (b) above.

4. Any individual offered conditional clemency or granted a pardon or other clemency under Executive Order 11803 or Presidential Proclamation 4313, dated September 16, 1974, shall receive the full measure of relief afforded by this program if they are otherwise qualified under the terms of this Executive Order.

Document Analysis

President Carter's Proclamation 4483 begins by noting the presidential power of the pardon granted in Article II, Section 2 of the United States Constitution, which is absolute. Carter's proclamation outlines the dates covered by the pardon, corresponding to the beginning of US escalation of the war after the Gulf of Tonkin Incident in August 1964, and running through the 1973 Paris Peace Accords and the expiration of the draft.

Carter declares "full, complete and unconditional pardon" to all persons in violation of the Selective Service Act. Carter excludes from his pardon anyone whose violation of the act involved "force or violence" and individuals were who "agents, officers or employees of the Military Selective Service system." At the conclusion of the document, Carter also includes anyone offered "conditional amnesty" under President Ford's executive order who meets the conditions of his pardon.

Although it is not mentioned, Carter's pardon does not cover military deserters (estimated to have reached a half million individuals) or others who broke the law resisting the war while in uniform. The Executive Order 11967, also reprinted here, simply outlines how the pardon shall be carried out, primarily by the US Attorney General, dismissing all indictments covered by the pardon.

Essential Themes

Carter's pardon of draft evaders was controversial. Some Americans were outraged, especially many who served in Vietnam and veterans of previous wars. The term "draft dodger" has acquired the stigma of cowardice and lack of patriotism despite the fact that many who chose exile came to the decision after deep soul searching and from an alternative patriotism, which saw the war as an immoral departure from American ideals. Others argue that those choosing exile are more precisely described as "draft resisters," while those who sought legal ways of avoiding the draft more accurately fit the idea of "draft evader" or "draft dodger."

Choosing exile did not come close to approximating the hardships and dangers facing those who went to Vietnam or chose prison; however, exile often entailed far greater hardships than experienced by the benefi-ciaries of legal deferments. Some told of being unable to visit ailing parents or to attend the funerals of loved ones back home. About half of those living in Canada drifted back to the United States after Carter's pardon. The other half chose to remain in Canada. Many Canadians hail these US-Canadians for their contributions to Canada and continue to look with pride at Canada's role as a sanctuary.

—*Robert Surbrug, PhD*

Bibliography and Additional Readings

Bourne, Peter G. *Jimmy Carter: A Comprehensive Biography from Plains to Post-Presidency.* New York: Scribner, 1997. Print.

Dickerson, James. *North to Canada: Men and Women against the Vietnam War.* Westport, CT: Praeger, 1999. Print.

Hagen, John. *Northern Passage: American Vietnam War Resisters and Canada.* Cambridge, MA and London, UK: Harvard UP, 2001. Print.

■ The Vietnam Veterans Memorial

Date: proposed 1981; erected 1982
Author(s): Maya Lin (artist); Jan C. Scruggs (organizer)
Genre: proposal; work of art

Summary Overview

The Vietnam Veterans Memorial, today one of the most revered monuments on the National Mall in Washington, DC, was once a very controversial work. Built in 1982 through the efforts of Vietnam War veterans hoping to erect a memorial to their fallen comrades, the design selected at first raised doubts in the minds of veterans groups, the public, and elected officials. Maya Lin, a Yale architectural student who won the design competition with a unanimous vote from the project's governing board, proposed a memorial consisting of two black granite walls containing the names of the dead and intersecting at a broad angle in the middle, while sloping downward to the ground at the edges. Conservatives denounced the design as a misguided political statement—a sort of anti-monument—and demanded a more traditional work consisting of a statue and flagpole. Both "the wall" and the statue were eventually erected, and soon afterward, the controversy dissipated as visitors came to appreciate Lin's unique design and the honor it pays to the dead and missing of the Vietnam War.

Defining Moment

The United States paid a heavy price for its military defense of South Vietnam. More than 58,000 US troops were killed or listed as missing, and some 300,000 were injured. All in all, some 2.7 million Americans served in the country over the course of the conflict, creating a vast pool of returned war veterans needing to adapt to civilian life. Moreover, unlike previous wars when those who had fought on behalf of the United States were welcomed home and granted favored status and access to socioeconomic opportunities, during the Vietnam War, veterans were treated poorly. The war had challenged many Americans' basic beliefs about themselves and their country, including that the United States was a force for good in the world and that there was nothing it could not achieve. With Vietnam, a crisis of conscience arose when it became clear that policymakers and military leaders were capable of faulty decisions and indefensible actions, and that, moreover, we seemed to be losing the battle to a poor, undeveloped country in a far off corner of the world. The war became more and more unpopular as time passed, and as a result, returning veterans were not given the respect they deserved. Indeed, in some cases, they were looked down upon by opponents of the war as tools of a suspect government. More generally, the vets were reminders of a grim episode that many Americans preferred to forget.

Some veterans became activists and sought to turn this picture around. One of them was Jan Scruggs, a moderately disabled Army veteran who obtained a master's degree in psychology after the war, but still had trouble finding a job. Critical of meager government efforts to assist vets in reintegrating into society, and disturbed by the shoddy treatment afforded vets generally, Scruggs developed a view that America's "final recovery" from the war depended on a "national reconciliation." Further, he suggested that a national monument was needed "to remind an ungrateful nation of what it has done to its sons."

To that end, Scruggs organized a group of veteran activists who worked to bring a memorial to the National Mall. Contributing $2,800 of his own money to the cause, Scruggs eventually managed to obtain over $8 million in private contributions. In 1980, through a bill sponsored by Senator John Warner of Virginia and Senator Charles Mathias of Maryland, Congress authorized the Vietnam Veterans Memorial Fund, with Scruggs at its head. A panel of eight judges, none of them Vietnam veterans (in order to eliminate bias), was set up to evaluate design proposals submitted as part of an open competition. Four basic rules were established for the memorial: 1) it could make no political statement; 2) it had to fit in with the landscaping of the site; 3) it had to suggest a place of contemplation; and

4) it had to contain the names of the dead and missing. Over 1,400 designs were submitted. When the winning design was announced on May 1, 1981, the name Maya Lin was projected into history as the youngest—and most controversial—artist ever to be granted a spot on the Mall.

Author Biography

Maya Ying Lin was born in Athens, Ohio, in 1959, the daughter of Chinese immigrant parents who taught fine arts and literature at Ohio University. Lin studied at Yale University, where, as an undergraduate, she entered and won the competition for the Vietnam Veterans Memorial in 1981. Subsequently, she received a master of architecture degree from Yale and an honorary doctorate from Yale and several other prominent universities. Today, she continues to work as an artist and designer and has a studio in New York City.

Jan Craig Scruggs grew up in Bowie, Maryland, and, during the Vietnam War, served in the US Army's 199th Light Infantry Brigade. After his military service, he received a bachelor's and a master's degree from American University in Washington, DC. He founded a fund to build the Vietnam Veterans Memorial in 1979 and received Congressional authorization for it a year later. Today, Scruggs continues to serve as CEO of the Vietnam Veterans Memorial Fund and speaks about veterans and veterans' affairs.

HISTORICAL DOCUMENT

Original Competition Drawing.

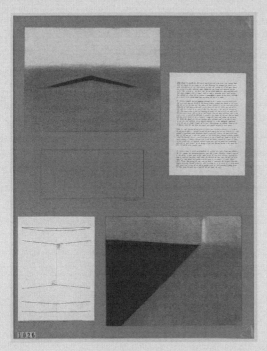

Original Statement by Maya Lin.

Walking through this park-like area, the memorial appears as a rift in the earth, a long, polished, black stone wall, emerging from and receding into the earth.

Approaching the memorial, the ground slopes gently downward and the low walls emerging on either side, growing out of the earth, extend and converge at a point below and ahead. Walking into this grassy site contained by the walls of the memorial we can barely make out the carved names upon the memorial's walls. These names, seemingly infinite in number, convey the sense of overwhelming numbers, while unifying these individuals into a whole.

The memorial is composed not as an unchanging monument, but as a moving composition to be understood as we move into and out of it. The passage itself is gradual; the descent to the origin slow, but it is at the origin that the memorial is to be fully understood. At the intersection of these walls, on the right side, is carved the date of the first death. It is followed by the names of those who died in the war, in chronological order. These names continue on this wall appearing to recede into the earth at the wall's end. The names resume on the left wall as the wall emerges from the earth, continuing back to the origin where the date of the last death is carved at the bottom of this wall. Thus the war's beginning and end meet; the war is 'complete,' coming full-circle, yet broken by the earth that bounds the angle's open side, and continued within the earth itself. As we turn to leave, we see these walls stretching into the distance, directing us to the Washington Monument, to the left, and the Lincoln Memorial, to the right, thus bringing the Vietnam

Memorial into an historical context. We the living are brought to a concrete realization of these deaths.

Brought to a sharp awareness of such a loss, it is up to each individual to resolve or come to terms with this loss. For death, is in the end a personal and private matter, and the area contained with this memorial is a quiet place, meant for personal reflection and private reckoning. The black granite walls, each two hundred feet long, and ten feet below ground at their lowest point (gradually ascending toward ground level) effectively act as a sound barrier, yet are of such a height and length so as not to appear threatening or enclosing. The actual area is wide and shallow, allowing for a sense of privacy, and the sunlight from the memorial's southern exposure along with the grassy park surrounding and within its walls, contrib-

ute to the serenity of the area. Thus this memorial is for those who have died, and for us to remember them.

The memorial's origin is located approximately at the center of the site; its legs each extending two hundred feet towards the Washington Monument and the Lincoln Memorial. The walls, contained on one side by the earth, are ten feet below ground at their point of origin, gradually lessening in height, until they finally recede totally into the earth, at their ends. The walls are to be made of a hard, polished black granite, with the names to be carved in a simple Trajan letter. The memorial's construction involves recontouring the area within the wall's boundaries, so as to provide for an easily accessible descent, but as much of the site as possible should be left untouched. The area should remain as a park, for all to enjoy.

Document Analysis

The proposal by Lin is remarkable for the degree to which the finished work conforms to the original plan. Oftentimes, artists' and architects' initial conceptions are modified as a project takes shape. The outcome in this case is all the more remarkable given that Lin acknowledged later that she did not know that much about the Vietnam War—she was quite young at the time—yet she did know that it was a divisive conflict that tore at the American social fabric. Thus, she envisioned the memorial as a kind of giant knife cutting a gash into America, creating a "rift in the earth." At the center of the work are the names of the first servicemembers who lost their lives or went missing during the conflict, while the remainder of the names, as noted in the proposal, proceed chronologically to the right, pick up again at the left edge, and conclude at the center, bringing the list "full circle." The sequence of names thus functions as a kind of diary of the war, a day-by-day, week-by-week, month-by-month accounting of the fallen. This approach proved to be a powerful one, in practice, because it allowed living veterans to see the names of their dead service mates assembled in one place according to the action in the war, the "battle," in which they were killed. In fact, "seeing" the names is only part of the story, for what happens in practice, nearly universally, is that visitors put a hand to the name and rub their fingers over the incised letters. The act becomes a powerful reminder of the physical

person—the friend or loved one—now gone from the visitor's lives.

Lin notes that the polished black granite walls, set, as they are, into the ground, are meant to act as a sound barrier, creating an aura of privacy and allowing for contemplation. And, indeed, even with some 4 million visitors per year—one of the highest visitation rates in the Capitol—the Vietnam Veterans Memorial is often considered a special place by visitors because of the aura of quiet reverence that surrounds it. The formidable black granite wall serves as a kind of permanent barrier between the dead and the living, the earth below and the surface above. Lin does not mention this in her proposal, but the highly polished surface of the granite permits the visitor to see a reflection of him- or herself facing the wall and viewing/touching the names. This effect generally adds to the intimacy of the space, the uniqueness of the moment, and emphasizes the boundary separating the visitor from the deceased.

Besides touching the names, another ritual that developed soon after the monument was erected was that of leaving a memento below the name of a friend or loved one. Over the years the National Park Service, which oversees maintenance of the monument, has collected thousands of these mementos, ranging from combat boots and love letters to cigarette lighters and children's drawings. A further detail that was added to the monument during final deliberations was the use of a small diamond symbol next to a name to indicate "deceased" status, and a small plus symbol to indicate "missing in action." Upon confirmation of death—for example, through the identification of recovered remains—the plus sign is converted to a diamond. Lin also notes that the eastern wall points to the Washington Monument and the western wall to the Lincoln Memorial. This visual effect, however, is less commented on by visitors than are other aspects of the memorial; nonetheless, it is appreciated when pointed out.

Essential Themes

The predominant theme of this work is the deep rift created by the war and the need to honor the dead and missing at the conclusion of the war. Initially, critics of Lin's design focused only on the first aspect—the rift—and could not appreciate how the work paid tribute to the fallen. A number of conservatives and veterans lambasted the design, calling it "a black gash of shame," a "degrading ditch," a "nihilistic slab." They commented on the fact that the memorial was black and below ground in a city of white marble. Some veterans objected to Lin herself as the creator, both because she was a young student and, in a darker vein, because she was the daughter of Chinese immigrants—the vets had not forgotten that China had supplied aid to North Vietnam and was itself a communist country. James Watt, secretary of the Interior in the Reagan administration, at first refused to authorize construction of the memorial, but eventually accepted a compromise solution whereby a more traditional statue and flagpole would be included at the site. The eight-foot bronze sculpture of three servicemen by Frederick Hart was originally proposed for the apex of the wall (the center), but under pressure the organizers allowed that it could be situated on a small hill a short distance away. It was unveiled in 1984. Nine years later, in response to calls by female veterans and women's organizations, another sculpture by Glenna Goodacre was added nearby to show the contribution of nurses and women generally. Finally, in 2000, a plaque was added to remember veterans who died later (for example, from Agent Orange exposure) as a result of their war service.

In comments made years later, Lin observed that whereas traditional war monuments seem to place war—and victory—in a respectful light, her monument was meant to be bleak and honest so as to serve as a "deterrent" to any future war. This is perhaps what rankled the critics; victory and "war pride" are nowhere to be seen in the Vietnam Veterans Memorial. The artist wanted to make death and loss the centerpiece of the work, and this she did. She effectively separated the warrior from the war, which turned out to be a message that Americans needed to hear in order to begin the healing process and achieve reconciliation regarding the war. Many veterans and others attended the dedication ceremony in 1982, and they embraced the memorial as a place for catharsis, a place to come to grips with the overwhelming tragedy of the war. The memorial was soon hailed as an aesthetic triumph and soon came to influence numerous state and local war memorials erected in subsequent years.

—*Michael Shally-Jensen, PhD*

Bibliography and Additional Reading

"History of the Vietnam Veterans Memorial." *Vietnam Veterans Memorial Fund*. Vietnam Veterans Memorial Fund, 2015. Web. <http://www.vvmf.org/the-memorial-history>.

Lin, Maya. "Making the Memorial." *New York Review of Books*. NYREV, Inc., 2 Nov. 2000. Web. <http://www.nybooks.com/articles/archives/2000/nov/02/making-the-memorial/>.

Nicosia, Gerald. *Home to War: A History of the Vietnam Veterans Movement*. New York: Crown Publishers, 2001. Print.

Piehler, G. Kurt. *Remembering War the American Way*. Washington, DC: Smithsonian Books, 2004. Print.

Scruggs, Jan C., & Joel L. Swerdlow. *To Heal a Nation: The Vietnam Veterans Memorial*. New York: Harper & Row, 1985. Print.

APPENDIXES

Chronological List

Web Resources

digitalhistory.uh.edu

Offers an online history textbook, Hypertext History, which chronicles the story of America, along with interactive timelines. This online source also contains handouts, lesson plans, e-lectures, movies, games, biographies, glossaries, maps, music, and much more.

docsouth.unc.edu

A digital publishing project that reflects the southern perspective of American history and culture. It offers a wide collection of titles that students, teachers, and researchers of all levels can utilize.

docsteach.org

Centered on teaching through the use of primary source documents. This online resource provides activities for many different historical eras dating to the American Revolution as well as thousands of primary source documents.

edsitement.neh.gov

An online resource for teachers, students, and parents seeking to further their understanding of the humanities. This site offers lesson plan searches, student resources, and interactive activities.

gilderlehrman.org

Offers many options in relation to the history of America. The History by Era section provides detailed explanations of specific time periods while the primary sources present firsthand accounts from a historical perspective.

havefunwithhistory.com

An online, interactive resource for students, teachers, and anybody who has an interest in American histor

history.com/topics/american-history

Tells the story of America through topics of interest, such as the Declaration of Independence, major wars, and notable Americans. Features videos from The History Channel and other resources.

historymatters.gmu.edu

An online resource from George Mason University that provides links, teaching materials, primary documents, and guides for evaluating historical records.

history.state.gov/countries/vietnam

From the Office of the Historian, Bureau of Public Affairs, United States Department of State, a guide to U.S.-Vietnam diplomtic relations including numerous documents relating to the Vietnam War.

law2.umkc.edu/faculty/projects/ftrials/mylai/mylai. htm

A site devoted to the trial of the My Lai defendants and other matters relating to the My Lai Massacre.

memory.loc.gov/ammem/index.html

Covers the various eras and ages of American history in detail, including resources such as readings, interactive activities, multimedia, and more.

ocp.hul.harvard.edu/immigration/

A Harvard University web-based collection, this site contains a large collection of primary sources on immigration to the United States, including 1,800 books and pamphlets, 13,000 pages from manuscripts and 9,000 photographs. Documents from the 1920s include Emergency Quota Act and the Oriental Exclusion Act.

pbs.org/wgbh/americanexperience

Offers an array of source materials linked to topics featured in the award winning American Experience history series.

pbs.org/wgbh/americanexperience/lastdays/

Another PBS/American Experience program called "Last Days of Vietnam," about the 1975 effort to safely remove U.S. citizens and Vietnamese supporters from Saigon as it fell to the communists.

pbs.org/wgbh/amex/vietnam/

From the award-winning PBS series American Experience, an online companion to *Vietnam: A Television History*.

si.edu/encyclopedia_si/nmah/timeline.htm

Details the course of American history chronologically. Important dates and significant events link to other pages within the Smithsonian site that offer more details.

smithsonianeducation.org

An online resource for educators, families, and students offering lesson plans, interactive activities, and more.

teachingamericanhistory.org

Allows visitors to learn more about American history through original source documents detailing the broad spectrum of American history. The site contains document libraries, audio lectures, lesson plans, and more.

teachinghistory.org

A project funded by the US Department of Education that aims to assist teachers of all levels to augment their efforts in teaching American history. It strives to amplify student achievement through improving the knowledge of teachers.

ushistory.org/us

Contains an outline that details the entire record of American history. This resource offers historical insight and stories that demonstrate what truly an American truly is from a historical perspective.

vietnam.ttu.edu/

From Texas Tech University, the Vietnam Project offers a variety of documents, oral histories, and other resources relating to the Vietnam War.

vvmf.org/

This website provides information on the Vietnam Veterans Memorial in Washington, D.C. and other information on those who served (and died) in the war.

Bibliography

Ahern, Thomas, Jr.. *Vietnam Declassified: The CIA and Counterinsurgency.* Lexington, KY: U P of Kentucky, 2010. Print.

Allison, William Thomas. *My Lai: An American Atrocity in the Vietnam War.* Baltimore, MD: Johns Hopkins UP, 2012. Print.

Allison, William Thomas. *The Tet Offensive: A Brief History with Documents.* New York: Taylor & Francis, 2008. Print.

Ambrose, Stephen E. *The Wild Blue: The Men and Boys Who Flew the B-24s Over Germany 1944–45.* New York: Simon & Schuster, 2002. Print.

Anderson, Terry H. *The Movement and the Sixties.* New York: Oxford UP, 1996. Print.

Ang, Cheng Guan. *The Vietnam War From the Other Side: The Vietnamese Communists' Perspective.* London: Routledge, 2002. Print.

Appy, Christian G. *American Reckoning: The Vietnam War and Our National Identity.* New York: Viking, 2015.

Barrett, David M. *Uncertain Warriors: Lyndon Johnson and His Vietnam Advisors.* Lawrence, KS: U of Kansas P, 1993. Print.

Berger, Dan. *The Weather Underground and the Politics of Solidarity.* Oakland, CA: AK P, 2006. Print.

Berman, Larry. *Lyndon Johnson's War: The Road to Stalemate in Vietnam.* New York: W. W. Norton, 1989. Print.

Berman, Larry. *No Peace, No Honor: Nixon, Kissinger, and Betrayal in Vietnam.* New York: Free Press, 2001. Print.

Berman, Larry. *No Peace No Honor: Nixon, Kissinger, and Betrayal in Vietnam.* New York: Simon & Schuster, 2001. Print.

Berrigan, Daniel, Robin Anderson, & James L. Marsh. *The Trial of the Catonsville Nine.* New York: Fordham University Press, 2004. Print.

Bilton, Michael & Kevin Sim. *Four Hours in My Lai.* New York: Penguin, 2003. Print.

Bird, Kai. *McGeorge Bundy and William Bundy: Brothers in Arms.* New York: Simon & Schuster, 1999.

Birtle, Andrew J. "PROVN, Westmoreland, and the Historians: A Reappraisal." *The Journal of Military History* 72.4 (October 2008): 1213–1247.

Blair, Anne E. *Lodge in Vietnam: A Patriot Abroad.* New Haven: Yale University Press, 1995. Print.

Bourne, Peter G. *Jimmy Carter: A Comprehensive Biography from Plains to Post-Presidency.* New York: Scribner, 1997. Print.

_____. & Brian VanDeMark. *In Retrospect: The Tragedy and Lessons of Vietnam.* New York: Vintage Books, 1996. Print.

Brinkley, Douglas. *Cronkite.* New York: HarperCollins P, 2012. Print.

Brinkley, Douglas. *Tour of Duty: John Kerry and the Vietnam War.* New York: HarperCollins, 2009. Print.

Brocheux, Pierre. *Ho Chi Minh: A Biography.* New York: Cambridge University Press, 2007. Print.

Burrough, Bryan. *Days of Rage: America's Radical Underground, the FBI, and the Forgotten Age of Revolutionary Violence.* New York: Penguin P, 2015. Print.

Burr, William, and Jeffrey P. Kimball. *Nixon's Nuclear Specter: The Secret Alert of 1969, Madman Diplomacy, and the Vietnam War.* Lawrence, KS: University Press of Kansas, 2015.

Busby, Horace. *The Thirty-First of March: Lyndon Johnson's Final Days in Office.* New York: Farrar, Straus, and Giroux, 2005. Print.

Campbell, Karlyn Kohrs. *The Great Silent Majority: Nixon's 1969 Speech on Vietnamization.* College Station, TX: Texas A&M University Press, 2014. Print.

Caputo, Philip (1999). *A Rumor of War.* New York: Holt.

Carland, John M. "Winning the Vietnam War: Westmoreland's Approach in Two Documents." *The Journal of Military History* 68.2 (April 2004): 553–574.

Chomsky, Noam. *Rethinking Camelot: JFK, the Vietnam War, and US Political Culture.* Cambridge, MA: South End Press, 1993. Print.

Clarke, Thurston. *The Last Campaign: Robert F. Kennedy and 82 Days That Inspired America.* New York: Henry Holt and Company, 2008. Print.

Cortright, David. *Soldiers in Revolt: GI Resistance During the Vietnam War.* Chicago: Haymarket Books, 2005. Print.

Cronkite, Walter. *A Reporter's Life.* New York: Ballantine Books, 1997. Print.

Dallek, Robert. *An Unfinished Life: John F. Kennedy, 1917–1963.* Boston: Little, Brown & Company, 2003. Print.

Dallek, Robert. *Nixon and Kissinger: Partners in Power.* New York: HarperCollins P., 2007. Print.

Dancis, Bruce. *Resister: A Story of Protest and Prison during the Vietnam War.* Ithaca: Cornell UP, 2014. Print.

DeBenedetti, Charles & Charles Chatfield. *An American Ordeal: The Antiwar Movement of the Vietnam Era.* Syracuse, NY: Syracuse UP, 1990. Print.

Dickerson, James. *North to Canada: Men and Women against the Vietnam War.* Westport, CT: Praeger, 1999. Print.

Duiker, William J. *Ho Chi Minh: A Life.* New York: Hachette Books, 2000. Print.

Duiker, William. *Sacred War: Nationalism and Revolution in a Divided Vietnam.* New York: McGraw Hill, 1994. Print.

Eldridge, Lawrence Allen. *Chronicles of a Two-Front War: Civil Rights and Vietnam in the African American Press.* Columbia, Missouri: University of Missouri Press, 2011. Print.

Foley, Michael Stewart. *Confronting the War Machine: Draft Resistance during the Vietnam War.* Chapel Hill, NC: University of North Carolina Press, 2003. Print.

Freedman, Lawrence. *Kennedy's Wars: Berlin, Cuba, Laos, and Vietnam.* Oxford: Oxford University Press, 2002. Print.

Gardner, Lloyd C. *Pay Any Price: Lyndon Johnson and the Wars for Vietnam.* Chicago: Ivan R. Dee, 1995. Print.

Garrow, David. *Bearing the Cross: Martin Luther King, Jr., and the Southern Christian Leadership Conference.* New York: William Morrow, 2004. Print.

Gitlin, Todd. *Sixties: Years of Hope, Days of Rage.* New York: Bantam, 1987. Print.

Glennon, John P., David M. Baehler, & Charles S. Sampson, eds. "Foreign Relations of the United States, 1961–1962, Volume II, Vietnam, 1962." *Office of the Historian.* US Department of State, 2015. Web.

Goodwin, Doris Kearns. *Lyndon Johnson and the American Dream.* New York: St. Martin's Press, 1991. Print.

Greenberg, David. *Nixon's Shadow: The History of an Image.* New York: W.W. Norton, 2003. Print.

Hagen, John. *Northern Passage: American Vietnam War Resisters and Canada.* Cambridge, MA and London, UK: Harvard UP, 2001. Print.

Halberstam, David & Daniel Joseph Singal. *The Making of a Quagmire: America and Vietnam during the Kennedy Era.* Lanham, MD: Rowman & Littlefield, 2008. Print.

Halberstam, David. *Ho.* Lanham, MD: Rowman & Littlefield Publishers, 2007. Print.

Halberstam, David. *The Making of a Quagmire: America and Vietnam during the Kennedy Era.* Lanham, MD: Rowman & Littlefield, 2008.

Haldeman, H. R. *The Haldeman Diaries: Inside the Nixon White House.* New York: Putnam's, 1994. Print.

Herring, George. *America's Longest War.* New York: McGraw-Hill, 1996. Print.

Herring, George C. *America's Longest War: The United States and Vietnam, 1950–1975,* 3rd edition. New York: McGraw Hill, Inc., 1996. Print.

Herring, George C. *LBJ and Vietnam: A Different Kind of War.* Austin, TX: University of Texas Press, 1994. Print.

Herring, George C. *LBJ and Vietnam: A Different Kind of War.* Austin: University of Texas Press, 1996. Print.

Hersh, Seymour M. *Cover-Up.* New York: Random House, 1972. Print.

Hess, Gary. *Vietnam and the United States: Origins and Legacy of War,* rev. ed. New York: Twayne Publishers, 1998. Print.

"History of the Vietnam Veterans Memorial." *Vietnam Veterans Memorial Fund.* Vietnam Veterans Memorial Fund, 2015. Web. <http://www.vvmf.org/the-memorial-history>.

Hung, Nguyen Tien & Jerrold L. Schecter. *The Palace File.* New York: Harper & Row Publishers, 1986. Print.

Hunt, Michael H. *Lyndon Johnson's War: America's Cold War Crusade in Vietnam, 1945-1968.* New York: Hill & Wang, 1996.

"Interview with Eldridge Durbrow, 1979." *Open Vault.* WGBH Educational Foundation, 2015. Web. <http://openvault.wgbh.org/catalog/vietnam-078fff-interview-with-eldridge-durbrow-1979-part-1-of-2>.

Jacobs, Ron. *The Way the Wind Blew: A History of the Weather Underground.* New York: Verso, 1997. Print.

Jacobs, Seth. *Cold War Mandarin: Ngo Dinh Diem and the Origins of America's War in Vietnam, 1950–1963.* Lanham, MD: Rowman & Littlefield, 2006. Print.

Jamieson, Patrick E. "Seeing the Lyndon B. Johnson Presidency through the March 31, 1968, Withdrawal Speech." *Presidential Studies Quarterly* 29.1 (March 1999): 134–49. Print.

Johnson, Lyndon B. *The Vantage Point: Perspectives on the Presidency, 1963–1969.* New York: Holt, Rinehart and Winston, 1971. Print.

Kaiser, David. *American Tragedy: Kennedy, Johnson, and the Origins of the Vietnam War*. Cambridge, MA: The Belknap Press of Harvard University Press, 2000. Print.

Karnow, Stanley. *Vietnam: A History*, 2d ed. New York: Penguin Books, 1997.

Karnow, Stanley. *Vietnam: A History*. New York: Penguin, 1991. Print.

Karnow, Stanley. *Vietnam: A History*. New York: Penguin Books, 1984. Print.

Katz, Andrew Z. "Public Opinion and Foreign Policy: The Nixon Administration and the Pursuit of Peace with Honor in Vietnam." *Presidential Studies Quarterly* 27.3 (Summer 1997): 496–513. Print.

Kaye, David. "April Is a Big Antiwar Month on Campus and in Nation." *The Daily Pennsylvanian* [Philadelphia] 2 Apr. 1968, 84th ed.: 1, 4. Print.

Keefer, Edward C., ed. "Foreign Relations of the United States, 1961–1963, Volume I, Vietnam, 1961." *Office of the Historian*. US Department of State, 2015. Web. <https://history.state.gov/historicaldocuments/frus1961-63v04>.

Kent State: The Day the War Came Home. Dir. Chris Triffo. Single Spark Pictures, 2000. Documentary.

Kent, Stephen A. *From Slogans to Mantras: Social Protest and Religious Conversion in the Late Vietnam War Era*. Syracuse, NY: Syracuse University Press, 2001. Print.

Kimball, Jeffrey P. *Nixon's Vietnam War*. Lawrence, KS: U of Kansas, 1998. Print.

Kissinger, Henry & Clare Boothe Luce. *White House Years*. Boston: Little, Brown, 1979. Print.

Kissinger, Henry. *Ending the Vietnam War: A History of America's Involvement in and Extrication from the Vietnam War*. New York: Simon & Schuster, 2003. Print.

Kurlansky, Mark. *1968: The Year that Rocked the World*. New York: Ballantine P, 2004. Print.

Ladenburg, Thomas. "Sink or Swim, with Ngo Dinh Diem." *Digital History*. University of Houston, 2007. Web.

Le, Quynh. "Vietnam Ambivalent on Le Duan's Legacy." *BBC News*. BBC, 14 Jul. 2006. Web. <http://news.bbc.co.uk/2/hi/asia-pacific/5180354.stm>.

Lin, Maya. "Making the Memorial." *New York Review of Books*. NYREV, Inc., 2 Nov. 2000. Web. <http://www.nybooks.com/articles/archives/2000/nov/02/making-the-memorial/>.

Lodge, Henry Cabot, Jr. *As It Was: An Inside View of Politics and Power in the '50s and '60s*. New York: W.W. Norton & Company Inc., 1976. Print.

Logevall, Fredrik. *Choosing War: The Lost Chance for Peace and the Escalation of War in Vietnam*. Berkeley: University of California Press, 1999. Print.

Lucks, Daniel S. *Selma to Saigon: The Civil Rights Movement and the Vietnam War*. Lexington, Kentucky: The University Press of Kentucky, 2004. Print.

MacLear, Michael. *Vietnam: The Ten Thousand Day War*. Toronto: Methuen.

Mann, Robert. *A Grand Delusion: America's Descent Into Vietnam*. New York: Basic Books, 2002. Print.

Mansfield Foundation. "Mike Mansfield: Great American Statesman." *The Maureen and Mike Mansfield Foundation*. The Maureen and Mike Mansfield Foundation, 2009. Web.

McCormick, Anita Louise. *The Vietnam Antiwar Movement in American History*. Berkeley Heights, NJ: Enslow, 2000. Print.

McNamara, Robert & Brian VanDeMark. *In Retrospect: The Tragedy and Lessons of Vietnam*. New York: Random House, 1995. Print.

McNamara, Robert S. *The Essence of Security: Reflections in Office*. New York: Harper & Row, 1968. Print.

Michener, James. *Kent State: What Happened and Why*. New York: Random House, 1971. Print.

"Military Advisors in Vietnam: 1963 Lesson Plan." *John F. Kennedy Presidential Library and Museum*. John F. Kennedy Presidential Library and Museum, 2015. Web. <http://www.jfklibrary.org/Education/Teachers/Curricular-Resources-Image-List/High-School-Curricular-Resources/Military-Advisors-Vietnam.aspx>.

Miller, Edward. *Misalliance: Ngo Dinh Diem, the United States, and the Fate of South Vietnam*. Cambridge: Harvard University Press, 2013. Print.

Morgan, Joseph G. *The Vietnam Lobby: The American Friends of Vietnam, 1955–1975*. Chapel Hill and London: University of North Carolina Press, 1997. Print.

Moser, Richard. *The New Winter Soldiers: GI and Veteran Dissent During the Vietnam Era*. New Brunswick, NJ: Rutgers University Press, 1996. Print.

Moss, George Donelson. *Vietnam: An American Ordeal*. Upper Saddle River, New Jersey: Pearson Prentice Hall, 2006. Print.

_____. *My Lai 4: A Report on the Massacre and Its Aftermath*. New York: Random House, 1970. Print.

Nguyen, Lien-Hang T. *Hanoi's War: An International History of the War for Peace in Vietnam*. (The New Cold War History) Chapel Hill, NC: University of North Carolina Press, 2012. Print.

Nguyen, Phu Duc & Arthur J. Dommen. *The Viet-Nam Peace Negotiations: Saigon's Side of the Story*. Christiansburg, VA: Dalley Book Service, 2005. Print.

Nicosia, Gerald. *Home to War: A History of the Vietnam Veterans Movement*. New York: Crown Publishers, 2001. Print.

Oberdorfer, Don. *Senator Mansfield: The Extraordinary Life of a Great American Statesman and Diplomat*. Washington, DC: Smithsonian Books, 2003. Print.

Oberdorfer, Don. *Tet!: The Turning Point in the Vietnam War*. Baltimore, MD: Johns Hopkins UP, 2001. Print.

Olson, Gregory A. *Mansfield and Vietnam: A Study in Rhetorical Adaptation*. Lansing: Michigan State University Press, 1995.

"Paul Potter." *50th Anniversary Conference—A New Insurgency: The Port Huron Statement in Its Time and Ours*. University of Michigan, n.d. Web. <https://www.lsa.umich.edu/phs>.

Perlstein, Rick. *Nixonland: The Rise of a President and the Fracturing of America*. New York: Scribner, 2008. Print.

Phillips, Jak. "Top 10 Nobel Prize Controversies: Nobel-Winner Wrangling, Henry Kissinger." *TIME*. Time Inc., 7 Oct. 2011. Web. <http://content.time.com/time/specials/packages/article/0,28804,2096389_2096388_2096386,00.html>.

Piehler, G. Kurt. *Remembering War the American Way*. Washington, DC: Smithsonian Books, 2004. Print.

Potter, Paul. *A Name for Ourselves; Feelings about Authentic Identity, Love, Intuitive Politics, Us*. Boston: Little, Brown, 1971. Print.

Prados, John. "JFK and the Diem Coup." *The National Security Archive*. George Washington University, 5 Nov. 2003. Web. 29 May 2015. <http://nsarchive.gwu.edu/NSAEBB/NSAEBB101/>.

Prados, John. "Kissinger's 'Salted Peanuts' and the Iraq War." *National Security Archive*. National Security Archive & George Washington University, 2006. Web. <http://nsarchive.gwu.edu/news/20061001/>.

Report of the President's Commission on Campus Unrest ("Scranton Commission"). Washington, DC: US Government Printing Office, 1970. Print and Web.

Rottinghaus, Brandon. "'Dear Mr. President': The Institutionalization and Politicization of Public Opinion Mail in the White House." *Political Science Quarterly* 121.3 (2006): 451–76. Print.

Rudd, Mark. *Underground: My Life with SDS and the Weathermen*. New York: William Morrow, 2009. Print.

Rusk, Dean. *As I Saw It*. Ed. Daniel S. Papp. New York: W.W. Norton & Company, 1990. Print.

Sale, Kirkpatrick. *SDS: The Rise and Development of the Students for a Democratic Society*. New York: Random House, 1973. Print.

Schlesinger, Arthur M., Jr. *A Thousand Days: John F. Kennedy in the White House*. 1965. First Mariner Books edition. New York: Houghton Mifflin Harcourt Publishing Company, 2002. Print.

Scruggs, Jan C., & Joel L. Swerdlow. *To Heal a Nation: The Vietnam Veterans Memorial*. New York: Harper & Row, 1985. Print.

Shafer, D. Michael. *The Legacy: The Vietnam War in the American Imagination*. Boston: Beacon, 1990. Print.

Shawcross, William, *Sideshow: Nixon, Kissinger and the Destruction of Cambodia*. New York: Simon and Schuster, 1979. Print.

Sheehan, Neil (1988). *A Bright Shining Lie: John Paul Vann and America in Vietnam*. New York: Vintage Books.

Siff, Ezra Y. (1999) *Why the Senate Slept: The Gulf of Tonkin Resolution and the Beginning of America's Vietnam War*. Westport, CT: Praeger.

Small, Melvin. *Antiwarriors: The Vietnam War and the Battle for America's Hearts and Minds*. Lanham, MD: Rowman & Littlefield Publishers, 2002. Vietnam: America in the War Years Ser. Print.

Small, Melvin. *Antiwarriors: The Vietnam War and the Battle for America's Hearts and Minds*. Lanham, MD: SR Books, 2002. Vietnam: America in the War Years Ser. Print.

Snep, Frank. *Decent Interval: An Insider's Account of Saigon's Indecent End Told by the CIA's Chief Strategy Analyst in Vietnam*. New York: Random, 1977. Print.

Sorenson, Theodore C. *Kennedy*. New York: Harper & Row, 1965. Print.

Sorley, Lewis. *Westmoreland: The General Who Lost Vietnam*. New York: Houghton Mifflin Harcourt, 2011.

"The Antiwar Movement." *Ushistory.org*. Independence Hall Association, 2014. Web. <http://www.ushistory.org/us/55d.asp>.

"The United States and Ngo Dinh Diem, 1954–1963." *The Vietnam Era*. Woodbridge, CT: Primary Source Media, 1999. Web.

Tucker, Spencer C. *The Encyclopedia of the Vietnam War: A Political, Social, and Military History*. 2nd ed. Santa Barbara: ABD-CLIO, 2011.

US Department of Defense. "Soldier Missing from Vietnam War Accounted For (Newton)." *Defense POW/MIA Accounting Agency*. Department of Defense, 8 Jun. 2015. Web. <http://www.dpaa.mil/NewsStories/NewsReleases/tabid/10159/Article/598458/soldier-missing-from-vietnam-war-accounted-for-newton.aspx>.

US Department of State. "Foreign Relations of the United States, 1958–1960, Vietnam, Volume I." *Office of the Historian*. US Department of State, 2015. Web.

Useem, Michael. *Conscription, Protest, and Social Conflict: the Life and Death of a Draft Resistance Movement*. New York: Wiley-Interscience, 1973. Web.

VanDeMark, Brian. *Into the Quagmire: Lyndon Johnson and the Escalation of the Vietnam War*. New York: Oxford University Press, 1995. Print.

Varon, Jeremy. *Bringing the War Home: The Weather Underground, the Red Army Faction, and the Revolutionary Violence in the 1960s and 1970s*. Berkeley and Los Angeles: U of California P, 2004. Print.

Vietnam: A Television History: Episode 8, "Laos and Cambodia." Dir. Judith Vecchione, Austin Hoyt, Martin Smith, & Bruce Palling. Nar. Will Lyman. Boston: WGBH, 1983. Documentary.

"Vietnam, Diem, the Buddhist Crisis." *JFK in History*. John F. Kennedy Presidential Library and Museum, 2015. Web. <http://www.jfklibrary.org/JFK/JFK-in-History/Vietnam-Diem-and-the-Buddhist-Crisis.aspx>.

Vietnam War with Walter Cronkite. Nar. Walter Cronkite. Marathon Music and Video, 2003. Documentary.

Warner, Geoffrey. "Lyndon Johnson's War? Part 2: From Escalation to Negotiation." *International Affairs* 81.1 (January 2005): 187–215. Print.

Westheider, James E. *The African-American Experience in Vietnam: Brothers in Arms*. Lanham, MD: Rowman and Littlefield Publishers, 2007. Print.

Westmoreland, William C. *A Soldier Reports*. Garden City, NY: Doubleday, 1976.

Wirtz, James J. *The Tet Offensive: Intelligence Failure in War*. Ithaca, NY: Cornell U P, 1994. Print.

Young, Marilyn B. *The Vietnam Wars, 1945–1990*. New York: HarperPerennial, 1991. Print.

Yuravlivker, Dror. "'Peace without Conquest': Lyndon Johnson's Speech of April 7, 1965." *Presidential Studies Quarterly*. 36.3 (2006): 457–481. Print.

Zaffiri, Samuel. *Westmoreland: A Biography of General William C. Westmoreland*. New York: William Morrow, 1994.

Index